IDENTITY AND CONTROL

IDENTITY AND CONTROL

HOW SOCIAL FORMATIONS EMERGE
SECOND EDITION

Harrison C. White

PRINCETON UNIVERSITY PRESS

PRINCETON AND OXFORD

COPYRIGHT © 2008 BY PRINCETON UNIVERSITY PRESS

PUBLISHED BY PRINCETON UNIVERSITY PRESS, 41 WILLIAM STREET,

PRINCETON, NEW JERSEY 08540

IN THE UNITED KINGDOM: PRINCETON UNIVERSITY PRESS, 6 OXFORD STREET,

WOODSTOCK, OXFORDSHIRE OX20 1TW

LIBRARY OF CONGRESS CATALOGING-IN-PUBLICATION DATA

WHITE, HARRISON C.

IDENTITY AND CONTROL : HOW SOCIAL FORMATIONS EMERGE /

HARRISON C. WHITE—2ND ED.

P.   CM.

INCLUDES BIBLIOGRAPHICAL REFERENCES AND INDEX.

ISBN 978-0-691-13714-8 (HARDCOVER : ALK. PAPER)

ISBN 978-0-691-13715-5 (PBK. : ALK. PAPER)

1. SOCIAL STRUCTURE. 2. SOCIAL INTERACTION. 3. SOCIAL INSTITUTIONS.

4. SOCIAL NETWORKS. 5. SOCIAL CONTROL. I. TITLE.

HM706.W55 2008

303.3'3—DC22   2007041874

BRITISH LIBRARY CATALOGING-IN-PUBLICATION DATA IS AVAILABLE

THIS BOOK HAS BEEN COMPOSED IN PALATINO TYPEFACE

PRINTED ON ACID-FREE PAPER. ∞

PRESS.PRINCETON.EDU

PRINTED IN THE UNITED STATES OF AMERICA

3   5   7   9   10   8   6   4   2

CONTENTS

DETAILED CONTENTS

THREE

Three Disciplines   63

Commonsense illustrations lead in to three prototypes.

FIVE

Institutions and Rhetorics   171

Institutions guide but need not be benign. They can emerge from ongoing styles and feed into regimes with rhetorics built up for and around control, by tribal elders and Roman orators alike.

SIX

Regimes of Control 220

Regimes, which embed disciplines, generalize their valuation orderings.
Kinship roles, like everyday roles, evoke a rhetoric, whereas a kinship
system calls up a regime with narrative.

SEVEN

Getting Action   279

Breaking through the crust of common sense thrown up out of identities
seeking control: getting control over control.

ACKNOWLEDGMENTS

ALTHOUGH the title is unchanged, I offer a thoroughgoing revision of my 1992 book, as suggested by the changed subtitle. I do incorporate much new material, but coming to understand more clearly what I had been trying to argue is what has kept up my momentum in rewriting and spurred me to develop important new connecting ideas.

Professor Scott Boorman of Yale University proposed in 2003 that I revise this 1992 book. I was reluctant; he came to stay in New York for a month to argue the case on blackboard and by copious notes on content. Then for several summer weeks in Paris, Scott continued discussion in the idyllic setting at Reid Hall, in the Columbia University Center for visiting scholars on leave, which continued to be a generous host thereafter too. Scott agreed with the case study foundation; he counted fifty-eight major plus eighty-odd minor presentations in the 1992 book. Scott's contribution to this edition is widespread; in particular, his reasoning influenced chapter 4, "Styles"—a central chapter not only in its placement but also in its significance for the theory.

What finally decided me to undertake this revision was Michel Grossetti's suggestion that I clarify the 1992 book as he began to translate it into French. He hosted me many times at his University of Toulouse, where I held a Chaire d'excellence Pierre de Fermat, and Michel contributed much advice of his own.

I am deeply grateful to both counselors, especially since this final product is rather different from what either would have chosen. My third crucial counselor has been Professor Richard Lachmann of State University of New York—Albany. His vision was close to mine, and his advice at key choice points was always terse, decisive, and constructive.

Two contributors are named for each chapter in the table of contents. I ran a graduate seminar on *Identity and Control* in 2005 and then again in 2006. Frederic Godart, who is now also co-translator for the French version, along with Victor Corona, were in the first group and then continued informally with the 2006 seminar, which came to constitute a wonderful working group. Indeed, the exact assignment of person to chapter is a bit arbitrary, since all contributed ideas throughout.

Some of the case studies surveyed have drawn at least in part on various earlier forms of the present theory. Several, as you will see, are doctoral theses in sociology at Columbia with which I had some connection. Peter Bearman was often the principal adviser to these

Ph.D. candidates, and fortunately he has also frequently given me ideas. Two other recent applications, by Yally Avrahampour (2007) and by Petronille Reme (2005), draw especially on my book on markets (2002), which is kin to *Identity and Control*.

I was helped by, and am grateful for, the insights and assessments offered in published reviews of the first edition—Abbott 1994; Boudon 1993; Calhoun 1993; Meyer 1993; Stinchcombe 1993. And I benefited very much from the thorough readings and analyses in three doctoral theses that have been devoted to *Identity and Control*: by Daniel Harrison (Florida State University 2000), by Matthias Wachter (Swiss Federal Institute of Technology Zurich 2001), and by Reza Azarian (Stockholm University), the latter of which has now been published (Azarian 2006). Stephen Brint (1992) earlier published an assessment of my work leading up to the 1992 book; Baecker (1997) offered what I see as a preview to this second edition.

Over the past year, Corinne Kirchner of Columbia University made invaluable editorial contributions, as well as substantive suggestions, to this book project, including the final copyediting. And thanks to freelance copyeditor Joan Gieseke for her astute and meticulous copyediting work.

Of course, I continue to owe all the debts that I recorded in the lengthy preface of 1992, which gives earlier background of ideas that also appear in the present book.

What I came to understand only when well along in this revision was the emergence of entirely new depth and power in network analysis and theorizing in American sociology and other social sciences. Along with this came my recognition of major new theoretical depth in European sociology, notably in Bourdieu but also in Luhmann (who in 1992 was still little translated into English). So the somewhat carping tone of 1992, complaining about the state of social science, gives way to a celebratory tone.

PROLOGUE: PREVIEW OF THEMES

FROM STUDIES of sociocultural process of interest this book distills and integrates analytic themes. "Of interest"? To whom? Use "observer" as placeholder for the great variety of perceivers (personal or not) who may, singly or jointly, figure in and/or influence and/or unobtrusively observe:

What is going on here?
What matters, to whom?

For each ongoing sociocultural situation some implied searchlights from the different chapters of this book give us cues. We work outward from situations rather than impose boundaries.

The data-mining of Quentin Van Doosselaere (2006) will suggest how, over two centuries, a capitalist trade economy spun out in networks around medieval Genoa. And closer to home, on a smaller scale, we'll watch Andrew Abbott (1999) tease out (as analyst, as observer, and also as participant) how a department and discipline emerged, in decades of orientings and dealings and commitments, as a robust cloud of common sensibility—the "style" discussed in chapter 4—around a scholarly journal nested in the University of Chicago. Other studies and observation suggest that similar portrayals and themes can also apply for much smaller scopes in sociocultural time and space.[1] Altogether, chapters 1–6 offer six distinct viewpoints (or takes or humors or framings) on sociocultural process. Metaphorically, these are "takes" on us as schools of fish in a vast river, with tributaries and shoals and yet also some great depths.

The principal question for this book is *How*? My colleague Charles Tilly recently published an enticing book simply entitled *Why*? It seems to me that *Why*? is becoming the easy question for social analysis. An analyst can drown in thousands of answers, sought and unsought, since all studies are geared, trained, socialized to say why, to give reasons. These can just cancel out, leaving the play with *How*? which is to insist on setting, context. Now Tilly builds on earlier foundational labors, not least by Lazarsfeld and colleagues at mid-century Columbia, to tease out, then probe further, how folk approach causality. And four years earlier Tilly gives equal billing to how and why in a book on stories to which I return in chapter 2.

---

[1] This is a principle of self-similarity, as brilliantly laid out by that same Abbott in a chapter on "fractal analysis" in *Chaos of Disciplines* (2001).

Geographical factors count in social process, of course, along with equipment and weather and myriad other factors including skills and know-how. Their impacts as settings appear only indirectly, as refracted by the dynamics and topology of social process, viewed anew in each chapter. This book gives them little direct attention in order to instead develop deeper accounting of social process in its own terms.

Horizons

You may already know something of social network analysis (chapter 2 here), a major advance in sociology and anthropology over the past half century, and this is indeed bedrock for my spinning out social space through this book. Identities, which are the nodes, trigger out of struggles for control as they seek footing with each other (chapter 1), and so co-evolve along with networks in one and another tangible domain of activity. What is seen in searchlight focus depends on context, embracing for example some degree of reflections from other networks, along with their at least partly distinct identities.

Our metaphoric river consists in stochastic flows of events. Ties and identities alike are bathed in uncertainty among crosscurrents from situations, on up through births and deaths. Switchings thus are endemic, across combinations of network and domain. Situations may be imbricated across multiple network-domains of identities. Signalings lead to utterances and thence stories that cluster for each network-domain as a set, able to account for happenings within those ties.

Participants, too, probe cohesion and connectivity among ties and may come to perceive boundaries. Subsequently, identities and ties may string and profile under some circumstances (see chapter 4) into what you and I think of as persons.[2] Or the process of interest may go on to bloom into a style, or instead mature as the institutions dissected in chapter 5.

Levels

Actions may, instead of lolling around among network ties, directly build up a disciplinary unit (chapter 3)—for example, a production team. Such a team may be so robust that it figures as an identity itself, on a new level, nonpersonal, enabling a whole new level in continuing

---

[2] The late Niklas Luhmann powerfully theorized (1995) how identity dances with identity in a relational tie (without, however, paying much attention to the network that emerges: see his chapter 10 and also Fuchs [2001a, b, c]).

process. Paradoxes abound here, since the new level requires and presupposes at once an embedding into and decoupling from context. And a discipline may adjoin another example or another type of discipline.

And still further levels conjugate. A higher-level network can grow, for example, among nodes that are disciplines. A style is itself recognizable as a new level, an identity with a new sort of internal constitution. The publics induced and presupposed in constructing identities and networks in chapters 1 and 2, can also be seen as a zero level. The possibilities are myriad, and dizzying, as indeed they must be for an accounting of our vast "river."

The idea of context, its spread of reference, is now seen to have a vertical, depth aspect. But each one of the six chapter views can be put to service over and over, even with the same case; so there is no precedence ordering among the six. For example, chapter 5 will argue that a production market discipline, introduced in chapter 3, actually presupposes and must induce a style on its downstream side. And, of course, the process in focus, along with attendant context, can evolve and switch, such that a different view becomes appropriate.

The horizontal aspect of context affords a different sort of proliferation, such as networks abutting a given network. I pause to note that there are alternative constructions of these metaphors, "level" and thus horizontal/vertical, such as laid out in Breiger (2000).

Which view should capture the focus surely comes from what matters to those within the process, with its entailments of glimmers from context—horizontal and vertical. Judgment is required. In the final chapter 8, mathematical models are cited that can be of some assistance, with one view or another, in pinning down and testing the implications of framing in given context.

Embedding and decoupling for levels are confusing and difficult to trace. Enlarging the scope, as I do in the next section, will offer guidance. It should become evident that identity and control figure into each of the levels and processes as the core concepts. It will also become clear that the concept of authority as stabilizer of control can emerge only on a higher level.

Guidance from, and to, Linguistics

It is hard to doubt that language is a social construction (Halliday and Hasan 1976), and yet at this banquet until now language has been the ghost. All humans use speech, and more important, they always share some particular languages. What I assert and argue in these chapters thus can also be seen as specifying language usage. I foresee revealing correspondences between linguistic and sociological parsings of the great social river. Mine is a general frame of sociology, and the match should be to linguistics.

Nothing in my argument so far has implied English language. Mutual comprehension is the litmus test, but from earliest times languages remain messy spreads across overlapping and interacting tribes. And a first correspondence with linguistics, for some river, is between dialect or other sublanguage and social networks (e.g., Milroy 1980). Biber and Finegan (1994) survey a hundred studies, by linguists, of specialized registers of speech, ranging from radio sports announcers to Somali journalism. Phonetics and intonations and rhythm are harnessed along with their survey of lexicon.

Thus, linguistics surely helps to illuminate and specify the horizontal aspect of context. The real insights, however, come from another universal facet of language, namely syntax or grammar. All human languages are comparable as to complexity and flexibility as well as applicability.

Depth, along with embeddings, is the subtlest and most complex aspect of context. The previous horizontal correspondences work variously across one or more of my six framings. Now there need not be analogues in a language to these six views of sociocultural process, although I do make some suggestions in the following chapters regarding English.

My main guidance is that grammar (essentially any grammar) is an array of compact mechanisms for conveying fundamental meaning—mechanisms that are robust across both the horizontal and the vertical aspects of context. That makes sense for language as social construction. Concrete meanings supplied by lexicon evidently must be at least partly geared to specific situation. Functional theory of grammar (Halliday 1994) shows that deeper, structuring aspects of meaning come in invariant packaging, starting with the fact that grammatical words are a separate breed that come in a relatively few sets, each of a small number of items.

The truism is that each ongoing process of grammaticalization "leaches meaning" from that particular lexical item—for instance, the Anglo-Saxon word that over time turns into an English pronoun. A sounder view (Hopper and Traugott 1993; Levinson 1983) reveals the grammaticalization process as pragmatic adaptation. Pronouns join other "pointers" (deictic terms such as "here," "now") in supporting the easy transposition of messages from one situation to another.

These aspects of grammar also enable the switchings that are fundamental to building and maintaining identities and social process. So they supplement registers in pragmatics of horizontal context. The sentence or equivalent unit is, however, the core of making meaning, and thus of grammar.

The six views or framings (chapters 1–6) could not have evolved nor could they survive except for packing together, by means of each sentence, the essential distinct functions of a message. This is the province of word order among classes of lexeme, and of tense, mood and provenance of verb. They enable the six framings.

The very sketchy presentation of linguistics here will be expanded later, especially in chapter 5, and in a projected companion monograph. But this presentation supports a final main point (developed further in chapter 6 with reference to the theory of Luhmann). Each of the six views depends on the others so that embeddings are constitutive, not optional. In particular, social process even thousands of years ago could develop only in co-constitution with full-fledged language. As we will see, only within framing six could such dominance transpire.

Contextualizing Contexts

Sociocultural context is active, not passive; it gets negotiated rather than uncovered or invoked. This book construes context of a process seen from one view as drawing from instances of contexts found in various other views (chapters) besides itself. I develop this further in the conclusion, chapter 8, but already recognition and use of contexts within all kinds of ongoing scenes is at the core of chapter 7, which traces how constraints in chapters 1–6 get shaken by knowing agents.

Making the Majors (1998) is a brilliant specification by Eric Leifer of *how* a whole new independent realm, professional sports, gets built. It is an instantiation both of chapter 7 and of chapter 6, within a larger canvas of one hundred years of formations up and down the levels of chapters 1–5.

Historian Lawrence Stone (1972) makes a signal contribution to social science with his *Causes of the English Revolution, 1529–1642*. He has read, understood, cited, and made use of sociological and political science analytics. And Stone puts his hand on a core problematic, the complex interplay across varied periods of crossing projects and perceptions and mobilizations that yield a major disjunction. Yet at the end of his acute survey, Stone throws up his hands and just dumps the causes into three baskets: background conditions, long term; precipitating incidents, short term; and medium-term organizing in between. I hope this book provides a more helpful, a more discriminating framing for a turbulent dynamics perceived in hindsight as disjunction.

Three clock-times cannot effectively discriminate across embedding levels and the six views.

So much for prelude, which may be as useful and more intelligible for you as coda along with chapter 8. My hope is that you, the readers, will start trying out the approach in this book on your own observations, whether direct and daily or drawn from extended study, and I also offer quick sketches from my own experience. I borrow much in ideas. Altogether a hundred or so studies, often qualitative and historical, will be introduced. The originality is in how to parse one and another by drawing on the six distinct lenses of chapters 1–6, plus the view in chapter 7 of disruptions.

What to Do, and How

We need to figure out how to bring this text to bear comparably on a large enough population of studies to suggest, as well as test for, regularities, whether interpretive or demographic or cumulative. Payoffs from this text can include enhancement of observation by anyone whatever the background. But enhancing and adding to the few systematic claims offered here will depend on its use by and usefulness to other analysts. Most of my earlier books and articles (some reported on later) turn out in hindsight to be pretty consistent with the views I've reached now, but I think that explicit use of this text would have improved as well as speeded them up. I suspect that enrichment by combinatorial analysis (Crapo and Rota 1970; Cameron 1994) will be crucial even given much further development of simulation analyses. Some sort of Wiki sites or chat rooms may be helpful in these matters.

IDENTITY AND CONTROL

ONE

IDENTITIES SEEK CONTROL

IDENTITIES spring up out of efforts at control in turbulent context. But our everyday sense of reality then guides us. Being common sense, it enables communication among us, and thus makes our lives work. This book argues that "common sense" also obscures the social processes that lie behind us and our everyday perceptions.

An identity emerges for each of us only out of efforts at control amid contingencies and contentions in interaction. These control efforts need not have anything to do with domination over other identities. Before anything else, control is about finding footings among other identities. Such footing is a position that entails a stance, which brings orientation in relation to other identities. Biophysical context, of course, also impacts footings, most obviously as lines of visibility.

The control efforts by one identity are social realities for other identities. So this identity can be perceived by others as having an unproblematic continuity in social footing, even though it is adding through its contentions with others to the contingencies they face.

Thus, social contexts assert normality that is at odds with the improvisations and stumblings in direct experience. Perceived normality is a gloss on the reality of turbulent efforts at control by identities as they seek footings. Smooth social stories intrude into common sense. News broadcasts imply that everyday life is not newsworthy.

Researchers should put on different eyeglasses that unfold the complexities of the everyday. We often work outward from observation of some tangible pattern and can disregard notions of an overarching "society." At all scales, normality, and happenstance are opposite sides of the same coin of social action. **Sociology has to account for chaos and normality together,** and this book works toward suitably flexible framings.

Identity achieves social footing as both a source and a destination of communications to which identities attribute meaning.[1] Consequently, without footing, identities would jump around in a social space without meaning and thus without communication. Gaining control presupposes a stable standpoint for orientation. Identity be-

---

[1] Theorist Luhmann (1995, chapter 2) lays out a subtle yet precise argument for meaning emerging in co-constitution of communication among identities.

comes a point of reference from which information can be processed, evaluated. Footings thus must be reflexive; they supply an angle of perceptions along with orientation and assessments that guide interaction with other identities, to yield control. So all these processes among identities in their footings can be understood only as an inextricable intermixture of social with cultural spreads, out of which meanings are constructed jointly.

1.1. Identities Out of Events in Context

A firm, a community, a crowd, oneself on the tennis court, encounters of strangers on a sidewalk—each may be identities. Identity here is not restricted to our everyday notion of person, of self, which takes for granted consciousness and integration, and presupposes personality.[2] Instead I generalize identity to any source of action, any entity to which observers can attribute meaning not explicable from biophysical regularities. Those regularities are subsidiary to social context as environment, and persons will appear as bundles of identities.

I claim that all scopes and scales of social process induce themselves in some such fashion as the following: Identities trigger out of events— that is to say, out of switches in surroundings—seeking control over uncertainty and thus over fellow identities. Identities build and articulate ties to other identities in network-domains, *netdoms* for short. However, netdoms themselves remain subject to interruption from further switching with attendant netdoms. Thus, the world comes from identities attempting control within their relations to other identities. In their search for control, identities switch from netdom to netdom, and each switching is at once a decoupling *from* somewhere and an embedding *into* somewhere.

An Internet forum, as illustration, can flesh out this claim. There you can create an account in order to participate and use it. It's not the mere subscription but the postings that create your identity in a forum while linking you by stories to others and their comments. You don't exist in the forum as a whole person but as a user, contributing to the specific topic of the forum—e.g., football or sociology. Since you can have accounts in many forums, you can switch between them by logging out of, say, the football forum so as to log on to the sociology forum. We can see the forums as netdoms. The important point is that, although you log out, your identity in that forum, your account, remains, so

---

[2] The work of psychologist Mischel (1990) supports this turn away from common sense: see chapter 4.

your postings are not deleted by the logout process. In this sense, your activity has left a social trace consisting of the ties to other identities in the forum. But the interaction has just switched from one netdom to another.

The only moment in which you are less than a bundle of identities is in sleep. Each morning's awakening puts together a you that had been deconstructed within social and physical protections around sleep.[3] You reconstruct out of various identities triggered earlier in switches among topics amid ties with others. The same few general sorts of identity can be found here as in social context.

Many other tangible examples surround you: switches in and out of committee meetings, mealtime switches, shopping expeditions . . . The list is endless, and subsequent chapters troll through them. Communication remains central. Human social process typically orients around meanings of events and interpretations of relations among identities.

Speech presupposes language, and I aim for these chapters to provide a basis for appreciating how languages themselves emerged as by-products of the continuing spread of dances in identity and control. This communication need not be explicit speech—or even extension of speech by nonverbal means. For example, consider how students induct a newly arrived professor at a university into the implicit standards of grading and cognitive framing in curriculum for their campus (e.g., that technical but not historical sophistication is encouraged): none could articulate, and most are unaware of, the complex of pressures this subtle communication brings to bear. It is indeed effective control, but there is no intention there. It does not rely on intention to get fresh action, instead smoothing the new participant into the previously existing flow, the previously existing expectations.

Social organization is a by-product of the multiplication and the cumulation of these processes in control, which, inversely, shape how identities result from social process. The connections may be quite obscure, as in reshufflings of careers resulting from patterns of switchings in jobs. Also, identities and their contentions come wrapped up in and with larger contexts of many sorts (cf. Tilly *The Contentious French*). Interpretations emerge in patterns, weaving topics among identities and ties. When contending counteractions result in some dynamic equilibrium, even common sense perceives context as social structure. This is, for example, the case with kinship or social stratification.

Social organization has two faces: blockage and allowance of fresh action. The blockage can come from the intermeshing of identities de-

---

[3] There is great variety in these protective orders, from tribal fireside vigil to modern dormitory: see the extensive survey in Aubert and White (1959).

spite some latitude, some decoupling. The other face cuts open the Sargasso Sea of social obligation and context to achieve openness sufficient for getting fresh action. Each of us has experienced how hard it is to push even the smallest social organization in a given direction. By what means, and when, does it become possible to break through rigidity in social organization to get fresh action at large scale and small? How can one effect action by intention despite social context? Are there any reliable guides to getting action? But then again, if there are, would that not generate paradox? This book builds toward chapter 7, where recursive conjugations of control across levels are examined to identify ways to overcome, sometimes, that blockage of action that is built into social organization.

My central claim entails that the lives of these identities are stochastic flows over time whose primary shapers and switchers come from the others, not just in local detail but also as overall patterns and dynamics—as co-constituted context. It follows that blockage and getting action provide the key contrast necessary for making sense of the complex arguments to follow.

*1.2. Playground as Illustration

[In each chapter, with a section marked with an asterisk, I will point out how the studies there can also be seen from other perspectives. This playground example will be taken up again, more than casually, in sections 1.5 and 1.7, and in sections 2.2.1, 2.2.4, 4.3.2, 7.2.2, and 8.1.5.]

As an example both of how identities are formed and of how they help to create each other, consider children interacting across a playground. We can tease out some complexities from just this seemingly simple context. Dynamic models can be based and tested on observation of spatial patterns in free play of young children.[4]

Likely as not, the identity for a given child on this playground was triggered from contingencies during play. The child's identity links to other identities in the playground through stories in that setting (e.g., Tom is the bad guy who always breaks the toys of other kids).

Strings of children may be seen rushing along, some following a leading child, while in other sets each child is just tagging along after a friend known from neighborhood or home or school. If the children

---

[4] Joel Cohen's Ph.D. thesis (cf. Cohen 1971) is a notable attempt. And see the observations of adult freely forming groups by James (1953) as modeled by Coleman (1964; cf. White 1962 for critique).

are older, one can record some continuing networks of relations, of ties between pairs of children.

Or, a cluster of children may go about together because they are similar in their own and/or others' eyes. This recognition of similarity may be implicit, as when all the members are teenagers or each child is a fan of singer X; or it may be explicit, as when the group are Hispanics or are "fatsoes." Mostly these clusters are unnamed, even unrecognized. They depend on the kinds and degree of activity going on. Such clusters can come to be perceived as, and act as, identities, if they reappear repeatedly or in a variety of other contexts.

Certainly what you observe at a given moment is there only because of some underlying orderliness of process. This orderliness partially comes from, and is reflected in, talk. One can listen to the standard tales being offered across the playground in accounting for what this or that cluster does. Stories go along with expressing habits and habitus. But it is conflicts and inconsistencies in which a child finds itself caught up that start generating identity. With children it is not repetitive family domestic life, and not playing with the same bunch, but rather clashing gangs that cause, and work from, identities. A common set of stories, as we shall see in chapter 2, is what can meld such identities into a network.

This orderliness is also affected by the physical environment. How slides and swings are arrayed influences how children sort themselves into groups, with geometric ordering overcoming some social disorder.[5] And other identities of the children come from mismatches elsewhere between two netdoms like home and school, for example, when a kind of food newly enjoyed with peers at school is rejected when the child goes home. Or the mismatch may occur when the clothes that classmates insist upon, as their badge of belonging, are disdained by a parent at home who resists purchasing them.

Any identity comes out of the energy *for*, which becomes the energy *from*, bringing together many disparate bits, as when the child becomes the weird dresser in the parents' eyes.[6] Having an identity in the common sense of that term requires continually reproducing a joint construction across distinct settings. This is better described as having a bundle of identities. That is the dictionary notion of the person, a placeholder term embracing identities, often conflicting, from different settings.

---

[5] See Alexander (1964) and the actor network theory as elaborated by Bruno Latour and collaborators.

[6] Garfinkel (1967) emphasized this with counterexamples, odd probes such as knocking on a restroom door to "greet" its occupant.

Even though the playground is a casual setting, one can observe con-flicting identities and orderliness at the same time. If the playground is observed over a long period,[7] certain clusters of children will emerge repeatedly. This is what is meant by "finding footing" through control struggles. Choosing up sides for games will go on. This may partition children into teams, almost every child going to one team or another, but likely there will be a straggle of leftovers. Thereby identities find positions in relation to other identities. Together with the stories that tie them together, structure and meaning are produced. Any such crowd may partition anew, into teams, which make claims about spe-cialization in relations and tasks. Or the crowd may dissolve instead into casual chasing or gossiping. Neat accounts only faintly reflect the real turbulence, energized by unending searches for self and control. In this sense, the social never stands still. Identities couple and decou-ple, thus continuously creating social space and time.

On the playing field, teams may come to visit for tournaments. If so, grown-ups probably come along with the visitors, and this activates local adults to come out and spend time on the playground. These adults favor and slight various children, patronize them, according to how they themselves get caught up in the tournament. A much more elaborate social organization is created, or rather is shown to have been there in potential, and in the perceptions of some, all along.

1.3. Control and Structural Equivalence

The triggering of one identity activates control searches by other iden-tities, with their own impetus toward control of any and all exigencies, including each other's. Each control effort presupposes and works in terms of realities for other identities.[8] Endemic efforts at control are exactly outside any given identity, and are fitted into relations by drawing on the outputs of undisrupted identities. Observer always is in some interaction with observed.

On a small scale, identities in a grouping may come to be seen as structurally equivalent by themselves, and by still other identities. This equivalence may be because of a shared attribute, or because all are

---

[7] As has been done in a series of distinguished investigations in social science: e.g., Opie and Opie (1969); Maynard (1985).

[8] In Luhmann's words: "An important structural consequence that invariably follows from the construction of self-referential system . . . is *abandoning the idea of unilateral control*. There may be hierarchies, asymmetries, or differences in influence, but no part of the system can control others without itself being subject . . . any control must be exer-cised in anticipation of counter-control." (1995, p. 36)

tied to each other in a clique, but the basis may be more indirect and abstract. To gain footings means to fashion structural equivalence.

Control is both anticipation of and response to eruptions in environing process. Control projects participate in how identities array in social structures, with social order as a possible by-product. **Social processes and structure are thus traces from successions of control efforts**. In the words of Chanowitz and Langer (1980, p. 120), "Control is not something that we possess. It is some way that we *are*. . . . The exercise of control is a whole situation that cannot faithfully be fully reproduced as a number of parts or measures." And further, control efforts become entangled in ways that need not be visualized as projects of individual actors.

The accuracy of observing the process is enhanced through deciphering which identities are structurally equivalent with respect to context, overall or partial. And control can be equally real when it is fugitive, since it uses disorder as material from which to evoke order.[9] So control efforts are responses by identities to endless stochastic contingencies, to which others' control efforts add. Context is crucial; context is experienced rather than designed. This is why "power" is not the right term for these processes.

1.4. Netdoms, Networks, and Disciplines

Control efforts take place in demarcated social spaces. Netdom is a suitable descriptor: "dom" from domain of topics and "net" from network relations. Identities switch from netdom to netdom, finding footings in different networks in differing domain contexts.

The dualism of network and domain is essential, and make no mistake, it is a radical departure from common sense. We won't reach the singular "person" until chapter 4. And an isolated single "relation" or tie is accorded no reality outside the special historical and social circumstances so brilliantly portrayed by Luhmann in *Love and Passion*. Netdom is not a thing, it is experiential process, usually transitory but with impact so awesome that participants cannot bring it into focus. Luhmann in his general theory (1995) takes a parallel road of deriving social organization with use of a single term; and his "communication," like netdom, presupposes the mixture of relation and topic, plus understanding.

[9] If we assume with Luhmann that all events are fugitive and that they are the elements of social systems, then control becomes the attempt to constrain the possible events.

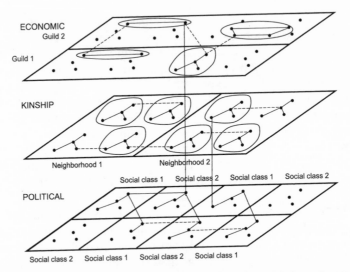

Figure 1.1: Netdom switching is not just for small-scale and informal settings, but is part of business and power life as seen in Padgett and McLean (2006). Concepts on figure are from this source, not from *Identity and Control*. Solid lines are "constitutive ties," dotted lines "relational social exchanges," and oblongs formal organizations. Dots are individuals.

We will repeatedly make use of studies of multiple networks in Renaissance Florence conducted by John Padgett and coauthors. Already here, without attempting any explanation yet of the case, I will exhibit a diagram—see figure 1.1—of theirs that you can interpret in terms of netdom switches. The constructs I am introducing are not meant just for small-scale, casual, and current processes.

Networks are overview reports from the dynamics of overlapping of, and transitivity in and across, netdoms. Each network is sustained through invocations by those identities of a common set of stories that explain away anomalies. Networks lay out the space of social action.

A further concept to be introduced in more detail in chapter 3 is disciplines.

Disciplines are self-constituting conveners of social action, which each induce an identity on a new level. In this book they are as important as networks. Disciplines build around commitments that constrain constituent identities, very different from networks with their flexible sets of stories. Disciplines are concepts about *processes* rather than about *structure* in sociocultural life. Depending on which discipline is at work, control struggles take place according to different rules and in different frames.

I introduce three different species of disciplines—Interfaces, Arenas, and Councils—around their distinctive valuations and contingencies. Much practical activity—whether the production of a frozen pizza or the dinner party in a country club—keeps on getting done and is shaped in all these venues. Disciplines can translate into normality and habit at some level. But chaos and accident are the sources and bases for all identities, and it is identities seeking control that fuels practical activity whatever the context.

1.5. Overview: Identities Out of Mismatch within Contexts of Control

Now that I have suggested the main paths, including networks and disciplines, through which to specify social process, let us look again at identities. Identity is produced by the contingency to which it is a response, an intervention in the process to come, at whatever level and in whatever realm. Seeking control is not some option of choice, it comes out of the way identities get triggered and keep rolling along as process. So, basically, an identity comes along with its footing out of mismatch, by drawing on both observation and reflexive self-observation.

Such a mismatch can occur at many scopes and levels. A "position" is identity triggered a level up from its occupants. To illustrate: Recognition of the position of "presidency" is triggered by the mismatch between Jefferson and Washington, or for that matter between Reagan and Franklin Delano Roosevelt. One can see "troubleshooter" as an identity coming out of mismatch a further level up, and so identity can take on life through imputations of others. I hope, for example, that this book will be draped with an identity by readers, and certainly mismatches will be at the root of that process, mismatches with prior works and their identities, as well as with observations and debates among commentators.

There is need for a population dynamics of identities, quite distinct from current demography. But within any one of these many sorts of realizations of identities there will be heterogeneity. Within the same network, for example, identities will appear to differ in strength, visibility, and longevity. Such discriminations and their inventories must be keyed to particular studies, but I can make some general points. Rediscovery and reshaping continue for every identity.[10] An identity is as likely to target itself for a control effort as it is to target another identity.

---

[10] On disappearance of identities, consult the discussion of "case breakers" and "dead" cases by Bearman, Faris, and Moody (1999); and Bearman, Moody, and Faris (2002).

Now let us return to my initial sketch of just four general sorts of identities, four senses of identity. For simplicity, I discuss these identities as tagged to individual human beings. Their mismatches include the rushing and jarring of daily living, along with the contingencies of ill health and of arguments. I turn to four particular dynamics for individual identity.

Identity for a human begins as and from a primordial and continuing urge to control, which can be seen always, in all contexts. For example, a new child on a playground has an overriding need to find some sort of stable social footing so that the child can know how to act in an otherwise chaotic social world. This is not necessarily a harsh struggle over status and rank: only occasionally does this lead to bullying on the playground. Identity in this first sense is the expression in social context of the same urge for secure footing that in physical settings induces behavioral patterns of posture such as leaning forward when climbing stairs.

A grouping can also have identity in this first sense, exhibited in its solidarity. Seeking celebration for example can yield a label for a group. All chapters of this book invoke instances of this **first sense** of identity.

Identity with a second, more elaborate, and quite distinct sense occurs apart from networks. This sense is akin to "face." It is identity achieved and expressed or operationalized as part of some distinct social grouping in which each member has face just because it is a social face, one of a differentiated set of faces that together make up that grouping. The differentiation may be uneven and the grouping may be loose. A simple example is a group at a table in a dorm eating dinner: chances are these students know each other and are accustomed to eating together often, and so have come to tend to take certain stances—one as topic selector, another as clown, and so forth.

Here the grouping necessarily has identity as an entity on a distinct level. It is also recognized by diverse other identities and observers through, and as participating and communicating in, social process. Celebration of this identity builds narrative. Around identity in this **second sense** each discipline builds its more complex and sophisticated process.

The tension between identity and control can be seen as conformity versus creativity. Identities figure in fury and fear as well as sweetness and light, as aspect of identity seeking control and thereby becoming creative. This creativity corresponds to an additional, **third sense** of identity that builds on the first two. This is identity from frictions and errors across different social settings. This third sense of identity figures especially in the formation of network ties.

This third sense of identity arises from the central fact of social organization: each human lives switching among netdoms. Even as children, we mix with different groups while intermixing our living in different realms. Moreover, each of us continues in several different roles which cross between distinct realms, such as family and village and job and secret society, so that our actions and thence our selves crosscut these realms. Even as adults we do not often try to include all these realms in any one narrative we call career.

All this transports to a higher level, to description of position and the like. But there need be nothing unusual or esoteric in this third sense of identity. Return to the homely example of a child on a playground. The child may pick up a new way of wearing (or tearing) its clothes as being proper (an aspect of the second sense of identity). But then the child finds, upon arriving home, that peer-proper is not family-proper. Such contradictions—all the screwups, mistakes, errors, and social noise—in life are just what bring about establishment of identity in this third sense. It is a sense that each of us achieved when still a child, and it is in the third and first senses that any identity initially comes into existence.

Identity in this third sense is urgent; it thus both implodes and explodes with the greatest of energies. These are, for example, the energies which generate and which call forth artworks along with narrative creativity. This third sense of identity may be construed by an outside observer as critic, assessing the outcomes through a dossier indicating some broad range of possibilities.

This third, and crucial, sense of identity has no application in utopias, because identity in this sense arises precisely from contradictions across social disciplines impinging on the same actor, from mismatches and social noise. Literary utopias acknowledge the central fact of multiple roles for persons, but what makes them utopian is imagining individuals to be in roles that are combined in consistently prescribed packages.

There is also a **fourth sense** of identity, which is close to what is usually meant by identity in ordinary talk. This fourth sense of identity corresponds to an ex post account, after the fact, about identity; it is career seen from the outside. Whereas change is enabled by identities in the third sense, the fourth sense of identity is all about rationalization and about failures of action. And so the fourth sense combines with the third in network phenomenology.

Yet all four senses of identity attach to the same constructed reality, as emanations from mismatch as it becomes observed. Each sense weaves together layers of expression in myriad ways. These are ways that can change. A painting can reflect a second or a fourth (and boring) sense of identity, just as some story or play can suggest the interesting third or first senses; but the reverse occurs as well. It would therefore be silly to reify the four senses of identity, to set them up as separate personae, or wholly distinct sorts of positions. Narrative can and does weave them together; the narrator's business is to generate, for the time being, a larger sense of membership that embraces both auditors and author.[11]

1.6. Meanings Come in Switchings: Scientific Precursors

Netdom shows habit as surface. This is dual-sided habit, as one finds in Bourdieu's (1996a, b) construct of habitus. But now perception comes only with and from contrast, as a process (Gibson 1979). Thus, fresh meaning emerges for humans only with switching, as from one netdom to another. Switching is central to this theory and will appear again and again at different scopes and levels. Again this point is unorthodox, departing from common sense, but as I noted earlier I hope to show you that it unties some knots and riddles in existing social science.

I make only a partial claim for originality of this theory in sociology, since I think much the same root idea was found long ago in works by Garfinkel, by Cicourel, by Goffman and in linguistics by Halliday. Recently it is again being championed, by Vaughan (2002), by Powell (2002), and by Mische (2007; and see Mische and White 1998).

My radical innovation is different. **I disallow the bracketing, the setting aside, of context** when penetrating and following particular situations and episodes, whether commonsensical or Garfinkelian. Bracketing is in direct contradiction with how I conceptualize identity. Instead, I venture short-circuiting proposals in order to bring contextual reality cheek by jowl with particular situational encounters. I do this rather than endlessly trace out particular situations. I try to emulate playwright rather than narrator.

Psychological perspectives offer precursors too. I have already cited James Gibson. An early parallel is *Personal Knowledge* by Michael Polanyi (1958). That book argues that all knowing is an essentially tacit integration of subsidiary clues, *from* which we attend, into focal wholes, *to* which we attend. Much the same was also said by Fritz Heider, from whom sociologist Niklas Luhmann drew guidance, to construe social process as communication. Here I bring this insight still further outside the minds to dissect it into component social processes.[12]

---

[11] This also addresses the problem tackled by Bearman, Faris, and Moody in "Blocking the Future": see previous note.

[12] This extraction is supported by a recent study (Arnoldi 2006) of stock market derivatives. Futures of various sorts long have been around and actively traded, growing into the orgy of the 1990s that centered in sophisticated mathematical modeling. The

I will argue that linguistics provides the deepest-rooted evidence in support of switchings among netdoms. Its most direct evidence is the universality of deictics (grammatical pointers like pronouns, "this" and "that", "here" and "now", and so on). Careful examinations (as in Hanks 1990, 1993; Lucy 1993; as well as in Halliday 1994) suggest that deictics have evolved exactly to support coherence of discourse across switches in netdoms by providing terms that everyone can and does use to maintain footings with others through changes in netdoms.

1.7. Culture in Play, and in Emergencies

Speaking of meaning, where is culture in all this? Culture in the sense of museums and libraries is set aside for this discussion. I think of living culture as a process recognized in societal institutions and practices, which are taken up in chapter 5, as by-products but also co-constitutors of social process at all levels. The previous playground example could concern just some empty lot or field, but I was in fact thinking of a school or city playground, which would be subject to more or less explicit institution and practices, even aside from coaches and teachers.

Left to play by themselves indoors, young children often take on roles—mommy, doctor, nurse, cowboy, teacher. Developmental psychology attests to and elaborates this common knowledge. And recently sociolinguist Sawyer (1992) specified the discourse pragmatics that he observed over a year of observation.

One can conclude that from an early age, kids are made aware of more complex forms and higher levels of social process, over which they try to acquire some mastery. Their play is the beginning of the sophistication in transposition that everyone needs just to participate as a "normal" adult. Sophistication, however, is not the same as analytic awareness—such constant awareness indeed would induce stumbling instead of normality.

Accidents offer a different prism. Unlike children's play, they are not pretend switchings. In a city, an accident often evokes an emergency team and ambulance, which in chapter 3 will be modeled as a discipline. The injured person experiences a vivid switch to another net-

---

volumes became so huge and the markups so small that electronic trading from computer terminals replaced Chicago-style bidding auctions. What Arnoldi found is that the lack of face-to-face contact among a set of traders, with all its back and forth signaling through discourse and body language, crippled their intuitions and thus their actions: so much so that face-to-face contact was introduced again through various subsidiary auctions.

dom, and then likely a continuing succession of switches. Whether in Paris or Milwaukee, though, the situation will unfold according to much the same script from culture, inducing interlocking role behavior along the network lines presented in chapter 2.

Culture is being naturalized here as the product of social process. This is analogous to developments in information science, such as cybernetics early on, and general systems theory, especially as specified by Luhmann. There is also an analogue here to dynamic control theory, and to Kalman filters. The latter are self-learning, not just self-directing, programs.

1.8. Challenging Both Extremes

Within sociology and other social sciences, there is a strong resurgence of an individualist mode of theorizing under the label "rational choice theory" (Bueno de Mesquita and Lalman 1992; Coleman 1990; Coleman and Nowak 1986; Lindenberg 1989a; Riker 1982). Such theory takes identity for granted and ignores the nesting of contexts, and thereby tries to explain away control.[13] Some institutional economists themselves take exception to that theory (Favereau 2005; and see the volume by Lazega and Favereau 2001).

Rational choice theories build upon a myth of the person, as some preexisting entity, and focus on how choice is made and how choices interact, once made. But although one can usually impute ends from actions, these "ends" often are, despite protestations, mere by-products of previous history as adapted to current circumstance. These theorists need not deny this empirical weakness because they can point to the sheer scope of prediction possible on those assumptions.

The push toward some rational choice theory is in itself sensible. Indeed it is rational, because it mimics the push in other sciences toward what is called mean field theory.[14] This is an approximate theory of long-range order through calculation of self-consistent fields. At first sight, of course, rational choice theory might instead seem to ape models of short-range order which concentrate on immediate environs. But no, the long-range order of a self-consistent field is essential to the calculations in a theory of rational choice. This is because the goals and

[13] But see Hechter (1987) for an attempt at institutional explanation. And Pizzorno (1991) reviews exactly this difficulty in Hobbes.

[14] Also called the Mean Field Approximation, or Self-Consistent Fields; see de Gennes (1979) and Ziman (1979), and for an elegant and readable early account, see Van Vleck (1932). It is discussed further in the conclusion, chapter 8.

ends in fact have to be read out of a pattern, and only larger patterns will sustain such attempts. Although any self-consistent field approach attempts to take great care with local context, it is at the cost of the subtle correlations that are central to actual process.

Structuralism,[15] by contrast to rational choice theory, disdains events, as when it explains the United States without the War between the States, and that war—the Civil War—without Gettysburg, and the Third French Republic without Louis Bonaparte's Eighteenth Brumaire. Structuralism thus takes control for granted and tries to explain away identity. Structuralism builds from the myth of society as some preexisting entity. Neither rationalist nor structuralist approaches can give proper account of social action.

Abandon structuralism, including Talcott Parsons's attempt to derive social order from values guiding individual persons, and also abandon the view common in economic theory of social order emerging from preexisting individuals' efforts to achieve their idiosyncratic wants and interests. In my opinion, neither of these two approaches to social theory, themselves opposites, take persons seriously. As a result, neither can treat historical trends and cultural impacts with proper sensitivity. In contrast, my theory aims not just to sidestep the "structure and agency" problem, but to build on grounds of concepts that eliminate that problem.

It is silly to treat rational choice theory as the basic or general theory of social organization. It is just as silly to carp at any particular approximations it uses, and then refer to the carping as an institutional theory. All theory is simplification; scientific theory simplifies so as to uncover new phenomena. Rational choice theory has suggested new phenomena, and the present task is to determine contexts in which it is likely to be productive. Chapter 4 develops theory to ground these ideas about personhood and rationality.

1.9. Control and Social Space: Scientific Precursors

Now I go on to develop a more general claim. I will draw on natural sciences for analogies to this claim. Start with weather forecasting. My first article, as just a teenager, published in the *Tech Engineering News* of MIT, was about the initial introduction of radar to survey storm clouds. I continued to follow the blossoming of meteorology and became convinced that a fresh perspective was as crucial there as new technology. Now I try to bring a fresh perspective to sociology, and

---

[15] Whether in Parsons (1937) or Wallerstein (1980) or later forms.

encourage the reader to break out of some standard terminological frames in social science.

Social dynamics have peculiar features when compared with, say, chemical reactions. There is no single, unique, and isotropic space for context. The dynamics of control, while they are playing out, are also inducing and constructing their own "spaces." These accommodate possibilities of social action, which depend on perceptions and interpretations that must be communicated and are set only partly by the biophysical environment.

There are also similarities between social dynamics and chemical or other natural science reactions. Extension and shape get read by the analyst from observing mutual positionings. In both realms, positionings are pressured by jockeyings for control. There is spread across a field.

Topologies of social spaces are complex, varying over time and from one locale to another. Insights about a topology suggest leverages for control. For example, the military drill is one model of control, a model that subjects to caricature the preconditions and steps for control. In a drill, persons are induced to move in parallel within a little group which is both literally and metaphorically cut off from other social relations for a time. Alternatively, one can seek control from weaving a maze of uncoordinated and changing contexts around others. Chapter 7 develops these themes.

My general claim makes moves analogous to three moves made by physical science in supplanting Aristotle and his insistent common sense. The first key move was to divorce force from momentum so that unchanging momentum signifies no force. The commonsense reality of frictions is set aside in order to achieve analytic power. Coupled to that, the second move was abstracting from particular objects to universals, point masses, and the like. The analogous moves in sociology are to switching, as to momentum/force, and to identities as the actors.

The third key move was the later explicit development of Cartesian space, completely parameterized space, as the setting. This allowed physics problems to become formulated analytically, subject only to boundary conditions. The analogue being developed for social process is networks, a distinct new sort of friable, multidimensional space, with which a new and friable constitution of interpretive social time has to be interwoven.

Engineering disciplines also offer analogies. Implicit in Cartesianization was universal regularity of the time dimension, also found in engineering. Engineering need not imply predictable control. Perhaps closest to social science is chemical engineering, in which, it has always seemed to me, the highest art is just riding herd on enormously complex fluid flow processes.

1.10. Where to Go

An identity in a human being need not constitute person, despite being mirrored in the body and in the consciousness, in a mind. Minds fall outside the scope of sociology as I work it here.[16] And all sorts of identities are bound up with what "control" is in social surroundings. I expand on this in subsequent chapters around the following five theses.

Five Theses:

- Identities emerge from turbulence seeking control from within social footings that can mitigate uncertainty.
- Switchings are the vehicles of meaning for identity and control.
- Switching reckons in change both of social relations and of domain of association.
- Context gains in depth as identities embed into new levels.
- The fifth thesis is dual: context is constituted in and as patterns in dynamics across identities and control across levels for a situation.

I also expand on this in subsequent chapters around what become the following five senses of identity.

Five Senses of Identity:

- The **first** sense is identity as the smallest unit of analysis. Persons consist of a bundle of these identities. When this form of identity finds footing, one could replace the word *identity* with *position* in a netdom.
- The **second** sense is a connected bunch of the first-sense-identities. It exists only where first-sense-identities found footings and are thus object and subject of the attribution of meaning.
- The **third** sense is the trace of different identities in different netdoms. This identity is a report of, for example, a human being switching from netdom to netdom over time. It is the pathway a person, entity, or place takes through social time. If we could graphically sum up time as well as domain layers, we would see this third sense of identity.
- The **fourth** sense of identity is the interpretation of the third sense. If a person looks back on the netdoms and identities he switched into and out of and embeds this pathway in meaning, he produces the fourth sense of identity. This is what a person perceives to be his or her self—a narratively embedded history of a journey through different netdoms. If the third sense is, for example, the detailed account of the misfortunes of Oedipus's life story, the fourth sense is the realization

[16] Niklas Luhmann's system theory (1995), which I see as compatible with mine, does treat consciousness but keeps it segregated (his chapter 7). I discuss this further in chapters 4 and 6, and then start chapter 8 on this issue.

that he failed. It's the fourth sense that leads a psychologist to label a certain mind disturbance the "Oedipus complex."

- I will argue that there is yet another, a **fifth**, sense of identity with very different scope. It is a dynamic, self-reproducing amalgam across profiles of switchings in the first four sorts of mismatch. This fifth kind is on a distinct level that analytically is still more embracing than the level of discipline. This fifth kind, I will argue in chapter 4, is the form in which persons are realized.

My aim is theory that enables observation, expert observation attentive to all scopes and levels. Social organization is messy and refractory, a shambles rather than a crystal (cf. Sorokin 1956). There is no tidy atom and no clear-cut world, only complex striations and long strings that reptate as in a polymer goo. So my account challenges commonsense constructs of person and of society in order to search out self-similarity of social organization, according to which much the same dynamic processes apply over and over again across different levels and scopes.

But any level and scope can be constrained, and otherwise influenced by, and thus embed into, as well as decouple from others. Language, as both vehicle and outcome, is central in this process.[17] From time to time, I draw on linguistics for support that goes beyond coding of particular case studies, and I intend to devote my next book to social construction of language.

The importance of identity and control and switchings as primitives of the theory is manifest, and this has an important corollary. Since they arise around irregularities and amid contentions, they prove less responsive to averages than they are to dispersions, that is, to spreads across locale and degree of social connections and timing. For example, how long you wait in a queue depends as much on the dispersions of arrivals and of servicing times as on their means. On a grander scale, the volume of product an industrial firm ships out depends especially on the quality rank seen by buyers among competing producers who are eying each other; it is dispersions across flows, not averages, that trigger levels in prices, costs, and profits that sustain a set of production volumes in dynamic equilibrium.[18]

To reach such results, I first lay out network analyses in chapter 2 followed by construction of three disciplines in chapter 3. Then in

---

[17] For example, Hopper and Traugott (1993) argue this regarding grammaticalization, and Halliday (1994; and see Dejoia and Stenton 1980) has long argued this for language more generally.

[18] McPherson and Ranger-Moore (1991, p. 35) make a similar argument about sizes of organizations on the authority of Darwinian models of evolution: there in Hardy Weinberg equilibrium, the rate of change of fitness is equal to the genetic variance in fitness.

chapter 4 I jump to a conjecture on what sort of larger format survives as sensibility within stochastic social process. Chapter 5 illustrates what practices and institutions emerge, in some systems of implicit and explicit culture. Then chapter 6 turns to what regimes of control are able to establish themselves, with special cases of separate realms in law, economy, art, science, and even sports.

Chapter 7 is foil to all the prior chapters in laying out how to break through such formats sometimes to get fresh action. It may well be the most relevant chapter for those readers seeking to cut their way through the Sargasso Sea of conformity, which chapters 2–6 dissect.

This book draws on case studies, a hundred or so, diverse in scope and realm and period. Ragin and Becker (1992) organized a major discussion on issues in the use of case studies for social inquiry. I argued there that a case study concerns primarily either identity or explanation or control. Studies in the present manuscript conform to this classification, chapters 1 and 4 concerning identity, chapters 2 and 5 concerning explanation, and chapters 3 and 6 concerning control; chapter 7, however, crosscuts all three concerns.

• • • • •

I offer guidance about what lies "under the hood" of a social vehicle, and I hope that sheer curiosity will bring in some readers, with still others searching for guidance on practice and policy. The concluding chapter will begin with an overview, and you may wish to consult that, as well as the prologue, as you move along in the seven chapters.

The argument is intricate, somewhat unconventional, introduces some new terminology, and draws some unfamiliar distinctions. This is for the purpose of providing flexible tools in a supple framing to assist very diverse observation. I hope to hear from you about what does and does not work for you.

One of my contributors (see table of contents for their names) suggests that you be sure to read chapter 8, maybe even early, because it gives such a good overview.

TWO

NETWORKS AND STORIES

IDENTITIES seek control. Any identity may see control as slipping away and going to other identities. Each control effort presupposes as well as shapes some context of particular relations across identities, particularly in talk. The netdom described in chapter 1 is the local and short-term context for relations between pairs of identities. These relations are called *ties*. The present chapter canvases larger, continuing contexts in patterns of ties, called *networks*. "Network" has entered common speech as a verb, but only recently.

Social networks are traces from dynamics across netdom switchings. As two identities come over time to focus control attention upon each other, a stymied struggle can settle down into some story that marks a tie between them. A story is a tie placed in context. Stories structure switchings into accounts with a beginning, middle, and end (Tilly 2002); so story-making frames social time.

This chapter sketches how social process plays into, from, and around networks of pair relations. These relations are characterized by stories told in and about them, with meanings drawn from switchings between netdoms. Since actual settings and the switchings among them are endlessly varied, the description I give here must be kept abstract and general. Existing technical and substantive prototypes (e.g., Padgett and McLean 2006a; Lazega 2001) and canvasings can guide the reader for particular implementations. It is often convenient here to substitute *person* for the general term *identity*: see chapter 4 for the problematics of this substitution.

A network can be traced as similar stories appear across a spread of dyads. These ties are, in an incisive phrase from Podolny (2001), prisms for meaning as much as they are pipes for connectivity. In this chapter, we will look first at emergent networks, and then survey some ways that ties fit together with stories into networks. Next comes a discussion of how a network shakes out over time. Examples are then provided of how all this matters, before getting back again to the emergence of networks, this time referring to a new level of network. The chapter ends with a focus on the role of uncertainty.

2.1. Emergence and Tracings

Assessing connectivity is crucial (Freeman 1979) but may be problematic for a network that has only crude coding of relations. Coding itself commonly derives from a relation between observer and subject, namely the instruction about the criterion for reporting a tie, as in the Small World studies that follow. But we begin with modeling that derives ties from behaviors evolving over time.

2.1.1. Political Polarization via Staccato Network

Triggerings of identities also invoke communication with others as an aspect of seeking footings. Repeated communication between some pair can get recognized as a continuing relation when its frequency rises above chance expectancy in that context. The pattern of such ties across identities can become seen as a network engraved in some sort of public space with an identity of its own. Influences flowing through ties, and their impacts, are shaped by the network and in turn can reshape it.

Baldassarri and Bearman (2006) model how this may transpire when political issues that are already active in participants' minds are the subjects of communications. Repeated communication will include arguments and attempts at influencing the opinion of the other participant in a tie. A threefold stochastic model is proposed for showing how the choice of what issue to discuss, and with whom, shift along with the existing divergence of opinion. Baldassarri and Bearman ran large numbers of massive simulations of the resulting distribution and location of opinions in that public, across the menu of issues.

The point is to see how an extreme partisan polarization can come about even within a public most of whom take moderate stands on most issues. The crux of the study's findings is that, even with the majority moderate on most issues, this public can sift itself into rather segregated and homogeneously partisan blocs of opinion on one or a few hot-button issues. The simulations were run over hundreds and thousands of periods of discussion, and the output provided the full network on each issue at each period, noting the opinion level of each actor at each stage. Not always, but often, an issue or two sorted themselves out as hot-button without attribution of particular content.

This is a classic illustration of a way to use social network theory about how people interact to explain unintended outcomes that are paradoxical to common sense focused on *whys*. When you read Baldassarri and Bearman's full account, note how perfectly the setting of the model corresponds with the vision I have laid out in chapter 1. And also note how ties and their stories are generated in an endogenous process without need for the analysts to call on attributes or ideology. We will return again and again, in chapter 5 in particular, to the interpretation of *public* as referred to in this illustration.

2.1.2. Tracings of the Small World

Stanley Milgram (1967) and others (Pool and Kochen 1978) over an extended period (see Kochen 1989) developed and applied chain-search techniques to assess connectivity across both huge and medium-size populations. Subjects actually used rather than just reported ties. Milgram had each arbitrarily selected initiator, aim to reach a named target person—a stockbroker in Boston—with whom they were not previously acquainted, initiating a chain beginning with some acquaintance presumed to be more likely to know the target. Each successive contact was to select, and mail the instruction booklet on how to proceed, on to a next contact, reporting completion of that step by postcard to Milgram. The basic finding on chains was that an arbitrary pair could connect in about a half dozen steps, this within a population of one hundred million persons.[1]

The basic finding for phenomenology is that in our society, ordinary people made sense of and carried out an activity that to peasant societies[2] might seem a bizarre task. Coding a tie as "acquaintance" sums across some scope of specialized relations. It also sums up implications perceived from some range of past incidents from ongoing processes. And it folds in more intense relations with weaker ones.

It is not that the scope of acquaintanceship—the actual number of persons known to someone—necessarily differs by society. In all known times and contexts, from primitive tribes to empires, the scope of effective acquaintance, persons known in the relevant minimal sense, clusters around a median below one thousand. The six steps of separation found by several researchers seem to suggest a surprising extent of overlap among acquaintance circles around distinct identities. This is where intuition fails and explicit modeling is required. But this type of modeling is very demanding even with smaller populations, as was found in early modeling for epidemics (Bailey 1957, 1982).

---

[1] Dropouts from the searches terminated some chains falsely, but the distribution of chain lengths can be corrected for the resulting biasing (White 1970a).

[2] E.g., the Tallensi (Fortes 1945).

Those studies themselves come to the conclusion that more depth in the phenomenology of ties is required.

A generation later, Duncan Watts and colleagues (see Watts 1999; Watts, Dodds, and Newman 2002) established through extensive simulations of network formation how to characterize the evolution of chains abstractly. They surveyed probability models of tie formation within sets of nodes numbering one thousand or more. Watts guided his explorations with measurements of chains sampled from three widely different types of populations (co-castings in movies considered as ties; the power network of the western United States; and the nerve network of a worm species). Overlap was indeed important, in particular the degree to which the nodes connected to a given node were also connected to each other. Even a modest fraction of ties sent out to random targets was sufficient to generate shortcut chains that seem analogous to the six degrees of separation found with ordinary social worlds.

Milgram, however, was studying actual search behavior by subjects rather than measuring each of a large inventory of chains formed according to a probability model. The analogy is problematic, although people do search out the shortest co-casting chains in the Kevin Bacon Game. Watts and his collaborators subsequently adapted Milgram's chain-search technique to messaging on the Internet. Far more chains were initiated across far more targets across the whole world (again with somewhat arbitrary recruitment of the initiators). One study (Dodds, Muhamad, and Watts 2005) closed a glaring loophole in the technique by having each contact verify that he or she was indeed an acquaintance of that sender. Another study (Kossinets 2006) assessed chain reliability more generally. Later I describe classic studies by Rapoport and others and by Granovetter that differentiate acquaintanceship ties by coding them according to their strength.

Recent studies are also able to explore variations according to attributes of the message-senders, on each of whom a dossier was gathered. Watts, Dodds, and Newman (2002) propose an explicit model for how search is conducted by respondents, the first explicit explanation of searchability.[3] Grossetti (2005) studied networks in Toulouse, by interview and survey, and also pointed to the importance of common attributes and memberships in forming network ties.

[3] Because of Milgram's arbitrary selection of the initiators, and because of a very low success rate, Kleinfeld (2002) concluded that the Small World phenomenon is not empirically reliable. In a simulation, Watts (2003, chap. 5) came up with six as the median number of steps in a chain search, rehabilitating Milgram.

And a whole new domain of data, on mobile phone calls, has been probed (Eagle, Pentland, and Lazer 2007). Presumably that dataset, when combined with content-analysis programs from linguistics, could supply an empirical base for the Baldassarri and Bearman modeling described earlier.

Milgram appreciated bizarreness in our world: his Small World of acquaintanceships abuts the phenomenological world of Goffman and Simmel, who attuned us to sensibilities of life in city streets, constantly amid strangers on errands unknown to you and me. But to understand any world and its origins requires more than modeling Small World linkages; we should also be thinking in terms of, for example, vacancy chains among jobs, and kinds of exogamy/endogamy in kinship. It may be vacancies, not participants, whose moves reflect the underlying dynamics across organizational systems (White 1970b; Stewman and Konda 1983). And generalized cycles of exchange may dominate local titration in ties of direct exchange, as Bearman (1997) and D. White and Johansen (2006) have shown for some kinship systems.

The Small World can be seen as an artifact using social networks, more than it is an architecture in social networks. It should evoke in us queries about how the overall context constructs itself amid the diversity of mode, and multiplicity of level, extent and incidence, for which this book is trying to offer handles. Further discussion to respond to such queries is called for, and is provided by the discussion of contextualization that is in the final chapter.

2.1.3. Network Population as Process

Identities of actors and events come out of mismatches, and they embed among the ties spun in seeking control. These identities array in networks or, when there are many balancing condensations, give way to the vaguer catnets, a concept that I will introduce in the last part of this chapter, and to identities on new levels. The resulting ensemble can be called *network as population*.

Euphemisms—world, school, society, and so on—are often used for *population*, which is possibly the most deceptive term in the social sciences, just because it seems so obvious: "this set of people here." But a population of identities, each seeking control is, through these struggles, coming to specify its own social space, rather than boundaries being imposed arbitrarily, as an observer is tempted to do. Identities are embedding via some stories with respect to various other identities in a network population evolving during the course of continuing struggles for control. Ongoing demographic flows, births, and deaths, of course, are also refracted into these social networks, as are clusterings in neighborhoods and skills.

When a person strikes up a pleasant chat with a stranger at a bus stop, this does not constitute a network tie. What counts is that each identity is, and knows it is, committed to some entailment to still other ties. Take an opposite example. Even in present society, although you may not like or seek out your cousin, this person remains known socially as your cousin. Although you don't perceive a tie to this cousin, that person is embraced by cousin-hood in social reference.[4] The requisites are a domain context and also coordinate ties, which is to say, a network context. *An apparently simple pair-tie can be seen to be a considerable social accomplishment.*

Research often works outward from some tangible behavior patterns or topics such that it need not call for boundaries, implicit or explicit. Think of the qualitative work by Erving Goffman (1971), or even scan the quantitative studies in our journals. Networks could be used as method, metaphor, and form for such research (Knox, Savage, and Harvey 2006).

In most actual projects, sociologists need not trouble themselves with reifications such as society. Nonetheless, theorists insist that observers use some explicit framing, which need not conform to framings by those being observed. Niklas Luhmann (1995) developed an especially penetrating formulation, in the idiom of systems theory, around communication that is wary of environment. A new version presented in *Against Essentialism* by Stephan Fuchs (2001a) takes the key step of regrounding social construction in social networks.

A specification of *tie* as an overall, general pair relation, also called a *multiplex tie*, sums up implications for ongoing process that are perceived from some range of past incidents. Or, alternatively, each multiplex connection in a general network sums across some scope of specialized relations; it incorporates all types of tie.

Can observation of discourse suffice to identify ties and their network? Social networks are rooted in the reflexive nature of language in talk and as enhanced by the three *g*'s of semiotics: glance, gesture, and grunt.[5] Choices in networks reflect the representations that people have about those to whom they tie, as well as assessments of sacrifice, opportunity, and time.

---

[4] For further background on roles, see, for example, Nadel (1957) on roles in general, and Boyd (1991) and White (1963a) on kinship role networks, and Berkowitz (1988) on phenomenology, and Pattison (1993) on models.

[5] From this base can grow sophisticated realizations of solidarity, from what Doreian and Fararo (1998) formulate as "ideational" and "relational" aspects (also see White 2006).

A relation in a dyad can be expressed without stories. Subtle, real-time interactions in a pair-tie, a dyad-as-process, have many facets, but these do not necessarily require verbal expression by way of a story. Hand-holding is a nonverbal way of expressing a relation. It is simultaneously very personal and yet also manifestly public, seeable by anyone around. There are whole classes of other nonverbal ways, such as glances and grunts, to express relations, and thus to constitute a tie in the given population.

And such ties have different meaning and occur more or less commonly depending on the history of that particular network population. Moreover, the cast of characters should be expanded to include objects. Relations of various youths to a snappy roadster are indispensable to capturing the network dynamics in the movie *Saturday Night Fever*. So were the relations of the hero in the same movie (played by John Travolta) to a routine job and to the tailoring of his new suit. French sociologists have developed the insight about objects in a call for recasting theory of social networks (Callon 1998; Latour 1999).

How can a tie capture the ambivalence and complexity of interaction? What is being coded as "a tie" is dynamics from control attempts around a dyad.[6] Pair balancings of control efforts can become generalized as a set of stories held in common. And indirect ties can gain standing in some strings of ties and stories. Expectations grow up as to both content and participants in ties. To be in one relation is to be enmeshed in further relations to some of those tied to you and your alters, to know of further warranties and entailments, thus generating new ties with other identities. So a tie is as much a projection as a record. The result across all identities is a network as more than a set of identities and their ties.[7] And networks and ties are also shaped by storied shadows from identities that have vanished or did not come into being. That notion of potential, according to the wide choice social life leaves you, figures large in the accounts I will give later, of styles (chapter 4) and careers (chapter 5).

Even if the initial claim about network analysis is true, just how much leverage is demonstrated? A series of papers out of the "Add

---

[6] The underlying netdom switching patterns are the substructure. These relations are the unmarked form dual to the ties that are marked by stories. This is a dualism common across language (Battistella 1996). The unmarked is elusive, and the marked can seem artifactual.

[7] "Network" is retained as designation because of its familiarity, but it does have misleading, mechanistic overtones. Terminology in social science applications remains loose and unstandardized, despite compendia such as Wasserman and Faust (1994), and histories such as Freeman (2004). There are mathematical foundations in theory of graphs and binary relations (e.g., Berge 1962; Harary 1977; Ore 1965; Watts 1999).

Health" study recently took on this question across ties of all sorts (Bearman, Moody, and Stovel 2004, p. 46; Moody and White 2003, table 1). Also, Barry Wellman stands out as having devoted an entire career to exploring and documenting natural social worlds in network terms.

2.2. How Ties and Stories Mesh in Networks

Meanings that come from switchings fold into stories, which thus come from, and also become a medium for, control efforts in ties. Since social situations include stories, nonverbal relations, and instantaneous ties, I conclude that social networks emerge only as ties mesh with stories.[8] Particular ties and stories get spun off as by-products of some particular history, but I can offer some general guidance for specification and analysis.

I associate a single overall story, such as acquaintance, with a general network in multiplex tie, whereas stories specialized to types of tie may call up multiple networks. For participants, stories are the key, and they may suffice to discriminate among *types of tie*, resulting in multiple networks, as for kinship relations. A set of dyads may each exhibit several qualities of relation that may be discriminated and explicitly coded only by an analyst. He or she can factor the set into multiple networks.

Yet it may be that the whole set of stories proves necessary to sustain the metabolism of a single general network, such as of acquaintance. Participants may induce and call on a set of excuses and disclaimers and allowances that legitimate and keep viable a network of acquaintanceship. Walter Johnson (1999, chap. 1) was drawn to this conclusion concerning a chilling special case: relations in the slaveholding antebellum South. Concerning the stories from slaves:

> Some incidents appear so often that it seems certain they are stock figures. ... But these stock figures have a truth of their own to tell: they gesture at the way the world looked to people whose access to information and technology was limited. ... Whether or not every one of these stories was true (and we know some were), collectively they tell a truth. (p. 11)

And concerning court stories by others about slaves, from Louisiana docket transcriptions:

[8] But this is the conclusion of a researcher, an observer, and netdom analysis perhaps should be closer to lived experiences, foggy and fuzzy and elusive and stochastic. Such may be going on with the current reifications of social networks among business organizers and marketers, within the military, in everyday talk, and among social analysts.

> Captured in the neat script of a law clerk are conversations a century and a half old. . . . I have generally read the docket records as if they contained only lies. And yet these lies describe the circumstances of a specific sale in terms of a shared account of what was likely to happen in the slave market. A few stock stories supported much of the testimony. (p. 12)

Nothing is simple and clear-cut in process across social situations, but we can lay some bases for possible guidelines for analysts. The Internet forum illustration in chapter 1 opens out into different types of ties. For example, strength of tie derives from the number of direct responses to another user's postings, and/or from the intimacy of the content of communication. There is asymmetry if one user never responds to your comments.

And remember that incidences of types of tie are not some extraneous analytic matter. They are part of the armaments of manipulation for control. With general networks one looked for effects according to the absolute or relative efforts and resources devoted in ties, rather than to their specialized domain. Generally, multiplex ties also play into selfhood, as we will see later.

After canvasing stories, first consider two pairs of contrasting framings for the mesh of ties and stories, note variants within each, and then use the framings to cross-tabulate example networks.

Next we turn from meshes to sources and varieties of their stories and ties. The talking that underlies story-ties requires constant use of pronouns and other deictics, which are prominent in every language, no doubt because of their utility.

2.2.1. Stories and Ties

Each tie that persists encapsulates struggles for control. Each tie is a metastable equilibrium of contending control attempts, and as such it induces chronic reports. Ties portray connections, but these need not be once-and-for-all interconnections among fixed identities. Ties always reflect but also are implicated in activity, as seen by observers as well as participants.

As the reports accumulate, invoked also in other ties, they fall into patterns that tend to be accommodated as stories. A whole set of stories can go with or come from a type of tie. A *convention* (Lazega and Favereau 2002) is such a set of stories. Conventions emerge over time with networks of ties as their context. This process goes on right under our eyes again and again. The playground will have its neighborhood argot. The occasion and arena are there for a primitive language to emerge as a vehicle for contending accountings.

Rules of thumb, which often appear in packages (Simon 1945), are one form of conventions for a network. Rules of thumb are widely transposable across concrete social contexts and across frames of interpretation. Rules of thumb applied *here* affect the application of rules of thumb *there*, or their application here at other times. They are transmitted and vouched for along strings of interconnection in a network. A language makes them available in idioms and formulae. Rules of thumb can supply the story set for a network.

Regular life is shot full of contradictions. They are less obtrusive to adults than they are to children. The contradictions may even become invisible. Everyday life has trained us and supplies us with nice packages of stories. At any given time, we have learned to apply just some one of the set, and suppress memories of the switchbacks and changes that at other times we use and embroider to get along. Much of social science has been an auxiliary to this provision of packages of stories sufficient to account for most anything we find—but only by suitable ex post selection of one rather than another story.[9]

This explains how it is that stories have become so universal, how they communicate so effectively across diverse hearers and audiences (including social science). No one has made this section's case as well as Charles Tilly: I quote at length from his recent masterful reweaving of a generation's worth of sustained analysis:

> Effective explanations require the peculiar combination of skepticism about the stories told with close attention to how stories work. . . . Most of social life consists of interpersonal transactions whose consequences the participants can neither foresee nor control. Yet, after the fact, participants in complex social transactions seal them with stories. . . . Identities are social arrangements reinforced by socially constructed and continuously renegotiated stories . . . we can *contextualize* stories, which means placing crucial stories in their nonstory contexts and seeing what social work they do. (Tilly 2002, pp. x–xiv)

And from further on:

> Consider the place of standard stories in social construction. For reasons that lie deep in childhood learning, cultural immersion, or perhaps even the structure of human brains, people usually recount, analyze, judge, remember and reorganize social experiences as *standard stories* in which a small number of self-motivated entities interact within a constricted, contiguous time and space.

---

[9] Some social and economic theorists are working to adapt preferences and goal maximization to the realities of perception accommodated by stories. One rubric in this awakening is "framing" effects (e.g., Kreps 1988, chap. 14; Lindenberg 1989a, b).

Even if the individuals involved harbor other ideas, the embedding of stories in social networks seriously constrains interactions, hence collective actions of which people in those networks are capable. . . . They recast events after the fact in standard story form. (Tilly 2002, pp. 8, 9)

2.2.2. Mesh: Situational or Inscribed?

Political polarization from an emergent network, as in the Baldassarri and Bearman (2006) modeling example that I gave at this chapter's beginning, is a pure example of *situational mesh*. Ties are observed to congeal out of a soup of discussions, to emerge from cross-cutting situations. By contrast, kinship relations exhibit a mesh of significations that are *inscribed*, that can be transposed in setting or time. There are, of course, ranges of in-between meshes. For example, Small World traces chain together situations, but according to a criterion inscribed by the searcher.

2.2.3. Mesh: General or Specialized?

This contrast can also be expressed as *inclusive* versus *delimiting*. Small World traces here too are in between, since they mesh ties with all sorts of content but always under the rubric of recognition. But taking multiplex versus uniplex to be the relevant contrast instead obscures the importance of strength of tie, measured as a continuous cline; see the Rapoport example that I give later.

2.2.4. Source and Variety in Stories

A relationship gets interpreted in stories both by its members and by onlookers. Amy Shuman has traced this process in depth with a group of city schoolgirls. She records how stories over many months emerge through switchings back and forth between oral account and diary entries.

Considered more generally, how does this process come about? Identities perceive and invoke the likelihood of impacts from other identities, which are seen to do the same. These relations get coded from raw reports into various shorthands of discourse and deportment. Then sets of signals, communications on topics, get transposed from one situation to another. Eventually these sets can settle down into stories. These stories are fresh in any particular application, but they are also familiar from before and elsewhere, so that relational ties can indeed be recognized by stories.

Indispensable to all of this are resources in language: first, of course, discursive (Silverstein 1998) but also grammatical. The sentence is a marvelous mechanism for packing three strands of meaning into brief utterances that interact to sustain talk (Halliday 1994, p. 34). A sentence can carry a story, which can also draw on lexical distribution and on other cohesive resources of text (Halliday and Hasan 1976).

Stories include everything from the simplest line heard on the playground—"Ernie loves Sue, . . . true, . . . true"—through artful excuses and basic daily accounts and on through recondite nuggets of professional gossip. Stories are invoked, without hesitation, endlessly. But a story in itself does not suppose or require identities and relations. Gossip can be about the collapse of a skating rink roof under the weight of snow, or a shout that the surf is mounting, a call to the beach.

A story is at root an *authority*, a transfer of identity, which explains its binding to network.[10] This holds as much for respondents answering a survey as for civil servants issuing reports; therefore, social science must attend to this truth. Anything about which you tell a story can get reflected in a relation. Everyday time spent with stories, building and hearing them in gossip or whatever, suggests that they are crucial in social process.[11] And imbibing a formal story or film is so similar to imbibing "real life" that their authors and directors also, like gossipers in ordinary life, must have found effective shorthands for expressing identities and control in social relationships.

Stories can and do conceal projects of control. Failures too require accompanying stories. Even setting aside chicanery, concealment would still remain in social space. Every identity continually seeks control to maintain itself, and in that struggle breaks, as well as establishes, relations with other such identities. Both the tensions and their overcoming induce stories and may require sets of stories to characterize relations within a network.

2.2.5. Repertoires for Story-Ties

Differentiation of ties is not a passive, detached affair. Types of story-tie evolve as a by-product from endless trading off among different

---

[10] This idea is due to Pizzorno (1991).

[11] Some sort of social network may be uncovered for other social species besides man, for wolves and monkeys at least. One finds pecking orders and ties and certainly control struggles there (e.g., Wilson 1979; Wynne-Edwards 1985). These involve communication, but at a simple level that need not rise above the pheromone level of an ant society (Wilson 1970). This suggests that meaning and stories are what set human social action apart. Without stories, social action would have a monotone quality; there would not be all the "colors" that humans observe and use in social settings.

control efforts across identities. Multiplex networks initially report how the various identities have spread their presence in the course of these struggles. As struggles for control continue, the ties themselves, which report chronic states of struggle, are subject to splitting into distinct types of tie.

This factoring process can be illuminated in the abstract by an extensive literature based on observation of experimental discussion groups. Much of it is distilled by Bales (1970) through modeling. Before sketching two simple ways to characterize a tie or a type of tie abstractly, I turn to some of what we know empirically about repertoires.

Start with a focus on just those types of relations that are intense enough to persist indefinitely once established for a given ego. There seem to be around sixteen as a modal average. In early societies these relations were reckoned in a kinship frame. In those societies, above all, you have to deal with your in-laws, for one or more spouses at a time. The in-laws relate differently with your immediate kin, as well as the grandchildren, in ways you wish to monitor. The relative age of your siblings will circumscribe some of these choices.

A definitive study of hunter-gatherer demographics (Howell 1979, 1988)[12] finds about sixteen relatives recognized by a particular ego. Every kind of relation, practical and emotional, is construed in kinship terms in this mode of human social life.[13] Thus, sixteen is a good bet for the upper limit of distinct relations sustainable by human beings.

In current society but at much smaller scope, Sampson,[14] in his meticulous and fine-grained study of a monastery with its entering novitiate, differentiates eight types of tie, but he imposes them as a grammar of affections, which do not in fact all produce distinct configurations. This collapse to very few distinct types confirms extensive experience with sociometric testing on small populations: compare Bjerstedt (1956) on classrooms and Newcomb (1961) on fraternities. Regarding large populations, see Burt (1987), Fischer (1982), and D. White and Johansen (2006). In our own society, key ties are dispersed over peer, kin, work, neighborhood, and so on. Thus, many distinct sets of stories can earn recognition for different types of tie. But you still can-

---

[12] Her estimate, for an African setting, confirms the most detailed data available in print for Australian aborigines (Rose 1960).

[13] To this end, marriage choice is constrained in terms of kinship, as are residence and foraging. Howell's findings are not inconsistent with the little that can be deduced about early hominids by archaeological reconstructions.

[14] His thesis of 1968 has not, unfortunately, ever been published; see Boyd (1991) for definitive analysis.

not monitor across more than sixteen or so. From a survey of case studies one can argue for two abstract ways to discriminate among ties.[15]

First is the characterization of a tie as to *symmetry*. That is based on recognizing that the network metaphor is always a metaphor of flows. Information, support, and attitudes are a few of the "substances" seen as "flowing" through a network. Thus, simple codings of ties—even the basic coding of on/off—can yield useful assessments of what's going on in the network. Yet the number of possible patterns, networks, is huge, even for small populations or only on/off coding. Since each tie is a relation between two identities, an on/off tie has three states: besides being "on" from both sides, it can be asymmetric—"on" just in one direction, or "on" just in the other direction. This is the core of the abstract characterization of tie as symmetric or asymmetric.

Strength is a second way to discriminate ties. The multiplex tie can be distinguished by intensity level. At one extreme is the multiplex tie of sociometry and casual gossip. These are the ties of everyday networks spun out as in bars or acquaintances dancing, or on a playing field. These are overall ties as commonly perceived. The other extreme is the tie of maximum intensity. Such a strong tie embodies frequent interchanges and sustained perception between the identities, which perhaps helped to induce the identities. Strength of ties is the key aspect in the arguments I present later derived from results of the Granovetter and Rapoport studies.

2.2.6. Other Ways to Types of Tie

Tangible sorts of ties may be differentiated further. For example, a family tie may be extracted from a multiplex tie even aside from its strength or symmetry. But splitting open the multiplex tie is not the prime goal here, nor is abstraction the prime logic. The theoretical focus is upon how different types of ties are constructed socially.

A name for an identity makes it transferable at the same time as unique, so that a name is the primitive element of "position."[16] Similarly, a label for a juncture of identities, a dyad, makes it into a "tie" type, transferable. These latter colorings, the animuses of distinctive stories that give content to types of ties, can be borrowed from the valuations

---

[15] This is aside from self-conscious cultural formulations such as Duby's (1980) three realms. Others also relate type of tie to the concept of "realm," on which I quote Tillich (1963, p. 16): "'Realm' is a metaphor like 'level' and 'dimension,' but it is not basically spatial (although it is this too); it is basically social. A realm is a section of reality in which a special dimension determines the character of every individual belonging to it, whether it is an atom or a man." See chapters 5 and 6 in this book.

[16] Developed as a construct in chapter 8.

set up in the emergence of identity, as is illustrated in the next chapter. Again, the grammatical features of language are crucial resources.

Types of tie, then, can be explained and labeled, and their number can be estimated in terms of *specializations*. Specialization describes how the ecological is patched into the social—for example, in work (Udy 1970), where it has a technical or engineering cast. You are living in multiple networks, each limning a distinct realm.

Some network of all-purpose multiplex ties of low intensity is all that may be perceived by the actors involved, as well as uncovered by most research studies on a population. But upon further scrutiny, the ties may be seen to devolve into special networks, each a network of ties with a focus from a particular set of stereotyped stories. An identity can be very differently perceived in these different networks. In the playground domain with the peer type of tie, for example, a child may be perceived as on the offensive, a identity that may be compensating for its defensive role at home, where a different set of stories characterizes the kinship type of tie.

The analytic task is to sort out types of tie in a particular concrete population, using methods that are transposable. Discriminating among types of tie is a hallmark of expertness in the sociocultural milieu, but there are formal techniques to help an observer sort out the discriminations (cf. Burt 1987, 1990). Techniques are needed that go beyond both tribal kinship lore and early sociometric studies described later; we will return to this in section 2.5, the Modeling section.

2.2.7. Indirect Ties and Transitivity

Another universal basis for separate types of tie becoming recognized is the institutionalization of *indirect ties*, that is, ties compounded from adjoining ties. Participants and observers alike persuade themselves it is cogent to single out some such tie for a network of its own. A relationship grown beyond acquaintanceship implies sufficient familiarity with the other party to know to whom there is a further tie. For example, a friend's friend is a reality, gives orientation to action; yet the tie to a friend's friend need not be considered as a friend relation itself. Thus, a crude distance can be measured in steps away, given some calibration of intensity of relation required to code the presence of a tie. Some sense of distance and cumulation, of social space, is a by-product of and motivation for network thinking (Burt 1990).

Kinship is the premier instance: e.g., grandparents, cousins, uncles, in our Western parsing, or mother's brother's daughter, father's sister's daughter, or elder sibling's descendants, or mother's mother's brother's daughter's daughter and the like in various other kinship systems (Schneider 1968). In Riggs's *Thailand* (1966) two clientship ties, if both to the same party, generate, by observable processes on the ground, a nexus of behavior between those indirectly connected that is sufficiently distinct to be recognized as such. Thus is encouraged recognition in that society of other sets of parallel ties as a separable type (Riggs 1964).

It seems from the wide gamut of case studies available that the indirect tie will tend to be more homogeneous in intensity and in concrete attributes than the direct ties that occasion its phenomenological construction. One example, from the Norman feudal regime treated in chapter 6, is how magnates' conscious efforts to enhance recognition of indirect ties of fealty tended to generate a much more uniform quality of relation than held across the direct ties, which, however, still seem more uniform than in the preceding Anglo-Saxon regime. And what makes the ambiance of Thai society so distinctive is not the patronage tie in itself, but rather the universality of recognition of indirect ties carried to the bounds of total population: it is the limiting case of network population as universe.

A base type of asymmetric tie may change so as to no longer generate indirect relations. This was true in the Norman development of the mere household knight (see chapter 6). Indirect ties generated from symmetric ties are more likely to gain separate recognition; yet while indirect-tie formation can generate recognition of distinctiveness for new types of tie, at the same time the relevant scope of population tends to be enlarged, which in itself would tend to weaken recognition of distinctness.

When indirect ties get lumped in with the base type of tie, that network will fill in, of course. And ties of that type will then exhibit more transitivity. Such a partial tendency to transitive filling in is surely common. It has been noted in Small World studies, although those studies emphasize how sheer connectivity accommodates with local clustering.

This point triggers attention to another way to arrive at a single network. For this purpose, I introduce the notion of a "public" as an overarching realm in which only an overall, bland set of stories is invoked in relations. Think of Goffman's strangers on the stage of our city streets and subways. Or think of Peter Bearman's (2005) Manhattan doormen talking with apartment house visitors. The relations are muted and thereby transient and so widespread as to wash out distinctiveness in network incidence and in impact on other networks that those identities invoke.

2.3. Networks Sort Themselves into Types of Tie

Stories come to frame choices, from among the innumerable distinctions and nuances that could be imposed upon relationships in hindsight or from the outside. This is a dialectic of accountings in which distinct hues and distinct types of tie can come to be recognized.

2.3.1. Coupling and Decoupling

Networks are phenomenological realities as well as measurement constructs. The multiplex tie contributes, as a cause and mechanism of exchange, to allocation and to distribution more generally. For processes where sheer connectedness is the issue, multiplex network is suitable: this is considering tie as coupler. But ties also go with decoupling, which fits with factoring into distinct types of tie.

Coupling describes the way in which different parts of social structure are interlinked to work together, whereas *decoupling* designates the processes that lead each part to deal with some aspects of the "work" and to ignore others. These constructs are tools for explicating more clearly, and also generalizing, the old, still sound, idea of the importance of the division of labor as key to social process. In the Internet forum illustration used in chapter 1, logging out of an account is decoupling, whereas logging in is coupling.

Decoupling presupposes coupling, not least into networks of relations. The primordial tie was to your mother. There you found your first footing. That was the story told, which everyone took for granted. And then other ties of kinship came into your experience and helped shape identity, variously through bullying or succor or play, embedding you into a kinship network using multiple stories.

As any identity emerges out of social process, it couples onto other identities. When ties are severed or an identity degenerates, it decouples. Coupling means inclusion; decoupling means severance. Even this distinction is not simple to make. Perceptions are at issue and, of course, also control.

Contending projects of control, as these efforts generate stories, can disrupt routine. Such processes that loosen constraints attributed to control, yield decoupling. So decoupling induces a spread of alternative stories as menu. Then, as relations among identities get characterized by a set of stereotyped stories, they become a type of tie, specifying a network. Subsequently, when two distinct types of tie co-occur at a node, coupling is signaled to some degree between those two networks, yet some independence in sequences of action continues across situations.

Accuracy of perception within a complex social formation—perhaps measurable by the density of sociologists or of mothers-in-law?—increases the need for couplers-decouplers. This is because wide and widespread misperceptions, including ignorance, are principal conditions for several coupler mechanisms to work effectively. For example, many regularities of size distribution, such as will be discussed in chapter 4, are largely the cumulative results of random processes, yet their results are commonly interpreted as coherent signals of ability and leadership.

Coupling and decoupling do not deal with levels, with embeddings into new levels of identity, which I will take up later in this chapter, and in chapter 3. Coupling can be coded as the provision of channels between parts and aspects of networks, as with chaining of ties, as well as multiple networks. Decoupling can be seen, then, as the primary process, the exchange through these channels of different types of uncertainty.

Inhomogeneity of networks remains a challenge to measurement and perception despite attempts to sidestep it (Wellman 1981; Howell 1969), yet it may be a necessary aspect of rhetoric. Rhetoric must accommodate to inhomogeneity not only of networks but also of the rest of the context of that institutional system, as we will see in chapter 5. So pervasive decoupling must underlie any rhetoric, which therefore calls for a calculus of trade-offs among ambage, ambiguity, and contingency, as will be introduced at this chapter's end and in chapter 3.

2.3.2. Dynamics of Control

Stories serve to describe the ties in networks. These are ties of contention as well as of cooperation and of complementarity. There will be many distinct perceptions, many stories about particular ties and interconnections of ties. Stories serve to soothe identities' irreducible searches for control, which can be captured in stasis as stories representing ties.

New and additional control can be achieved by some actors when a network of multiplex ties becomes factored into distinct subnetworks of types of tie. One illustration is the trenchant analysis by Padgett and Ansell (1993) of the rise to supreme power of the Medici faction within the Florentine polity of the 1400s. They detail how particular stories became associated there with various distinct types of tie.[17] Everyone can see that the Medici did centralize control; what was less obvious is that they segregated ties to different dependents into different sorts of connections. This kept the dependents relatively separated and segregated, connected only via the Medici themselves, and therefore not a good base for success in the chronic counter-control attempts. In this dynamics for control, the nature of the tie is kept muddy, multiplex (see also the discussion of Leifer ties in chapter 7).

The combination of asymmetric and indirect modes for generating recognition of distinct types of tie, yields a richer variety of patterns than does indirect chaining of symmetric ties from overlaps. The latter tend toward a form of solidarity or mutual common reference. The former exhibit that also, as in the omnipresent formation of councils and courts among dependents at the same remove from a patron (for discussion of that process, see chapter 3), but furthermore, they may string into the mutually aversive chains of dependence that characterize clientelism (for that discussion, see chapter 6).

Factoring into distinct types of tie, along with reconnecting through brokers, is again seen to enhance control in the study by Karen Barkey (forthcoming) of the last two centuries of the Ottoman Empire. The scale is larger, and the contents of types of tie differ, but the sociologic carries through.

To recapitulate, identities become embedded into some story-ties with respect to other identities in a network population during the course of continuing struggles for control. Control struggles can open up a multiplex network into distinct networks for separate types of tie. The distinct types are as much perception by third parties as by the "ends" or nodes of a tie itself. The third party may be a native observer or an analyst. Under pressure from identities' interactions with one another, stereotyped stories emerge as social accountings that discriminate types of tie.

There is, among these several dynamics, a countervailing process: ties, once discriminated, may again be thrown back together into a common kind, with attendant acknowledgment of diverse and subtle multiplexities for particular exemplars. The Norman feudal example in chapter 6 describes processes mediated by money mechanisms where indirect tie rights are made fungible, available in a direct tie.

---

[17] Their paper is unusual in the number of types of ties distilled from the historical accounts. There are nine, and then the analysis goes on (1993, p. 17) to argue aggregation into two families, one of strong types of tie—each one tending to inbreeding in the sense of Rapoport traces—and the other a family of weak types of tie that cluster the actors quite differently, following structural equivalence.

2.3.3. MAN Triads and Other Subnetworks

There can be subnetwork population as process too. A host of external impacts can break off some fragment of a network as the focus of everyone there; I return to this in the last sections of this chapter. Any control regime that survives and can be observed, must also encompass strategic moves by participants, and these must involve a switch in type of a given triad. And ties centered around affect and emotions can impact one another heavily in an immediate locality.

Such triad analyses were pioneered by Davis, Holland, and Leinhardt (D-H-L) in various combinations (Davis 1979). They emphasized an interpretation of triads as triangles in which there is only one type of tie, which is either symmetric (Mutual) or asymmetric (A) or absent (Null). Even in a single triad, thirteen distinct patterns are possible.

These authors provide extensive statistical framing in which to evaluate, for particular populations, hypotheses about which of the thirteen patterns occur at greater than the likelihood of chance, and which occur at less than chance likelihood. Across a larger population of nodes, there obviously will be heavy overlaps among triads, which can obscure the picture. The analysts' explorations show that results are heavily influenced by the totals of M, A, and N edges across the population (hence, the designation as MAN); they control for this in evaluations. The observed distribution of triads by type in a network can suggest ideas about control there, based on this profile of the outcomes of struggle.

The focus of D-H-L is on the degree of transitivity predicted among the ties in a network. Similarly, a later colleague, Jensen (1985), derived algorithms for laying out likely conformations to transitivity of the whole network, as treelike structures, partial hierarchies. Theory can then seek interpretations for diverse substantive settings. I expand on this in chapters 3, 5, and 6.

Much the same setup can be given a very different interpretation, in which M now represents liking—call it the positive tie p; A represents ties of disliking; and N is the label for each pair without a tie. One can try to test the familiar conjecture from Heider balance theory that in any triangle without null ties, there will be either two ties of dislike, or none. This has been extended in various ways, around a tendency for each closed loop of like and dislike ties across the network to have only an even number of dislike ties. One can then show a tendency for the set of all nodes to split into two sets with dislike ties only between, not within, the two sides. That version of a MAN approach can be accommodated in the blockmodel approach taken up at chapter's end.

Triads are, of course, a special case. Many problems of network analysis (and not, of course, only social networks) require locating and factoring out subnetworks, in a range of sizes.

2.3.4. Siting through Stories into Social Times

Social structures are often made to seem the antipodes to, or at least unrelated to, details and nuances of sequencing in timing. This is in part because of the influence of structuralism (e.g., Lévi-Strauss 1969). Social times should instead be accounted as much part of structure as are network spaces. In the words of network theorist Granovetter:

> It is also important to avoid what might be called "temporal reductionism": treating relations and structures of relations as if they had no history that shapes the present situation. . . . *Structures* of relations also result from processes over time, and . . . without such an account, analysts slip into cultural or functionalist explanations, both of which usually make their appearance when historical dynamics have been neglected. (In Breiger 1990, chap. 2, p. 8)

Social process creates and defines distances for time just as it does for network. Social times are woven together with meanings, through switchings; so times go with stories as well as with relations. Stories cite behavior. Behavior guides stories. But, to quote the dictionary definition, "Behavior is action on specific occasions involving essentially external and sometimes superficial relationships." Story goes beyond behavior to weave interpretation into and around relationships, as they then interweave over time into network forms. Chapter 7 will look at problems of timing in "simple" exchange reciprocity, as discussed in Leifer (1990).[18]

The systems of tenses in language are, of course, key. They enable continuing updating of stories as social process continues. Meanings get written on network as palimpsest—that is, as tracings of what went before.

2.4. How It Matters

I will explore how all this matters through examining a few of the classic studies that gave teeth to social network analysis. The first two

---

[18] The vexed issues of exchange and reciprocity (Blau 1964; Emerson 1962; Macneil 1978; Newman 1965) require analysis of embedding as well, which is a kind of dual to timing. Ideology can entrap us in the notion that specific local exchanges are the "realistic" version that should be modeled. Contexts of broader scope for exchanges should supply further antidote to this ideology.

studies do not have the vividness that comes from ethnographic study of particular scenes as I present subsequently, but conversely, the quantitative ones can come to more reliable measures.

2.4.1. Rapoport's Profiles

Draw a network of ties among the children on the playground first encountered in chapter 1. Represent each child by some point as node. The network is then a set of nodes with connecting lines, each representing a tie between a pair of children. To define the tie, some cutoff is assumed on strength or persistence of relations in a dyad (Berkowitz 1982; Burt 1980, 1982).[19]

Another helpful abstraction is to fix the nodes in a social geography of rejection and affiliation, rather than having them rush around in the field. A final abstraction is to catch the pattern as ties in a matrix whose rows and columns for kids are in a social ordering that is not necessarily in line with location on the playing field.

Rapoport (1983) and associates (e.g., Foster, Rapoport, and Orwant 1963) brought networks to life for modern social analysts with an innovation for tracing networks. Long prior, sociograms, following Moreno, had been used to record small interpersonal configurations such as any teacher intuited in the classroom (Waller 1932). The question was how to extend the idea operationally to larger settings.

Rapoport proposed to measure large networks by frequency profiles of traces through them. The idea of tracing a string of ties would be anachronistic in some early or tribal societies—though not in ancient Rome or Persia. The issue is just who, in pairs, are interconnected, and just how, amid the diversity of many distinct and often incomparable frames of kinship, work, and play. In particular, who are interconnected by that most sophisticated of notions, sheer acquaintanceship.

To bound a setting is to introduce the arbitrary. Like Coleman (1961) before them, Rapoport and associates used a (junior) high school, the simplest and most accessible exemplar microcosm of the modern, polyglot social context. "Who knows whom," on one or another crite-

---

[19] One can get obsessed with measurement problems and prospects. The possible cues are legion. Eye movements can be as reliable as utterances (Duncan 1977) as indicators of ties. One actor need not be abstracting from behaviors in the same way as each other, or as an observer might abstract if called upon to articulate that social setting. Early on, Bjerstedt (1956) uncovered surprising robustness across kinds of sociometric probes. A sociometric network is no more than an observer's coding or recording of a set of relations between pairs of people. Any network is less than a map known and attended to by all of the actors in the network. There may or may not be names that are known. A network is a matter of fuzzy sets (Zadeh et al. 1975).

rion,[20] is asked and answered within this school, whose principal can ensure that each child is recording choices according to instructions. The size of this school, approximately one thousand actors, turns out to be apt: big enough to exhibit nontrivial connectivity and yet small enough to be manageable.[21]

What are the significant parameters, what is the social "shape" of this network representation, this indigestible mass of claims and verifications of who knows whom? As observers, we do not, for example, care which Suzy is most popular, although we may be interested in how divergent individuals are in popularity. The single most interesting question to Rapoport, and predecessors, was how interconnected the school of youths was and thus also how fragmented.

It is a question with limits. Social action always arises from accidents and speculations and gamings that become aspects of more far-reaching and crisscrossing projects of control. Later we report incidental observations of neighborhood bars and acquaintance dances. But Rapoport's traces are important tools of measurement, despite being divorced from particular incidents.

Rapoport exploited the combination of two ideas. First, conceive connectivity as how many people can be reached from some person, taken as a representative location within the population, and according to the remove, to the number of steps through intervening acquaintances. Second, distinguish ties from one another according to the perceived intensity of the relation.

Each idea requires many subsidiary notions to become operational. The conception must be based on sampling from a statistical ensemble of possibilities. Try out a number of randomly selected actors each as "the" center from which to trace out connections; useful parameters will then derive from averaging the resulting traces. Trace out a given sequence as far as it can go. Realize that from some Sam at the "center," one may reach some given Suzy by any number of distinct chains, sometimes through completely distinct sets of intermediaries.

According to the first idea, Rapoport presents a nesting of cumulative curves. Each reports the (averaged) percentage of the school that had been reached at the jth remove from the child making the direct choices. These are the children reached indirectly (and often repeatedly) through any and all chains of ties through whatever intermediaries, traced from the trial "center" who made the initial direct choice.

[20] In their choices, respondents prove not to pay much attention to the exact criteria stipulated—see previous note.

[21] As was mentioned in chapter 1, this is also the minimal size for relatively separable and independent populations in all sorts of contexts, from Australian aborigine on to modern village.

One curve traces just through the first choices, another traces just for the second choices, and so on. So there is a separate curve for each "order of closeness" of acquaintanceship choice. The profiles of rising connectivity constructed in this way are reported in the diagrams used by Rapoport and his associates.

The second idea was operationalized by having respondents list acquaintances in order of closeness or some such criterion. Rapoport then pretended as if the fifth choices, for example, really made up a world of their own, identifying a certain intermediate "level" of intensity. Thus, traces are given separately for each successive intensity level of ties.

The main message of the work is exactly in the neat nesting of successive intensity profiles in Rapoport's graphs. The monotonic rise in the number connected is definitional, and the eventual height of the asymptotic proportion of the total school reached may be rather erratic as a measure, even after averaging. What is fascinating is that the indicator of intensity, which necessarily is crude and may not be valid, distinguishes whole trace profiles so neatly.

Quality of life among students in the school may correlate more closely with the sheer relative incidence of the different strengths. The relative absence of medium-strength ties may go with higher incidences of bullying and marginalizing. And, of course, density of the absence of ties, which here was set by study design, will contribute information too, as I note later in the section on diffusion. Chapter 4 will further pursue this argument of quality as derived from profiles in order to operationalize *styles* as a construct.

2.4.2. Granovetter Ties and Medium Ties

Ask yourself this simple question: Should the profile for best friend lie above or instead below the profile for a choice of a weaker relation? Granovetter brought Rapoport's work to the attention of, and use by, the social science community through demonstrating that this was indeed *the* question. Moreover, Granovetter showed that it was most fruitful to simplify the question into weak ties versus strong ties; label this union of ties based on intensity, *Granovetter ties*.

Granovetter (1973, 1982) derived from Rapoport's results the conclusion that ties and network were intertwined in a manner that was, at first sight, paradoxical. Ties that were intrinsically weaker, more casual, yielded higher connectivity across the network: weak ties are strong. That is, the way in which weak ties spread themselves around is such that they connect a larger fraction of a world together than do the same number of strong ties spread out in their way.

Strong ties, ties given precedence by the issuers, are weak in the broader context because they do not bind as large a fraction of a world into a corporate whole in connectivity. Granovetter elaborated all the nuances implied. Strong ties did fit into strong, if tiny, corporates so inwardly turned as only to choose each of the few intimate others again and again without attention to the larger context of persons. Sum it up abstractly: Close-knitness of a network is highly correlated with involuteness.

Granovetter (1974) then showed that access to jobs was dependent upon the implications of these Rapoport traces, as no doubt could be shown for sexual access also. Not only are network perceptions shown to be intertwined with concrete networks, but also the accumulative impact of social structure is demonstrated. Granovetter captured so much attention because his results were not obvious; they could become plausible with thought, but they were not accessible to uninformed intuition.

We may discover that strong ties can subsist only between like actors, whereas weak ties of everyday networks may be incident between any pair of identities. But Granovetter ties, both weak and strong, are also multiplex connections between identities. Multiplex ties maintain themselves through narrative stories able to account for uncertainties, both physical and social. But a black-and-white portrayal as reflected in Granovetter ties can't accommodate cultural nuance and intermediate intensity. Granovetter ties instead deal with connectivity and clustering, as shown earlier.

Note that social times are also articulated by networks of ties. A strong tie, as seen from inside it, constitutes a continuing struggle for control between two identities, and this struggle defines the phenomenological present—which in terms of biophysical space-time is a fuzzy set (Zadeh et al. 1975) rather than an instant. For that very reason, it can sustain itself over long periods, years. Granovetter's weak ties are casual as seen either by others or by selves and may have only fleeting existence.

The focus of interest now becomes ties of intermediate strength. Any tie is defined by, induces, and responds to stories, but only as communicated in that dyad between identities. Control pressures within an identity also furnish a base of comparison of the strength of ties. Except when control pressures *between* identities either are smaller or are greater than the pressures *inside* them, stability can be anticipated for such networks. The inference that is relevant now is that Granovetter ties, weak and strong, are excluded.

All the other types of tie—those that are qualitatively differentiated—correspond to the whole intermediate range of social times, neither short nor long. Then is when multiple networks by type of tie can be recognized. Types of tie are factored as sets of stories. Any tie of intermediate intensity can be diffracted into one or more types of tie, where each type goes with a particular story from some set of stories, a menu.

So qualitative distinctions among ties hold just for intermediate periods as well as for ties of intermediate strength. One can confirm this by turning to how identities themselves distinguish types of tie, especially in complex and differentiated contexts. These are contexts that invoke unbundling overall relations into the types of tie.

One class of examples comes from working out connotations of the terms *favoritism, nepotism,* and *venality.* A variety of relevant studies (e.g., Kelsall 1955; Namier 1961; Mousnier 1971, 1984; Swart 1949) establish story sets and a time frame. Job placements, for example, commonly involve such unbundlings of preexisting ties that are neither weak nor strong.[22] This is developed further in chapter 6 with regard to professional regimes.

2.4.3. Hanging Out in Corporates

Networks contextualize identities, but connectivity is not the only basis for discriminating context. A clique, at one extreme of network topology, exhibits full interconnection of all pairs. This may come from or become marked by belonging in a group of comparable actors. Designate as corporate any such group in which membership is recognized. But this need not imply intimacy, since membership in a corporate is, and is perceived as, a state that is exactly to be taken for granted.

Membership presumes, as the norm, lack of questioning. *Character* is a suitable term for what membership is to reflect. As stories are seen to characterize identity formation in general, so gossip in particular tends to cluster around character as a member. Members of a corporate may be deemed structurally equivalent to one another on grounds of affiliations held in common.

Comparability is achieved and presupposed as character in a corporate group. Stability is to be guaranteed through ritual, as it does for clans in tribes. And a clique might bind into a distinct identity at a higher level, a development I will sketch in the next section. Then, in

---

[22] But that depends on overall context. For example, under clientelistic spoils systems (see chapter 6), no differentiation of skills may be recognized, and hence there is no unbundling of tie in awarding spoils. Note the institutional context is different here than in the job searches that Granovetter studied.

the next chapter, arena disciplines will come into the picture, as centered around a gradient superposed on comparability.

The important point is that corporate, in this sense, is very different from corporation in its ordinary current meanings, although it is true that such corporation may, but need not, contain various corporates. Corporation can be defined as formal organization (an institutional system in the sense described in chapter 5) and recognized in a rhetoric within a legal system. Take as a contrasting example, a body of professors in a long-established university, say the Faculty of Arts and Sciences, or of the Law School: at any given time, no doubt each will have some formal organizational and legal definitions, but these definitions will not account for, nor predict to, collegiality and commitment. Those qualities are governed by informal relations in networks and thus by corporates.

Nationalism presents somewhat the same distinction on a larger and hazier scale (Deutsch 1953). James Coleman (1961) reports on corporates with equal richness from a smaller and more specialized canvas, the American high school. In Coleman's account, it is initial networks among youngsters feeding in from diverse elementary schools and family clusters, which are overtaken by corporates that emerge among the children in straggly fashion. Coleman's substantive theme is the preoccupations and machinations of identities situated in these networks to become assimilated to the "right" sorts of corporates. These are the "in" crowds on a social level, specializing variously around clothes and clubs and hangouts and sports and so on. Of course, there can be more or less bullying too, correlating with differences in architectures across corporates.

Coleman's central vision is the importance of corporateness, above mere categorical identification, at the basic level of phenomenology. Adolescents above all are seeking a sense of belonging through emotionally grounded inclusion in the right sets. Coleman argues that school sports, especially in competitive leagues, are the single most important venue. Scholastic achievements were not broadly appealing, not foci around which youngsters wished to identify with a particular school.

And yet abstraction is what high schools engender regarding belonging, it seems from Coleman's comparative study of eight schools near Chicago. Younger kids have corporate identifications too, but these not only are usually smaller, they also are specific and concrete. High school induces one to perceive and to structure one's actions toward corporates that simultaneously are real and are abstract. These are precursor to larger arrays of attributes that become the building blocks of adult working life. Learning about belonging is not an easy task; expectations gyrate, and one can expect intense emotions to be generated. Rituals come into being within corporates, offering some privacy separate from the broader conventions.

Not just one sort of dynamic supports memberships in corporates. Go beyond Coleman's high school context. Think of neighborhood bars, which intermix network and corporate aspects. They cannot be reduced to just groups or to just networks.

"Neighborhood" can be vague and an amorphous context for distinguishing actors and their ties. So a bar can be a significant influence in shaping perceptions that there in fact exists a neighborhood, and who in what pairs are in that neighborhood as a penumbra to the bar. But what determines an establishment's going down this road of being identified with its locality? When, instead, is it identified as a gay bar or an ice hockey hangout or whatever—and when may several of these identifications all roll into one consistent compendium?

A tie to another who is habituated to the bar is a major avenue of initial attendance there. You may have heard some other way that your kind of person hangs out there. To become a neighborhood bar is to grow a particular kind of corporateness. Networks are pressured. Over time, persons in the paths by the bar, and the area around it, become very much more likely than others to get caught up in a tie or identification with the bar. Just as real, others who visit the bar simply by chance may not have ties and identifications proffered to them, but rather find signs of lack of welcome and even exclusion.

A neighborhood bar helps establish some corporate membership that operates largely from networks, the literal geographical locale being an amorphous field of possibility that is consistent with endless alternatives (see Wellman, Carrington and Hall [1988] for more extensive development). The corporateness is fuzzy, and in reality it is never inclusive of any complete local population. Wishful speculations and gaming calculations of social advantage underlie what we find; the supposed sociableness of drinking is less a truth than a stipulation conveniently shared among the speculations in the gamings.

2.4.4. Stratification

Intermixing of networks with corporate groups is endemic. These can be Small World or staccato networks, and may involve affective ties or work ties. Such intermixings can be seen to engender and shape the experience of social stratification.

Psychiatrist Elizabeth Bott (1957), in a landmark monograph, contrasted levels of well-being in their social lives, across a sample of married couples in England. This was a pioneering analysis in which Bott let the research findings guide her to the astonishing realization that social network structure dominated other more obvious attribute and situational factors. She identified two sorts of network context. In one, the husband and wife had much the same network of friends. In the other, each gender had a largely separate set of friends and thus were segregated in their sites of social interaction. There was a strong correlation to social class stratification, such that the couples with segregated networks tended to be working-class, whereas professional and middle-class couples tended to exhibit the joint network.

Now turn to a totally different setting and another classic study of stratification effects from network/corporates: Antal's study of Renaissance Florence (1965) is a prototype of how accurately past corporate formations can be reconstructed, even in medieval European cities. His study was focused on artwork production, and it shows how this cultural activity is very much enmeshed with the other aspects of, and stratification in, the round of social life. Thrupp (1948) had done much the same for all London guilds in a somewhat later time. Baxandall (1980) follows both prior authors in making brilliant use of art data for cities shaped around guilds. He builds from detailed studies of individual sculptors in their guild settings among a system of cities. Baxandall goes into detail about the cognitive bases, and economic context, of the particular jurisdictional joustings among separate but interdependent guilds. One can derive a sense of the stratification profile.

As Emirbayer and Goodwin (1994) argue with their "anticategorical imperative," network analysis can supplant the need for conventional categorical attributions of causation.

2.4.5. Ties and Selves

"Real selves" cannot be disentangled from "intimate ties" in modern social contexts. The modern concept of friendship is wholly aside from tit for tat, from favor for help. Silver (1989, esp. p. 274, 1990) provides a convincing argument and evidence for this evolution of friendship: he fixes its beginning as the Scot Enlightenment. Equate Silver's tie of friendship with the multiplex tie, the overall tie that we take for granted as the basis for civil and civic life.

This overall tie presupposes a lack of concern with the detailed balancing of obligations found in traditional formations. There is no tangible, concrete mechanism perceived as concerned with enforcement of obligation. This multiplex tie itself comes to seem a recent, modern innovation, along with a great desire to create "privacy." So it is ironic that its intimacy comes with pulling out of a particular realm of a type of tie, and shifting over into a "public" with a multiplex tie, probably without conscious awareness.

A tribal or feudal society does not know the luxury of a single, over-all tie that is not built into a concrete economy of obligation. Such social formations make use of relations, each part of which is lucidly factored out by audience and occasion—as kinship, as village, whatever. A mul-tiplex tie is a late and sophisticated construct, in this interpretation of evolution.

What the overall tie can bring about is the *person*. By this argument, which will be elaborated in chapter 4, the person is a late construct in perception. "Self" becomes the creation as well as the creator of person, with multiplex tie as the occasion for perception of a self. The tie of marriage is an example.

The key is that the multiplex tie requires, and contributes to, dispa-rate populations. Bott (1957) emphasized this point. She showed how to predict apparent changes in marital goals from underlying diver-gences in the interlocking between goals and concrete social relations. Marital style was read by Bott from the immediate context of social networks, which changed from couple to couple in London. A "joint" form of marriage relation was distinguished by Bott from segregated roles of domestic wife and pub husband. Only the joint form required each person to straddle different populations.

The world of romantic love is a precursor and correlate of the joint-form marriage. Romantic love is induced by the same modern contexts in which attitudes are reified. Love can be an induction of identity, but only as a metastable state. Romantic love is so important because de-velopment of this sort of subtle, ambiguous, gamed bond of some du-ration is a main path to unique personal identity in Goffmanesque so-cial contexts. Here is where the esoteric game theory that economists misplace onto "rational decision" might yield empirical insight.[23] Unique identities as persons are difficult to build; they are achieved in only some social contexts; they are not pre-given analytic foci.

Yet the modern multiplex tie need not be fraught with fearsome potency from balanced duress in gaming. Romantic love is merely rep-resentative of extreme examples, not of medians in multiplexity. (Some extreme examples, notably the feud, can also be found in tradi-tional formations.)

---

[23] It could be argued that the crippling of game theory is the worst effect of rational choice theory (for which see chapter 4). At its introduction by von Neumann, game theory had the potential of refounding the theory of social action. Unfortunately, it devolved into the hands of economic theorists. The results for many years were increasingly arid exer-cises, except in the work of Schelling (1978), who eschews systematic theory or modeling, and of Shubik (1984a, b). New developments are afoot, but effective game theory has to concern the induction of identities and disciplines, of social organization.

2.4.6. Modern Personhood

The modern vision of social milieus is exemplified by Goffman's (1963, 1967, 1971) and Simmel's (1955) strangers. These are persons who are so little reinforced by siting in specific social locations as to have only shadowy existence, to be creatures mostly bracketed, to be abstract actors triggered into concreteness only through encounters. Yet encounters can yield ties.

This modern type of vision fits as well in the province of romantic love, which at first sight seems so surely and purely a matter of one preexisting person intensely attuned to another. Perhaps. But in fact, the two persons are meeting in the Small World. This Small World has been emerging since around the time a phenomenology of romantic love was spreading beyond troubadour circles (Bloch 1977).[24] It is just when persons are shadowy in their social sitings that intensely personal attractions are generated, as Swidler (1986) and Leifer (1982) have argued. But this modern vision also reminds us that an identity may have just one or two facets or personae (out of its corporate self) exposed to observation at any given time. These facets are cobbled together, by the identity, from different frames, perhaps spun together in stories and yet decoupled as well.

Romances are outcomes of mutual searches among networks and groups that are keyed to occasions, to specific times marked by assemblages of persons as at acquaintance dances. Attention can be given, in social as well as physical perception, only to limited numbers of "contacts" at a time. Romantic acquaintanceship can be pursued only one "date" at a time. Romantic personages are a construct out of, a by-product of, distinctive eddies and enclaves that emerge as by chance in a Small World in which "eligibility" itself, perceived active participation, is induced by the states of queues in what can be visualized as a system of stochastic social servers.

Romantic love is a colorful topic. The same truths can be argued, however, about more everyday stuff of our life in Small World contexts. Attitudes are perhaps the most distinctive invention for modern contexts of social life. Substantial portions of time and cognitive attention are given to attitudes, as the adaptations and replenishment of hosts of notions on topics remarkably far removed from any tangible aspect of the actual daily living of the persons concerned.

---

[24] There are no person pheromones that signal one person as special to another; i.e., there is no doing ant societies (Wilson 1970) one better. A queuing system of stochastic servers (Kleinrock 1964; Riordan 1962) is a formal-modeling way to situate romantic love.

Persons become unique in identities, yet must be validated as stereo-types. So today to some extent the person *is* the attitudes. Each set of attitudes can be seen as distinguishing an identity.[25] Each such set can then find it comfortable to recognize and define as persons other such combinations, variously alike or compatible or neither.

Chapter 4 develops these matters at length. Here just note that mod-ern democratic politics and its incessant stream of "news," events made meaningful by episodic campaigns and elections, can be seen, in part, as contributing to the sustenance of personhood, to the creation of persons as distinctive combinations of attitudes that can be per-ceived as having meaningful continuity over time. Modern politics is a very inexpensive way to create the voters as civil persons, whatever the significance of the ostensible processes of decision and governance. Modern politics can be seen as a phenomenological by-product of the Small World. Milgram's (1977) use of persons whose name is not pre-viously known, to be the "targets" of search, do not seem bizarre to us as civil beings in part because we have come to attend to and "know" politicians as names remote from our direct experience.

Politics is just an example. Sports is another, or rather each is a cas-cading modern family of examples. Persons are defined and define themselves most easily and inexpensively, within the Small World that also yields romantic love, by what particular families of attitudes they penetrate into, as much as by particular attitudes upon topics appar-ently portentous enough that every person should indulge in a "hold-ing." Trivial Pursuits is a parlor game emblematic of an age.

2.5. Modeling Emergence of New Levels

Now look further into how to discriminate distinct networks with dif-ferentiated ties, in order to deepen insight into how sociocultural for-mations build. But corporates also deserve further examination, and we will also reprise and generalize the phenomenon of hanging out in groups, which do supplant networks in many evolutionary accounts of social organization.

Transitivity can be worked out in terms of a single network, the union of underlying differentiated networks being recognized in the overall type referred to as multiplex tie. But the last example from the playground showed how a multiplex tie can be factored into particular types of tie that differ as particular "flavors" of the relation. The Rapo-

---

[25] Combinatoric calculations show the number of possible combinations or sets to be astronomically larger than any human population: see Cameron 1994.

port model developed an intermediate approach in which each of the many degrees of friendship being reported by students was treated, quite artificially, as a separate network for multiplex tie, and we didn't examine the mutual impact of these "networks," just the differences in involution.

2.5.1. Cliques and Catnets

A new way to differentiate type of tie brings us back to the notion of corporates. This way discriminates a type of tie on the basis of the pattern of *overlaps* observed among identities and corporate groups. Especially in tribal contexts (e.g., Hart and Pilling 1960; Rose 1960), age and gender corporates spring into relief as intersections, such as "old men in councils." But Breiger (1974) proposed a general duality between person networks and corporate ones: for example, the earlier networks from co-casting invoked by Watts in his Small World study.

A generalization to group-as-common-attribute is in the literature (e.g., Feld 1981) and is being further developed and applied by the Watts team (e.g., Kossinets and Watts 2006); and see McPherson, Smith-Lovin, and Cook (2001). And absolutist France provides a rich tapestry of enacted and self-conscious corporate forms, based on underlying identities, and offers an array of overlaps. Mousnier (1984) magisterially surveys the inclusions and exclusions among those corporate forms that served to underline and define the importance of various attributes. This patterning provided the basis for that regime, as we shall see in chapter 6.

The anthropologist Smith has attempted (1975) to raise an entire general theory of social action just on corporates and their interlocks. Classic field studies of communities in our own day (e.g., Hollingshead 1949; Gans 1962) portray overlaps and exclusions and nestings that are less tangible than corporates. I suggest the term *catnet* as a general designation for such less tangible outcomes, generating meanings and interpenetrations of lives and ties. The following paragraphs flesh out this concept and the basis for the term.

Start with a limiting form to catnet. As the density of ties among a subset of persons reaches some threshold value, the subset may come to regard itself as having an identity. Most of the pairs in the subset may not be actively connected at any given time by network relation, but because of the perception of an identity, all relations will be regarded as present in a latent way. In other words, any member in a clique will feel free to "mobilize" a particular individual relation with another member in the clique.

A clique can continue to grow by the process of "folding-in" (e.g., Coleman 1957, 1961; Burt 1982). If one or more clique members have a friend in common in the network outside the clique, other clique members will tend to assimilate the additional person. When several types of network tie occur in a population, cliques can form in each. Folding-in processes now work across the different types of relations and tend to yield cliques with common membership across several netdoms.

Similarity in attributes will generate groups out of categories. Yet network ties will continue to be recognized, intertwining across categories without recognition of the network as such. Label this generalization and loosening of the corporate concept a *category-network*, abbreviated as *catnet*.

Given the tendencies in a catnet toward the focusing and alignment of relations, it becomes easier and more common to perceive indirect relations with a wider segment of the surrounding population. In the bar setting, you may feel that you have a relation to a stranger because last week you saw him there laughing with a good friend. The clique consisting of you, your good friend, and your other good friends, can then grow by folding in the stranger, the similarity of attributes being the bar you all visit frequently.

Now we can say much the same thing in more general, abstract terms: one reckons relations through clique memberships and the like—that is, through the latent relationships, rather than tracing out some of the usually long chains of concrete ties that would be necessary to "reach" most other persons in the population. The network comes to be projected in perception into a network among nodes that are clusters or cliques, with persons in a clique treated as equivalent unless there is some short, actual path to a given one.

Each person in the catnet system thereby secures a less fragile place in a social formation that is less definite but as ineluctable as any given identity. When particular concrete ties are disrupted, there are clearly acknowledged sets of other persons with whom new ties of equivalent sort can be acknowledged and mobilized quickly. Yet at the same time, the catnet system is more decoupled from random disturbance. Being surrounded by a wider range of reliable ties, a person can be less attentive to and concerned about every rumor and disturbance that passes along the concrete nets. Catnets are thus important controls over ecology.

In still larger scopes around it, a catnet tends to become perceived in a broader view as an entity that itself grows links and evolves into membership in a still larger catnet system. We each have had the experience of leaving one early-life stage and moving on to another in which our previous highly refined and detailed perception of network among the young peers we leave is quickly distilled into a lumped representation of that whole stage as an entity, a catnet. Such is one genesis of more complex social organization studied in later chapters.

2.5.2. Structural Equivalence and Complementarity

Structural equivalence is a more general concept than membership or network. It includes as a special case, but may be contrasted with, the cohesion of corporate interconnection (cf. Burt 1992b). It concerns mutual positioning: what partition into sets of identities would signal what partition of types of tie? Note the duality. Blocks of structurally equivalent identities are built according to tie profiles. For an explicit definition, consult Breiger, Boorman, and Arabie (1975).

There may be no ties at all between structural equivalents. Two lonely kids alike isolated on the fringes of a playground illustrate the pervasiveness of marginality in networks. Romo (1991) analyzes this as the "Omega Phenomenon." Also structurally equivalent are two "stars" who each reach out to gather the other kids into their respective orbits but have little to do with each other. Or structural equivalence can be abstracted from the particular others, so that two quarterbacks are equivalent even though there is no overlap between the kids in their orbits (Winship and Mandel 1984). The result is *positions*.

The central point is to look for a partition of a population, such that the nodes in each set tend to relate to the rest of the sets in much the same way: in the pure case, they have the same incidence of the same sort of ties into each other set. According to this principle, just call it *streq*, those in a set see the rest of the world the same way but need not even be aware of each other, much less be tied as a clique.

There is a dual aspect. Look at the types of tie and separately at each type of compounding, of the sorts we discussed earlier around MAN triads. This huge array of separate patterns found for compounding may itself be partitionable into sets so that there is streq on the ties too, dual to the streq on the nodes.

2.5.3. Blockmodeling

Computer implementations of intricate search algorithms called blockmodels are required to get usable results from structural equivalence, even with small populations. Structural equivalence is entirely relativist (for further discussion, see D. White and Reitz 1983). It requires bootstrapping. That is, equivalence among identities assigned to a given compound actor is determined only with respect to other compound actors—but each of them in turn is defined only with respect to the presumed existence of the others, including the initially given one. And this relativism is simultaneously dual with respect to the sorts of ties distinguished, from among the endless array of compounds, as being distinct in implications for social action. So searches have to be open-ended. For early expositions, see Burt (1978a) and White, Boorman, and Breiger (1976).

A blockmodel interprets multiple networks, one from each type of tie, in terms of a particular population.[26] Blockmodels parse distinct relational aspects among actors into feasible clusterings. This is the obverse of our focus earlier on establishing some continuity in character for multiplex networks. Each of these two foci has distinctive cultural accoutrements, and quite different procedures are appropriate for modeling and measuring structural equivalence groupings on the one hand, and on the other hand, continuity. Observer accounts are but sketches, offering just hints and clues. But this seems the promising direction for assessing how multiple networks impact social process and organization.

Now start again from the beginning in building up a substantive context for explicit modeling concerning structural equivalence. Coding of a tie is, at minimum, two names in brackets to indicate juncture. A name makes an identity transferable at the same time as unique, so that a name is the primitive of "position." But the child is more than the playmate represented by a named node in the playground network of chapter 1. Children also come from several elsewheres, from families, from schools, and likely also from neighborhood gangs. Each of these network populations of identities in which a given child is found may contain few or none of its other playmates from that playground. To represent the child as a whole takes a bundle of such nodes-in-contexts from beyond any one physical locale and any one network.

Maybe these bundles can be fitted together into roles, but the sustained abstract analysis of role theory by Nadel (1957) suggests we should be skeptical about that, even for an American playground. So do traditional statistical analyses. Qualitative accounts in textbooks are unpersuasive.

Social positions are presupposed by earlier role theory, but their provenance has been a continuing puzzle (Biddle 1986). One needs to look for a set of positions within network data as a bridging structure among distinct role frames. A role frame has to do with more or less

---

[26] I use the term *blockmodel* generically to refer to several distinct lines of development that are surveyed by Freeman, White, and Romney (1989). The one full-length monograph treatment is Boyd (1991).

fixed patterns of ties—no ties to the identities in a zero-block, and ties to those in a one-block—which give footings to the actors. And after all, until other role frames are activated, there is no phenomenological basis for discriminating roles in a given frame. One will not be seen as a parent until one is also a workmate or scholar or tribesman; you will not be seen as a playmate until you are also a schoolboy; and so on.

In the playground example, the child may be braggart, bully, docile follower, and the like, sorted out by some familiar complementarities held in tension, that may become recognized, amount to an institution, what Bourdieu calls a habitus, to which we return in chapter 5. Separately, in the home there is some menu of roles vis-à-vis parents and siblings. Separately again, among gangs there may be task leader, social leader, follower, and so on (Whyte 1943). A position then appears in each of several network populations of identities. The position may have some tag associated with it, such as, for the child, teacher's pet, or butt of ridicule, or big shot.

A particular position may bring together a set of distinct identities, from distinct networks. They are brought together into a more-or-less integrated whole. This whole can be tied to one account of social personality (Mischel 1968), as is done in chapter 4 after bringing in the dynamics of switching. This vision seems compatible with the structuration perspective advanced by the sociologist Giddens (1979).

Each actual implementation requires relational data from across some population, such as, for example, Gross, Mason, and McEachern (1958) collected long ago in studies of school superintendency positions, and on a much larger scale recently collected by Bearman, Moody, and Stovel (2004) in the "Add Health" study of high school social life.

2.5.4. Everyday Roles and Positions from Blockmodeling

Types of tie confound differences between relations with differences in their framing; that is, they confound distinctions in structural context for, with distinctions by, asymmetries and strengths and qualities in the pair ties. Even so, types of tie have face validity and enable effective prediction of changes in both relations and their structure. Theoretical interpretation leads to rediscovery of "role frames" as one of the most effective forms of constraint and control.

Blockmodels derive various possible implications for how multiple networks may imply aggregation of actors, and aggregation of types of tie simultaneously, into some articulated larger structure. Any such structure is one of an array of such structures latent in the context, dependent for activation upon impetuses of chance and control. Incidences of types of tie are, to repeat, not some extraneous analytic matter; they are part of the armaments of manipulation for control. Blockmodels identify different possible stable balancings of control projects within that population, separated from production pressures that stem from the biophysical ecology. The outcomes are possible partitions of the original population, and each partition defines a set of possible identities called blocks, which are candidates to become disciplines (chapter 3), if and when that partition emerges from control struggles. And relations between the blocks are candidates to outline a role frame, as discussed later.

Substantive interpretation, as in the previous section, invokes roles and positions. One can argue that a type of tie already by itself describes a role. Discourse in all the dyads for that type is being framed in one distinctive set of stories. I have avoided that claim, since the substance of role involves a pattern across different domains of discourse, and thus implies the complementary notion of position.

There are still other ways to assess and visualize overlaps and orderly ecology across networks, as we saw in the first section of this chapter. And this is equally true in formal and business settings: see Stuart (1998). Further advances along those lines will be cited in chapter 8.

2.6. Uncertainty Trade-Offs

Modeling tends to suppress the noisiness of reality. At this point in the discussion, confusion is to be treated as a lawful aspect of process, an aspect to be assessed. I refer to confusion from and across switchings through publics, around networks. Refined distinctions are needed as tools for this analysis. We can assess phenomenological confusion in terms of trade-offs. Make these trade-offs be between specifically social slack and specifically cultural ambiguity.

2.6.1. Ambiguity versus Ambage

Slack has too many extraneous overtones, of intentional carelessness and the like, to be effective as an analytic term, a tool of discrimination. Instead contrast *ambiguity* with the term *ambage*. *Ambage* designates slack in the sense of uncertainty in a purely social context. *Ambiguity* designates uncertainty in a purely cultural context. From its origins, the word *ambage* signifies winding or indirect and roundabout ways.[27]

---

[27] In previous centuries, *ambage* also carried meanings of concealment and deceit, but as the *Oxford English Dictionary* (1933, vol. 1) makes clear, that usage has become archaic. The established meaning is "circuitous, indirect or roundabout ways or proceedings, delaying."

Ambiguity can begin to be measured in spread across a set of stories. We can call that set a *convention* used in that network, as we already discussed in the earlier section on mesh (section 2.2.1). These conventions are not mere matters of perception. Exactly because a convention can be fit loosely to any situation, it is not subject to refutation by ongoing observation. Pressures for change of conventions will come as by-products of efforts at control. The conventions actually used, which are not determined by the social mechanics going on, can be expected to be very resistant to change (Lazega and Favereau 2002).

Ambage, on the other hand, concerns the concrete world of social ties, in networks of ties and corporates among nodes. Ambage can be operationalized in several ways.[28] A test of reliability of measuring ambage is needed. One test is correct prediction of the appearance of a tie of specified sort in some action context. This test applies separately for each participant and for observer.

Thus, ambage is dual to ambiguity: fuzz in the concrete embodiment as opposed to fuzz in the rules of perception and interpretation. One can see there should be some sort of trade-off between ambage and ambiguity. Consider how ties bundle and unbundle into types of tie. Blockmodeling treats reduction of ambage, measured through zero-blocks, and increase of ambiguity from adjoining larger numbers of initial identities into the one-blocks, the corporate nodes of a partition. Here, ambage decreases and ambiguity increases for an "involved" observer. The particular blockmodel predicted is one that has some intermediate level on both.

Other levels emerge. The nodes of a network, for example, may be identities or may be corporate blocks such as derive from a structural equivalence analysis such as blockmodeling. And you will see that the next chapters embrace regimes of disciplines crossed with styles that cross network populations. It is difficult to transpose the measures of ambiguity and ambage proposed earlier to the other levels, and the concept of publics needs reconstruing. But transposition of measures across such levels is essential to establishing self-similar theory that can hope to deal with the scrappy mess that is social organization. We will return to this in chapter 7 around discussion of agency.

Let us return to the discussion of coupling and decoupling in section 2.3.2. Note that going to parties is an analogue and prototype for the communion ceremony, which decouples ambage in the past from am-

---

[28] For example, Burt (1992a, parts 1 and 2) introduces several relevant measures. These center around the construct of redundancy, which, being more abstract than structural equivalence and more concrete than role equivalence, is a good basis for measuring uncertainty in specifically social relations.

bage in the future. Age grading and other seniority systems, when seen as a succession of cohorts moving through the same set of positions—e.g., generations—are a most obvious form of coupler-decoupler. What pattern and process of coupling and decoupling would prove robust, for example, among university departments each hunting for funds and prestige?

In complex societies, the law court is the institution most specifically concerned with coupling-decoupling. A judicial sentence on an individual is a coupling point, which from that individual's point of view, transforms ambiguity in his past role to ambage in his future role, whereas a duel or a killing in a feud does the opposite. A change in substantive laws operates in a similar way for social groups.

* 2.6.2. Diffusion

[In each chapter, with a section marked with an asterisk, I point out how the studies there can also be seen from other perspectives. Diffusion examples are taken up, more than casually, in the following sections: 2.4.1, footnote 7 of 3.2, 4.2.2, 4.5.6, footnote 4 in 6.2.2, 8.2.1, 8.2.3, and 8.4.]

Diffusion of information significant enough to trigger consequential actions observable across a population, provides a basis for assessing the evolution of types of tie in network patterns. Burt (1987, 1990, 2000) has built upon and summed up a tradition of study and modeling for diffusion of innovation. The tradition rests on a few definitive field studies. In particular, Coleman, Katz, and Menzel (1966) generated a reliable record of actual prescriptions of a new drug in a city by doctors whose network patterns they investigated: the strength of the study was its anchoring in specific events.

Bothner (2003) extends the paradigm to diffusion for new computer technology. Salganik, Dodds, and Watts (2006) bring the 1966 paradigm into the Small World framing of this chapter's beginning: with a huge population and experimental design, they are able to penetrate further into the extent of social suasion on adoption preferences. Morris (1993) brings diffusion via social networks to epidemiology. And Strang and Tuma (1993) take on modeling effects of temporal as well as spatial heterogeneity on diffusion.

Innovations generate ambivalence. High standing can come from adoption, but so can scorn, depending on what comes to be accepted as the worth of the innovation. That worth in turn is no isolated technical truth but rather is negotiated by the interaction of numbers of actors who adopt and are pleased, and it is also assessed with haughtier and more specialized verdicts likelier to shape cultural traces. To be crude, "early but not too early" seems an apt stance for those already of high standing, such as physicians as a group and within them the better-placed ones. The original study has much information and insight on corporate aspects of these issues.

There are ways to crudely allow for corporate effects, as Burt shows. But there are no data for discriminating networks by intensity of tie.[29] As often in social science, a good probe becomes unusable as the population being examined shifts from one that is inexperienced and low status, like junior high school students, to loftier adult persons of affairs. But, on the other hand, for much the same reasons, in the latter type of study population, timing becomes more visible in actions, and these tend to be actions that are consequential.

Adoptions of the new drug among this town's physicians, controlling for corporate statuses and effects, generate a mosaic in time that Burt (1987) shows to be interleaved with the mosaic of structural equivalence in social space. Network ties are identified from a single crude measure: with whom ego discusses professional medical matters among colleagues in the town. Social space is mushed into an artificial Cartesian representation, but that is done on the basis of the quintessential social relation of structural equivalence.

Structural equivalence asserts how important it is that two actors see and relate to—especially on similar topics—rather much the same set of other actors, if similarity in the views and acts of the given two is to emerge through a myriad of instant transactions. Close location in the Cartesian space conjured to the observer's eye boils down an average of a great deal of structural equivalence. Timing of major acts, such as first prescriptions of the new drug, should interlock with this array of locations in social space.

It does. A few clusters of doctors are so completely interconnected with each other in the cluster that stringing becomes cohesion and is indistinguishable from structural equivalence. And just here a particular tie of advice-giving, between a particular pair within the cluster, does not stand out and predict closer timing. Such a cluster is so saturated with closeness that more elaborated cultural and hierarchical influences intervene in decision making. Most physicians, as in any actual population of size, have little connection and thus not the raw material for much structural equivalence with most of the others.

A crucial set of physician dyads are intermediate in that they are rather close in the Cartesian space—they share, and are structurally

---

[29] As there was in Rapoport traces of different order: see section 2.4.1.

equivalent with respect to, many neighbors in the space—yet by no means do they cohere into a cluster of near-complete connectivity. Timing is significantly correlated just in these circumstances. A reported tie of professional discussion activates similar adoption dates just when the physician pairs are acquaintances, so to speak. Time has different social meanings and results according to its interpenetration with locale and topology of social space.

"Boundary" is seen to be a problematic concept for social phenomena, in time or space. Boundaries are both matters of perception and of construction and thus subject to speculation and to gaming. The physicians are demarcated only fuzzily on their own account, as is the community in which they are operating. In fact, it seems natural to think of several subpopulations of doctors, which overlap only partially and differ on locale and specialty and standing and age.

Further layers of embedding and of control (e.g., of "certification" and of "residence") must be invoked and recognized to yield an edge for analysis, and there is little sign of that in this particular naturalistic observation of diffusion of prescribing a new drug. Networks and corporates were uncovered as explanatory pointers in fieldwork and analysis among the physicians. In contrast, boundaries either were impositions of convenience to demarcate the field work, or pointed entirely outside the scenes accessible to this fieldwork, like regulations on issuing and recording prescriptions.

Our axiom is that ties and identities alike are socially constructed, not just imposed by observers. And multiple types of tie are generated, not just the overall multiplex tie. Thereby identities come to be perceived as embedded in more commodious network spaces, while at the same time being constrained by ecological space. Note that similar insights follow from the studies of tracing for the Small World. The principal conclusion is that processes even of diffusion, much less of manipulations for control, cannot be treated properly by a network stripped down to sheer connectivities. For a more recent overview of diffusion models, see Edling (1998).

• • • • •

The claim is that social network analysis adequately captures some essential aspects of the lived social experience toward which chapter 1 was directed. That claim originally rested on little evidence. It was bold and provocative, but two generations of research have now provided a menu of results and tools. Arriving at positive results despite noise from imperfect implementation of messy constructs brings me extra conviction. Results have reached beyond connectivity and clustering for general networks, on to aspects of roles across specialized networks, using structural equivalence and ambiguity assessments.

Control is the driving energy of identities spinning out social networks and coping with ecology. Stories emerge from interacting control projects as these build networks. Stories come from these energies to embody their spinning out; they give color to human social life, they shake it up. Ceremony and ritual emerge from social goings-on to smooth their junctions with ecological space-time; they, along with stories, derive from and build valuations. So network analysis provides only one window on social process and structure.

Yes, the lead insight regarding some situation in its moving context may come from this chapter 2. Parts of later chapters will point out especially close groundings in particular parts of this chapter. But more often, this book will instead call primarily on one of the other four framings offered in subsequent chapters. It is a mistake to cram other framings in under the rubric of network analysis, which is demanding and complex enough by itself. Networks supply some sense of social space to us as observers but only partial insights into social processes, which involve more complex interactions such as the *disciplines* taken up in the next chapter.

THREE

THREE DISCIPLINES

DISCIPLINES offer rules of the games that yield coordination in tasks in an otherwise messy world. Joint tasks of many sorts get done and keep getting done. Disciplines order ties between identities, enabling joint accomplishment of tasks. To persist and reproduce itself, any joint accomplishment must root in and emerge from some focusing, some disciplining of the *ties and talk*, as presented in chapter 2, among the *identities*, presented in chapter 1.

In chapter 1, we saw that a public was produced jointly as a forum for the fleeting netdoms—that are the phenomenological base of networks—and disciplines can emerge in such a forum as well. Consider how that can be: Durkheim has sold us on the primal necessity of deviance of at least some sort and degree. Such deviations can regroup, coming to constitute an invidious ordering around a valuation order that unfolds in talk around netdom switchings. The results are task groups as status systems, made up from socially patterned judgments around networks. The ties in these networks reflect interactions among flows of action, along with the ways they are judged by the participant identities.

This chapter focuses on processes, whereas the descriptions and models in chapter 2 were about patterns as outcomes. Those patterns did correlate with participants' interpretations, but little attention was given to the question, "What is going on here?" Which identities are doing what with whom and on what basis? By introducing the concept of discipline, this chapter shows how struggles for control, which in stalemate constitute ties between identities, can also evoke a whole new identity on a different level over the existing set.

This chapter proposes and elaborates three genres of joint disciplines. Varieties of public, ranging, say, from Goffman's strangers on a street to Habermas's citizens in forum, here give way to three disciplines proven able to accomplish joint tasks. For example, if Goffman ambled on down to William Foote Whyte's particular Street Corner (1943), he would have seen his anodyne public replaced as "arena," or as "council" discipline.

I begin with some everyday examples before developing the concepts further. Then the subsequent section traces the emergence of discipline out of network form: it sketches how struggles for control coalesce with and around some **valuation order** to yield a discipline.

Each discipline is a local status system with different bases of valuations and different systems of ties.

The succeeding section argues that each of the disciplines necessarily **embeds** a task into a context that embraces not only outside relations (with recipients, observers, clients, plaintiffs, etc.) but also the physical and engineered environment. Disciplines embed into their operational environment on three dimensions: dependence with respect to the operational environment, differentiation among identities, and involution.

Later sections lay out each of the three disciplines separately. These presentations are laced with case studies as well as theoretical elaboration. Trade-offs in uncertainties are discussed throughout. Then at chapter's end, I begin to show how disciplines switch and hitch and stack as larger social process builds.

Disciplines can be seen as status systems that are made up simultaneously of evaluative judgments and of network patterns created by interaction of those judgments with task flows. For initial orientation, I turn to familiar university settings to provide a commonsense "take" on each genre, along with a label.[1]

For an **interface** discipline, task flows are production, which may be of material goods, but could be lectures or briefs, oral or written, in a university or a law firm. Evaluative judgments tend to be from the impacts on the flow of these products (e.g., scientific papers) out of that status system to a larger context and the usefulness seen from returns back (e.g., citations, fame, flow of graduate students). This is the valuation of **quality**. In turn, particular instances (e.g., law firms) as wholes could get swept up into some discipline on a higher level (hierarchy of fees among Chicago law firms practicing real estate law): chapter 6 portrays such further embeddings, which influence as well as build on functioning of the local discipline.

In contrast, the Greek letter fraternities and sororities (or "houses") in American universities are organized around judgments involving inclusion and exclusion, the affirmation of group boundaries and thus the **purity** of those inside contrasted with the danger of those outside. These judgments induce an **arena** discipline. One might be willing to work in a laboratory with a non-Greek ("independent" is the euphemism), but one would not want to dance with or marry one. These houses constitute a university status system of selecting future friends and lovers. The flows across university boundaries relate this system to larger systems of inclusion and exclusion (e.g., by generational connections to adult country clubs, Rotary clubs, coming-out parties, etc.).

[1] Adapted from a review by Arthur Stinchcombe (1993) of the first edition.

TABLE 3.1

Genre	Process	Valuation Order
interface	commit	quality
council	mediate	prestige
arena	select	purity

Indeed, members identify it as a marriage market, the flows in being largely unmarried and the flows out either engaged or "eligible," and thus it also becomes an arena on a higher level.

In university councils, people such as deans and research entrepreneurs compete to shape issues as well as for dominance over resources. Within these **council** disciplines, judgments center on **prestige,** in the sense of perceived capacity to influence corporate action. Judgments involve bets about others' power as well as about their "soundness" in corporate political matters. Such councils relate to the outside through regulating the flow of people and resources into the control of the local system.

The basic notion, then, is that these three different kinds of local status systems are disciplines with different bases of valuation and different systems of ties that coordinate what is getting done. Networks around councils tend to reach out to control resources and people, whereas networks in arenas tend to break off at boundaries to avoid introducing impurity into the group. And the interface pumps flows from outside upstream to downstream outside. Each genre of discipline points to its prototype process: participants **commit** to producing flows in **interface**, whereas in **council** they **mediate** among proposals, and in **arena** they **select** from candidates.

Table 3.1 correlates these with the label and valuation order for each genre of discipline.

I build pictures of disciplines using constructs that are realizable for different scopes, histories, and levels. Although some explicit and detailed models are proposed, accounts of disciplines perhaps serve best as heuristic guides to observation (including those folded in among participants' own discourse). Here, flexibility enhances scope of use. The following detailed discussions of each genre will, for example, offer variants on the prototype process and valuation order in table 3.1, as did the introductory three examples. Neat and precise discriminations are at odds with the stochastic messiness of social life.

3.1. Emergence

Valuations are the idiom in which irregularity gets replaced by discipline. Each discipline is a mechanism of social action that configures an identity, but only as adapted to some context. It is a discipline of process toward accomplishment from, in, and for that operational environment. The earliest example is a work group, such as one for hunting or gathering. Networks themselves grow around (and with) work and other material production, as these open out into ties and stories. Disciplines also emerge in contexts more purely sociable, divorced from work, such as the children's playground of chapter 1. How a discipline emerges also presages the forms in which it continues and reproduces itself, and it points toward a process distinctive for the continuing discipline of that genre.

To begin, consider some homely examples of discipline process: namely, meals as social processes. A sit-down urban dinner party among professional couples is an example of an *arena discipline*. It is concerned with establishing yet bounding some sort of identity of the evening with a set of stories that index professionalism. So status ordering on purity is at play.

A church supper, by contrast, can be considered a *council discipline* ordered by *prestige valuation*. There is unending concern with balancing and disciplining conflicts among factions. At the same time, the integrity of the congregation as a church is being reaffirmed.

A cafeteria at mealtime can be seen as an *interface discipline*. This is the production discipline, effectively delivering foods into people arrayed to receive them. An interface mediates between social worlds. In many places in the chain of food production and service there are interfaces: interface is generalizable to multiple levels. For instance, the checkout counter at a fast-food restaurant doles out hamburgers and such in return for money. They do this with minimum contact, the interaction being mostly stereotypical. The stereotypes hide the complexity of the networks on either side—in the worlds of food manufacturing and services, and in the worlds of the customers. I return to this in chapters 5 and 6.

On the one hand, control is attempted over specific occasions in social context. And on the other hand, control induces efforts to verify or regulate by comparison with some standard, if only implicit or relative or historical. This is how discipline emerges out of contention. And discipline extends over multiple occasions. For example, Ochs and Taylor (1992) show, from a hundred case studies in America, how a family's dinnertime typically engenders narrative that reinforces a political order—what I have called a council discipline.[2]

---

[2] Don Steiny suggested this fit.

3.1.1. Valuation Order and Narrative

Switchings among netdoms (from chapter 1) underlie the general mechanism in which discipline emerges from network context. Valuation order is also key. One can try to infer and induce the valuation by looking at story-sets active in the local discourse.[3] Standard stories for networks can settle out across situations and then transmute into narrative.

There are common elements across sets of stories in the networks being drawn into an emerging discipline. Stories vary, but some framing by valuation is taken for granted. As a discipline emerges, the taken-for-granted valuation order becomes hegemonic.[4] It is this hegemonic quality that can afford the discipline independent standing as an entity, as an actor on its own. For example, *The Right Stuff*, which is both title and theme of Tom Wolfe's novel (1980), exactly captures the inarticulate hegemony of a valuation, as prestige among a group of test pilots.

Focus first on the origins of a council: contentions for control can trigger each other across netdoms within the initially bland setting of a public. Some of the players are sociometric stars with many ties and thus potentially wide influence toward setting an agenda. As they recruit each other into joint discussion on those topics that they argue are central to the situation in that public, some consensus emerges among them as to their efficacy in setting agenda and settling disputes through such discussion.

Such consensus can crystallize into a valuation ordering among them by **prestige**. Such ordering of them as **council** prioritizes their own interventions and, as this prestige order gains legitimacy in others' perceptions, it inhibits efforts by outsiders to gain a direct say. Dispersion, then, is based on internal social prominence: attempts at influence by outsiders are eventually directed along ties to council insiders. This is a messy affair of repeated trial runs, as to topics and ordering, before any council discipline coalesces, but thereafter feedback is biased against deviation from council guidance.

Deviance and variation are the original raw material from which discipline emerges. It gets crafted across control struggles that trigger net-

---

[3] For observer, more than for participant, the inference process is laborious, in both sampling and transcribing various communications as well as coding them: see, for example, Carley (1993).

[4] Luhmann makes a similar argument: "On the highest attainable level of establishing expectations, one must, by contrast, renounce all claim to establishing the correctness of specific actions. One works only with—or talks only about—*values*. Values are general, individually symbolized perspectives which allow one to prefer certain states or events" (1995, p. 317).

dom switches. Dispersions are key, rather than averages. These are dispersions in time, switchings, as well as within network standing. Durkheim long ago noted:

> We have only to notice what happens, particularly in a small town, when some moral scandal has just been committed. They stop each other on the street, they visit each other, they seek to come together to talk of the event and wax indignant in common. From all the similar impressions which are exchanged, for all the temper that gets itself expressed, there emerges a unique temper—which is everybody's without being anybody's in particular. That is the public temper. (Durkheim 1947, p. 102)

Dispersion is, of course, also key for emergence of an **interface** genre. This is dispersion not on internal social prominence but rather in access through ties outside, both those offering supply to, and those seeking delivery of, production. Discussions are around perceptions of how the members can utilize these external relations, and the valuation order has to conform to perceptions from the external contacts, which is to say order by **quality** of product. The repeated trial runs before successful establishment, if any, can be anticipated by an external observer who looks for structural equivalence, streq, maps. The quality order disciplines commitments members make, by some trade-off between quality and volume of delivery with quality rank.

Arena discipline can come out of dynamics between hostilities and likings in netdoms. Some are perceived as gatekeepers and come into array according to how stringently they exclude, as they select for successive degrees of **purity**, the valuation order. Any number of particular arenas can emerge from trial runs out of an initial configuration of netdoms. No order or membership is predetermined, rather they are emergent.

3.1.2. Tie Dynamics and Disciplines

Now stand back for a general look at tie dynamics. The evolution of patterns across types of tie reflects incidence and distribution of control struggles. The results of this evolution can be modeled, crudely, through the differing frequencies of emerging compounds in types of tie on the population. Such is the rationale of the Davis-Holland-Leinhardt triad census approach (MAN) from chapter 2.

Such pattern can also be assessed by examining the incidences of various compoundings across all types of tie (Boorman and White 1976); for example, clustering of friends' enemies ties may overlap enemy but not friend ties, the balance hypothesis that was also laid out in the MAN section of chapter 2. In this assessment, structural equivalence suggests possible partitions into identities.

Each partition specifies a split into sets, each of which, pressured by similar influences being compounded from the other sets, might trigger perception as itself an identity in social action. A blockmodel is a conjecture as to such a partition: see chapter 2 again. Each of these sets of nodes making up a blockmodel may become a corporate identity, under some mechanism of process, some genre of discipline.

But how is clustering into specific discipline identities to be understood? There is no necessary implication that such compound actor is cohesive, is bound together positively, or is even aware of "itself." At some given time, character as an identity may not have been demonstrated in participants' eyes despite structural equivalence as to interrelations with other corporate actors across all the sorts of tie. This means that embedding remains an open issue.

The disciplines cumulate control pressures such as are implied by the pattern of observed ties (see Burt 1978b). Faulkner's (1983) account of evolutions of moviemaking teams in Hollywood is an example. These teams combine different sorts of specialists, and Faulkner reports sequences of memberships for project after project.

The basic fact is the astronomical number of possible dynamic configurations. Rather than searching out which ones lead to this or that discipline, I argue for identifying the disciplines that prove able to reproduce themselves. **The real point is not how a particular example of a discipline came into being, but rather the mechanism for that species, which then inhibits breaking out of the mold.**

Padgett and McLean (2006a, b) have recently reported on a massive study of changing socio-political-economic organization of Renaissance Florence over a century and more. They interpret it as the emergence of capitalism (a somewhat similar study for medieval Genoa is taken up in detail in chapters 4 and then 6). They offer a wealth of circumstantial detail to support their interpretation, enough so that one could look and test for discipline configurations. Their point is also, on a larger scale, that the significant organization is one that reproduces itself.

3.1.3. Other Perspectives

First, a brief review of the genres. An interface gains identity via production and continuing delivery of a tangible flow of social productions. For instance, in a hunting group in tribal context, members are identified by quality of the meat they bring back, whereas in each embodiment of the arena, the ordering can sift itself apart and together into new identities characterized in purity valuation. The embodiment for the council is the formation of alliances and counter-alliances in mobilization to retain existing valuation in prestige. This focuses dynamics around valuation order.

Other sorts of dynamic should be considered. Each type of tie from chapter 2 may be distinctively involved in the formation of some genre of discipline as a species of identity. We may find some correspondence between, on the one hand, the three universal ways or modes of induction for tie types suggested there from case studies, and, on the other hand, the three genres of discipline we sketch here in chapter 3. Asymmetric tie suggests the interface species; overlap tie suggests the council species; and indirect tie suggests the arena species.

It is also instructive to match this abstract partition—based on asymmetry, overlap, and catenation of ties—with a substantive partition common in the literature (e.g., Laumann and Pappi 1976)—business, honor, and professional, respectively. But it is a distortion of the social material to argue for the neat and tidy in either discriminations or mappings—except as imposed by the analyst for purposes of inferential computation.

Disciplines are not free-floating molecules, and we now need to specify how they embed into context during struggles. But before asking just what this term *embedding* signifies, we should examine how uncertainty plays into these struggles.

3.1.4. Decoupling and Contingencies Shape Uncertainty

Discrimination between uncertainty in cultural contexts and uncertainty in social contexts is subtle and elusive, as we saw in the previous chapter. Processes in discipline emergence compound this because of the importance of contingencies from other aspects of the operational environment, subsumable as biophysical, geographical, and technological. Chapter 2 supplied an illustration: each blockmodel sketches one possible partition into disciplines that results from pressures indicated in networks of ties. But other contingencies, biophysical ones, have an impact on the outcome and are themselves affected by the changes in network among disciplines. Stories emerge accordingly in sets to accommodate diverse outcomes. Chance effects thus proliferate and assume interpretive guises and social forms with incidences that are correlated. Decoupling is essential.

Decoupling is basic to networks, as we saw at the end of chapter 2. Coupling is more obvious to trace in strings of ties, but decoupling is equally important, as it is the buffering of one chain of actions from another. Chance combines with network and story to yield patterns of decoupling and embedding. Decoupling is the phenomenological face of what a calculus among ambage and ambiguity and contingency can assert analytically.

The general source for decoupling is attempts by identities to establish comparability as they seek footings. These efforts have a paradoxical character: comparability is established for perceivers (other identities) only through the most strenuous efforts at superiority. Attempts at dominance are exactly what set up the arena of contention within which comparability falls out as the unanticipated by-product.

One is surrounded by examples: professors vie for distinction and thereby become as peas in a pod to students in their classes; physicians strive as individuals—and also in much the same process as specialties—for prestige, only to thereupon become perceived as interchangeable. Burger King, McDonald's, Wendy's, and so on induce a new category of equivalence, the fast-food restaurant, exactly and only by striving to be better than each other—which requires, and therefore induces as presupposition, being comparable.[5]

It follows that uncertainty as to contingencies in the operational environment must also enter into any equation in ambage (uncertainty of social position) and ambiguity (uncertainty of meaning). This is contingency from the physical world of work together with its social exigencies, from which the social spaces have spun out initially. Thus, ambage and ambiguity both exist only as a follow-on to contingency. For development of this theme, see Stark (2001).

Any equation must sustain three very distinct variables; the equation must be in contingency as well as in ambiguity and ambage.[6] Ambage is especially associated with the connection between identities and network populations; ambiguity goes with aspects of connections of production disciplines with networks; and contingency, in a natural environment sense, is associated with how identities play off production discipline. These are not assertions about single disciplines or identities. These are tendencies that seem diagnostic in our social world of disorderly "gels and goos" as compounded by gaming.

[5] There may emerge, as by-product, some one or more formulaic statements of the comparability. Here, for example, the formula may be expressed as a reshuffling of the time order among phases—say, preparing, ordering, paying for, eating—which are standard in all restaurants. But the comparability emerges, first and painfully, as product of unceasing strivings for control by identities. In the present illustration, these can be seen, in agreement with the principle of self-similarity, not only as between concrete establishments but also at another level, such as among franchises (cf. Bradach and Eccles 1989).

[6] This deserves full mathematical development along lines akin to information theory: see e.g., Brillouin (1962).

The subjects of these three measures for aspects of uncertainty are active processes, not natural flows. They are active processes among interactive identities. "Gaming" is the current idiom for interacting manipulations. Manipulations trade on the concretely contingent as well as on social maneuvers and interpretive ambiguity. Manipulations often key on weather and shortages, for example, which provide convenient excuse-stories. Such gamings require, find ready, and resupply ambage, ambiguity, and contingency, all three of which are its raw material, its medium, and its product. So a calculus of ambage, ambiguity, and contingency taken as a set is necessary. Section 7.3.2 will develop these themes further.

"Equation" and "calculus" are being used as conventional shorthand for a much more complex interplay among "variables." These latter are assessments that may or may not prove to be measurable like temperatures. It is difficult enough to assess uncertainty in an objective or engineering sense, as Tukey (1977) tells us. Shannon pioneered measurement of symbolic uncertainty, here termed *ambiguity*, in information theory, but only in limited aspects (for an appreciation and development, see Hofstadter 1979). And the overwhelming scope and subtlety of social uncertainty, of ambage, is a theme seen in Knight (1921) and von Neumann and Morgenstern (1944) and Schelling (1960).

From its introduction in the first chapter, decoupling has been reserved for where contingency has at least some role. Material situations are where time, and thence stochastic process, has the greatest importance. Unfortunately, the greatest technical gaps in social science are in models for stochastic networks (for assessments see White 1973; Boorman and Levitt 1980), which are indispensable for capturing coupling and decoupling at the same time.[7]

3.2. Embedding

Embedding is mutual discipline that sifts out of chaotic crisscrosses of attempts at control. Embeddings seed on now this happenstance and now that one, but once established they can induce continuance of the discipline through repetition and imitation. Embeddings take couplings to a higher level. Embeddings occur at many scopes: for macro

[7] There are beginnings: on search in networks (Boorman 1975; Delaney 1989; Kleinrock 1964), on diffusion in networks (Boorman 1974; Burt 1990; Bailey 1957, 1982), on statistical mechanics of networks (Erdos and Spencer 1974), and on parallel distributed processing models.

and political economy, see Evans (1979), and for geographical perspective, see Brenner (2004).

Embeddings surround us in many varieties. They overwhelm us and thereby become hard to pin down for explicit analysis. Consider two examples of the embeddings in which our social lives are enmeshed. The first has to do with geographical space. Think back to the last "snail mail" envelope you addressed. The first line may be an identity taken as being independently fixed, no doubt a person with name, and the last line similarly will have some fixed location from geography. But the second line was, say, "Apartment 231," while the third line was, say, "1603 Redwood Street," and thus this address you wrote was exactly an embedding. By itself "Apartment 231" means nothing much, and so too "1603 Redwood Street," until each is embedded into the complete address.

For the second example, turn to time. How was your weekend? What is your day like on Wednesday? Again here, your life is shaped around an embedding you are not even aware of, now into a framing of time. Here the social construction is of days as defined through being embedded into a seven-day week. Only in an intensive care unit or a submarine or another of Goffman's total institutions can you partially escape. The week is hegemonic, in that it is utterly taken for granted.

And these examples remind us of the other side: embedding has as complement decoupling in some other respects. Recently, for example, I drove into a small city I was already acquainted with, along what I thought was my standard approach road off the highway. I circled for an hour, completely disoriented because I had, in fact, entered along another highway connector. I was embedded in one view of the street grid, but that decoupled me from the view natural from the other connector. Embeddings can fail and switch.

Decoupling is a converse to embedding. Social life begins with triggerings of identities, each of which comes from embedding a discipline of constituents but which then is decoupled in seeking control in its ties. That is, the discipline for an identity embeds its constituents while simultaneously offering them decoupling as some insulation from and brokering to the context.

Decoupling is also a complement to coupling, as we saw in the previous chapter. This can be confusing, so return to the illustration given there concerning the Internet forum. Logging out is decoupling. Brief log-ins with minimal contents to a number of other accounts would count for me as couplings. Whereas extended log-in to continue and develop ongoing discussions in that forum would count as an embedding.

In an influential article, Mark Granovetter (1985) presents a convincing account of the gist of embeddings as being social extensions and involvements amid networks, in which embedding is given overtones of emotional involvement and fuzziness. Yet this does distract one from the possibility of a new level of actor emerging: an embedding can be sharp and crisp, and it can also disrupt as well as nest in with networks.

By contrast, linguists are clear about the emergence of levels but neglect much of Granovetter's social extension because of their focus on the dyad. In the words of M.A.K. Halliday:

> Embedding is a mechanism whereby a clause or phrase comes to function as a constituent within the structure of a group, which itself is a constituent of a clause. Hence there is no direct relationship of an embedded clause and the clause within which it is embedded; the relationship of an embedded clause to the "outer" clause is an indirect one, with a group as intermediary. The embedded clause functions in the structure of the group, and the group functions in the structure of the clause. (Halliday 1994, p. 242)

The notion thus includes "recursion," since a clause may have clauses within it, which in turn may have clauses in it. For instance, "The man Sally saw was tall" has the subclause in it: "Sally saw the man." If you think of companies, divisions, teams, and so on as simply "organizations," then they can nest as well, because each is just an organization within an organization. Likewise, disciplines can become identities that in turn can be disciplined.

Further exploration of the nexus of embedding with decoupling is needed.

3.2.1. Embedding with Decoupling

Failure invokes the dramatic demise of an identity. In this sense, failure couples control to identity, whereas forgetting and referral are less dramatic erosions of identities. Failure is a basic social invention, which turns boundary condition into source of action. Any process of triage supposes and allows for failures as components. Failure is key to boundaries, but that is secondary to its generating change in embedding among levels.

Embeddings surround us. They indeed overwhelm us and thereby become hard to discern in explicit analyses. Overtones of the term *embed* as used in ordinary discourse incline us to miss the very induction of a new level of actor that is central. Granovetter (1985) presents a convincing account of social extension and involvement as the gist of embedding; yet this is a two-dimensional portrayal, as it were, a portrayal that neglects the emergence of new levels of actors from embedding. By contrast, linguists are clear about the emergence of levels but neglect most of Granovetter's concept of social extension because most of them focus on the dyad.

"Embedding is a mechanism whereby a clause or phrase comes to function as a constituent *within* the structure of a group, which is itself a constituent of a clause." The relationship of an embedded clause to the "outer" clause is an indirect one, with a group as intermediary. Analogously, the relation of a downstream actor in production market economy to the upstream supplier of the producer it buys from is indirect, mediated by a market, as will be developed further in chapter 5.

The puzzle of generalized exchange, which traces to Durkheim but is more specifically rooted in theories of Lévi-Strauss has motivated studies upon which my present line of inquiry depends. Notable studies (Rose 1955; Hart and Pilling 1960) that delved into aboriginal kinship as economic organization culminate in Bearman (1997). Recognizing this analogy supplies further insight into the possible emergence of distinct new level of actors. Production markets, from chapter 5 and later in this chapter, are analogous to sections in classificatory kinship systems (White 1963a), but need not have analogies in every kinship terminology.

Let us look more closely at mechanisms. Embeddings can result from each actor's **not only knowing entailments and warranties in his relationships, but also being known to so know**. Thus, the firm may become subject to, and be known to be subject to, the hegemonic pressure exerted by the others engaged in the continuing reproduction of a distinct identity as market. Such a market is itself embedded within networks in ways that at the same time constrain the actions of firms. Such a market is an actor on a distinct level, and yet firms are still partially decoupled.

Embedding can build a public subculture across actors at both levels within a particular sector of markets, even though commitments and decisions remain tied into catenations and compoundings of particular ties. The subculture recognizes, and personalizes, actors of different levels, while at the same time providing customs of switching from the calculus for one to the calculus for another.[8] Participants in the various markets act as if embedded in a curious web of cocoons (see Tilly 1996

---

[8] Cf. White 1995; Mische and White 1998. For examples of tracing this sort of evolutionary history for structural equivalence in networks, see Anheier, Gerhards, and Romo (1995), Baker (1990), Boyd (1991), Breiger (1991), Faulkner (1983), Giuffre (1999), and Pattison (1993).

for an analogous term) among markets that also come to constitute a self-consistent field, such as discussed in section 4.5.4. Yet the quality ordering is a property of the mechanism of the market as a whole, core to its identity. There is a transmutation of hitherto entailed ties into market parameters. The market is in effect projecting a new, more abstract sort of tie. This is the asymmetric envelope that is recognized as a market profile. Warranty and entailment on the level below are thereby abrogated, as to addressee if not interpretive content.

3.2.2. Embedding in Operational Environment

Any species of discipline can be analyzed abstractly, but its actual functioning requires embedding in an operational environment. By its identity, a discipline induces designation from outside, perhaps by literal naming, enhancing this awesome integral of embedding. The components of a discipline and their interactions are taken for granted, invisible; ordinarily, they become visible to participants or others only in failed disciplines.

A name for a discipline establishes the commonness in action perceived among the entities making it up, which is one side of embedding; but a name also establishes commonness in relations to the setting of the discipline, and that is the other side of embedding. Disciplines are perceived and characterized as embodiments of processes, but they presuppose and generate a larger setting with which they interact and wherein they embed. I have called this setting the operational environment.

Measures that encompass this second side must be developed in order to go on and explore still larger social formation, among identities at a higher level, as we begin to do at chapter's end, but the measures must reflect the first side as well. Each identity becomes a joint formation that reconciles the social spaces with whatever is the ecological impetus. It is this dual process that motivates the term *embedding*.[9]

---

[9] Talcott Parsons, in his later work (see chapter 6 for the earlier Parsons), developed a positive theory of social system as self-similar system. He specified nested sets of functional structures as universals. This was the AGIL scheme: Adaptation/Goal attainment/Integration/Latent pattern maintenance. Mark Granovetter suggests that there should be a mapping into my discipline species. A possible mapping to the three species of disciplines is G to interface, I to council, and L to arena. The correspondent to Parsons' Adaptation is of another kind: it is the adaptation of social organization, taken as a whole, to the biophysical ecology. One can argue for a more general correspondence of AGIL to my principal constructs: G to production, I to network population, and L to identity. However, there appear to be no analogues in Parsons to mechanisms of decoupling, apart from his "generalized media of exchange."

Any identity embeds to a new level of identity only through its discipline, but it continues being subject to ecological incident as well as to social unravelings. Struggles by identities take place in space as well as in netdoms. Geography must play some role too. A big wedding, say, will roll up many hunks of social networks into the same hall and there may engender new ties and clusters. But it is all too common for social theorists to treat space as unproblematic.[10] For example, in a collection of views on sociology of culture (Desan, Ferguson, and Griswold 1989) both Pierre Bourdieu and Alain Viala (cf. p. 292) accept physical space as the obvious arena of social action, just with the "forces" changed from their physical form. Field investigators in social science fortunately do better.

Hackman's (1993) studies of interactions among three-person crews in airliner cockpits can serve as a prototype for interrelating social with physical space in small scale. And physical settings do give an easy start for visualizing social networks: for example, the playground in chapter 1. Yet, distant pen pals may share only their love of certain authors. Social networks need be controlled by ordinary physical space only episodically. Understanding disciplines requires social specification of context. And analysis seeks abstraction of any given embedding according to several aspects.

3.2.3. Involution, Differentiation, and Dependency

Any discipline survives only as it settles into its context, both social and technical. This settling is an embedding wherein the context provides the support enabling the discipline to reproduce itself. I see three dimensions of this embedding into the operational environment, the same set of dimensions for any of the three genres: dependency, differentiation, and involution.

Any discipline that is accomplishing a joint task manifests some degree of **dependence** with respect to the operational environment. This dependence may be an absolute parameter of separation, as often applies for an arena discipline. Dependency can be seen as the extent to which the particular discourse in stories within the discipline, as well as physical activities, interdigitate with the external. For the interface discipline, the measure of dependence becomes some ratio parameter of contrast between upstream and downstream, yet at the same time

---

[10] This is so except for some geographers (Haggett, Cliff, and Frey 1977), but geography is out of fashion! Part B of Appendix 2 in the 1992 edition of this book surveys models of space.

there will also be some degree of differentiation in the embedding of context across particular members of the discipline.

Differentiation is how spread out the constituents embedding into an identity become on the appropriate valuation. Members channel attention toward those of higher prestige, who also may attract more attention from the outside, so differentiation determines visibility.

The third aspect of embedding is the **involution** of the discipline among other disciplines observed, the extent to which its embedding is shaped by ricochets from network processes in and around other disciplines. It reflects the stringing together of identities by chains of ties that close back on their origins, and so impact the valuation ordering in the given discipline. Involution can also be viewed as specialization.

The place of any particular discipline can be plotted as a point in the three-dimensional space that is implied by these three measures. Examples will be plotted in such spaces in chapter 8. Note that although the valuation order itself can be seen as an embedding, it is in a different key. It embeds the members with each other in a single dimension, which, however, is different for each genre.

To recast the argument: the three dimensions will have different importance in one genre from another. Within each genre, the outcomes of discipline embedding will be less sensitive on one dimension than the other two. The focus of the interface, for example, is pumping production, and this **commitment is not so much affected by change in involution**, which falls outside their focus. Whereas a council discipline, by its collegial nature, tends to be opaque to the outside so that **decrease in the extent of differentiation has only limited impact on the council**. As to the arena, its raison d'etre is separation from the impure outside so that **changes in dependence have less import on the arena**.

It may help to think of the embedding of a given discipline species in terms of a triangle, with each of the three dimensions as one vertex. See figure 3.1. There are three triangles, one for each species. The triangle for interface disciplines shows a perpendicular from the vertex for involution to the line between differentiation and dependence: think of that line as really the edge-on view of the whole plane defined by dependence and differentiation variations for a given value of involution. Since interface mechanism is least sensitive to involution, one can approximately plot, as in figure 8.2, examples in just three planes, for high and medium and low levels of involution. The same logic applies to the other two.

Readers may wish to sketch out plottings of particular examples for a discipline, either their own or examples from these chapters, in actual three-dimensional graphs such as in figures 8.2, 8.3, and 8.4. There is

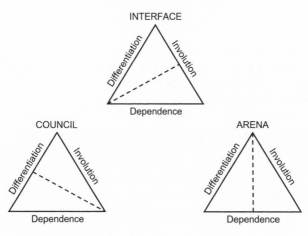

Figure 3.1: Embedding ratios for three disciplines

stricter justification for such placements of disciplines themselves rather than of the larger formations about which I hazard conjectural placements in figures 8.2, 8.3, and 8.4.

The number of constituent identities in a discipline may be small, as for a work group. But in some operational environments of a given genre, the valuation order may support discipline across a large set. Empirical application can accommodate idiosyncratic placements of identities along the valuation order of that discipline, in predicting accomplishments; generality for the genre mechanism comes through representing placements in terms of a gradient, a profile. These remarks should illuminate the placements of diverse examples in figures 8.2, 8.3, and 8.4 in section 8.3.1.

To recapitulate: a discipline presupposes some orderliness of perceptions by its participants. The control struggles that create and surround these identities, and to which their disciplines contribute, settle out variously in networks and also in styles, institutions, and regimes. Obversely, pressures from those larger contexts reach in to affect some orderliness of perception by a particular discipline as an entity. It is this dual orderliness that is reflected in the embedding measures. The three genres of discipline—the interface, the arena, and the council—are the configurations that proved robust to all these perception pressures, above and below, across varied contexts.

Now I expound each genre separately. One variety of each genre will be developed in some detail around a published study. But **the main emphasis in each of the three sections is the sheer variety of applications possible with that same core mechanism**. The three genres together can illuminate much of social life.

3.3. Interfaces

Physical production and biophysical reality matter, and work is the human adaptation to them. Much of life is work (Udy 1970), and work takes place in physical ecologies. Work and its contingencies provide a major coupler between the purely social and the biophysical. But much of work also involves coping with other identities and their control efforts, often also through interface disciplines in social context.

But war too matters and is endemic. In military operations, the basic interface is with the enemy, and the classic though not sole way of dealing across the interface is the engagement. One commits to the engagement, but in seeking disequilibrium may turn either upstream or downstream.

Asymmetry underlies all the variations of this commit interface. Asymmetry is built into the form. On one side individual flows are being induced, drawing on suppliers amid jockeying for relative niche position; the other side is (possibly disparate) receivers appropriating the aggregate flow. The flows are always into the one, disaggregate side and then on to the other. The social perceptions that discipline producers into order come from both sides of the interface, but behavioral cues to specific niches are on one side only.

Embedding into a new identity, which for the other two discipline species is a by-product, here in the interface is the focus. A set of actors can become comparable, become peers, through jostling to join in an interface on comparable terms. They commit by joining together to pump downstream versions of a common product, which are subjected to comparison by them and by the downstream. Children competing in hopscotch or reciting for a teacher, mathematicians in a test for a prize, manufacturers of recreational aircraft for the U.S. market, actors in a play—all can be examples of commit interface.

The word *interface* connotes passing through and transformation, as does the word *membrane*. But interface discipline is without the latter's implication of a sharply demarcated material body; instead, an interface is a mutually constraining array of contentions for control that yield as the net result a directed flow, a committed flow. Interfaces are the most transparent of the three species. The key parameters in explicit models prove to be variances, so that the average sizes of the flows being generated through this interface are divorced from the self-reproduction of the interface.

Quality captures connotations of the transitive ordering induced in such interface disciplines. This valuation ordering cannot be sustained by the induction and routing of average flows.[11] Instead such valuations provide scaffoldings for dispersions in social formations that then prove able to reproduce themselves.

3.3.1. Supervision and Identities

The "span of control" in modern bureaucracies is an unusually explicit formulation of the mechanism side of the commit interface, as distinct from the quality ordering. A superior is, aside from concrete abilities and achievements, also a placeholder, a symbolic representation of subordinates' embedding into a new joint identity. Their identity is as comparable peers with common, or rather parallel but differentiated, goals embedded within a common social production.

Embodiment like this of the interface as a tangible distinct actor, who represents the new embedded identity indicated by the designation "supervisor," lays the ground for subsequent further embeddings. In these, the supervisor can fold in together with others so as to become comparable peers embedded in yet another new identity, also a commit interface. Or the chain of embeddings can be initiated from above, in which case it can and usually does switch from one to another of the three species of discipline.

Pressures from contending efforts at control are so strong as to also support so-called inverted supervision. Here, a set of peers interact with no common structuring beyond having a common subordinate. This common underling may be a research assistant or a secretary. Or, at a different level, the underling of several personality components may be a sexual drive. In any case, the "underling" may increasingly come to cue actions of all and thereby achieve de facto apportionment and so supervision.

The commit interface is robust to both external and internal control projects. The equivalency in peer positions subjects insiders to very strong discipline by the comparable others. Effective oversight comes from those similarly located, and thus conversant with the information and perspective the subject is bringing. Supervisors symbolize authority but are substantively more important in linking to other levels of

---

[11] Reference group theory long ago came to the view that it was dispersions in rewards among actors, not averages, that drove social action in small groups. In the classic formulation, from the Stouffer et al. (1949) study of World War II military, anticipation over time was equally important with dispersion. Recently, Tversky and Kahneman (Kahneman, Slovic, and Tversky 1982), among others (Lindenberg 1989a), have revived this notion.

disciplines and context. Even the accumulation of authority through a supervisor is difficult.

Interfaces are directly concerned with identities. Since identities in action are refractions of what does not fit neatly into social organization of network and discipline, there normally is a multivalent correspondence, as regards authority, between identity and any tangible actor. There is more than one correspondence between interface and identity, even fresh identity.

Interfaces yield substantive outputs as well as comparative standings, and this distracts attention from the new integral identity on different level. Competition is about the importance of doing slightly better than your peers who in the larger context are so very similar to oneself; what is not necessarily signified is the strength of the new identity created by the competition. Within a supervisory structure as example, a tale is induced of potential antipathy toward the supervisor. That tale exactly conceals the fundamental effect of commitment through the interlocking externality of peers' impacts upon each one of them, as the production of social action proceeds.

3.3.2. Production Market and Quality Order

Production markets can be seen as extensions of simpler situations. Material production quite generally comes in these interface disciplines.[12] Here, the receivers are a distinct set, and the context is not relaxed and sociable. The hunting or gathering groups described for tribal contexts (Firth 1935, 1978; Lee 1979; Udy 1959; Rose 1960) are early realizations that have analogues in sports teams (Leifer 1990) and in children's games (Fine 1979; Opie and Opie 1969). The basic mechanism does not require or presuppose distinct roles among the producers with explicit cues and assignments. Rather, a spread of performances is induced by attention of producers to differential preferences by the other side, who can turn off their attention (or more tangible payments for production).

The same phenomenon of commitment can be seen on a much more massive scale in modern markets for manufactured products. The term *product*, whether light aircraft or frozen pizzas (Leifer 1985), has no independent reality as a technical or engineering matter. Its reality is induced only through the commitment of producing firms into being peers in a differentiated set that organizes terms of trade around an

---

[12] This example will be picked up in later chapters. As more scope and depth are introduced into the theory, production market in its larger contexts will provide a running example like the playground of chapter 1.

induced order of quality among the producers. Note the analogue to the humble example of children competing in hopscotch or before their teacher. The industrial production markets from the previous century up through today are exemplars of commit interfaces.

Take some production market as a particular institutional realization of the commit interface. Such a market is an ongoing social act. These markets accomplish the feat of reproducing themselves to continue month after month just by their coherence as social acts (Leifer 1985; Leifer and White 1988). Nothing is passive about this. The producer firms, which usually are the actors in modern markets, are giant pumps expensively committed to spouting continuing flows of products more or less unchanged.

The set of pumps, the market as super-pump, is built up only in interaction with, and confidence in, provision of an orderly and continuing social setting with buyers. The production market must induce, at the same time as it renders comparable, distinctive flows from a to-be-determined set of producers into the hands of an array of buyers becoming accustomed and committed here. This social process is what induces a definition of "product" from the common properties of this flow.

Some decoupling of relations lubricates choices and bargainings made in a production market. But in any interface market, the transaction flow with upstream, procuring, is distinct from, but coordinated with, that directed downstream, selling, so that market process invokes not only the peer producers but also two other layers of actors. There emerges a collective identity, associated with, rather than opposed to, decoupling.

Supply and demand are not operational concepts here. Supply equals demand, after the fact each time, as a tautology. But it is the variation among producers in qualities, and the difficulties each confronts in production, that shape the interface that motivates and sets the terms of trade. I have laid out explicit models for this variety of commit discipline, the production market (White 2002, 1981a, b).

The interface here consists in the observable spread of terms of trade being achieved by various producers with their distinctive flows. At the simplest level, these terms are revenue for volume shipped, leaving aside variant models for a line of related products that any given producer may supply. Gossip can supply to each producer an estimate of most of the terms achieved by peers.

For the market to reproduce itself, each producer must continue to see its pair, revenue, and volume, as its optimal choice from the menu of observed terms of trade. Only this menu is known to be sustainable by the buyers, who themselves are comparison-shopping. Terms of trade lie on a commonly observable shape that cues actors into niches by their own preferences that yet are agreeable across the interface. Call this shape a **market profile**.

Myriad requests and searches, each perhaps minor to its originator, cumulate into an overall pressure on some market of producers who are each baffled as to the overall response from across that profile to their particular product. Each firm seeks a footing for itself from some location along a profile that is traced through the set of choices (volume, revenue) already made by all the firms. So the profile is an interpolation through the array of prices according to total volume of production. Thus, an industry builds an identity that is perhaps as binding upon its constituent firms as is authority within a clan or bureaucracy.

Location along a market profile can be designated as a niche, a footing for that firm. The breadth of a firm's niche translates into some spread in quality around its index value on quality, and perhaps also some spread in time horizon. Firms caught up in a given market are also **decoupled** from having to be bound to habitual ties downstream. This is because the firms' rivalry in a market, and as a part of a market, insulates their commitments to particular deliveries of production flows downstream.

All this has to find expression in a common idiom, stories circulating among them. Each firm is unconcerned that other markets, which are home to those with whom they transact, are cushioning those transactors in like cocoons for transactions still further along. I return to this decoupling in chapter 5.

3.3.3. Embedding a Profile

The interface is being accepted by the embedding side. The latter is the arbiter of the competition, of the relative performances of the producer firms, and thus of the shape of the profile. But the interface as a whole is not in competition with other interfaces, like its firms are in competition with each other. The ironic implication is that a production market thus governs only the *relative* sizes of differentiated flows, not the aggregate size of flows combined. The aggregate size is a by-product of accident—that is, of the detailed incidents and situations that figure in the process of establishing the curvature of the profile. So aggregate "demand" is also, so to speak, an arbitrarily induced by-product.

That need not be true of all interfaces. Return to the earlier illustration of disciplines in meal-taking. Like the cafeteria, a fast-food restaurant will be an interface, with probably a rather flat profile across its workers. The fast-food restaurant from one chain will, as an entity, also be caught up in an interface of larger scope with competing restaurants. Fast-food restaurants will work to establish that they are comparable to others with which they compete: that is their point. So one sees that interfaces, like other disciplines, may recur and thus get embedded at successive levels.

There is varied basis in detailed phenomenology, in the perceptions of actors, for estimating parameters within a model across the niches of the firms within the interface, embedded in network. Some especially concern the "pull" and "push" of flows of intermediate goods. Estimation is not easy. How many paths of access downstream and upstream are afforded by the observed networks? This must be assessed and predicted not just from the density of connections but also from their involution.[13] Other parameters map comparative assessments of different firms as to perceived quality. Estimates of those parameters will derive not only from the involution and density of ties in a network but also from overlaps in the incidence of different types of ties representing distinct bases of relation.

The set of values on a quality index identify firms at a given period. This pegging by quality sets off further mulling over identities by some or all firms. Yet the quality ordering is a property of the mechanism of the market as a whole, core to its identity.

Processes of decoupling and embedding supplant birth and death of particular actors as foci. Demography is not the point. Decoupling is essential to the paradoxical duality of markets and firms as being both embedded in tangible networks among concrete actors while yet simultaneously being actors with scripts for relations that are transposable and interpretable.

3.3.4. Other Examples and Control Profiles

There is a stripped-down variety of this commit species that is just the reflexive form of a human group putting on a performance for itself. One modern example is the discussion group; there has been a tradition of systematic measurement of interaction profiles (Bales 1970) across the group that permits quantitative analysis (Breiger and Ennis 1979). A village meeting in India (Mayer 1960), repartee in a barber shop, lunch table conversation, all illustrate relaxed social contexts in which this or another genre of discipline can be found.

---

[13] Standard computer software packages are available for making such estimations (e.g., UCINET and STRUCTURE). The greater difficulty is devising fieldwork techniques for efficient specification or estimation of a network, which will require astute devisings of sampling frames for networks (Wasserman and Faust 1994).

By their construction, interfaces do not control for averages and cannot be programmed to yield prespecified flows. Instead, interfaces build their dynamics around the spread of contributions across the comparable set. The commitment characterizing an interface is best portrayed by how variation in members' properties correlates to the curvature in profile. Mutual attention of peers is directed toward jockeying for relative positions that yield each one a distinctive niche.

It follows that the interface can exert control through the shape of its profile, only given skill in manipulation of social organization. Only variances and their ratios constrain the curvature of the interface when it is operating autonomously (White 2002). But rewards, separately and in aggregate, depend upon the average, somewhat accidental outcomes; so there is a latent motivation to try to shift interface in concert. The shift can be accomplished only if the acceptable shapes of profile are retained, so that they become envelopes for achieved control profiles. Participants can make systematic use of these facts: see Eccles and White (1985) for how chief executive officers use these interfaces in achieving control over leading subordinates.

The interface comes in many other varieties, other institutional embodiments. "Star" systems, in entertainment and elsewhere, grow out of interfaces where embedding induces perceptions of events that are greatly exaggerated from the view of actors producing them (Faulkner 1983). Even where the differentiation or dependence is limited, as among starlets in entertainment, there is the same pressure to generate events sufficient to embed them with a skewed distribution of fame despite undetectable differences as judged within the interface. These star systems can be seen as closely analogous to the industrial markets.

The interface is a species with still more dresses than these few special types of competition or formal supervision, or the analogous pair of production market and Hollywood scene. Sitting around in a bull session or other conversation group is being in a commit interface. The institutional costume may be similar but the process shifted, or the reverse.

Actors ordinarily do not perceive and react to higher-order measures like variances; so this, like the other two mechanisms, must be realized through forms that are perceived and estimated directly in everyday terms. A model and its context must be specified in some detail to examine how this can occur.

3.4. Councils

The council genre of discipline is centered on a process of balancing contending but ever-shifting coalitions. Such is the focus, for example, in the logistics of mounting war, perhaps its toughest aspect. One escapes control through single centers by preset formulae. Instead, preexisting strings of dependency feed into an unending process of corralling and allocating: all the while the dynamics of contention keep this discipline going up and down in scale.[14] Mediation predominates over straightforward mobilization: this is mediation between identities, of course, but also between goals and regarding amounts of resources.

An early place to see the workings of this discipline is in the kinship lineage, an extended kin group with corporate rights whose allocations are balanced and rebalanced in a mutual discipline of mediation:

> Our starting point is not the organized corporate group or the fabric of continuity and stability in the social structure (part 1, cf. Fortes 1945) but the individual . . . the standard forms and processes of person-to-person relationships . . . the gradation of rights and duties in jural and ritual relations in which lineage segments emerge as corporate units . . . every person belongs to a hierarchy of lineage segments lying between the maximal and minimal limits of his maximal lineage . . . relevant to his conduct in different degrees and according to variations in the social situation . . . even when only a segment of a lineage emerges in any corporate activity its status and functions are influenced by the total lineage field, including at the limit the field of clanship. . . . Conversely, a lineage always functions as a combination of segments, not as a collection of individuals of common descent. . . . Every lineage segment represents a dynamic equilibrium of mutually balancing segments. It must be emphasized that these distinctions are not made by the natives. . . . The Tallensi have no term for the lineage . . . units of Tale social organization can only be defined by reference to the way in which they emerge in corporate action in relation to other like units. (Fortes 1949, pp. 10–11)

---

[14] In the production economy context discussed at the end of this chapter, as well as in later chapters, the mediator discipline is visible in procurement and supplier networks (Corey 1978; Porter 1976; B. Shapiro 1980; Walker 1985). In that context, too, this discipline evidences the clientelist qualities developed in political contexts in section 6.5. There, regime as larger context is seen as shaping constituents, as well as the reverse etiology of buildup to which the present chapter is devoted. Clientelism is a term for dependency, especially in political institution, built around strings of connections such as are latent chains in mobilizations. Since the mediation discipline has indefinite boundaries, it is natural to liken it to clientelist control regime, a more intricate system. Trust is more prominent and problematic in the larger system than in a mediation discipline, but the logic is similar. The discussion here and later oversteps the bounds of a discipline proper and will be taken up in the further discussion of uncertainty trade-offs in sections 5.2.2, 5.6.1, and 5.7.1, and in sections 6.1.3, 6.8.5, and 6.8.6.

These lineage disciplines are not preset but rather are invoked as to membership and type of tie and occasion. The discipline in this genre is from an ongoing and interconnected and changing set of mobilizations and conciliations. The stories and identities being induced are about claims, and the content of social process activates chains of these claims.

Thus, council disciplines revolve around conflicts and contradictions spread over time. Theorizing these conflicts and contradictions will help in specific technical modeling: see, for example, chapter 9 in Luhmann (1995).

3.4.1. Mediation through Prestige

Council discipline is the closest to the purely social. Stories associated with this discipline center on the allocation of resources, both material and social. The concern with mediation is seen in some gathering-and-foraging party as much as in a formal council with purely political concerns.

The social processes are urgent ones, though the overall identity being induced and embedded by this discipline often aims at time-rooted claims, and an appearance of immutability. Though not as urgent, the playground of chapter 1 also provides illustrations of council discipline. Children do not just appear at random, and where they appear is significant; over here they move into particular productions, but over there it is unstructured play activities, and mediations are required. Named street gangs give further color and recognition to what is a universal—namely, the interactive, the riposte nature of councils.

Correlation among involved identities is key as both the source and outcome of mediation. To mediate is to induce similarity, in actual social enactment, even though the story told may be a unique claim. This is so because, objectively, mediation is always a reciprocating process of inducing like claims and commitments in responses to those of other actors (these claims and commitments need not be verbalized). One can best equate mediations according to whether they yield equal differentiation across all the claimants. Council discipline is what anthropologist Adrian Mayer discusses as action-sets and quasi-groups (1960).

Any effort at mediation, for an innocuous purpose as well as a weighty one, is latent mediation of what others might mediate. Mediation feeds upon itself, induces counteraction and structure to any triggering action. This is as true among the Nuer of old (Evans-Pritchard 1940) as among our big business folk (Bower 1986), or in government (Bearman 1989; Namier 1961). It is just as true on playgrounds with their diverse yet persistent subcultures of conciliation (Opie and Opie 1969).

Thus, mediation cannot exist as an actual social process except in a set of foils and counterfoils. Mediation means tangible wrestling about claims that ostensibly are fixed and abstract. Mobilization also means inducting other actors via commitments that are unrelated to claims. Rather, these commitments focus on successive scopes of alliance and opposition from concrete commitments.

The arena discipline is an inverse, of sorts, to this mediation discipline, the council. Participants in an arena are not embodiments of the rooted interests of factions, as in a council. Selection within the arena has actors functioning off to one side in obscured cliques of matchers, and there is mystification by systematic doctrine in the purifier format (e.g., committee or profession) of the arena. In the mediator-council, and only there, can each direct participant also invoke ties of dependence.

3.4.2. Factions and Autocracy

Factions and their endless maneuverings around control of substantial outcomes are the substance of the council mechanism. There is never a solution, a permanent alignment of factions, for that would contradict the central process. Mediation and realignment goes on routinely in continuous adjustment. It is a context in which changes are embedded as routine. Members enter into and leave particular dependencies, as well as the council structure itself, whatever the stories told.

An identity's standing within the council is tallied according to how many successes are being accumulated in close encounters, what some Native American groups referred to as "counting coup." The Roman Senate of Republican days (Syme 1939; Gruen 1974; Badian 1958, 1985) is an apt illustration of how this counting of coups worked out, persisting over centuries. In its heyday, the Senate was remarkable in its marshalling of small initiatives, leery of grand gestures, as it encroached its way into dominance in Italy and beyond: this rested exactly on subtle re-mediations among ever-shifting confrontations of honor-seeking aristocrats caught in the hold of mediation pattern that lasted for centuries.

In the special case of autocracy, any external or public differentiation—spread in standing among all but the autocrat—is squeezed to nil. This remains true no matter how much effort is expended in jockeying for standing among a servile elite around the autocrat, be it

Holmes's "autocrat of the breakfast table" or an Ottoman sultan (Findley 1980).[15]

As a further example, the council power mechanism is central to the segmentary lineage systems exemplified by the Nuer, who exist in a homogeneous context near the upper Nile that offers little scope for involution. Here, it resembles action in the Roman Senate but in simpler clothing. It can also be seen in a whole array of segmentary kinship systems—along with their analogues in boards of directors (Burt 1983; Levine 1972, 1989; Mintz and Schwartz 1985; Mizruchi 1982, 1984; Mizruchi and Schwartz 1988; Palmer 1984). In Evans-Pritchard's words:

> The outstanding structural characteristic of Nuer political groups: . . . the distinction and individuality of a political group is in relation to groups of the same kind is a generalization that embraces all Nuer local communities, from the largest to the smallest. . . . The relation between tribes and between segments of a tribe which gives them political unity and distinction is one of opposition. (Fortes and Evans-Pritchard 1949, pp. 282–83)

An essential mechanism among the Nuer is the feud, which is endlessly particular to pairs and need not induce any recognizable status ordering. There is endless breaking and recalling of old alliances and identifications, all as circumstances change.

Council disciplines are more stochastic in operation the more complex the overall economy and technology in their context. Among the Nuer, exactly the same genealogical descent lines and groupings can continue indefinitely as the grammar in which power adaptations are made through fission and fusion—seen as moving further back up a descent line or further down. In more complex environments, there is a greater density of disciplines being worked up among a comparable number of actors. This greater density will have the effect, especially in the council form with its dependent strings, of shocks that unsettle particular alignments without changing the overall discipline.

Power is often the idiom of the story set for the council discipline. The explicit demonstration of power is only occasional in the actual operation of this discipline, in any of its variants. While displays of power are only occasional, they are awesome in actual encounter.

---

[15] This contrast with exemplars of "counting coup" seems to be illustrated by the distinction between French and German intellectual cliques as sketched by Lepenies (1988, p. 268): "The ecclesia invisibilis of the Georgeans (followers of the charismatic Stefan George) in fact had about it as much of the French 'chapelle,' the demonstrative academic-cultural defensive alliance congregated around a patron, as it did of the informal, indirect and thus all the more influential coterie of an invisible college."

This occurs when there is, temporarily, fully joint action and perception by the constituent and competing strings of dependency whose representatives or embodiments constitute the council. This is overwhelming when it occurs, not just when there is a great imbalance among constituents' resources but because of hegemony of the council as integral identity with monopolization of the reality perceived by all "involved."

Trust presupposes power; power is built out of trust in council disciplines.[16] But power over engrossment and disbursement of social and physical material can be seen as what mediation points toward. Without mediation discipline there is no power, but very often without anticipation of power there is no mediation.

* 3.4.3. Lazega's Law Practice

[This case study will be reported in some detail and then discussed again under other rubrics: in sections 3.7 and 4.4.2, and in sections 6.3.2, 7.7.3, 8.2.4, and 8.5.2. This is parallel to the treatment of other sections marked with an asterisk.]

An American big city law firm centers on providing advice. Advice to its clients is shadowed by the pervasive seeking and offering of advice from one partner to another. None of these are isolate events, advice is developed and repeated, has history, and one line crosses with another, so that resolution of some sort is needed. It exemplifies a council discipline in operation, but close scrutiny is required.

Close scrutiny is just what Lazega (2001) supplies in his monograph.[17] He uses several idioms, which are compatible with council discipline. He begins with the problem of fission, articulating part of how this council discipline works:

> Well-knitted teams—that is subsets of members who recurrently belong to the same task forces—become a threat to the organization because they can defect and take away with them valued members and clients. . . . Collegial organizations solve this problem . . . by allowing some niche members to reach firm-wide status through the accumulation of one type of resource, and the establishment of a balance of power between these

[16] Compare Baldwin (1978) and Lasswell and Kaplan (1950) for accounts that are, however, not referred to explicit social formations.

[17] Besides the detailed analysis of one partnership, Lazega surveyed a whole range of firms in this city, with help from various law professors and the like. So the book could also be invoked in the next chapters on style and rhetoric. And indeed the firm is large and diverse, so that complete analysis must embrace features not tied to council discipline.

members with different forms of firm-wide status . . . consists in systema-
tizing the division of leadership work—that is, status inconsistency . . .
particularly through a process of destabilization of task forces and circulation of associates (members but not partners). (p. 39)

And he later amplifies:

Members competing for status also reached out of their niches. By doing
so they both gained some autonomy and created, at the overall level, a
cohesion-based integration process of "stitches" bridging sides separated
by internal boundaries. (p. 199)

And he reports the following results:

First, members influential in policy discussions in partnership meetings
tended to be cited as important professional advisers and important pro-
tectors of the common good, and were considered by many to be friends.
. . . Secondly, members—including young and entrepreneurial partners—
considered important to others as strong co-workers . . . tended also to be
sought out often as professional advisers, but did not put in many billable
hours. These were often rain-makers or finders who were in a position to
distribute large amounts of work to others. Finally, there were solo operators who happened to bill and collect individually enormous amounts
during the year, but tended to be prima donnas. (p. 262)

Lazega backs up this portrayal using several bodies of systematic data,
plus extensive, confidential interviewing. He extracts meaning from
this large corpus through use of several standard techniques of network analysis[18] and network diagrams using structurally equivalent
sets of actors as the nodes (e.g., figures 3.1 and 4.1, pp. 103 and 163).

Lazega also collaborates with Pattison in devising powerful statistical
framing (Lazega and Pattison 1999) to test how incidences of several
types of tie influence one another, also allowing for effects from attributes of individual members. "Cooperation is systematically amenable
to structural analyses at the dyadic, triadic, and overall levels" (p. 131).

Finally, he developed an imaginative new sort of sociometric question about who a respondent thought had what kind of control and
then what sorts of levers he would use to influence action there. Krackhardt was his collaborator (Lazega and Krackhardt 2000) on new scaling techniques to portray these results, as in figure 7.3, p. 214.

---

[18] Some were described in chapter 2. But Lazega does not employ blockmodeling, for
the reasons he lays out in note 12, p. 308; I assess this divergence in section 4.4.2 on
professionalism.

Lazega presents summary assessments that fit this firm into council discipline:

> Status is not only based on seniority and money; it has a particularly strong dimension of prestige, of symbolic recognition of a member's contribution, and of ongoing critical judgment about members' quality. (p. 272)

And Lazega also invokes embedding and decoupling, as well as identities:

> The existence of social niches means that one must learn to personalize (embed) and depersonalize (disembed) work relationships and business transactions. (p. 272)

This is not only a convincing portrayal of a council discipline, but also a model, as was the Sampson monastery study of chapter 2, of research both rigorous and insightful. The quality of the data is central: it was by persistence over years that Lazega won unusual access to confidential data, including access to policy and individual member financial performance.[19]

But there is more to say, and this case will be carried forward through subsequent chapters along with the examples of children's playground and of diffusion. A tangible, detailed study like this makes it obvious that reality comes neither cut up into separate cookies nor laid out in cleanly separate levels. And as to discipline species, we argue in 5.6.4 for Lazega's firm as a member of a production interface, as a big law mill competing to churn out cases of various sorts. Then, when it attends more to the judgeship core of law, the firm orients around purity and is also an arena discipline.

3.4.4. Ambiguity in Council Disciplines

Discipline in councils is highly ambiguous. There is little in the way of systematic doctrine. Connectivity seems essential to power; the key is to be tied to the right faction through the right connection, whether in the Senate or in a family business. However, when normal reshufflings of factions are traced over time, it becomes clear that the essential aspect of structure is structural equivalence. No factions and alliances ever stay the same. In the end, what counts is the likelihood that your connections will be mobilized because of parallel hostilities and re-

---

[19] Even so, Lazega was unable to get accounts of selections to partnership, and he had to settle for retrospective sociometric reports on coworkers. Depth and accuracy in field investigation remain enormously difficult to achieve.

flected interests with dominant sets of other factions. The combination of fission-fusion with stringing-dependency tends to generate aversive pillars as a by-product of structural equivalence.

The awesome yet ambiguous power of council disciplines is concurrent with an openness and flexibility of agenda. Each council, miniscule and local as it might be in some broader survey, is sovereign in its own concerns. These concerns are limited in and by concrete fact, but they are not limited by any systematic doctrine or rationale.[20] In particular, there is little interpenetration of one council by another, in dependencies and in various wrangles and quarrels.

As with any discipline, context shapes the process. Imagine a context with maximum differentiation, maximum contrast of upstream over downstream appreciation: mountains out of molehills, the context insisting on imputing great differences in status between actors and strings, even though their attributes are not much different as separately measured. An example is clientelism, as described by Riggs (1966–1969), common at all levels in Thailand. Riggs brings out that the strings of dependency are normally short, with dependency being very much personalized rather than leading to retinues. Thai clienteles are not specialized.

Another example of context shaping process in councils is seen in the *commissaires* of Renaissance French absolutism. These councils make and carry out wartime military requisitions (Hintze 1919; see Eccles and White 1988 and chapter 6 in this book). Dependency is higher, indexing the much higher attention that *commissaires* devote to producing what the fighting forces need as compared with insouciance of Thai patrons to clients.

Take another example that is medium on dependency and also tends to show high involution rather than sensitivity to context: Hollywood's production system is built around the council-mediation mechanism. This was analyzed and documented by Faulkner (1971, 1983), using a modern system of social structure measures derived from blockmodels, and compatible here. At first sight, it might appear to be a marketplace, an arena-purifier, but it is the same specialists who come together again and again. They get rearranged into new packagings of skills for each new production. Major figures find minor ones, from the same or other expertises, and bring them in tow into these packages. There is heavy inflation of tiny initial differences in standings.

In council disciplines, trust is required, and power is constructed. The two presuppose each other. Mobilization spreads from some be-

---

[20] In Nadel's terms from chapter 4, role summation is common.

ginning link, which at the same time will trigger other, apparently distant links whose actors perceive relevance to their own social locales. This is what underlies the mediations that reconcile divergences. As a result, some distribution, tangible or symbolic, of inputs and outputs is coming into place. Only a limited degree of equality through sharing is built into mobilization through the mediation processes.

Trust is presupposed and observably justified by some form of historicized tally. This tally cumulates into a type of tie that is weighted by its history in a succession of chains of mobilization. There is an institutional inflation, as compared to other standards, such as arena ones. This is inflation in that the claims of different ties, if called all together at once, would bankrupt the situation more clearly even than a rundown of confidence would bankrupt a bank.

3.5. Arenas

The arena discipline selects and matches, typically in an episodic fashion. In the playing-field case, formal teams may be only two in number, but the number of clusters going into and out of selections and matchings is various and shifting. Selecting here is concerned with variously perceived real tasks—throwing passes versus line play and the like—and corresponding degrees of social "fits." This transpires before the stylization of formal teams is achieved.

For many sorts of tasks, longer-lived and more complex teams, configurations enter into matching and selection for viable arena discipline. These selections are also often visualized as (and may in fact take place in) literal arenas, physical contexts given social identities from the matchings. The same extends to other realms, such as acquaintance dance, or the production of Broadway musicals (Prince 1974).[21] Diagnosis of your current ailments, legal or medical, are other modern exemplars of the infinite variety of dress in which these selection disciplines come, disciplines built out of exclusion for purity ordering.

Comparabilities are the foundation of all three genres. A cohort in age as it moves along through some age-graded mobilization exemplifies how participants make themselves available through preestablished comparabilities. In arena disciplines, these comparabilities are probed to turn up and then match complementarities. The talk tends to be about esteem, a purely social aspect, whereas the actual concerns in the productions being put together are with complementarities that

---

[21] See later for the former, and for the latter the previous chapter, and chapter 6 in White (1993).

may include the biophysical. The complementarities assessed can range from simple pair matching on over to a full team of specialties.

For a large-scale example, turn to Pierre Bourdieu's analysis of the process of examining candidates for the Grandes Écoles of France in *The State Nobility* (Bourdieu 1996, parts 1 and 2). For smaller scale, return to the playing field of chapter 1: in choosing up sides, the straggle of children are sorting out, from network context and proffered identities, the sorts of contributions and degrees of expertise that different kids can bring. The actual team may be a commit-interface, a reification and symbolization of the new identity being created. But the choosing is based on a preceding select-mechanism of the arena discipline.

3.5.1. Acquaintance Dance

For council discipline there was one extended empirical exemplification, Lazega's law firm. For arena the concrete example of acquaintance dance will be followed by two others (3.5.2 and 3.5.3).

An acquaintance dance or mixer provides an example of the arena discipline.[22] Whole entering classes at one or more colleges may be brought together, exactly to generate still further ties and networks out of random seeding of dyads. An acquaintance dance invokes some rotation of partners for the dance floor, perhaps with opposite circles and then switching of dyads at the stopping of music.

It is instructive to contrast the dynamics here with those for neighborhood bars, discussed in the previous chapter. Clientele of the neighborhood bar evolve from working networks toward corporate forms. In contrast, in the acquaintance dance, corporates are worked about to generate ties, which modify networks. In this there is a duality.

The acquaintance dance is a limiting case that invokes the explicit coordination required for bureaucracy and the like. It is but a first step in a proliferation of introduction settings of adult life nested within one another and across one another. These go on among elites and in esoteric settings as well as everyday, with gender as only one example of attribute selected on.

Individuals within an acquaintance dance may seek more restrictive corporates within the initial mass. More specialized mixers are likely to follow. More spontaneous versions are common. Boys and girls use any occasion of corporate commonality as a basis for exploring and forming couples. Men and women do so as well, usually in more complex contexts of organization.

---

[22] This ceremonial form may be disappearing, its replacement not yet clear.

3.5.2. Gibson on Turn-Taking

The most potent social discipline you experience is one that you can't articulate because you so much take it for granted. This is even though, or rather because, it is part of your habitus, in Bourdieu's formulation. David Gibson (2003, 2005) has established that turn-taking in oral communication is such discipline, and I will argue that it fits the arena genre in particular. As with Lazega's study earlier, I offer considerable detail.

The valuation implicit, I argue, is decorum, good manners, keeping face, and letting others do the same. This valuation is a form of purity, and therefore the genre of discipline is the arena.

Gibson observed fifty thousand turn-takings in committee meetings (many committees, each in many sessions). He concerted these into successive pairs of turns and then converted those into an inventory of "participation shifts." The key is what the participation shift suppresses, what it does *not* code: first, the participation shift omits the names of speaker and of target in a given turn, being concerned only with the switching between that turn and the succeeding one. It looks only to whether a party in the second turn (and, if so, which of the two there) coincides with previous speaker or target in the first turn.

Second, this participation shift (PS) also ignores the topic and content of either turn, except for any throat clearings (discourse markers like "Oh . . ." "Well . . .") by the second speaker in seizing the spot.

And third, PS suppresses information on the duration of either turn (although that is stored in the computer along with, of course, Gibson's list of names for members—but without any transcript of topic).

Gibson thus created a grammar of turn-taking, akin to the grammar of pronouns in regular language. These are momentary "pronouns," just S marking speaker and T target in the first turn. Interest initially focuses on whether the second turn just switches S to target and T to speaker on the second turn, and indeed in a good 40 percent of the PS, such answering shift is observed.

There is another piece in this grammar. Gibson also coded whether a turn had all conversants, the whole group G, as target. (These are committees of bank managers who don't brawl or all talk at once: Gibson does not code any instance of G being the speaker on a turn.) About 30 percent of all the individual turns are undirected, that is, with the group G as target, so that 70 percent are directed. In the PS grammar, for pairs of turns, whereas only one-tenth of the PS had G as the target on both turns, one-fifth of the PS had G on the first turn only.[23]

[23] Indeed, the percentage of PS with G as target in the first turn only is about the same, 40 percent, for PS with an individual as first target who then reciprocates as speaker back to the first speaker as target.

Yet only about 5 percent of the PS had G as the target only on the second turn; there is a pronounced asymmetry. That is the clue to how the grammar works. Gibson took the bare string of turns and coded them as simply directed d or undirected u (G as target). He constructs and tests a null hypothesis that the occurrences of d and u are independently distributed. In the whole corpus of fifty thousand turns (which differs by only one from the number of PS!), the null hypothesis is rejected and indeed the probability of du is substantially less than the probability of ud.

The real point, however, is that the big divergence, the big effect, is segregation. That is, d's cluster together as dd Participation Shifts a bit more than expected, but especially the u turns cluster together into uu Participation Shifts very much more than expected. This outcome means that there must be a lot of interaction effects back up at the level of PS, which validates Gibson's intuition to look for grammar there. His task was to explore these interactions and then interpret them: see Gibson (2003). The notable results are how participants manage to shoehorn and piggyback into speaking via invoking just those active in immediately preceding turns. A bare 3 percent of PS have two entirely new persons in the second turn.

The concern in this discipline manifestly is selection. The valuation implicit in this discipline, I proposed earlier, is decorum, good manners, keeping face, and letting others do the same, which I interpret as a form of purity. So the discipline uncovered is of arena genre.

The pattern of findings has face validity as a discipline of turn-taking, a discipline so engrained as to be unnoticed. A discipline should also predict to other aspects of social behavior. Gibson (2005a), in a second piece, using data on network ties, shows that indeed there are strong correlations between role in PS grammar and role in networks, particularly in networks of authority ties.

Social living is complicated, and there are many aspects of the lives of these managers not captured by the discipline that governed their group interactions. That does not make the discipline any less real, nor does it excuse the researcher from bringing to bear other constructs— these constructs could be from the other chapters or from the other two disciplines in this chapter—all of which may be visible in Gibson's settings (see also Gibson 2005b, 2005c).

3.5.3. Arena Markets and Production Markets

A selection-arena brings together actors who may be disparate and inhomogeneous into a setting that is socially constructed to emphasize formal interchangeability so that actors are viewed as comparable.

That is why your earliest conscious experience of this discipline may have been choosing up sides for a game amid a bunch of kids on a playground. And the pure-exchange market distinguished by economic theory (Newman 1965) is a mediated version of choosing up.

Exchange markets on all scales are obvious arena disciplines. The actors are there to make matchings, which can be of the most variegated sorts and which can appear as flows and/or stocks, or services, or intangibles. Consider a lawn sale, or for that matter a village market. Money, while it eases barter, also obscures the underlying social form. From an operational social viewpoint, what is being created are dyads that can "produce" what they both want only by acting together.

By contrast, within the interface discipline, production is relatively unproblematic for individual actors. The focus of production markets, as an interface discipline, is to induce orderly reception and interpretation of the flows the producers generate via a clear precedence order among the producers according to quality. The arena discipline is the obverse, in which the social production, exclusion and recombining, can be accomplished only (and in diverse ways) from joint activity; so matching together into pairs, or more various teams, is induced. Mating is the homeliest example. "Supply matching demand" is a syllogism for the arena market; it is at best an ex post rationale, a tautology for the production market.[24] This is true for any scale, true whether the discipline is of firms or of persons.

In the commit-interface discipline, producers eye only each other, as reflected in terms of trade achieved, with the buyers adding confusion: the interface operates as a one-way mirror. In the selection-arena, in contrast, either you are in the arena, or it is opaque to you. You are equally "in" whether a seller or a buyer or both, and sellers are no more active than buyers in establishing proposed terms of trade. Select and exclude are obverse and complementary operations here.

There is also a basic difference in time construction. The production market presupposes and requires unremitting attention to the flows and to the interface by the producers, whereas an arena market can come in discontinuous and self-contained sessions. All those present in an arena are equivalent, rather than "marked" by side and fixed in niche by quality. Yet attendance at an arena may be fickle.

Note that linguistics can offer some guidance on criteria for discipline membership. The issues are subtle, as in the distinctions between marked and unmarked. Battistella (1996) does a good job of laying out elaborations of that distinction since its early classic statement by

---

[24] Supply matches demand is called Say's law: see Morishima (1973) for a trenchant dissection.

Roman Jakobson (1990). For a social application, see Salzinger (2004). A central aspect is ambiguity not just in categorical assignment but in whether any assignment is called for: intuition is helped by reading in the *Brown Book* by Wittgenstein (1965).

Price seems like the natural idiom for matchings and selections. This is so much the case that we expend great efforts to impute and realize a monetary format even when remote from any economic context. But a more general way to view the ambiance of the arena discipline is as purity: after selecting or excluding particulars from a whole bunch, the bunch becomes more pure—for instance, selecting nuggets of gold from a pan of ore or picking debris out of a rice harvest.

3.5.4. Fame and Chance

Selection-arena disciplines are robust with respect to eruptions of control projects, whether from within or from without. The robustness comes from the multicentered structure, combined with the fluid and stochastic nature of flows into and among clusters. Size distributions of freely forming social groupings within an arena have proved robust (James 1953; Coleman 1964; White 1962), and on larger scales too, this is evidence of robustness across attempts at manipulation.

Arena disciplines are flexible for accommodating various and unexpected actors. The problematic for this species is identity formation for clusters. Selections into clusters of complementarities can be apt, can constitute, from an observer's viewpoint, effective social constructs in future production, yet they may come with inadequate induction of identities.

It is for this reason that fame, in various shadings and spreads, so often is articulated in matchings and selections. Fame can be purely social and arbitrary. Fame can supply a sort of universal currency of identity, a flexible spread of identities among the straggle that are matching into clusters. Fame is a way to make purity ordering tangible.

Chance, the stochastic, is attracted to and helps induce the selection-arena discipline, which most often we conceive as an exchange market or a garage sale. This arena seems chancy and disorderly, even socially problematic, yet it is an effective and predictable regulator of real network flows.

3.5.5. Arenas as Purifiers

Purity valuation frames the operation of arena disciplines. Selection is a sort of purifying. *Exclude* is the complement of *select*. As the metaphor "arena" suggests and "purifier" language reinforces, examples of this discipline cover a vast range from an office cocktail party to diplomacy among nations. Iterative realignments of alliances are arena dynamics, which underscore the inevitability of compromise but also of ambivalences. For example, ducking frustration in arena settings may lead to successively imputing "impurity" to former allies.

Modern communication technology, by proliferating audiences and possibilities of communication and affiliation more generally, is also proliferating arena disciplines. Take Google as a prototype in the Internet environment that affords virtually unlimited possibilities for affiliating and also for distancing. Using the Internet link structure and network measures to rank value of Web pages and relevance to topics, Google ranks (purifies) pages according to how many links it receives, as well as by weighting the links according to the "importance" of the Web site that is doing the linking.[25] Google emerges as an identity shaped in arena discipline. Implicit here is a distinctive degree of fluidity: indeed, it is weak ties in the sense of Granovetter that blend best with arena, not strong ties with their more fixed architecture.

Membership in purifiers can vary from the most temporary and casual to the most permanent and rigid. There is a tendency to concentric shells of membership. The inner shells are the most pure, have the most weight in evolving changing standards of matching. For example, when creating page rankings, ties from "important" pages have more weight. Purity is created by achieving matchings that become defined as pure.

Purifying occurs off to one side, out of the mainstream, with the most pure out of the mainstream. The general purpose of purification is known and indeed disseminated. On the other hand, the arena of the selections and matchings is opaque from outside. And just how and why particular sets of selections are made need not be visible to each other. That is, the rules and standards evolve and change across the disparate population that the purifier exists to make comparable.

A village caste council in India (Mayer 1960) is a selection-arena that explicitly emphasizes purity ordering. Its business is endless small matchings and adjustments of ceremonial requirements. This example, like exchange markets and indeed disciplines of any species, occurs as one among many other of its type. This reminds us that disciplines of all genres are analytical devices that presuppose as they also imply aspects of the larger context. Disciplines do not come solo.

This fact of pattern goes hand in hand with the character of story-set used. The caste example is one in which particular purifiers indeed

---

[25] See Google Web site explanation: http//www.google.com/technology/index.html.

refer to and imply particular others, so that they imply a larger rhetorical structure. The caste example is extreme in the explicitness of concern with purity, to the extent that there is an ideology tied to a religious institution to undergird it.

Another sort of example is the office of chief executive officer (CEO), which evolved in business over a fifty-year period in the last century (Chandler 1962; Fligstein and Fernandez 1988; Vancil 1979). Like all real evolutions, it was blindfold. At first it seemed but an innocent alternative to "president"; it seemed at most an example of title inflation, where both CEO and president could bask in apex glow. Perhaps it also served to ease retirement transitions. "President" itself was an uneasy concept. President was a temporary managerial servitor, in an environment of "owners" unlimited in term, and too many tried to assimilate to the time horizon of owner.[26]

Analytically, the CEO indeed is a selection-arena discipline. The CEO was not the hands-on manager and decider of operations, but exactly the fixer, the healer—and thereby the controller, given appropriate networks of committees and offices below,[27] which is to say that the CEO is a purifier. Over a single decade (Vancil and Green 1984), the CEO came to be more and more commonly designated as a small committee of interchangeables who are to function in what we have described as the purifier way, as the selection-arena discipline, selecting for issues, choices of strategic importance.

At another extreme, consider committees with which you are familiar in your own practical life. They too are purifiers, in a broad range of situations. The committee enables placements to be made in much less constrained ways; that is, committees may serve to pull, from out of the main flows, streams of problems and opportunities and bring them to one side where matchings can be made (cf. March and Olsen 1976). Because the functioning, although not the provenance, of a committee can be private, existing memberships and networks can be temporarily suspended in devising rationales for matchings and selections. The formal equality within committees, which neutralizes age and status and tribal distinctions and the like, is important to the flexibility.

Common also as purifiers are arenas defined as uncommon, centered on an inner core of purification specialists. A gathering of elders may

---

[26] It eventually became clear that this mere change in terms went hand in hand with a shift to a very different, a larger physiology of control, to the multidivisional form from the scalar functional one: see discussion in chapter 7.

[27] In chapter 7, this shift to CEO is also shown to be exactly a shift to use of arena disciplines in a new lattice of control.

function as a purifier in dealing with ill health, matching complaints to treatments. A gathering similarly may mediate conflicts, seen as a purification with wisdom. A gathering may similarly be consulted and consult concerning sin and matching sin with apt contrition. In otherwise very different societies and rhetorical systems, purifier arenas of any of these kinds can be given explicit formal standing.

In this era, such "uncommon" purifier arenas are professional settings (see Abbott 1981, 1988 and chapter 6 in this book). Doctors heal, judges judge, priests offer sacraments, each in formalized settings fitting arena discipline. A joint, opaque arena of matchings underlies the formal setting, but the potential interventions from many and varying actors are not obvious. In each there is a logic of purity akin to that in the caste situation, keyed to an "inner," because more permanent, body of allowed practitioners. There is little tangible connection between the body of doctrine kept up to sustain purity definitions, on the one hand, and the tangible matchings of victim to remedy, or of actor to another actor or to material parcel. Thus, the setting can be understood as a discipline rather than some mere offshoot of overall arcane cultural prescriptions.

3.5.6. Ambiguity versus Slack in Arena Disciplines

Professions and committees are examples of the arena discipline. Arenas orient around purifying. In all purifiers, there is a decoupling of external status from internal standing. Within the purifier, the practitioners—temporary or permanent—are operating in a collegial mode. There is no tendency toward inducing status discrimination within the purifier. Practitioners as such tend to have special standing when viewed from outside, and this is associated with a tendency to impute differential status among practitioners—which need have no relation to any internal standings.

The opaqueness of a purifier permits it to seek matchings that can reduce social flexibility and unrootedness. At the same time, it provides rationale for ambiguity being kept fixed, or even fixed up, as seen from outside. The very same committee members who may have just artfully patched up a social tie may, back "outside" the committee, not see that; or similarly, not see how they have rigged a generally accepted cultural rule. The unusual degree of social confusion within the purifier is necessary to obfuscate the ambiguity that, according to the formal cultural rules, is being introduced by purifier action.

A purifier is a structure whose system of operation offers a high degree of slack. That is, there is not a tight constraint on timing; there is not a tight constraint on the amount of attention and other resources given to this or that situation. "Slack" is shorthand for uncertainty in social context. One further observes that not even the overall total consumption of attention and other resources is subject to much constraint. We have all noticed that committees tend to go on for unpredictable lengths of time, with unpredictable partition of attention by item. They are subject, even against formal rules, to being convened exceptionally.

High slack is a corollary of the purifier's being out of the mainstream of everyday business, available for unpredictable claims for social fixes. Open-air markets are another institutional embodiment of purifiers, here where the "hurt" to be fixed is a material one. The pure theory of exchange applies (Newman 1965). But this pure theory concerns only the formation of "prices" that are internal to the purifier operation. Left out is the huge slack built into the arbitrary times, occasions, and membership in the pure exchange arena—the swap meets and lawn sales of current times, or the village fairs of Skinner's Asia (1964–1965) or early Europe or Africa (Smith 1975).

It may be because of high slack that one finds purifiers so often in whole sets—say, lattices of committees for a larger environment. On a longer timescale, careers are being negotiated more or less explicitly. High slack permits the subtle and endless probing and estimation that lead to invitations and acceptances, and possibly to careers. But this points beyond particular disciplines to the rhetorics of chapter 6.

3.6. Households, Family, and Gender: Bringing It All Together

A family in the everyday sense, around its meal table, exemplifies council discipline. Yet also, gender is sorting out according to arena discipline emerging from ongoing networks. And above all, so too is production of children along with work amalgamated as interface discipline. Of course, all three figure in later chapters too: gender and family build into and from the institutional system of kinship (see chapter 5), and often also with the control regimes of chapter 6 (see Hamilton and Biggart 1990).

Household discipline undergirds much of traditional work institutions (Udy 1959), which exemplifies historicity in disciplines. So this section is in every sense evoking how disciplines, indeed all the constructs we work with, invoke and affect context of all kinds. This section is a preview of the general look at contextualizing in chapter 8.

Gender calls up gendering of all sorts of items in stories. Gender is a major symbolic resource: the grammar of most languages attests this, and for some like French and Spanish, scream it out. At the same time,

gender also gets stretched out, as if taffy, into one cline and another—
for example, along the degree of femininity or masculinity with age,
for both sexes.

3.6.1. Meld of All Three Disciplines

Patriarchy and domination call forth each other across some meld of
gender and household with family discipline. And all three often figure in the institutional system of production economy (Udy 1970) and
of polity control (Padgett and Ansell 1993).

Demography, when it is guided by theory and history (Hammel and
Laslett 1974), beyond mere bean counting, needs to give an account
that is integrated across all three disciplines. Network population itself
melds all three. Macro redundancies, such as across age/period/co-
hort, build out of all three (Ryder 1965). Ours is not like an ant society
(Wilson 1970): ours is a species with continuous rather than discrete
generational spread. All our social formats, as proposed in chapters 1–
7, are pushed and stretched by the persistent and yet erratic injections
of babies, and thus new identities.

As we shall see in chapter 8, the network population context feeds
back into shaping the meld of disciplines. This is true as to network
topology, but also as to structure of spread over time. Family discipline, for example, has to stretch over extreme fluctuation in relative
age and kinship transitivity. And, of course, the geography and ecological setting of the network population correlate with variants of
each discipline.

3.7. Inventory of Disciplines

Yet the melding of disciplines is not unique to family setting. Lazega's
monograph on a law firm supplies tangible exemplification. Yes, it was
seen earlier as council discipline. But Lazega goes out of his way to
bring out the playing out of the other two valuation orders. The firm
depends on bringing in new business and elaborating existing counsel,
which can support interface discipline around such commitments.
Nonetheless, this seems secondary to council discipline, since the
"rainmakers" are by no means hegemonic. And certainly this set of
lawyers is concerned with excellence in legal thinking. Some partners
win honor from that, so one can argue some presence of arena discipline, but a Supreme Court panel is not what they are emulating.

Beyond the focus thus far on a single genre of discipline, I claim that
there is nothing esoteric about them. They are everywhere, in all

scopes, all realms, at all levels. The trick is to penetrate the bland mirror of common sense to track them in motion. I will practice what I preach by looking for disciplines right at home, in the most familiar aspects of my life—or rather, at work, not home.

But first I take up general difficulties in taking inventory, even if just for the playground of chapter 1. Already with networks there are puzzles about how to inventory. The previous chapter described (2.3.4) an elaborate parsing of larger pattern in a network in terms of constituent triads. Perhaps that can be brought to bear on disciplines, each of which obviously must invoke triads selectively in distinctive ways.

Each discipline folds into the contexts of any other disciplines within the social process being observed. At the same time, netdoms among its constituents are influenced and reshaped. The sets of stories that characterize ties borrow from valuation orders in environing disciplines, just as disciplines get hitched to one another through network ties, preexisting or new, between constituents.

And any such hitchings between disciplines are only one part of the larger configurations taken up in subsequent chapters. Network-populations and their disciplines interpenetrate through migration and conquest and many other processes, from which control struggles emerge on a new scale. These struggles settle into reproducible social formations that are so far not describable from constructs and measures developed in these first chapters. Three new approaches that probe different aspects of robust articulations of network populations are required. At the very end of the chapter, I examine tournaments and liminal occasions, which furnish two extremes that bound the larger social formations in the succeeding three chapters: extreme constraint and extreme looseness.

One general difficulty in analysis is fuzziness in the disciplines to be inventoried. A closer look at catnet will help clarify this issue.

3.7.1. Catnet as Residual of Disciplines

A discipline as actor comes in and out of activity, being buffeted by thrusts of control efforts by self and others. When can a discipline maintain identity as integral actor with energy shaped from its embedding? In disciplines (as in netdoms), meaning gets shaped through switchings. Discipline, once emerged, is tracked as narrative within discourse. So discipline pulls on and is pulled by ties, in and across networks. The resulting potpourri sometimes manages to keep reconstituting itself in distinctive profiles of meaning, such as we turn to in the next chapter.

In some contexts, there may be no sustainable variety of any species, as modeled here, according to then-current observation. Disciplines themselves can be identities with social ties, and at the same time participants within such a discipline can be identities as well. Thus, some network of ties can appear connecting entities embedded on different levels. It is only while a discipline is in action and hegemonic that its context and contingency minutiae (in the form of ties and networks of ties) may fade from the focus of attention.

When clear-cut disciplines do not emerge, one can expect not only a profusion of identities of limited durations but also much more prominence for looser forms of social organization. There are other representations of social space and contingency that surface where identities cannot be grounded in terms of niches in disciplines. Attributes, of actors or of events, become more prominent in the absence of place in an articulated mechanism of discipline. Stereotypes—that is to say, categorical attribution of character—appear among actors and events.

Catnets appear in the absence of stable, well-formed disciplines. But Lazega goes out of his way to bring out the playing out of the other two valuation orders. In earlier work (Schwartz 1966, 1967), the term **catnet** was coined to capture the involutions among network interconnections and personalization of attributes. Chapter 2 already introduced catnets. Persons recognize indirect connections that are implied by the set of pair relations, assumed common knowledge, which can be represented as a network. But these indirect connections are recognized only in part, and over a limited number of removes. These indirect connections are reacted to in concrete terms rather than as well-defined new types of relations. The principal result of the evolution of a catnet is the definition, in the eyes of participants, of structural equivalence as a guide to the perceived system. A simple example is the development of cliques in a network of friendship.

The rather diffident theory of social interaction elaborated by Niklas Luhmann (1995, chapter 10) can be operationalized in terms of catnets. One can see that the catnet construct is a path around the portrayal implicit in this chapter that disciplines have disjunct memberships. It is a path toward the style construct of the next chapter, as we will see.

3.7.2. In My Own Experience

Many years ago, as a young faculty member, my views remained commonsense ones, with lots of stories of villains and heroes and shenanigans and especially goals, along with elaborate plans to achieve these goals. Underneath, I slowly have come to see, the reality is self-perpetuating disciplines whose activities often seem immune to the best-laid plans, even of the majority and the powerful. This was crystallized very recently, during a visiting professor research stint at the University of Toulouse–Mirail, when my collaborator and host insisted that I write an extensive account of how American academia worked, for delivery to a hall full of interested but bemused French graduate students and faculty.

My own disciplines at work center in the Department of Sociology at Columbia University. We just now are having two faculty meetings for evaluating graduate students. I experience these as a council discipline, with a certain amount of jockeying and horse trading as to whose protégé and whose field rates best.

Yet just at the end of each meeting, the department chair calls a different meeting to order. It also is a faculty meeting, but only of senior (tenured) professors, called to examine recommending possible new senior hires. So I am switched to a new discipline, one that I experience as an arena discipline, with discussion and argument centered on whether this and that candidate and their works are truly sociology and truly of high quality that fits with our profile.

In an appointment at a secondary branch of a state university system, my department would be concerned with undergraduate teaching, in large classes to meet deans' enrollment targets. I think I would experience this primarily as an interface discipline, both in faculty meeting and in classroom teaching. The undergraduate teaching in Columbia sociology has until lately been secondary to the graduate teaching and especially to our research, so I have rarely felt myself in an interface discipline.

For most of us in the Columbia department faculty, research looms larger than teaching, though graduate mentoring ties in closely with the research. I do not experience this research side of our life as a discipline. In some respects, it is very much a matter of networks among research specialists, labile and often hazy. The present department arena discipline does figure here episodically, as one thinks of possible recruitments. Yet when we are called upon to referee manuscripts for publication in major journals, there is some experience of interface discipline, whereas it is arena discipline when we ourselves strive for such publication.

But the main influence of academic departments is of a different kind: it is the spread of acquaintanceships from many years spent in other departments, as well as this one—now including ties then with students of that period as much as faculty members. In the next chapter, I characterize a very different sort of social formation, a stew that seems to me to capture best the research aspect of work life as I experience it. In chapter 6 I lay out in some detail how I think the whole university research faculty package works out into an institutional system. There I further examine the contexts that prove to embed the disciplines that figure in the stew.

That is enough to give you some tangible flavor of observing and analyzing through the lens of disciplines. Note that disciplines abound, and one finds endless hitchings and stackings, and very clearly also switchings so common as to be ritualized. Yet one does have to concentrate, and have some experience, to energize the lens and make it convincing.

Surely you can explore for yourself how to add in the many other facets of university social process that bear on disciplines. Consider the separate and parallel professional schools, and distinct subpopulations of students. Interdisciplinary teaching, especially of required courses, is a disruptor of departmental insularity, along with the endless reaches of larger faculty governance.

3.7.3. Tournaments and Liminality

In concluding this chapter, I bring in some new aspects that will help set the stage for later chapters. Larger social contexts have been presupposed in earlier chapters, both in examples and in analysis, and now here. Before turning to particular institutions and regimes, preliminary insight comes from viewing larger contexts in extreme forms. We look for a zero and an infinity. Tournament and Mardi Gras are two extremes that permit assessments of contingency, ambiguity, and ambage, cleared of intricacies of historical specification. Both extremes evidence the dialectics of embedding and decoupling.

The tournament is a conscious enactment of a pecking order. A tournament is a set of pairings among a population (Moon 1968; Erdos and Spencer 1974) in which, within each pair, one dominates the other. The pairings are to be strictly divorced from positions in other social networks and thus from institutional position. The outcomes of pairings are to be arrayed to permit inference of a transitive ordering from the outcomes. A perfect, or near perfect, dominance ordering is one in which if one actor dominates a second who dominates some third, then the first also dominates the third in direct paired encounter. Call this a tournament: it defines a transitive order. Examples from casual observation come to mind, such as among children on the playground of chapter 1; other examples are imposed by fiat, as in organized sports.

Liminality, on the other hand, following Turner (1974), is exemplified by Mardi Gras, where all normal rules are suspended. This is a suspension conceded as legitimate by all. Liminality exemplifies decoupling and embedding in an extreme form that is the opposite of that for tournaments. Any and all network populations may but need not impact encounters during Mardi Gras.

Liminality is signaled by ceremonial boundaries; that is, there is a self-conscious embedding within an explicit culture, usually by rejection. At the same time, the period of liminality serves to interrupt causal chains of agency and gaming. Usually this suspension holds only for some short, very specific period.

Liminality is a decoupler for agency even while it embeds in overall context. One can see this duality in Turner's Mexican fiesta, in student strikes, in pilgrimages (Christian 1980), in masses, in reunions, around a stage, at imperial apotheoses (Cannadine and Price 1987). Liminality copes with phenomenological confusion.

These two extremes, of tournament and liminality, are perfect converses. In the tournament, the social standing of each actor is totally clear. This is a state of zero ambage, and there is, as a result, complete ambiguity as to the cultural basis of the social standings, as argued further later on. In liminal formations, on the other hand, there is zero ambiguity because there is an agreement on an extremely simple "new" culture of rules. Usually this is just an erasure of previous rules. At the same time, there is complete indefiniteness in social patterns of relation and thus extreme high ambage.

While liminal occasions mush together disparate and remote swirls of action, tournaments break apart larger contexts. Ambage is suppressed at the cost of erasing verifiable cultural content as criterion of dominance. By-products, such as hierarchies, may emerge in the larger context around the tournaments. Various tournaments, each with relatively arbitrary cultural bases, can be fitted together, in resultants of projects for control. Chickens do their flock's pecking order sincerely, but unlike humans they have no capacity to concatenate tournaments into ladders of mobility and hierarchies of control.

Utopias are the imagined, long-term versions of liminality, compromised to various degrees for plausibility. The dictatorial utopias, the Orwellian 1984s and the Walden II's, are as much liminal as the happily communal ones. It is not clear that liminal formations are observed in any other species. Mathematical modeling by stochastic process and encounter matrix should be feasible (along lines analogous to Landau's cited in chapter 8), but there is no set of empirical findings to give bite to the analysis, in which symmetric ties would replace the asymmetric dominance ties.

What is clear is that liminality is common if not universal in known human societies.[28] It appears to be an episodic formation.[29] Why the contrast with dominance hierarchies? Liminality appears endogenous, in that no external pressure or trigger seems needed. Yet liminality is episodic, presumably from endogenous pressures of decay. Dominance tournaments are often extremely stable, in structure and even in exact mapping of member to rank, yet except in stupid species, where there are dominance hierarchies as a coupling between biophysical and social, tournaments are ceremonial contrivances not engendered in the routine operation of a social formation.

Liminality and tournaments both emphasize discontinuity. Time in social life has a picaresque quality overall, picker-up in ambiguity and ambage as at a cocktail party, but moment by moment it is remorselessly Markovian (Feller 1968; White 1973). Memory, whether as vengeance or forethought, interrupts the Markovian quality only occasionally, with most of the generation of the picaresque coming, for each actor, from interruptions through gamings by others.

Liminality produces the illusion of an enlarged present in which Markovian chains are broken. Tournaments impose an enlarged present by fiat. Tournaments make mock of preceding continuities of interdependent action. Complete linear orders of precedence, complete sets of pair dominances without ambage, are antithetical to experiences of time and sequence and interdependence.

[28] See Turner's cross-cultural survey (1969).

[29] However, sleep, it can be argued (Aubert 1965; White and Aubert 1959), is a liminal social state.

FOUR

STYLES

A SENSIBILITY is how style presents itself in experience. For the observer, style may become apparent as an interpretative tone, deployed by native expertise. As such it exhibits a distinctive texture in social process, sensed by those immediately involved. Analytically, style can be of any scope and level: it is a scale-invariant concept. And whatever the scope, two basic aspects of style come intertwined: (a) the interpretive tone along with (b) the feedback dynamics. Style is not transposable, though it may get reconstituted.

Style is immediately available through attending to the sensibility that goes with texture in life. Some family mealtimes are homely in style. Graduation ceremonies are formal in style. I will always remember the style around Harvard Yard in mid-April 1976, where Elysian weather accompanied both extreme social stress and mellow discourse to form a unique texture. But style is not to be seen everywhere—not, for example, in administrative routine of a business day or deployment of an army battalion.

Style generates its own context and so is involute, constituting a boundary, in contrast with the network population of chapter 2 (see 2.1.3). Style also differs from the disciplines of chapter 3, whose survival and properties depended on how they are embedded into contexts. Networks need not persist just as they happen to be thrown up by stochastic eruption, any more than a particular discipline, with its projected identity, will persist and reproduce itself independent of social context, which is in turn made up of networks. These social contexts are necessarily stochastic.

Style transcends and commingles network populations and disciplines via peculiar patterns of switchings. Despite being a self-reproducing context and a self-contained identity, style can change through stochastic social processes across diverse constituents among networks and disciplines.

Social temporality emerges, basically, from a profile of switchings across netdoms. Whereas identities can be like musical notes that struggle for a melody, and discipline embeds these identities in the larger context of a genre, style is the rhythm of social life. Metaphorically, identities contextualized in disciplines make up the melody to which style adds temporality. Couples dancing close, for instance, are in a style, and so are teenagers jumping around on the dance floor.

Styles encompass a wide range in scope, scale, and level. Style can characterize strategic actors as well as whole social contexts. Hence, a style is scale-invariant—or "scale-free" in the sense laid out by Abbott (2001). Like those "Russian dolls" that are identical in shape, pattern, and colors, but differ slightly in size, style offers a nested structure. Thus, for example, a person, in the ordinary sense that we avoided in chapter 1, is a style. Pithy conversation may establish a style, such as in a Paris salon or a research discussion group. Successful mobilization toward a political end embodies a style, perhaps differently around the cause of human rights than around the cause of ethnic autonomy. Expertise attends to style as interpretive tone, as will be argued later; however, rational choice theory seeks mobilization of rationality as the style for expertise.

My initial examination of sensibility will end with two large-scale studies of womankind. Then we turn to three studies of style emergent in networks of commerce. Next comes an examination of person as style, followed by the argument that rationality itself is a style. These discussions motivate, then, taking up general ways to appraise and measure social spaces and profiles. One main focus is how best to observe styles, personal or other, and to locate them in some ecology.

The divisions in this chapter—and the book—are not conventional. The numerous and diverse examples spread across conventional framings of social life as found in textbooks. In particular, this central chapter is cited in the next three chapters, as well as having been foreshadowed in the previous three chapters. Indeed, analysis in each chapter of the book must, given the nature of social process, presuppose and draw on findings from the others, as I show visually in the final chapter (see figure 8.1). Not surprisingly, many studies to be reported will be large and heterogeneous, not neat and focused.

After thus spelling out approaches to recognizing ecology, I will explicate more general selves and also communities as styles. Then we return to observing emergence and change with three further studies of style, where the cultural is intertwined with the social. To cap that, I will offer a general proposition.

The whole range of studies we will cover flesh out the initial definition of style and illustrate how style and control interpenetrate, which is the main topic of the final section.

4.1. Sensibility

Style is a profile of the commingling of network relations and discursive processes across switchings that result from and also shift situations. Temporality in the social world comes from style, from the rhythm of profiles of switchings. This temporality is not time as we ordinarily think of it in the count of hours and minutes displayed by a clock. Rather, it is closer to a tempo in music. A conversation can exhibit a style, which may be bland, as in "making talk" or just chatting, or may instead track and trigger vivid episodes through domains across some situation. As in music, a conversation can have a specific rhythm, a specific sensibility that is the signature of its style; similarly, the issue is whether a field of recurring discourse sustains and reproduces a distinctive rhythm of social interaction.

Relevant here, at a completely different scope, is Randall Collins's magisterial survey (2002) of philosophies' social constitutions, spread over millennia and continents. His study documents successions of what I have termed council disciplines, as well as cross sections within those disciplines, but not an overall style. Instead, he shows that a sensibility establishes itself, again and again, which one now sees from a long perspective as the hallmark of a civilization.

I shall analyze styles with much the same tools whatever the scale, size, or level of living, whether in a large organization or in the playground example from chapter 1. At the micro end, Bourdieu's "habitus"—as a matrix of "perceptions, appreciations, and actions" (Bourdieu 1977, p. 83)—is analogous to style, as it also predetermines interpretive tone. Conversely, styles can shape, bend, and mark bodies as well. Styles can be thought of as specification of how individuals live their lives: in this view, individual lives emerge through an ongoing process of combining understandings of situations with sets of practices arrayed across lives embedded in social networks. Bourdieu proposes habitus as the signature of a person (1996a,b), whereas later in this chapter, I argue for person as style.

At the macro end, toward the close of this chapter, come hieratic styles observed across fields of army, church, and colonialism. Such styles encompass vast numbers of networks, across disciplines, and unite identities around unique sensibilities.[1] Bourdieu's "field"—in some of its aspects—refers to manifestations of such broad style.

Styles both couple and decouple actions among network-populations that overlap in physical space. Styles are set off by and thus ap-

---

[1] However, the concept of style is not to be confounded with the concepts of habitus and field. Although all three concepts invoke orderliness of perception and action, they differ in the way they qualify orderliness. First, style—at its core, a stochastic concept—is in itself a source of innovation and change. Style itself does not change easily yet offers options for getting action. Second, style—because it is a scale-free concept—can be applied to a whole range of contexts and social formations that the other two concepts do not allow taking into account.

pear in the midst of complex overlappings and switchings of networks and also of disciplines. In that sense, they are analogous to identities. But styles are envelopes, as I specify in a later section, created from innumerable attempts at control by identities—envelopes that, once created, limit and funnel control. The environment in which they appear is one of stochastic incident and process among actors.

In the next section, I present exemplifications of sensibility. I begin by examining the potential for style in the small and everyday events, such as conversation, after which I turn to organizational settings to show how interpretive tone shapes and is shaped around expertise. The section winds up with two evocations of massive, yet focused, change in sensibility in the historical record of the United States.

4.1.1. Style as Texture of Social Dynamics

The contexts in which identities lie are shaped by their attempts at control, which—if the identities survive and concatenate—can be represented by ties in networks, along with disciplines. What matters is the texture of the process as reflected in the context created from contingencies surrounding their disciplines and ties. Social organization becomes heterogeneous, not tidy, as it survives stochastic flows of contingencies. All this leads to fluid social contexts, only some of which prove able to reproduce themselves as styles.

Identities are differently positioned in one and another network so that multiple networks must impact each other. Two actors who are joined by one type of tie may have no connections in other types, or they may have connections there to third parties that appear complementary to their joint tie. Thus, in chapter 2, I investigated impacts from multiple networks, deploying the concept of structural equivalence, which gives little purchase with a single network. I argue that most of the real-time dynamics play out for the overall network of multiplex or general ties, as in Small World searching. So the continuing texture of social living appears in styles.

Style is a generalization of network that traces along strings of ties and may reshape the connectivity aspects of network. Like stories, style characterizes the rich phenomenological texture, the fabric of lived experience of identities among populations in networks and disciplines. Style may supply a particular idiom for the orderings by values in disciplines, but it also presupposes and specifies some complex layering of networks within and across levels. Networks made up alongside disciplines are a new realization of network, at a new level of analysis. Here "levels" characterize the different kinds of control patterns in social process.

If one takes into account the messy nature of social process, then it is misleading to presume a hierarchy of levels; rather, one must acknowledge that any given level mixes with others in actual context. Nevertheless, analytically one may contextualize and distinguish style with regard to other levels as follows:

- In contrast to the predictable, organized nature of disciplines (chapter 3), style reproduces itself as stochastic social process across ties and domains.
- In contrast to institutions (chapter 5), which are settled and stabilized through norms, styles are more ephemeral in their patterning. Thus, styles are more likely to offer "leaks and cracks," which open opportunities for fresh control and thereby beget action (as distinct from sheer change: chapter 7).
- In contrast to regimes that can be purposively enacted (chapter 6), style is stochastic in nature—it may emerge, or not.
- Most essential, because it concerns the building blocks of identity and control, style embodies an identity in a fifth sense.

A main challenge, which this chapter can help meet, is how to pin styles down with measures that are transposable and yet still tangible to intuition.[2] Profiles across populations are static reports that I use as measures. But their significance is derivative, relying as it does on the reported outcomes of dynamics of switchings across networks and disciplines and thus domains of interpretations. Indeed, profiles are frozen moments carved out from continuing dynamics within which their actual significance rests.

It is also true that style is more a theoretical construct than a realist concept that evokes and sustains self-evident measurement. Style is a

---

[2] As intuited by Mannheim ([1929] 1936), social sciences have need for an analytical construct such as style. Social scientists tend to overestimate the generality and persistence of patterns they observe—what Fuchs (2001a) calls the "essentialist fallacy"—and thus to see durable and constraining formations where a flexible and subtle concept such as style may be required. This general problem corresponds to three specific observer errors that can occur when searching for style. First, native theories of style can be informative, but building on them may be a tricky task. As Bourdieu would argue, there is an epistemological gap between what the researcher and the native can see; what is "obviously obvious" to the native may not be to the observer. Second, observers may see styles where none is present. This relates to the aforementioned "essentialist fallacy." Third, observers may omit styles and pay attention to other social formations that are more easily perceptible, such as institutions, without realizing that styles can "ooze" from them and be confounded with them, especially in native accounts. The two last points raise the question of finding analytical boundaries for style. This chapter offers many examples that can help define these boundaries, but leaves the broader question open for subsequent research.

construct in the sense of Quine—a construct that does not exist "in reality" but rather guides, specifies, or unifies hypotheses.

4.1.2. Style and Conversations

Style presupposes decoupling among actors and events, as in conversation. The smoothly interactive system by which we take turns in conversation rests on and presupposes decoupling as well as coupling. This intricate dialectic has been explicated systematically in many studies.[3] For example, in chapter 3, I assessed Gibson's extensive data set on turn-taking in a more formal setting.

Is a conversation a matter of style and form, akin to a sketch in art? Or is it more an embodiment and building of one or more social ties, whether seen in council or tryst or deal-making? Where does conversation come from, how can it be generated and sustained? Must a conversation coalesce around rhetorical figures—need it rely on metaphor and synecdoche to tease the ambiguity of life?

The issue is how to conceive personal conversations. Must one *bring* an identity to a conversation, or does one *grow* identity during conversation, or can one *share* the identity of a conversation? Is an audience in some sense crucial to conversation? Does conversation permit or encourage or insist on three-and-more-way involvements? How do dramatists and other authors "create" conversations? Did Erving Goffman believe in conversation, and did George Herbert Mead?

What is the demography: must a really good conversation be a descendant, have progeny, have affinal kin—or rather does it have an entourage (see later in the chapter)? Must a conversation be episodic? Can it exist among changing partners? Does it end, or does it merely dissipate?

May conversation be but a Western specialty? Was it invented in Greece (Kitto 1958)? Was it revived in the Renaissance or earlier in the troubadour period (Bloch 1977)? Is the Parisian salon still alive? If so, how has it transmuted? Are political gossips and intrigues still intertwined with literary erudition?

What is the analogue, if any, to conversation in music? Is shoptalk ever conversation? If it occurs among scholars of the humanities, then does it also occur among natural scientists? Do teenagers converse? Do authors converse? Can a Barth or a Geertz be conversing in the act of observing?

Can conversation be nothing but questions?

---

[3] Consult, for example, Bilous and Kraus (1989); Duncan (1977); Kent and Shapiro (1978); H. Sachs in Rawls (1989); Wilson (1989).

Answering each of the preceding queries requires some theory of control across identities in network populations. Within such theory, conversation is part of the dynamics, exhibiting and shaped by style. Conversation helps turn aside or postpone the usual social science formulations of persons as pre-given integrals, as stasis. In particular, personal conversation demonstrates the realities of decoupling as well as embedding at the smallest scales of size and time.

Switchings between one particular domain-in-locality, one netdom to another, shape the texture of social living. This is notably true of much personal conversation, but it is also true at broader scope, for network population. For example, contrast one town with another, or with a city, as to their sleep regimens (cf. Aubert and White 1959). As a second example, consider auction markets of many distinct species:

> The need to increase social distance in some auctions points up the fact that while communities are common to all auctions, there is considerable variation in the number of distinct communities to be found within a given auction as well as the way these various communities are interrelated. There can be a strong community of buyers, as in the New England Fish Exchange; a strong community of sellers, as in thoroughbred auctions; or a strong mixed community of buyers and sellers, as in wholesale automobile auctions. There may similarly be secondary communities such as the community of fish captains present in fish auctions; thoroughbred owners at horse auctions; and the loose, temporary community of casual buyers present at most art and antique auctions . . . there are buyers who attend auctions as purely self-interested individuals with a desire to buy certain goods for less than their assumed value. These buyers, in part because of their indifference to the communal dynamics of the auction, seldom get the items they want at their price and are usually disregarded by the regulars . . . their relevancy to the whole auction process remains minor because their low bids do not hinder or interfere with the communal process of determining value and allocating goods. (Smith 1989, p. 75)

These observations can be verified through observing personal conversations, considered in sets that partially overlap in time and attendance, and surely can be extrapolated. Similar analysis can apply to communities, as developed in a later section. Overlap among conversations supplies a sort of feedback that can spur evolution of style (as well as spur differentiation of cross section in network population).

4.1.3. Interpretive Tone around Expertise: Fashion and Warfare

Style is the flavored and colored phenomenological texture of commingling of network populations and disciplines. In this regard, it is a context for interpretation and expertise. As a profile, style distinguishes itself from stories (chapter 1) and rhetorics (chapter 5) because it does not refer to specific contents but rather to specific patterns or matrices of perceptions, appreciations, and actions.

Consider two examples, one around fashion and another around warfare (White, Godart, and Corona, 2007, forthcoming). In the former, style appears primarily as a matrix of taste, whereas in the latter it appears more as a matrix of action.

Fashion is a two-pronged notion. First, in the sense of a process of change in clothes, slang, and so on, it refers to the current version of a social calculus of style. Second, in the sense of adornment and choice in clothing, it is primarily about matching of appearances to social contexts. In both senses, the conventional core of fashion is cultural expertise:

> Levels of expression measured according to the norms of the day . . . but also . . . interactions between the framework established by formal conventions and the contents and themes it accepts or questions according to the period or current. . . . And it is obvious that stylistic choices are not only personal choices . . . but are also positions taken vis-à-vis society. Burlesque, for example. (Viala 1988, p. 262)

Intersections of social calculi of style—that try to integrate appropriate matchings of appearances and contexts with the unfolding of trends—yield calendars that are common across identities of different scopes. They also yield other computations that may supplant prices (Aspers 2001). In other words, styles guide both individual switchings of clothing items, that amount to switchings across netdoms, and aggregations of identities around common clusters of sartorial elements in a manifestation of what some cultural sociologists would call "subcultures" (see, for example, Ferguson 2005).

Fashion is an apt illustration of style as a scale-invariant concept. At a micro level, fashion is the expression of a person as style, a profile of switching, or individual sensibility. At a meso level, fashion specifies social contexts and inscribes individual identities in lasting stylistic patterns of taste. Fashion at a macro level can be seen as a cumulation of multiple styles into a profile. The melding pushes up ambiguity—an uncertainty in the rules of interpretation—and thus goes with lower ambage—or uncertainty in social relations—as interrelated actors converge toward the same behavior. From this point of view, fashion is style purged of person. Ambage is reduced as skirts rise and fall together, at the cost of heightened ambiguity about meaning. The sensibility of fashion is the rhythm of its seasonal change. Temporality is thus the outcome of style.

Anyone can be an expert in fashion, but fashion designers are experts among experts. Their expertise amounts to not only an expertise of contextualized choice but also an expertise of translation—the deployment of an interpretive tone. Fashion designers translate identities of different scopes into clusters of sartorial elements. Their creations are therefore aesthetic assertions of their personal styles as well as the expression of different scopes of identities in their environment. A designer's sensibility will match with the sensibility of surrounding identities through the look of his or her designs. The matching of designs and tastes at a micro level happens through styles created as envelopes at a macro level.

Warfare is another apt example of how styles transcend and specify social contexts. The focus of military organizations is some battlefield: consider it here in all the contemporary complexity of physical warfare, and also virtual warfare. Organizations as social contexts disciplining identities shape combatants' styles. Traces of these styles can be found in rhetorical devices used by these organizations to sustain their identities as well as in lethal interactions with the enemy. Expertise on the battlefield is expertise in switchings according to stochastic evolutions—the "fog of war"—of the environment. It is an interpretive tone in action in a highly uncertain and dangerous environment. The style of a military organization is the result not only of a multitude of encounters on the battlefield but also of interactions in other contexts such as the political sphere. Memories of victories and lost battles shape behaviors through the rhetorics of chapter 5. Styles provide the context of their own change.

Now let us turn to history.

4.1.4. Nineteenth-Century American Womankind— in *Market Sentiments* and in *Protecting Soldiers and Mothers*

Each of the two books just referenced with abbreviated titles displays the emergence and consolidation of a distinctive style across the United States. *Market Sentiments: Middle-Class Market Culture in 19th-Century America* (Nelson 2004) focuses on women's process of making themselves at home in a realm previously thought male—the urban economy. *Protecting Soldiers and Mothers: The Political Origins of Social Policy in the United States* (Skocpol 1992) does the same, but with regard to the political arena. The latter deals mostly with the second half of the nineteenth century, whereas *Market Sentiments* starts about 1830. The books differ also, even with respect to their overlap in periods, in that Skocpol gives great attention to the Midwest, in contrast with the greater focus of Nelson's *Market Sentiments* on the Northeast and South.

Men do figure in both books. Each author shows how particular men became enmeshed as part of what I define as a style. There are, of course, some particular organizations involved and a good deal of conscious organizing. But what is striking about each book is how a particular zone of sensibility best characterizes the reality. Neither author had any notion of my approach, which makes it all the more striking how well their accounts fit with the account of style given in the first part of this chapter.

The heart of *Market Sentiments* beats around a series of oxymorons: sentimental value; domestic economy; fancy work; marriage market; education business; moral sentiment. New melds were created, as dichotomies eroded: stranger/friend; production/consumption; character/status; property/propriety; sentiment/pragmatism. There are several apotheoses including Valentine's Day and the middle class amid a characteristic rhythm of bankruptcies and panics overridden by massive migration into cities and city life.

Teaching of fancy-work, for pay, replaces oral culture. Whole new crafts and modes of transactions are celebrated in charity fairs. Crassness is banished with the rise of the ladylike woman unlike any European image. Turning to Nelson's own words—I will give three excerpts here; then in chapter 5, I will take up a fourth excerpt that identifies tangible agency enabling this mobilization of style.

The first excerpt offers a vignette:

> In 1849, Esther Howland, the daughter of a prosperous stationer and insurance salesman in Worcester, Massachusetts, started manufacturing and selling fancy valentines. Intrigued by the imported valentines . . . Esther saw a business opportunity. . . . In an interview with the *Boston Globe* toward the end of her life, Howland described her business as an extension of a woman's ordinary leisure production, characterizing herself as more of a maternal figure than a managerial one and noting that several of the girls who worked for her were family friends and even lived with the Howland family. . . . Esther's mother took advantage of her husband's printing business and published *The American Economical Housekeeper and Family Receipt Book* (1845). . . . By the mid-nineteenth century, the market had become more than the sum of market places, and a culture of the market had developed that influenced a broad spectrum of social interactions. (pp. 1–3)

Second, some overviews:

> The anxiety about moral authority prompted an increase in economic advice, particularly in the form of fiction, to try to reassert a restrained version of sentimentalism in the face of the excesses of the newly prosperous. . . . The fluctuations of the economy and a discomfort with European definitions of class hierarchy based on birth encouraged prosperous

Americans to dissemble their claims to status and displace their definition of class hierarchy onto cultural and economic criteria. . . . The fluctuations of prosperity played an important role in the dependence of these men and women on cultural definitions of class that could transcend temporary economic difficulties. (p. 5)

The third excerpt sets up a transition to Skocpol's *Protecting Soldiers and Mothers*:

Sentimental rhetoric was useful as a tool of reform because it insisted on a universal recognition of moral sentiments and reframed traditional forms of social and economic hierarchy in cultural terms. (p. 15)

Skocpol introduces her argument vividly:

During 1989 I finally experienced the gestalt switch that allowed me to pull together *Protecting Soldiers and Mothers*. At last I understood that . . . [g]ender relations and identities were not just a footnote to my overall story; they were centrally intertwined with the structural and cultural patterns of American politics. . . . My state-centered theoretical frame of reference had evolved . . . as I had grappled with . . . the transformation over time in the issues, social identities, and styles of politics that succeed (or fail) at influencing agendas of political debate and public policymaking.

The argument germane to our focus, emergence among women of a style, is in her part 3 and centers there in chapter 6, "Expanding the Separate Sphere: Women's Civic Action and Political Reform":

Social circumstances and political arrangements . . . facilitated middle-class women's consciousness and mobilization, and encouraged women to make collective and hegemonic demands—that is, demands not only for themselves but also on behalf of the entire society. . . . During the nineteenth century, both a sharply gender-based division of labor and Protestant evangelism encouraged American middle-class women to form voluntary associations to deal with matters of social welfare as well as their own well-being. . . . Even as . . . females were barred from electoral and party politics in the world's first mass democracy for males. . . . Operating without votes, women became civically involved in a polity where plenty of "space" was available for new forces who favored collective as opposed to distributive policies. . . . Outside . . . yet in many ways in parallel . . . female voluntary federations increasingly pursued legislation that American women boldly claimed was in the moral best interest of society as a whole. Maternal values were projected from homes and local communities onto the agendas of state and national politics. (p. 318)

Skocpol denies that getting "equal rights" was perceived as the primary concern for reform, so this style is not of one piece with the feminism of the last decades of the twentieth century. Nonetheless, one could explore whether profiles of switchings were sufficiently similar to warrant assimilating this style to the feminism template.

Both the Skocpol and the Nelson accounts offer depth in several senses: depth in historical time as well as sprawl across regions. These combine into portrayals rich enough to calibrate depth in social process. Mobilization builds upon prior or parallel mobilization, binding networks among higher-level actors to personal networks, and binding sensibilities to underlying sets of stories. Styles emerge from networks.

* 4.2. Commerce Grows as Style

[In each chapter, with a section marked with an asterisk, I point out how the studies there can also be seen from other perspectives. These commerce and trade examples are taken up again, more than casually, in the prologue and in sections 6.5.2, 6.9, and 7.5.3.]

Style appears in diverse settings and scopes, as much in commercial dynamics on large scale as in cultural prescription in smaller scope. Consider a first example. Two or three distinct new industries have been emerging around biotechnology, around new foci made feasible by the advances of molecular biology (Powell et al. 2005). Important in this example[4] are contractual commitments between pairs or among sets of actors, commitments as to venture capital or joint development or marketing agencies and the like. Each new industry could be the triggering of an identity, a new industry as an identity embedded from one of the three crisp discipline-mechanisms, with the clear boundaries implied in chapter 3.

But there may be too many independent actors involved for such discipline to be likely, since participants would have to key on one another's actions as signals of quality position. Also, there are many potential products being developed, which could string together through their inputs and outputs in some sort of catnet (see section 2.5.1), even though, alternatively, each could separately key a specific market. What remains clear is that there are social networks of ties spinning out among all the actors (identities, persons, other disciplines and organizations). These networks suggest that some sort of economic community is evolving—a quasi-market that is becoming a style.

Now turn to examples that are large-scale in time and scope, explorations of how specific styles—in this case, self-interested action and commercial rationality—emerge out of dynamics in decouplings from social contexts, and switchings across netdoms.

---

[4] Four studies are reported in Nohria and Eccles (1992).

4.2.1. British Trade around the East Indies

Trade in the past across long distances was hazardous; the extent of hazard as well as of possible reward depended on routing. Often the context called for some coalition of traders to be established for particular voyages if only for insurance purposes. Often, a diversity of goods was involved because the two ends of a route would put different goods on offer, except where specie was the quid pro quo.

Erikson and Bearman (2006) have published a long-term study of all the thousands of sea voyages conducted by the English East India Company (EIC) over the century and a half of its independent existence. These voyages went halfway around the world. What routes did ships follow? How did this network across the travels of many ships evolve?

One might think this was a matter of centralized decision making by a precursor of our modern large firms, and it is true that the EIC board had unusual power and clear focus. But there was too much uncertainty—from Dutch and other rivals as well as from the sea itself and from the destinations—for that to work well. Captains had to be trusted in voyages lasting a year or so, and they in turn had to rely on various agents on ship and at ports. Information was slow in coming and feedback was limited.

The striking conclusion of Erikson and Bearman's study is that, in fact, the evolving pattern of routes that was actually followed had little to do with EIC central direction. Early on, the EIC had to concede autonomy to captains and other of their agents to conduct some trading on their own in order to motivate them as well as to enhance the quality of information guiding voyages—in a sense it was personal "malfeasance" feeding the EIC's commercial success. The agents often invoked these rights so that they could fit in extra side trips across the reaches of Asian markets. In short, the real story seems to be unfolding around an emerging commercial style. Captains, by decoupling from the stated objectives of the EIC central direction and by embedding in other social and cultural contexts, triggered a style central to modern capitalist pursuits. Consider this example as partially parallel with another large commercial empire in the making, to which we now turn.

4.2.2. Mediterranean Trade Takeoff—Medieval Genoa

Through and beyond the 1100s, the city-state of Genoa transformed itself from feudal warlordism into a hub of vastly increasing sea commerce. There is no abrupt or clear shift to this Genoese supremacy. Now, thanks to the work of Van Doosselaere (2006), for the first time we have extensive and systematic data on transactions, more than ten thousand of them, from which to trace out and decipher changing network configurations and style of commerce.[5]

Peaceful and advanced, the hitherto dominating Middle Eastern commercial circuits were kept by their habits from opening to the possibility of trade on a much larger scale. Indeed, in this respect they were unlike the Genoese who organized their sea ventures by way of interchangeable *commendas*.[6] By contrast, the Middle Eastern traders' commercial practices—their very own commercial style—had responded to the enormous uncertainty that faced all commerce, by relying on inbred networks of relations that were based on trust, which in turn was guaranteed through kinship, ethnic, and religious contexts (Greif 2006). The brash Genoese newcomers broke through into what became a new configuration leading to trade on a wholly new scale. Their flexibility in occupations was woven around their *commendas* into a distinctive new style. The new commercial practices were related to the Genoese ability to pool larger capital together and to deal with longer and riskier trading routes.

This new Genoese configuration was exactly a style in my sense:

> In examining the 12th and 13th century commenda's data sets, one is immediately struck by both the large variety of people involved in the long-distance trade and the occasional nature of their activity. . . . The participants' diversity expressed itself in the variety of places of origin [within Genoa territory], occupation, status, and even of gender [women constitute up to 12 percent at one period]. It is in this light that the ubiquitous saying *"Genoese therefore merchant"* should be understood . . . only a very small—albeit growing—minority made commerce their primary activity. That long-distance trade was most likely a side activity for many persons is evident in the case of all those artisans who showed up only once in our data set." (pp. 112–14)
>
> The variety of occupations and the fine specialization of functions in certain industrial fields hides a fundamental medieval reality: Most men, even artisans, would not easily fit in the modern pigeonholes of occupational classification because they were all capable of devoting themselves for extended period to activities as diverse as agriculture, war making, or house building. . . . This fluidity of occupation was especially evident in Genoa because it was the sea, above all, that presented the primary eco-

[5] Genoa is practically unique in having retained notarial and related evidence on a large scale, and myriad scholars' contributions enable Van Doosselaere to decipher handwritings and trace persons and their sociopolitical settings with some precision.

[6] Genoese trade was mostly carried out through *commendas*, that is, simple temporary equity partnerships among at least a principal and a traveler to carry goods on a voyage. The *commendas* were an institutional envelope through which the new Genoese commercial style could emerge.

nomic opportunity, and sailing seasons or military ventures could at any time draw the Genoese far from their regular occupations. As evident by the countless employment contracts that are almost exclusively for the duration of a single round trip voyage, many artisans took leave from their occupation to find temporary employment on ships. In doing so, thousands of Genoese gained a direct taste of the more sophisticated overseas exchange economy, which they could then bring home to share with their kin and neighbors. (pp. 124–26)

The fluidity of occupations in Genoa enabled sailors to engage in risky sailing endeavors, triggering an innovative and specific commercial style. Genoa commerce is a style, a stochastic whirlpool rather than some organization—a matter, if you will, of the typical variability of weather as the symbol of sensibility. Profiles of switchings across occupational netdoms form the core of this style.

Padgett and McLean (2006a) look on land, not sea, and look to Florence not Genoa, but it seems to me their research also uncovers a style in an emergent period of business innovation, around banking partnerships. This is a style of the defensive sort I will discuss later under the label "segmentary." These partnerships insulated banks from catastrophic risk and thereby dramatically improved liquidity and credit among competitors, enabling Florence as a whole to lock in a lucrative international financial role as "the banker of Europe."

Observe that both this and the previous study are tracing the emergence of a new type of rationality to the emergence of new ends, along with decoupling from previous social embeddings. Furthermore, these transmutations of commercial rationality reach out in widening circles as part of the emergence of modern capitalist pursuits. In turn, the new capitalist pursuits centered on production markets that are the result of decoupling from traditional ways of producing, and embedding in new networks of suppliers, producers, and buyers (White 2002; White and Godart 2007). Switchings rise to new prominence in the searches for profitable business, and so do decouplings shielded by partial embeddings in other cultures, communities, and organizations. The diffusion of commercial rationality as a specific matrix of perceptions, appreciations, and actions was facilitated by the travels of EIC "malevolent" captains as well as of Genoese crews. Public mode becomes more tangible, on a new level and with newly large scope.

4.3. Person Grows as Style

The point in this section is that the ordinary person, so called, is a late and sophisticated product resulting from the interplay of larger social formations, of populations. This conception is to stand on its head Durkheim's call on religion. Every person is a god, since a god is exactly any actor required and generated at the intersection of multiple social worlds. For social science, thinking of persons acting like atoms makes as much sense as asking gods for predictions.

Persons, in the ordinary sense of the term, thus are neither the first nor the only form in which identities appear. Much theory in social science stipulates persons, takes them as preexisting atoms.[7] In contrast, this book builds from chapter 1 on toward twin conclusions: (a) that persons develop only under special social circumstances, which come late historically,[8] and (b) that personhood is a compounding across identities in several senses.

Switchings and profiles will be invoked in making the case that personhood is a style, parallel to the case made in the next section about more inclusive actors. You, the reader, are a social construction in a practical and current sense, as much as are communities. And, as I elaborate later, this is a construction across some gamut of situations in context of networks and disciplines, as a style.

Styles presuppose integrated skills at perception that are held only by human beings. Humans have capabilities for signaling and memory and the like beyond those already invoked for all identities. Memory is a biological algorithm for decoupling actions over time, an algorithm from which language can emerge.

But these human skills need not come packaged as persons, in the sense current today. Such persons come into existence only in a complex stochastic environment. Human actors rally around valuations in constructing and interpreting disciplines; but the irony is that persons

---

[7] These atoms perhaps can be equated to souls, the ideological invention of the Christian Church over long centuries. Means-ends schemes seem to be transpositions of the church's beautifully wrought theology of the soul. Even among sociologists, this methodological individualism is currently close to hegemonic, as Keyfitz and Keilman argue: "Of course, no one will argue that individual persons (the parts) do not exist. But it is certainly true that they behave differently depending on the context. Applying Capra's thesis to household demography might therefore imply that one should study the network of relations between individuals inside (and outside?) the household, in order to understand the behaviour of the individual—and many sociologists will wholeheartedly agree. Is our present preference for the individual as the object of analysis mainly due to the attention the individual receives in Western society?" (in Keilman, Kuijsten, and Vossen [1988], p. 277). Just so.

[8] Durkheim's account of the transition from a mechanical solidarity to an organic solidarity resonates with the theory of personhood developed here (1947). For Durkheim, societies characterized by mechanical solidarity exhibit almost undistinguishable individuals. "Individuals" in the modern sense—persons—need an advanced division of labor and a high degree of social distinction to emerge.

come into existence only, as I argue later, through the exigencies of a stochastic environment built on quite other principles than the valuations to which persons, once formed, continue to orient. Moreover, this construal of "personhood" can and will be extended to other scales.

4.3.1. Etiologies of Persons

We return now to develop further and somewhat differently the views on identity developed in chapter 1. The emergence of identities from irregularities and their mismatches has been traced by Firth (1957) even amid the smooth life of the isolated island of Tikopeia, isolated on a Melanesian atoll. These are natural irregularities caused by storm or other upsets to the island's fishing, and also social irregularity from the degradation of some tribal members' health status, or from randomly triggered brawls. In his reports across two generations concerning this tribe, Firth weaves an account in which one sees persons emerging only dimly and partially in their own eyes. Persons become vivid and real only in the consequences of, and as by-product from, bridging across to distinct populations, whether of the society studied by Firth or Asian sailing-bark crews.

For the much more complex tribal spread across the hills of upper Burma, Leach (1954) painted a very similar picture of how persons emerged—and faded. They did so by sequentially invoking and ignoring two competing forms of social portrayal, *mayu* and *dama*, which appeared and then faded as a by-product of eddies of social action. Populations analytically distinct, though only partially segregated, were bridged by actors who maneuvered from one to the other according to the political situation. Persons as identities are triggered by turbulences, and persons as styles emerge from switchings across network populations.[9]

With reference to cities also, in our own day, ethnographic fieldwork confirms these ideas. Personal identity can come from turbulences in early life that result from and carry over into several realms—family and neighborhood and the like. Willis (1977) gives a vivid characterization of this process for working-class British teenagers. Many, if not most, of these teenagers participate for long periods in social scenes in which

[9] Anthropology may dominate history on this point. Our access to other ages through what we call history is not usually sufficient to reconstruct social milieus and contexts in which then ordinary persons would have appeared. There are, however, exemplary studies that appear to support the conjecture about identity; for examples, consult Tilly (1978, 1990) and his students on contentious assemblies, Bynum (1987) on medieval spiritual life, and Howell (1998) on power and wealth in the medieval low countries.

they never step outside routine role performances; thus for them, personhood is never induced or invoked, despite inevitable chronic mismatches among alternate role performances and role complementarities.

The chapters on ties and disciplines as well as these later chapters may sound aseptic and impersonal, and much too elaborate. But in fact, our separate consciousnesses as persons result from and are caught up in these mazes. Each "I," in the common parlance, is a more-or-less rickety ensemble; it is firm and whole only temporarily—and in temporality—as a facet of one particular constituent discipline or tie energized in some situation. In a specific context, we may recognize some particular self operating in one or another of the three species of discipline. But, overall, persons are aptly seen as the walking wounded, who evolve out of stochastic processes of continuing bruisings and coalescences among networks and disciplines.

4.3.2. Identities and Persons

Persons come into existence and are formed as the result of overlaps among identities from distinct network-populations. Identities and network positions do prefigure persons, but persons emerge only as the contexts become more sophisticated. Persons build in terms of styles across distinct populations. Conversation prefigures personal identity.

Return again to the playground example of chapter 1. A network spreads through many nodes, but it need not catch up all the nodes embedded in any given identity. A child as a person, itself a compound of identities, comes late in sequences of other disciplines of family and gang. Personhood would never have emerged in the child had it not also been placed as a node in some other networks than the playground, in networks across some other populations as contexts. Conversely, a personal identity may touch on many networks but does not encompass all of any network. A personal identity presupposes distinct networks—not just in different locales, but also with different tones. Consider, as illustration, games versus storytellings right on the playground.

Identities are the basis from which persons are constructed. Identities are triggered by turbulences. They are contingent by-products from mismatch between embeddings of disciplines, on the one hand, and contingencies in ecology and network histories on the other. Identities are as real as actors pulled into the complex interlocking of gels and strands of social process and organization. But persons are special: for example, not all the sorts of actors under consideration can converse, despite the fact that they all have identities.

"Person" should be a construct from the middle of the analysis, not a given boundary condition from the start. Personhood has to be accounted for by sociology, which means specifying contexts where it *may* enter, where it *will* enter, and where it *cannot* enter. But in most present social science, "person" is instead taken as the unquestioned atom. As I suggested earlier, this is an unacknowledged borrowing and transcription of the soul construct from Christian theology.[10] Before general theory in social science can be attained, "persons" have to be assimilated as being but particular embodiments of one class of socially constructed actors.

It is through common style that persons link across network populations. Like style in general, personhood tends to reduce ambiguity—to sustain orderly interpretive frames and decrease uncertainty in meanings—at the cost of increased ambage or uncertainty in social relations. However, with style such a trade-off must allow more for contingency. Ordinarily, persons and styles coexist, but the charismatic is a person purged of style, a manifestation of unpredictability in profiles of switchings. This fits with Weber's (1978) conception of charisma as an innovative force that challenges everything traditional. Note, however, that being purged of style does not mean the absence of style. The charismatic person stands above styles and integrates them in unpredictable patterns, a very strategic perspective indeed.

4.3.3. Learned Helplessness

An extreme denial of style as person is spelled out in the concept of learned helplessness. Learned helplessness (Seligman and Garber 1980)—in which adverse situations give rise to an inability to cope with such situations even if escape is possible—is the empirical accompaniment of consistency in role; for adults it is the analogue of the state of innocence for children. If you are in a wholly consistent social position, if you and your compatriots have roles that actually do dovetail, you have no basis for, and no irritant-generating capacities for, dealing with the unexpected. You are helpless, helpless outside the confines of your tied roles. You are not a person.

The issue is slippery. If one has a role, does one gain or lose control thereby? It is slippery because "having a role" can be just a story. If the story is an instance of a set among which an actor can change easily, one may be able to gain control. If the story is a fixed one, the actor loses control, whether or not the story is, on the surface, an attractive one.

[10] Christian theology worked out "soul" during centuries when a strikingly dual polity was emerging in its region, and this secular context helped shape and limit the construct. But the ultimate fixity of the soul, carried over to hobble social science, was a Pauline theological imperative.

The puzzle is mixed up with the standing of goals and the like. If one gains action by having and following goals, then having a definite role should contribute to gaining control.[11] But on the contrary, control, according to the present argument, comes out of and only out of fluidity of role, because then one does not have "goals" imposed upon oneself by the social process.

Learned helplessness has an unpleasant ring to it, taken alone; yet it is engendered by what is quite literally the utopian situation. Utopias all share the trait of roles fitting together. And though negative utopias may seem unpleasant, they are as bland as utopias in removing the basis for identity.

Regular life in some accounts is a utopia. Regular life seems to supply you at any time with an accounting, a story of what is going on and where you fit. If this were the whole story, there would be no triggering by happenstance, and you would not be in existence as an entity outside of prediction. You would not have an identity; you would not need it—any more than you would need an identity in a utopia.

Learned helplessness can recur in an abstract sense at some higher level of social formation. Not just persons but other social actors can be subjected to it. It need not be naive; it may be part of efforts of control, and of getting action. The psychologists' concept of learned helplessness should be elaborated and generalized by other social sciences.

Learned helplessness as an extreme opposite of person as style conversely suggests that the best exemplar of person as style is a figure whose core is strategic flexibility and thus unpredictability: Napoleon comes to mind. The French emperor is a classic example of getting so completely captured by his charismatic personality that it collapses down into an identity. At the same time, his military genius signaled an ability to stand above styles and play with them, to be a person without style but with many styles. As with many extreme cases, a paradox arises.

4.3.4. Mischel's and Burt's Persons as Identities

The general point is to distinguish neither between great personages and ordinary persons nor between the latter and corporate actors. On the contrary, it is to pierce the mysterious carapace that common sense allows the ordinary person. Network analysis suggests such "ordinary person" is a location within complex arrangements of social processes.

Recent research in personality has led to similar conclusions, as also have developments in psychodynamics.[12] The classic view, shared by

[11] For this argument, see Bailey and Morrill (1989): their example is the emergence of the "skinhead" role on the streets of contemporary Britain.

[12] For an assessment by a sociological theorist, see Swanson (1988).

both trait and psychodynamic approaches, was that the gist of the person was stable and broadly generalized dispositions that yielded substantial differences between individuals within the same social situation. By the late 1960s, extensive research had shattered these core assumptions. Yet the theories—that is, the cognitive constructions that persons have about themselves and others—were found to have consistency and continuity, and they

> suggest a world in which personality consistencies seem greater than they are and in which the organization of behavior seems simpler than it is. . . . Actuarial methods of data combination are generally better than clinical-theoretical inferences. Base rates, direct self-reports, self-predictions, and especially indices of relevant past behavior typically provide the best as well as the cheapest predictions . . . and usually exceed those generated either clinically or statistically from complex inferences about underlying traits and states. (Mischel 1990, pp. 113ff.)

According to Mischel, the focus has become

> the idiographic nature of each person interacting with the specific contexts of his or her life. . . . Indeed, the tendency to focus on dispositions in causal explanations soon was seen as a symptom of a "fundamental attribution error" committed by laypersons in everyday life, as well as by the psychologists who study them. . . . Going beyond lip service about the importance of person-situation interaction to generate and test theory-based predictions of those interactions became and remains high on the agenda. (Mischel 1990, pp. 115ff.)

Indeed so, but personality psychology remains grotesquely naive about the constituents of "everyday life."

Much the same conclusions about the person are drawn from some sociological investigations by Ronald Burt, where he approaches persons from the outside, in field studies of managers in competition for careers. Burt (1992a) writes a primer for effectiveness in social action that is at the same time a theory. He jumps directly into tangible empirical materials: in particular, mobility of individual managers in hierarchies (and, as an analogy, interconnections of various industrial markets within economic flows). The myth of the person—with specified goals and a drive to optimize—seems to be accepted. But it is from analysis of dependencies evidenced by relative movements and flows in networks that Burt induces his central construct: this is the structural hole as used in his book's title (which can be generalized to structural autonomy).

> You are one of the black dots in the dark gray circle; but the dot isn't all of you. It is a piece. Specifically, it is a piece of you that is redundant with

structurally similar pieces of other people. . . . The other black dots at the center of the network would be the other professors connected to the same clusters of students, colleagues and administrators. The distribution of holes in this network defines the structural autonomy you have. . . . Still another piece of you . . . involves another network. . . . As a physical entity, you are an amalgam of these structural pieces. . . . But structural autonomy exists for each piece of you defined by a network of others concerned with that piece. . . . At a higher level of aggregation, structural autonomy . . . with a functional division, . . . at a lower level . . . jobs could have been subdivided into project networks. (Burt 1992a, p. 144)

As Burt points out, the structural hole replaces the "weak tie" of Granovetter and Rapoport. But I argue that this is exactly because the idea of weak tie relies on person as construct, whereas Burt is forced into constructs much like identities seeking control, with persons as by-products only under some structural conditions. It is no accident that persons—as Burt here portrays them—suggest "the perfect spy" spelled out as normless cipher in John le Carré's novel with that title.[13]

Furthermore, the nexus of ties that Burt has shouldering aside person as chief actor, this nexus resembles the disciplines of chapter 3. In particular, his generic third party calls to mind a council discipline. The point is not that these various theories are the same as each other or as the present theory, but rather that, despite different stances toward the myth of individual persons, the substantive contents of the prime constructs arrived at are similar. All the theories must depend on specifying what mixes of distinct contexts—including regime and institution—can coexist, and how they may shape persons into existence.

These network perspectives are not inconsistent with one stream in social psychology (Gergen 1985).

4.3.5. Persons as Styles

The ordinary person is a late construct, by the standards of archaeological reconstruction of societies. Persons are like pottery. Pottery provides not just an illustration of style, but what seems from an archaeological perspective to be the principal early vessel of style. Pottery came in relatively late, and in some places it came along with persons (Nissen 1988), although in some, before persons (Luhmann 1995). Pottery combines the story aspects of style with physical

---

[13] *A Perfect Spy* is a 1986 novel written by British author John le Carré.

substrate in transparent form. The correlation continues to this day (Dauber 1992). Persons in seeking control cannot and do not attempt to deal severally with the enormous, astronomical array of paths and influences upon them. Instead, they come to deal with combinations that limn their styles.

Persons work with sets of perceptions and appreciations both of their own and of others' situations, social and physical. Such sets are styles if they exert constraints like molecular disciplines, though in a more sophisticated context. Only some such sets prove able to reproduce themselves, thereby demonstrating that the constituent identities accept them as objective constraints.

Style goes with a patterning in physical space that survives turbulence and reproduces, and likewise for style in social spaces of ties or stories and of values or roles. And formations at higher scopes must be reaching down with contextual pressures as styles through any particular discipline to effect an orderliness of perception. The converse applies from lower scopes, where, for example, conversations as prototypes become elaborated into further disciplines or styles of perception. The three species of discipline—the commit interface, the select-arena, and the mobilize council—are those that have proved robust to all these perception pressures, from above and below.

Stories are generated as explanations along with the embeddings within network and habits that all together can define a style for an individual actor. A person and a style can define each other, and the same duality obtains up through larger social formations. Styles can have still smaller or much more encompassing concrete referents, such as conversations and communities, respectively.

Individual actors watch one another within disciplines and social networks and imbibe patterns in how to maneuver and how to account for the maneuvers in stories and values. Thereby individuals acquire a style, as they jointly reproduce profiles through their mutually patterned actions. Gearings for action, intentional and unintentional, rely on common styles in profiles and switchings.

Style and turbulence presuppose each other. In the Simmelian milieu of strangers on downtown streets, style is the only skim on the surface of chaotic social process. Styles as by-products of turbulence arise across many ranges of incident and network, and across the many levels mixed up in social organization. The social economy of different relations is not developed only or primarily at a level of individual dyads and actors. A style may come in as a distinct counterpoint in combining and embedding disciplines into an overall topology with networks.

4.4. Rationality

Work gets done. Decoupling, not rationality, is the prerequisite. The decouplings must take endlessly different specific forms and be endlessly repeated, because decouplings go in tension with solving social equations of relative arrangements. Each work group, each slash-and-burn settlement, each metalworker circle in a city, in short each production setting inherits, every day and with each generation, a strangling embedding in social arrangements computed on grounds other than work; and each such inheritance must in some fashion be decoupled. The choice of one or another technical path of production is of subsidiary importance. Even the choice of goals is secondary, because it is illusory.

Earlier, in chapter 1, I argued that rationality—instrumental rationality in Weber's sense (1978)—was better understood as a style, an important style but certainly not the predominant one. Ends and goals are a pattern of deposits from social process. Rationality comes into play only after this deposition. Ends appear exogenous, but instead of being a constraint on social process, they rather are a dependent part of the social process that is unfolding. In this sense, ends are endogenous.

It should be possible to allow for this endogeneity. Proper structural theory should fold in but reinterpret rational choice. The kind of social formation, the context, must be uncovered, and this in turn should lead to prediction of what specific sort of means-end schema, if any, gets commonly used within that formation, as adapted to specific locales, and at specific points in social calendars. Rational choice does not drive social action, but neither is it epiphenomenal.

4.4.1. Contexts for Rational Choice Theory

Rational choice theory as presently in vogue is modeled on neoclassical microeconomics (e.g., Mansfield 1968, 1975). It focuses on the "individual," as chapter 1 already pointed out. But individuals come out of relations, out of skills in relations that are disdained by the theory. "You" and "I" and others are gotten together by our contexts of practical production and control, as much as we construct those contexts through social action. The economist Kreps's (1988) hero Totrep (Trade-Off Talking Rational Economic Person) is a straw man.[14] Economist Olivier Favereau (2005) asserts this too.

---

[14] Some versions of rational choice (e.g., Dahl and Lindblom 1953; Shubik 1984a, b) are not so myopic.

As causal guides, means-ends schemas can lead afield, but the impetus to adopt rational choice theory is natural in a scientific frame. Means-ends schemas do accommodate to dynamics. Means-ends schemas are at the root of the calculi of motivation, which at present supply almost the only systematic theory in social science (MacPherson 1962; Parsons 1937) that is also quantitative (Coleman 1990). And a convincing case can be made for the importance of these schemas in particular contexts, as does, for example, Pocock (1975, p. 309) and also Padgett both with Ansell (1993) and with McLean (2006) concerning Italian Renaissance settings.

Rational pursuits along means-ends chains remain important, but such pursuits are secondary to the engendering of ends. A main goal or end of action is control, and control need not have explicit intermediate goals any more than does some feedback control system in engineering (Bryson and Ho 1969; Leigh 1987). The history of an effort at control is concerned entirely with sequence in finding and sustaining leverage. Even long-term goals having much explicitness are inapt for control in the social context, and at the extreme—say, in the context of teenagers hanging around—control may not refer to any goals even indirectly, since means-ends schemas may not capture any of the variation found there.

Ends, and means-ends chains, are perfectly sensible constructs, but they are of only tactical help in uncovering social action. That is the practical objection to rational action theory, and also to many other role theories. An actor's social existence comes to pass only through embeddings that specify ends as well as support identity, embeddings that are matters of friction and mismatch rather than of induction into roles. Rationality should be seen primarily as a by-product from reading larger-scale patterns. Recognizing context is the crux.

The real risk is that means-ends schemas may stand in the way of proper observation by social scientists, the more particularly because these schemas have trained our perceptions of existence. To use goal and means as the guide to observation and analysis is to mislead oneself, to turn away from the sources of action toward by-products of the glossing, the explaining away, that is natural to social process. Explicit ends may be built up, with difficulty, together with means, out of stray materials at hand, but they might just as well be bypassed, letting meanings come from colorings of action by stories. And among the identities rubbed up from mismatched productions, events are as ineluctable as actors.

Both goal and personality as concepts miss the central point. Similar strictures apply to concepts of means, which also abstract from events.

Structuralism in the form of role theory takes embedding seriously. But structuralism treats embedding as decisive by itself in isolation, and so structuralism is misled through inattention to contingency. Structuralism is as much a danger to observation as is individualist rational choice. Embedding should not be confused with rhetoric, with wishes encapsulated as justice (Zajac 1985). One succeeds or not, and now rather than then, according to one's position in a concrete context, and that is in part an aspect of embedding in identities as well as being a network matter.

Goals are the problem with rational choice theory. The independence—and thus reality—of goals in themselves must be questioned, not just the degree of rational pursuit or the efficiency with respect to goals. Ends are supplied stochastically by the shifting embeddings in which actors are caught up over time. These same embeddings also frame means-ends chains, which can be important in much the way presumed by rational choice theorists, although more care is needed in specifying the dual embeddings in physical and social space. But such chains are limited in scope by their embedding; they show dependencies, not causalities.

4.4.2. Professionalism and Speech Registers

Professionalism cannot be apprehended without attention to how it embeds in social context. I argue that professionals can be recognized in much the same way as people in a line of business, or for that matter Marxists of a particular political line, by their drawing on a distinct speech register. But professionalism is special; it is not confined to any one realm of discourse, nor is it constrained within any particular setting or by a particular code. Professionalism is a style recognized in and from the distinctive context that it subvenes, a context that grafts deference relations onto provision of service valued for existence, not by test. So it is the syntax of deference rather than the content of its lexicon that singles out professionalism.

Professionalism is thus concerned particularly with the nesting of meanings, with, so to speak, the mobilization of meaning. Connotations of professionalism include obsession with appearance and form. Recall that chapter 3 argued that same concern by the mediation discipline, the council. And it so happens that the principal exemplar offered there was the law firm Lazega studied, which surely counts as professional.

I am presenting style as an analytic construct, so that professionalism should not be sentenced to jailing next to business within current usage as to how to label. This and other familiar claims I share with previous standard analyses such as by Sarfatti-Larson (1977) and by Freidson (1986, 2001). Those analyses also do not confine themselves to any particular one of the professions commonly recognized, such as law or medicine. Widening the perspective can improve discrimination and aid categorization. It is true that switchings and their profiles are appropriate measures of harried life in conventionally recognized professions. But surely they are found elsewhere too—say, among tour guides.

4.4.3. Rationality as Style

Rationality cannot be discarded as a concept, as an explanatory heuristic, any more than the reader and I can deny our quite sturdy identities as persons. But the significance of rationality is mainly as a rationale for both selves and observers in patching together action (Swidler 1986).

Rational choice is one preferred story-line today among us as natives, and the same holds for us as theorists. In chapter 1 this theory was shown to complement the structuralist theory of values, the latter of which might appropriately have been the focus of critique forty years ago.[15] These theories are, respectively, micro and macro explanations that share an underlying ontology of "spirits." If carried to an extreme as utilitarian and utopian explanations, respectively, each theory rests upon angels—that is, upon spirits both disembodied and independent.[16]

There is an absurdity here. To be interesting, rational choice theory should concentrate on possible new decisions, on change. But explicit goals or preference orderings, which are essential to the means-ends schema of rational choice, are appropriate and relevant only to entities that are inert as well as isolated—angels, in short. The situation for the theorist is bewildering, which is just the context in which one expects styles to loom large, whether it concerns a native or a theorist, displacing a prior story-line.

---

[15] Comparison with alternative theories of social action helps prepare the ground for a new approach.

[16] Both descend through the *philosophes* from medieval theology. In the words of Carl Becker (1932, pp. 30ff.): "[A]t every turn the *Philosophes* betray their debt to medieval thought. . . . They dismantled heaven, somewhat prematurely it seems, since they retained their faith in the immortality of the soul . . . there is more of Christian philosophy in the writings of the *Philosophes* than has yet been dreamed of in our histories . . . the underlying preconceptions of eighteenth-century thought were still, allowance made for certain important alterations in the bias, essentially the same as those of the thirteenth century." I only wish Becker's judgment of us moderns was true for social science: "The rise of history and of science were but two results of a single impulse, two aspects of the trend of modern thought away from an overdone rationalization of the facts to a more careful and disinterested examination of the facts themselves."

The central paradoxes in current social science concern rationality and person and contract, all of which presuppose stratification and other stigmata of embeddings in a complex world. Similar paradoxes involve the structuralist conjecture. Both approaches try to deny the independent reality—which is both enabling and constraining—of an indefinite number of intermediate levels of control. Both approaches also bypass the reality of several different frames of interpretation and accountings. Rational choice theory needs revision so as to be able to accommodate various styles to varying contexts.

The temptation to bypass rationality should be resisted even though it is subsidiary to meaning. Where, as in ties of romantic love, change and subtle calculation are everything, the apparatus of preference orderings and "goals" seems malapropos, but the style of rationality can still be observed. Performance skill involves more subtle interactions than are entertained in the main traditions of rational choice theory (Coleman 1990), but it subsumes that turf too. Ties in such settings are of the nature of resonance modes within social echo-chambers among characters that call for and induce validations in a ritual of style.

When rationality is seen as a style, it becomes more useful. Macneil is judicious in his approach to rational choice theory, which he, appropriately enough for a law professor, treats as but one phase, or style, of an overall theory of exchange:

> Only the most aberrant social behavior, if that, ever appears altogether lacking in some element of exchange, direct or indirect, short-term or long-term. As many views of exchange and its nature exist as there are viewers, but two in the non-Marxist world stand out as apparent polar opposites. One is the utilitarian position that exchange enhances the individual utilities of the participants respecting the goods being exchanged. The other is that certain patterns of exchange—categories of reciprocity— enhance social solidarity and *not* individual utility respecting the goods being exchanged, whereas other patterns enhance such individual utility and harm solidarity. . . . Man is both an entirely selfish creature and an entirely social creature. . . . Man is, in the most fundamental sense of the word, irrational, and no amount of reasoning, no matter how sophisticated, will produce a complete and consistent account of human behavior, customs or institutions.

Which all leads to a compromise solution:

> Getting something back for something given neatly releases, or at least reduces, the tension. . . and solidarity—a belief in being able to depend on another—permits the projection of reciprocity through time. (Macneil 1986, p. 569)

Macneil states the individualist objection to individualism: "individualist" because this "solidarity" is conceived as a taste or mood of
individuals.[17]

Few analysts are so foolish as to invoke a means-ends schema as
universal. This would deny inconsistency and passion in intentional
action.[18] But even if one conceded the universal use of means-ends
schemas, rational choice theory would be of limited validity. Action—
what is to be explained about social formations—comes from ignorance and incoherence as much as from their opposites. Halevy writes:
"The historian, that latecomer, is a fortunate man: he knows everything
and does not waste his time on unwarranted apprehensions. His objective detachment distorts his accounts, for the riddles and unknown
quantities of the moment are lacking" (1974, p. 36).

Rationality is misapprehended. Rationality follows in the train of
identity. Pressure for control comes from identities, themselves triggered often by pressures from other identities.[19] Chance in the realm
of work and practical production also triggers identities. Styles may
emerge across the complicated contexts that result, and it is exactly as
such a style that rationality gains its relevance.

It is meaning, not rationality, that is the focus of most social organization. Meaning comes into being only as accommodation to patterns
of social action that have been able to reproduce themselves. Identities
are rafts cobbled together out of leftovers to face cross-tides of circumstance. Sustenance of identities requires comparability of and meaning
between identities, so that meaning is the focus of insight for projects
of control. The useful way to treat rationality is as but a special case of
meaning, a case of limited scope.

Now we can begin over again, with a critique of everyday epistemol-
ogy for the personal relation. Courtesy, as Goffman long ago observed,
grants to the other in an encounter some "face," which becomes a facade concealing disparities among fragments of identity. Many of these
fragments get displayed in stories across locales of networks and
ranges in disciplines. It is through grabbing hold of, and dropping,

[17] Some sociologists make this elision, too: "If we know the categorical identities of
the person that are relevant to his or her society we then, as W. Lloyd Warner often
asserted, know all we need to know about the person as a member of the society" (Warriner 1981).

[18] Pareto (1935, 1966) is the preeminent expositor of the nonrational assessed alongside the rational or logical; for further development, see Levy (1948).

[19] The tradition of experiments on self-justification contains elegant exemplifications
of rationality following from identity: see the witty review by Weick (1968). And for
revealing case studies at three different scopes, see Allison (1971), Eccles (1981d), and
Powell (1985).

identities that stories come about to begin with, and it is through stories that identities can be connected into persons.

The way in which courtesy grants face is through story-sets able to
furnish explanations for any action, which thereby loosen constraints
upon the actor. "Ends," "preferences," "goals," and suchlike as are
found in one or another story are thus partly afterthoughts, traces of
manipulation and rationalization. Yet rationalization is a style and, like
any style, is valuable.

4.5. Social Spaces, Boundaries, and Profiles

We can see that measurement and specification of context is not some
secondary technical matter, but part of theorizing style. A style tends
to inculcate distinct sorts of perceptions and appreciations that go with
certain profiles of interaction among personal actors. One expects constraints on what concrete social arrangements, what profiles and disciplines and networks, can house the story processes whose interpretive
profile is termed a style. Styles come enmeshed in boundaries, and
some social calculus of uncertainty is needed once again. The test of
any such calculus is predicting change.

Changes in expressions can be triggered by environment or by group
and individual whim. But change in their structuring as a package,
change in style, is difficult because style is coordinated to a stratification system. A style has settled in only through continued reen-
actments. No change in style can take place without change in organization of networks and values, together with profiles, as I develop in
the next section.

4.5.1. Styles around Knots and Jet Streams

Knots can vex us everyday, on or off a sailboat. Powerful topological
analyses are available to guide their interpretation in the most varied
contexts (Atiyah 1990; Crowell and Fox 1963; Graham, Grötschel, and
Lovász 1995). Ten years ago I wrote (White 1997, p. 64): "a person
may come to be seen as a knotted vortex among social networks. . . .
It is not just persons that can emerge as actors from knot theories."
Abbott develops much the same intuitions around his construct of
braiding (2001).

Chapter 1 posits identities as by-products of mismatches, which is
to say of tangles in situations. Not all identities come of tangles that
are knotted, but I am now arguing that persons do. Like Abbott, I acknowledge the difficulties at present of operationalizing these meta-

phors for application in social science. Of course, networks here are not built of string so the idea of a knot depends on some mutual con-strainings of ties, and much the same is true with disciplines.

But knottedness can enrich and complete the construal of identities as emerging from mismatches. The knottiness of a situation breeds identities, which can also be seen as simplifications of the scene that enable participants and other observers to dope it out. Herbert Simon surely would have been drawn to this satisficing perspective, and would urge that his beloved stochastic processes can provide robust modeling.

There are still further directions. Back in 1970, I urged in a book on vacancy chains that knottedness of embeddings of vacancies across a large system of persons and jobs could be the aptest measure of in-breeding for elites. Figure 12.1, and the contrast of table 12.6 with table 12.5 in that book (White 1970b), are first steps toward such portrayal and measurement.

The jet stream can now be seen as a phenomenon of knottedness:

Jet streams are concentrated, intense, elongated flows that often contain most of the kinetic energy in a flowing fluid. . . . A mysterious property is that they can act as flexible material barriers, inhibiting mixing across their axes.

They are pervasive features of Earth's atmosphere and oceans . . . ob-served to occur spontaneously on rotating planets whenever stratified at-mosphere of oceans are forced into turbulent motion. . . . A new theoreti-cal paradigm explains the abundance of jets in a simple manner . . . it captures long-range interactions that are crucial for forming and stabiliz-ing jets. . . . Both jet formation and the inhibition of mixing are completely enigmatic in terms of standard turbulence theory.

Strong, compact anomalies . . . in swirl or shear (including planetary ro-tation) . . . are carried with the jet flow like a chemical tracer. . . . These structures are the familiar pancake-like vortices of cyclones. (Baldwin et al. 2007)

I argue that mutual blockings among local social flows arise analogous to the mysterious inhibition of mixing across jets.

4.5.2. Triage

Style is most potent and yet most slippery to specify at a middle range of scope, such as for instance in triage. One example of triage is admis-sions practices in hospital emergency rooms. When, to whom, and how an arriving claim thrusts itself upon attention calls for constantly moni-toring the current congestion and activity across a structure of treatment locales, which is itself changeable and negotiable. This monitoring requires acute attention to and guesses about origins of arriving claims. Thus, triage combines a context for control into an approach to control by indirection.

This triage binds the purely social in with biophysical contingencies.[20] Triage is a special pattern of attention to complementarities among arriving claims. Triage implies a dependency of the chooser upon a skeleton of other identities and their support structure. Triage thus implies a pattern of responsibility. For example, assigning a gunshot victim to a nursing station treating bacterial infections is not responsible. This responsibility emerges as a pattern of evaluating claims not from the views of the claimants but rather from views of the interactions, and the interactions of interactions.

There are many terms for structures that may afford triage—board, committee, council, counselors—but the complete ambiguity in use of these terms corresponds to the difficulty in analyzing triage. There is also much variety and ambiguity in terms for the accompanying operational systems.[21] For a tangible example of unplanned triage on macro scale, see Stark and Vedres (2006).

Triage can be highly formalized and elaborated, as in a system of appeal courts culminating in some court of final appeal. Triage can also take crude, unplanned forms. Switchings remain the focus, and they invoke and play off identities and networks of all sorts, and may recruit disciplines. Indeed, triage seems to invoke a mix of all three disciplines, arena for prioritizing, council for provider agreements, and of course interface for delivering service.

Triage is a process highly dependent upon timings. Consider, for example, the implications of the seating strategies of airlines. Taken as an example of triage, they show as a package that intentional forgetting is one prime component of the responsibility process in triage. Another component of triage that they suggest is arbitrary referral to some earlier history, jumping over a better present claim. Both forgetting and referral can be used in triage process as part of the ongoing attempt to balance and optimize timings.

---

[20] It is a special case of work, in Udy's (1970) formulation, and is thus subject to what he describes (1990) as the universal paradox of work organization.

[21] Existing economic theory is all too likely to assume away the existence of options in triage: contrast the assumption by economist Carlton (1979) in a prize-winning (!) essay on vertical integration—"Because a firm will always choose to use its own inputs first"—with the sociologist Eccles's report on triage in business (1985), based on observation in the field, in which he insists that managers as often shun as seek inside sourcing, depending on political context for control efforts.

4.5.3. Perceptions and Observers

Styles are in part the residues of native analyses or folk theories. No human observer of any social formations is truly outside the quandaries of style, since whatever scientific or other priestly garb is worn is itself constructed analogously. For example, topology and stochastic processes are two opposite scientific styles that analysts can use to try to make sense for each other of the messes of turbulent social polymer gels. And each has some commonsense analogues. Stochastic outcomes of social formations can be parsed in terms of native styles, and surely there is also some topology from theatre for style.

At one extreme, attitudes are a form of decoupling that yields fluidity sufficient for style. Attitudes are passive, however explicit their claim to goal and ordering, and attitude patterns change only in slow, accretive fashion. Yet particular attitudes can gyrate to accommodate events to stories and comport with a style.

At another extreme, decoupling attends generational replacement. If generations came as discrete events, and so were absolutely separate and distinct cohorts, as among locusts (Wilson 1970), there would be less confusion in embedding and hence less scope and occasion for decoupling. Such creatures, no matter how "intelligent," would have little occasion, for example, to develop career systems.[22]

In the control struggles that create and surround them, identities presuppose, and their disciplines contribute to, possibilities of order in larger contexts. Styles can be used to describe such a context, but not as a formation with definite stipulations such as in a discipline. A style refers to context as if it were in the analogue of a gaseous or liquid state.[23] Stochastic models (Feller 1968) are one apt vehicle for the observer to use in modeling and understanding style, which emerges out of what is going on as disciplines get hitched, networked, and aggregated. Impacts on disciplines from these larger environments[24] earlier

[22] Surely an apt topic for an Ursula LeGuin science-fiction novel!

[23] The distinction is like that drawn by the demographer Watkins (1990).

[24] It may be possible to characterize these environments with some construct modeled on temperature, which is the premier parameter that interlinks localities for condensed states of matter, and even gases. In bioecological phenomena, analogues to temperature—and even temperature itself—have proved themselves. And in engineering design, the Wiener feedback ideas of control theory exhibit some parallel to temperature. Interchanges among ambage, ambiguity, and contingency, through decoupling mechanisms begin to hint at temperature, and stratification systems are a self-reproducing social organization under such exchange. But social formations emerge as insulation in between counteractions of identities seeking control, insulation that is too extreme to permit a temperature that pervades a whole system. Style does permeate across levels but, in contrast to temperature, style allows for continuing inhomogeneities that result from blocking action.

were characterized abstractly in terms of trade-offs in specialized un-certainties around embedding and decoupling.

4.5.4. Social Spaces

Ties make up, together with disciplines and their embedding mecha-nisms, social spaces. Continuations through some form of signaling elicit the corresponding possibilities of social time. Before those whom we take for granted as distinct actors impinge upon our everyday con-sideration, there is already being constructed and perceived much so-cial space. Whatever the level or scope of the actors involved, counter-actions have interacted to generate the sense of structured possibilities for further interaction, which is just social space.

Contingencies are the origin of identities and their searches for con-trol. Contingencies are thus sources of social organization and its spaces—which are not pre-given Cartesian spaces. Indeed, social spaces are continually being rebuilt and torn down, over and over again, with everyday and demographic contingencies at the root of both tearing down and reproducing.

The central problem is that these spaces are simultaneously the envi-ronment for, and the result of, social action. The conundrum is how to stipulate a context in social action for disciplines and ties and values that by their cumulation produce just that stipulated order. Call the solution a "self-consistent field." Field is used in analogous fashion in natural science theory.[25] Style as defined in this chapter is enacted in or as such a field. Field is used in much the same sense by Pierre Bour-dieu as a foundation construct of his theories. In *Rules of Art* (1996a), he works out with care the formation and autonomization of a field of stratification in nineteenth-century French literature.

The physical spaces that are analogous are crowded spaces.[26] It is not the empty heavens but rather crowded insides of cells, organisms, or semiconductors that are called for as analogies. Social spaces are contexts in which identities and interactions locate in the unfolding of projects for control, which ricochet off continuing impacts of physical events. Isotropy does not exist, but rather levels and catenations and

[25] The closest analogue is with physics and chemistry of matter, where the conundrum is subjected to increasingly elegant solutions: as to process, by statistical mechanics (Huang 1963), and as to architecture by various mean field approximations (Ziman 1979; de Gennes 1979).

[26] Economic theory as contextualized by Samuelson (1947) made the regressive step to homogeneous and isotropic field constructs, as in gravity or electromagnetism, a step back from the institutionalist perspective of Marshall (1891) or Chamberlin ([1933] 1962), which both induce perception of crowded, irregular, and scrappy spaces.

interlockings. The social generates its own distinctive spaces of possibilities, even though they are somehow intertwined with physical-biological spaces.

4.5.5. Mixture and Switchings of Disciplines

Decoupling provides occasion for switching. Indeed, decoupling can be seen as the special case of switching-out without establishing where-to. Alternatively the after-state can be seen as undifferentiated blandness, a sort of innocuous public.

Chapter 3 segregated constituents in an interface discipline away from its context in the very step of correlating the mechanism across upstream, downstream, and cross-stream. It seemed that the discipline's business claimed the complete attention of its constituents, so there could be no overlap or mixture or even switching of disciplines. And it seemed furthermore that each species invoked similar story-sets, drawn from a common realm of interpretation.

Now, however, style captures how those myriad disjointed contexts of disciplines, along with networks, can fit together, thereby constituting itself across some self-consistent field. Put more concretely, a discipline that survives and does its business indeed seizes the attention of its constituents, but constituents live in and thus switch to other realms. Two of the case studies in chapter 3, the law firm and turn-taking, make it apparent that even a clear-cut discipline can invoke and overlap with other disciplines, as will the Mische study in chapter 7.

As social action by given identities continues around a particular site, it may, after first being captured in one variety of a discipline species, then shade into another variety. Or this action may switch over into an exemplar of a different species. Faction and autocracy may transform, for example, from council over into arena.

For example, it would appear from a study (Eccles and Crane 1988, developed further in chapter 7) that American investment banks in New York used to be actors in a council discipline but then fitted into arena disciplines. This occurred when the network context changed and enlarged internationally, and as identities of the issuers of and investors in debt also changed along with their story-sets. By contrast, American commercial banks have remained characterized by interface disciplines. On a smaller scale, purchasing agents within American industry have not only switched but also oscillated between discipline species as distinguished here (see Corey 1978; Pooler 1964).

The same process can be traced in different disciplinary species—for instance, agency as process. One aspect of agency, supervision and "inverted supervision," will be discussed in chapter 7 in terms of varieties of interface discipline. There the horizontal, peer aspect of agency is emphasized. When the vertical and cumulative aspect of agency is predominant, some variety of mediation discipline is likely to figure. Compounded agency is, so to speak, just one arm of the mediation octopus cut off and treated as independent and free-standing.

Note the similar conundrums encountered in chapter 2 regarding networks. Type of tie is analogous to discipline species except that it built its own context as that type of network. Chapter 2 started with the overall, single network and then faced the conundrums of fitting it in with types of tie. The overall network is a special case of self-consistent field, as is the specialized network. Style is a self-consistent field that folds these in along with disciplines sited among them.

A revised construct of environment is needed. Boundary remains as problematic as it was for network, for the reasons given in chapter 2. The revised construct must still serve both to frame action within itself and to summarize itself for action outside.[27]

Size profiles are one representation of order from stochastic process, in fact the simplest one. These profiles do not include the before-and-after, nor the in-and-out of actual system mechanisms. A profile reports a social formation in terms of mere distributions of constituents (Blau and Duncan 1967). A profile presupposes stable outcome along with stochastic process. Such a profile is useful in analysis only because decoupling establishes both flexibility and robustness, to degrees upon which Zipf (1949) insisted long ago.

Let us begin with a tangible historical example, and then turn to abstract modelings for the impacts from profiles and depths.

4.5.6. Envelope from Profiles

Aggregation into populations is best seen as a continuing process, not a static matter of putting beans in bags. An economy, for example, grows as some painful accretion of styles out of original disciplines and networks, through a process with contingencies that yields a profile of

---

[27] This environment, like a network population, exhibits complicated overlappings. Population ecology suggests instead a sharp partition, as of distinct biological species. Whole populations, each as defined by recurrent and patterned interaction, then may combine to constitute a super-population, within which each may be affected variously by biophysical ecology. One early statement of population ecology is Hannan and Freeman (1989). In their approach, actors each may be an organization or other large formation of human persons, whose appearances and decays are to be modeled in terms of physical as well as social context. They apply the basic work of Levins (1966), for which E. O. Wilson (1979) supplies phenomenology. For approaches applying mathematical genetics to related social topics, see Boorman and Levitt (1980) and Lewontin (1974).

occurrences. The population is recognized through a size distribution that is the by-product of counting and sheer accumulation—profile as size distribution—without any embedding via discipline and tie.

And network population need not be the only social construction of population. A prototype is the pattern of congestion in a city's road network. For some road network, a simple analogue can be drawn. A queue length across the set of intersections is the size distribution. Green-light times, in number of cars passed, could be the control parameter, with the analogue to status distribution being the profile of acceptable delays.

The term *envelope* captures the idea that it is only the outer limits of the cumulation of contingencies that has impact. This is a new sort of embedding where there is no re-forming of identity, but rather a factual accumulation that shapes or reflects a constraint on action that is comparable to embedding.

The envelope that an observer can draw as the high-tide line of contingencies is thus one operationalization of population. A population then defines itself by the aggregate produced from contingencies observed across networks linked one to another through common actors—actors established through interaction among discipline, identity, and network, possibly as positions. A city can be defined as the population within which interactions are observed to yield a stochastic pattern of congestion that reproduces itself (White 1973). Control over population definition, over boundaries, can thus be achieved by influencing the topology of the network of flows (Kleinrock 1964).

The same principles apply at very different scales. Take the layout of aisles and wares in a supermarket. By changing which products are neighboring, paths of movement and perceptions of customers can be reclustered, so that a different set of (micro) populations emerges within the store. Perhaps yuppies segregate out as a population in their movements away from young mothers with their children and from retirees, whereas before it was drinkers, the poor, and ordinary middle class. And this is a similar process of population formation by establishing the location and product alignment of supermarkets across a region of neighborhoods.

On a larger scale, too, a product is an aspect of population clusters mutually induced among actors and products and subject to some control through the ecology. This is what market is in the larger sense, and perhaps economic theory can someday be brought back into connection with this network reality. A Leontief input-output matrix could be derived as the result of carrying this principle to national scope (Carter 1976). Burt (1990) carries the approach yet one step further by specification of sector boundaries from organizational principles.

Manipulability of population boundaries is not unlimited. For example, an accident (Calabresi 1970) is a natural population, a cluster of contingent happenings and context. An epidemic is a large-sized social accident (Bailey 1957, 1982).

The diffusion of the use of a medicine (see chapter 2) can be seen as a species of epidemic. Here too the populations involved—in this case, professionals and users as mediated through a third population of agents (Coleman, Katz, and Menzel 1966; Burt 1990)—are best defined reflexively, as the contingency envelope of the stochastic processes of influence and action spreads. Reanalysis (Burt 1988) of the classic initial study underlines the structural effects of topologies.

These envelopes can be specified in narrower focus as well, where differential involvement with different species of discipline may become apparent. A tie of influence and dominance from one actor to another may chain though several actors treated successively as intermediaries. Whatever factual connections, of the diffusion sort described earlier, obtain as a result, joint perceptions of the concatenation of links into a chain can have major impact on continuing action. Such a perception is likely only in mediator and commit disciplines, councils, and interfaces. Reputation or fame, on the other hand, is a perceived result of clustering of ties to the same node, and envelopes of prestige like those of fame get recognized as significant only in the match and mediation contexts, arenas, and councils.

Return to the supermarket product-display example. It is an established rule of thumb that one-fifth of the products account for four-fifths of total sales. The rule is robust in that it holds whether one discusses "brands" within a so-called product or discusses distinct products, which implies being scale-free (Abbott 2001). This supports the earlier contention that categories like "product X" are socially induced rather than neutral "technical" facts. This particular rule of thumb is widely, but by no means universally, known. The rule is a profile that marks a significant decoupling in the merchandise system, whether or not particular actors or disciplines explicitly compute in terms of it. Such a size-distribution profile is a surface sign of the likelihood of finding a style.

4.6. General Selves: Actors, Personages, Personal Consciousness

Both actors and events are socially negotiated; both are derived from ongoing productions. Both can cumulate into new actors and events. Both can also partly shake free of context through decoupling mechanisms. It is this derivative nature of actors and of events that encourages the theory to be scale invariant.

4.6.1. Scale-Free Personal Styles

Control efforts are attempted every which way across levels resulting from embedding. The idea of levels comes with embedding, but social spaces are not tidy layerings, and actors on presumably different levels can relate directly through control projects. It is all the more important that the analysis be universal, or self-similar, so that the same terms and analyses apply at all scopes.[28]

It is not self-repetition at successive levels in a system that can be claimed. Levels build up in social formations as by-products of inter-acting control struggles. "Actor" can become anything from a multina-tional giant firm to a Goffmanesque creature of the brief encounter. It is for this reason that stories can operate as gears, as transcribers between actors and action on different levels. Scale invariance has been queried; for example, in the study of Italian city-states:

> The real state, the state felt all around one in the form of potent commis-sions or as a source of income (via speculation on the Monte), existed in the corporate and individual holder. . . . Nothing in the Florentine consti-tution emphasized the principle of indirect representation. . . . The contact with power was direct, immediate, sensory. (Martines 1968, pp. 391–92)

But on the other end of scale, whether in interpreting international re-lations (Ashley 1980) or in perceptions within sports leagues (Leifer 1991b), the personalization of embedded actors such as states (Tilly 1975; Wolin 1987) is universal. The plausibility of this personalization is evidence for self-similarity across levels.

Persistence through crisis is where identity emerges. Mere an-nouncement of a new business, or a sports team, or a farm, or a lineage, or a political patronage line, cannot effectuate an identity for some cor-porate actor. The new compound actor will not be taken seriously, con-sidered to have the inertia and staying power of an identity, by others and by its own constituents, until after some nonlinear eddy of affairs, some crisis. Ian Watt (1957) traces the rise of the novel as exactly this sort of birth from irregularity: the principle carries over from person to larger sort of identity, and thus the construct of corporate personage is justified.

Clinical psychologists are forced to cover this same ground and are aware of levels in formation of corporate character—and also of unique identity—even within a human being. Consider two different develop-

---

[28] For similar arguments on self-similarity, restricted to a macro scale, see Bergesen, Fernandez, and Sahoo (1987) and Caporaso (1989).

ments in clinical psychology. Stage theory deals with acquiring and evolving corporate characters:

> When a mother responds to anxiety with the intention to relieve it, she brings the culture of embeddedness to the defense of a given evolutionary state (the state of equilibrium). . . . She directs herself to the individual . . . rather than to . . . the movement of evolution itself. She responds to the protection of made-meaning rather than to the experience of meaning-making. . . . Support is not alone an effective matter, but a matter of "knowing," a matter of shape, as well as intensity. (Kegan 1982, pp. 125–260)

In contrast, group therapy (e.g., Napier and Whitaker 1978) deals with, as well as works in, subtle and ambiguous ties as the generator and base of unique identity formation.

On the one hand, Kegan's book adapts Kohlberg's stage theories (1981) of learning to a personality theory of four stages. Each stage should be seen as a theory of character, which is an essentially corporate matter of joint learning, necessarily concerned with rituals. On the other hand, theories descending from Freud's therapy approaches, such as Erikson's discussed later, take as their focus problematics and gaming in a pair. Thus, ironically, group therapy follows one side of Freud to achieve insight into unique individual identity in a way not available to stage theories.

The lines between personal and corporate blur.

4.6.2. Personage: Strategy and Intimacy

Personages evolve as corporate actors, compounds of identities. Disorder that is apparently unneeded and unusual in the context is a clue to shifts in the personage. Strategy and intimacy are involved, strategy and intimacy that cross distinct social worlds, that cross institutions. Intimacy seems to be a delicate by-product of exactly the multiplicity from strategy that can permit simple beliefs among some array of third parties. Intimacy is, of course, a situation of lowered ambage, and the strategy invoked increases ambiguity.

A biographer of President Lyndon Johnson comments on his important base of power in Senate years as follows:

> The biggest, the most efficient, and most ruthlessly overworked and the most loyal personal staff in the history of the Senate. . . . Those who made up that staff found that working for Johnson subjected them to unpredictable expressions of feelings. One minute he would turn right around, give him an expensive gift, and say to him "You know you are my right

arm. . . ." Johnson justified his violent swings in feelings and conduct by the need to keep his staff continually off-guard in order to ensure that they would not relax their efforts. Everything—from staff meetings to rides in his car—was by invitation only, allowing Johnson to arbitrarily freeze out or bring in anyone at any time. Yet if one of his staff decided to leave, Johnson would become desperate, begging him to stay, attempting to bribe . . . to pressure . . . so the aide who thought of leaving remained, per- haps because he felt he had acquired the intimacy that Johnson had hith- erto denied him. (Kearns 1976, pp. 78–79)

Kearns is looking from LBJ's side, but the strategy-intimacy ties may have been asymmetric, in tune with the hierarchic structure of Senate leader and his staff. An earlier account of Johnson (Evans and Novak 1966, pp. 410–12) comments on anomalies in his relation as new presi- dent with the press. There were sudden summonses and bizarre privi- leges here too, but the overwhelming tone is a consistent one of unin- terrupted wooing. The outcome (which Evans and Novak are confused by) is exactly a failure to build intimacy, a failure on either side to thus establish identity.

Around the world from LBJ, "big men" in New Guinea mountain tribes appear to develop a strategy for intimacy and to achieve identity in a similar way, according to one account. Strathern guided his field- work "by reference to Radcliffe-Brown's definition of alliance relation- ships . . . those which are characterized by an interplay of conjunction and disjunction, by antagonism and yet by mutual friendship and aid. Such relationships occur between persons who are outside the sphere of incorporation relative to each other." Ceremonial displays and os- tentatious conveyance of gifts, called prestations in the literature, are held scattered around, with one or another increased according to the strategizing of big men. There are numerous preliminary negotiations of who is to supply what to which others, and what they, variously arrayed in tribal distance, deign to accept.

But prestations themselves are always part of a further sequence . . . of alternating between a number of partners. . . . I distinguished between the main flow of prestations between a number of partners. . . . I distinguished between the main flow which is the moka chain proper, and auxiliary flows, which can be thought of as further "ropes of moka" attached to and feeding into the chain. (Strathern 1971, pp. 121–33)

Strathern emphasizes the strategizing and gaming from which moka emerges; for example, "a deputation of engambo Minembia men came to big-man of Kawelka Kundmbo late in July 1964 and complained strongly that he had not yet given pig-moka to them; had he done so in time they could have passed his pigs on to the Kitepi to whom. . . . such demands are part of the general effort of gamesmanship which is put into moka relations. . . . Each side knows fairly well how far to insist."

In addition to contributing to and representing political maneuvering among hierarchies amid tribal composites, Strathern's account is also a specification of one, albeit restricted, cycle of actions that can be seen as economic; someday they may be woven by some native entrepreneurs into the beginnings of a putting-out economy. Any economy anywhere is built only from such tangible mechanisms brought into some resonance with work and its cumulation; consult Granovetter (1985), and earlier Polanyi, Arensberg, and Pearson (1957).

Strathern's account also shows how intimacy[29] is bound up with creations of identity as by-products of superficially erratic mixtures of actions.

> The large size of prestations is partly a result of the desire to show temporary superiority and dominance over them . . . in this context, moka gifts are a true functional alternative to warfare. . . . Indeed, if one group were overwhelmingly "defeated" in moka exchanges it could become politically dependent on the victor; hence recipient groups, in order to retain their independence, *must* reciprocate. [And] [a]llies are also rivals, competing for prestige through the size of their reciprocal moka gifts.

Strathern sums up the "rope of moka":

> Donors' formally announced intention is often to compensate the recipients . . . to make them "feel good" again. But underneath the formal rubric a good deal of antagonism may show, especially when the social distance between donor and recipient groups is great. This point might lead us to suppose that the largest gifts, expressing the greatest antagonism, would be made to *major* enemies. But . . . between these there is insufficient trust for groups to risk very heavy investments in each other. . . . The upshot is that most effort is put into prestations to groups which are allies . . . but are also in some way politically and socially opposed.

Personages form from strategic ambiguity in maintaining intimacy in ties. This etiology can be illustrated as well in U.S. national government as in the New Guinea highland—or for that matter on any basketball court. This same process is at the root of the creation of stories that tell about identities as a core part of ordinary social life. There is

---

[29] There is a striking similarity to what Leifer (1991a) calls local action among skilled players.

a paradoxical combination of ambiguity and intimacy that must be there to weave together stories and establish the fascination from which personage can emerge. Resulting stories are likely to come in sets that accommodate each other.

4.6.3. Entourages

An entourage centers on a noteworthy figure but expands to some depth, even extending into historical time.[30] The topic of entourages, like the schematic playground example carried through from the first chapter, illustrates a fundamental tension between individuality in the sources of action, on the one hand, and constraint from the larger context, on the other hand. The topic of entourage also illustrates three further themes of this book: that action precedes and generates actors; that control comes from identities; and that variabilities serve as causes.

Entourages will also serve as introduction to person in the next section. Historians have developed diverging tracks for dealing with persons, arguably because of the uncertain scientific status of person as concept. We can summarize the debate as follows:

> Human beings are not ignored [by the *Annales* school], of course, since the study of history is by definition the pursuit of knowledge and understanding of men, but the focus shifts from individuals to their context. . . . Lucien Febvre wrote in his *Combats pour l'histoire*: "The historical individual . . . or more exactly the historical personage develops in and through the group. . . . Fernand Braudel went considerably further . . . in terminating his massive *Mediterranean and the Mediterranean World in the Age of Philip II*, he argues that the great king's death had no effect upon the established trends of Spanish history. (Church 1976, p. 97)

This *Annales* position is doubly ironic. Studies of ordinary persons, even in such apparently detailed form as psychoanalysis, are not and cannot be undertaken with the resources needed to report the larger social context for their action. "Movers and shakers" of earlier eras can be reconstructed, and indeed even better than current elites. It is more likely to be for past ages than for the current scene that "professional investigators," scholars and/or scientists, have enough clout and perspective to gain full access to elite life and the full context. But it is just such study that undermines the *Annales* conceit that fresh action of importance did not emanate from such as Philip II, Pippin, and so forth. The next chapter will make it evident that the *Annales* approach

---

[30] I borrow the term from Hull's study (1982) of the crowd around Kaiser Wilhelm I.

is suited to the history of, but only of, corporatism, or more generally, of institutions.[31] Let us examine whether the approach will function with the entourage, or its simpler variant, the personage.

4.6.4. Making History

Turn to a very different biography of a historical personage, Rowen (1978) on the great Dutchman, John De Witt. It is the very turbulence of the Cromwell-Orange period, when the Netherlands emerged out of an ambiguous fog of towns and polders, that created the identity of De Witt.

John De Witt started out as a bright young man from a middling line of patricians in a city of medium importance. He learned to operate among contending place-seekers in the unrationalized mazes of pensionable offices that made up Holland and the lesser provinces. He carried on extensive administrative routine in a turbulent time. All these fit together from separable contexts into a distinctive personage, De Witt[32]:

> The government led by De Witt should not be seen, however, as an emanation of his personality. . . . De Witt as councilor pensionary exercised his leadership not only by the undoubted power of his words and his skill in manipulation of the system, but also by the existence of, not a modern organized party, of course, no more than its competitor, the "[Prince of] Orange party," but a clique or a congeries of cliques . . . and it always remained a narrow party of the elite. (Rowen 1988, p. 98)

This personage was importantly an expression and creation of the larger convolution that was the United Provinces wound around Holland; it was not a mere person, no matter how able and multifaceted. Yet this personage was such an exceptional success at creating control—out of thin air as it seemed to his contemporaries, especially to smoldering royalty—that it is hard to deny unusual individuality to De Witt as central person. De Witt notably embodied a double genius: he contributed, as an equal among other great European mathematicians, a complete theory of conic sections.[33]

---

[31] The *Annales* approach is, in some respects, a throwback to an older form of history, the annals, which, rather than fitting the myth of history-as-a-general-form, suits well only to value-centered corporatism—corporatism which, as observed on the ground, is a shambles of high ambage, by the argument made earlier.

[32] See Rowen (1978) (e.g., p. 28 on the maze and p. 252 on the identity).

[33] Perhaps De Witt would today have contributed a mathematical theory of control covering issues such as those sketched in chapter 6 in this book, but perhaps not, since particularity may have been key to his method and his cognitions on control.

Nonetheless, across this same century there is striking evidence for the claim to personage as being shaped primarily by social confluences. Until a generation before, very much the same personage had been dominant, centered on another extraordinary human person, Oldenbarnevelt (Rowen 1988, p. 37). The social confluences, the system then, were also congeries of cliques, in "a political current . . . that is usually called 'republican,' but more precisely was 'Staatsgezind' (literally, 'in favor of the States') and denied the sovereignty either of the 'people,' however defined, or of the House of Orange" (Rowen 1988, p. 37).

As if to confirm the similarity conjecture, even the human fates of the two central persons were identical: both were assassinated by royal interests, Oldenbarnevelt under judicial guise and De Witt by the agency of a street mob. The context had changed considerably in concrete terms, and they were different persons, but the personages were parallel.

4.6.5. Personal Consciousness

Personal consciousness should seem a strange affair, not a familiar matter. Persons in the modern sense come to be generated only as by-products of an era of large-scale frictions among distinct network-populations, styles, and other larger formations. I conjecture this is also true of consciousness in an individual, which is not the same as claiming person to be style.

Usually there is not the evidence, nor the patience, to establish or refute this conjecture with precision. Surely it should be easiest to do so for a mystic or theologian, whose business it is to be self-conscious about their consciousness, their soul. Martin Luther came out of such an era; and enough is known to permit examining his personhood, which some masters have done.

Historians re-create Luther, like other "world historical" figures, as a strain point at confluences of significant social tides. They do not agree on some true underlying uniqueness and strength of the person but do offer re-creations of the entourage. And specialists in theological history (Oberman 1981) are engaged in a revisionist debate as to the originality of Luther's ideas and of Luther's systematic formulation, as opposed to a revived perception of liveliness across late medieval nominalist theology preceding Luther. But they too will join in an "as-if" account of Luther's importance, minimally as an expression of the oncoming major cultural reformation.

Erik Erikson contributes a highly original view of the importance of dynamics in young Luther's family constellation, which is fed into, rather than used to contradict, the historical and theological perspectives. The book *Young Man Luther* was unusual both in its impact and in its authorship by a psychoanalyst (Erikson 1958). Erikson's accomplishment illustrates one major theme: each social reality, of whatever scope, is caught up in and affected by other scopes. Erikson is convincing on Luther as being quite literally created as a person by cross-pressures of his immediate family life, as both interpreted and, simultaneously, concretely shaped by the late medieval theological and institutional context. The person as a pearl shaped in a family as a bivalve of turbulent flows: this could have been Erikson's subtitle. But the real point is to read Luther at length to see the riveting intensity of his anxiety about his soul, as a real-time, chronic continuing process in what is surely a consciousness.

4.7. Communities

Communities can be seen as built out of identities rather than out of persons. But style can also characterize a community. Silver (1989, 1990) argues that distinct identity as a person in the modern sense followed from rather than created the multiplex or general tie, and this can extrapolate to community from the configuration of general ties across identities. We draw on careful analyses of the concept of community related to diverse examples, and then turn to issues of exclusion and overlap clarified by an extended case study. Then the next section on emergence of style will begin with two community studies.

Consider this analysis of the concept of community:

> We need to develop a conceptualization of community which allows us to penetrate beneath simple categories . . . to see a variable of social relations. . . . The relationship between community as a complex of social relationships and community as a complex of ideas and sentiments has been little explored [p. 107]. . . . What is important about "sense of belonging" is . . . his modification of consideration of alternative courses of action on the basis of the communal relations to which he belongs. (Calhoun 1980, p. 110)

Then he goes on: "The self-regulation of community is dependent on dense, multiplex bonds. . . . The crucial issue is the breakdown of the structure of hierarchical incorporation which knit local communities into the society as a whole" (p. 115). We can recast Calhoun's point. Earlier forms of community had types of tie well defined and built into explicit disciplines, so that a sense of community was superfluous. The development of multiplex tie from community to other actors is what induces and permits the appearance of community persona akin to the modern individual person.

A large-scale exemplar of the signaling argument for identity is how "lost," "saved," and "liberated" communities are not successive stages, but rather alternative structural models:

> Many scholars believed that community ties were now few in number, weak, narrowly specialized, transitory, and fragmented. . . . These scholars feared that community had been "lost.". . . Others argued that people gregariously form and retain communities in all social settings. . . . By the 1960s their "Community Saved" argument had had much the better of the debate. . . . Both the "Lost" and the "Saved" arguments assume that a flourishing community can only be one that replicates the standard image of pre-industrial communities: densely knit, tightly bounded, and mutually supportive villages. But such bucolic imagery not only disregards widespread preindustrial individualism, exploitation, cleavage, and mobility . . . but it also restricts the criteria. . . . Scholars who have avoided this mislabeling . . . argue that large-scale specialization and personal mobility have "Liberated" community—encouraging membership in multiple, interest-based communities predominantly composed of long-distance friendship ties . . . people are not so much antisocial or gregarious beings as they are operators. . . . Each model speaks to a different means of obtaining and retaining resources: direct use of formal organizations (Lost); membership in densely knit, all-encompassing, solidary groups (Saved); or selective use of specialized, diversified, sparsely knit social nets (Liberated) . . . all three models are likely to be reflected in current realities to some extent. (Wellman, Carrington, and Hall 1988, pp. 133–35)

These are alternatives for community identity; they constitute a story-set for it. This set of stories is, in fact, used both in common parlance and also simultaneously in professional jousts by scholarly analysts within their own world. The set of stories clusters around some value(s).

There is community as identity of a personal sort at still larger scope and higher level. Identity acquires theophany, covenant, and law before gaining the most universal recognition, as for example Jehovah (Jahweh in Gottwald 1979, p. 94). All three of these aspects—pronouncement, reciprocal commitment, and rules—presuppose and can be observed only in social context. Social context is not opaque like the "insides" of persons, and so it is requisite for the three aspects even with respect to a particular human person. All three aspects presuppose value. This is true even where the "actor" is least personal.

There is an analogue to community at smaller scale. Ties are the detritus of discipline formations. Ties are fragments of what might have

locked into disciplines, thus yielding identities enabled to generate social action. Within a discipline there are strong connections among the
constituting entities, which may themselves be identities, so that other
types of connection exist between identities. These connections are mutual pressures that come to fit together so as to support some transitive
order, perhaps some personhood.

4.7.1. Overlap of Communities

Community can but need not bear a label, and even a very familiar
label need not signal community formation. But a stigmatizing label
(Link and Phelan 2001) is likely to induce as well as signal community.
Mignon Moore offers a spread of reports on the intersection of two
communities, black and lesbian, often still subject to stigmatizing. The
cross-pressures are intense and distinctive, such that her observations
can lead to deeper insight into features of general social process that
stay opaque with other contexts.

Moore offers fieldwork of depth and care reminiscent of the monastery and law firm studies described in chapters 2 and 3. There is some
quantitative observation and some report via impersonal survey, but
the core is a multiyear participant observation of multiple aspects of
daily living among this network population. The site is New York City,
and she observes across hundreds of occasions and locations and
across a wide range in age, class, education, and ethnicity within race.

One focus is family around children; the other is formation of intimate relations. Either focus generates the same finding: black lesbians
are an aspect of black community, black style in my terms; they reject
the lesbian style that they adjoin to feminist style, perceived as an
aspect of white style. No doubt one of the causes is the extensive,
though not complete, segregation of housing by race. Whether cause
or consequence, there are sharp differences in belief pattern from that
of feminists.

Whatever the causes, though, can core empirical measures be teased
out that support the finding? Yes: the signals of self that settle out for
negotiation of love partner. Within feminist lesbian style, it is a no-no
to rely on cues of femininity common in the wider society. Black lesbians, however, both in explicit report and in behavior, are comfortable
with settling into a dyad polarized by masculine and feminine. To be
more precise, the term *masculine* evokes unease and the term *transgressive* is substituted (not the term *aggressive*).

The general argument made earlier that intimacy is inextricably
bound up with subtlety continues to hold, however. In Moore's words:

In today's society women have a significant range of styles that are considered acceptable, and this is different from the 1950's when the simple act of wearing pants or short hair marked someone as having masculine presentation. The categories of femme, gender-blender, and transgressive now have the most meaning when they are presented in a context where lesbians are present. It is in the larger group of black lesbians that the subtleties which often accompany a femme or gender-blending presentation of self are made clear. Athletic jersey and baggy jeans on women as they walk down 125th street in Harlem or Flatbush Avenue in Brooklyn do not mark them as lesbian on the outside, but reveal their membership in a gender display category once she steps into a convention center or nightclub filled with black lesbians. In trying to understand how black lesbians are negotiating the organization and meaning of gender display, I found that it is desire, not feminism or politics, that takes center stage. . . . Most women, when asked if their sexuality was tied to feminism, had not consciously linked the two.

But she goes on to point to a subtle shift nonetheless in the significance of polarized dyad:

In the past, butch-femme roles eroticized and structured sexual interactions around the principle of gender difference. Gender presentation is defined more broadly now, and is no longer primarily a means of structuring sexual interaction. However . . . Black women take very careful pains to consistently present the same type of gender display over and over again because they are looking to create a particular aesthetic self, and the norms of the community require a consistency in their gender presentation. . . . Transgressive women are socialized by other lesbians to make sure their button-down shirt hangs behind the belt buckle, or that the scarf under the fitted cap is tied to show their hair in a specific way. Femmes learn to wear jeans that are fitted at the hip, and often tie a-line shirts (also called "wife beaters") in the back to create a more alluring look. (Moore 2006)

Through continued switchings you get socialized.

4.8. Emergence and Change

A style does not come easily. Experiences summarized in social networks and histories spread particular actors across diverse arrays of disciplines. Across positions within social organization, some social vision, some style, gets locked in for a while by the enormous pressures of joint living with others. The history of a style is interwoven with some complex of social formations in an ecology even for ostensibly purely cultural realms (Baxandall 1975, 1980). Joint action has to shape and generate perceptions into consistent patterns.

Some orderliness of perception is presupposed and supplied in any style. Change from one style to another has to trace itself out in some phenomenology of trust. *Trust* is itself a term for a clustering of perceptions.

An illustration within big business firms comes from Eccles's study (1985; and see Eccles and White 1988) of transfer pricing practices between divisions. He shows the predominance of "buy, or at worst make" over "make, or at worst buy" as a rule for procurement, and shows that this predominance centers on considerations of fairness. Division managers, in this era, prefer to buy from other firms rather than from other internal divisions. The then current scene of managerial competitiveness within the firm was not such as to encourage trusting internal arrangements. This was the style of their rationality. In other current business localities, the rationality style comes to incorporate trust. For a business illustration, return to the field study of auction markets cited earlier:

> This format [devised by the economist Vickrey], though mathematically well supported, is practically never used. The reason normally given is that it is too complex. Yet the more complex English knockout system flourishes. The true reason for its disuse might well be that the aim of this system is to maximize bids, whereas the purpose of the English knockout and other systems used in real auctions is to ensure fairness to all participants. (Smith 1989, p. 72)

The next chapter suggests that Vickrey's format, which cannot sustain itself, is an attempted rhetoric not a style. It is disrupted by mismatch between stories and changing networks, but it may resurface as it accompanies some evolution in style.

The first two extended examples that follow concern transformation of community. Then we develop a general proposition, which will lead into an extended cultural case study.

4.8.1. Berlin and Vermont

Examine how identity emerges for a particular community, or actually two, chosen as very different in period and ambiance.

Sophie Muetzel seized on the coming move of the German government from Bonn back to Berlin—in the late 1990s—as an opportunity to study in experimental fashion how identity gets (re)shaped. She reasoned that newspapers would be central in this process, and indeed a number of German newspapers, only some in Berlin, began mounting campaigns to win footing in Berlin. Most of them agreed that a key to this was shaping perceptions of readers, and everyone else, as to what Berlin would be—certainly not a sleepy provincial backwater like Bonn.

Muetzel tracked the various newspapers over two years, as well as the public discourse through interviews and also direct inspection. She adapted blockmodel algorithms (see chapter 2) to assess trends and differences in the campaigns (2002, 2005).

What is clear is that no authority, no government agency, not even any association of newspapers or of journalists could control this process. What Muetzel has studied is the evolution of a style. A sensitivity specific to Berlin remained, but of a new sort, a possibility opened up partly by chaotic juxtapositions and disjunctions between newspaper positionings and government changes.

The other example is the evolution of an identity for colonial Vermont (which split off late as separate from the colonies of New Hampshire and New York). Henning Hillman studied this through archival reconstruction of social networks there over a key decade. Debt relations were important; so were political alliances and church standing as well as, of course, kinship. He too presents systematic quantitative analysis with the idea of understanding how Vermont could come and hold together as a community despite radical geographic and economic as well as cultural disjunctions, nearly into two parts.

Again, the story to be told is of a style that emerged out of chaotic cross-currents. Interaction between national and local has still more bite. No one thought of Berlin as possibly pulling off as an independent (city)-state and/or joining Poland.

The idea of the Berlin area pulling off to join Poland is analogous to the idea of Vermont in its earliest days, say, joining Canada. Henning Hillman (2006) studies early Vermont, but he concentrates on the internal structuration of Vermont. His archival data search establishes that extension of credit, within this cash-starved frontier region of land title disputes, underlay how Vermont mobilized, drawing some analogy to Schwartz's (1976) account of later Southern Populism around cotton. The central lenders evoked some coherence into competing blocks across a variety of diverse relations and loyalties. This cut exposure of Vermont to centralizing manipulation from the national level exerted through brokers.

In his words:

> My main argument is that the power of brokers may be undermined by local coordinators whose role is distinct from brokerage between factions. Coordinators are elites who bridge gaps between otherwise disconnected

members *within, rather than between* network factions. Such coordinators forge the kind of strong local alliances that participate in, rather than succumb to state-making initiatives. . . . This study demonstrates how the success of coordinators over brokers in eighteenth-century Vermont channeled the translation of local alliances and identities into national politics without eroding the fabric of local social structure. The national battles between Jeffersonian Republicans and Hamilton Federalists fell on an already fertile ideological soil within Vermont. In this setting, local coordinators could use their personal relationships of economic patronage to align democratic western pro-Vermont New Lights (within Calvinism) and conservative eastern Yorker Old Lights into consistent factions. (Hillman 2006, pp. 3, 4, 41)

Well and good, but that does not begin to capture the confusing richness of the Vermont tapestry laid out in his doctoral thesis (Hillman 2004). Especially it does not capture the Vermontness, the distinctive sensitivity, marked by stubborn independence that carries down to this day. Paradoxes define Vermont. The western edge (think Bennington), which is cut off by mountains from the rest, nonetheless is avidly anti–New York, while the eastern edge is Yorkist. The latter also harbor some royalist loyalties and mix Anglicanism with Old Light but yet accede to the coming nation, while the former harbor the Green Mountain Boys (i.e., terrorists) who aim for radical independence. I place the case in this chapter because I think the convoluted and disjunctive history and profiles of switchings sustain a diagnosis of Vermont as emerging personage, style.

4.8.2. Styles Must Mate to Change

Now explore a general conjecture: requisite for a new style is an intermediate period of overlay and melding between preexisting styles; it is followed by a phase of separation and rejection, whereby the previous ones may reestablish, possibly leaving a newborn style. Some orderliness of perception is presupposed and supplied in these large formations around styles, and change between one and another is thereby made difficult. One example is the emergence of impressionism in the nineteenth century, a style that eventually displaced existing ones centered on the French Academy (White and White 1993).

This new style became worldwide and hegemonic around its ideology of the avant-garde (for which consult Crane 1987). But the old, the Academic system in its day was also hegemonic around its own categorizations by content, function, and means. One could not continue to live in the same perceptual world through the change: in this case, one had to literally see differently. And concurrently, the social organization of art production had to come to be seen in an entirely different light. We return to this case in later chapters.

The point is that interventions about symbols as about ideas can never be separated from social formations among specialized cultural producers themselves (Peterson 1976). The cultural producers' own use of "style" as a term captures both the created coherence and the claimed decoupling from social formations. I develop this next in a second case study, described in more detail.

4.8.3. The Story of Rock 'n' Roll

Ennis (1992) has supplied an enormously detailed and persuasive account of the breaking through of rock 'n' roll music as a seventh wave within the genre of American popular music. The first six waves fall into two groups, three smaller, deeper, and purer source streams: jazz, gospel, and folk; and three larger, commercialized popular genres: country, black, and mainline pop (each has several synonyms and variants and historical tracks). As they become well established, styles such as these come to be the signature of an institution (Becker 1982; Hirsch 1972; Peterson 1976).

One can discriminate for each style of song a distinct complex of production together with audience and distribution and critic. The complexes vary in how much they tie to broadcasting, to records, and to live performances, and as to commercial versus nonprofit sponsorship. The principal split is between the first three and the last three, but Ennis makes a case for a separate institution for each of the six.

Rock was a scene of "reaching up" to get action, in many different respects at once. Rarely have so many streams of critical discourse, tutored or not, popular or not, agreed so emphatically as to the lack of value of an innovation! In part this was because rock evolved out of resonances with the concerns of a depressed minority, adolescent youth.

Ennis tracks how the initial songs of what in hindsight is a new style struggled into limited acceptance. One key was new technology that permitted much more audience differentiation, and tapped newfound purchasing power of adolescents in the mid-1950s. Another key was the generation of a looser kind of local circle of performances that supplied enough base for new technical resources, with which novel items could be broadcast without gatekeeping by established centers.

Intelligent and conscious maneuvering was there, from agents and disc jockeys marginal to the existing circles of self-supporting professionals in administration (agentry) as well as production and performance. But the key was spontaneous pickups crossing one stream of popular music into another, without necessarily leaving imprint on the established lists of top sellers. Only this endless crosscutting between different streams, protected by obscurity, brought enough artistic resources to bear to sustain a new form, which by the nature of its audience had scope of motifs more limited than usual.

The maneuverings were reachings-up into established—and highly irritated—scopes of distribution and critique. New social forms were created. Local circuits of dispersed small clubs sustaining local radio stations were sufficient to sustain existing separate streams and generate trial cross breeds (of which rock 'n' roll was but one). But the seventh wave would have subsided unless producers reached up into the broadcast network level of a Tin Pan Alley, and unless the creators of seventh wave music brought new musical resources to bear to make the limited substantive content of lyrics less limiting.

The evolution of rock 'n' roll was a paradigm of searching by structural-equivalence. From the beginning it generalized across styles, it self-consciously cut across boundaries, including the basic black-white split of American popular culture. A new sense of stratification came into play; adolescents for the first time asserted a standing, even a preeminence on important dimensions of perception.

4.9. Style as Control

There are two styles of cumulation that are accompanied by frequent, open efforts at control. Generalist oversight forced up out of the clash of specialized committees marks the style that I designate as "hieratic." I designate the other as "segmentary," from the tribal kinship pattern that exemplifies it.

Both styles reflect processes of guiding others' perceptions into relatively few and relatively segregated equivalence sets, or clusters. These are clusters both in reflexive analyses of ongoing actions and control attempts, and in similarities of perspectives as observed by outsiders. I will focus on the hieratic and just interpolate a brief sketch of how the segmentary style differs.

4.9.1. Hieratic Style

The hieratic is a generalization of interacting attempts at control that recognize and make intentional use of decouplings; so hieratic control is offensive, whereas segmentary control (detailed later) is defensive. In hieratic style, events segregate out into equivalence structures comparable to and parallel with partition of actors into structural equivalence sets. Autocracy is but the utopian extreme of the hieratic; autocracy is an attempted solution without intermediaries to the problem of wresting control. This extreme can furnish a basis for story-lines whereby control efforts feed into a broader effort at getting action, which can be tracked through deference in language, for instance (Agha 1993).

And so the hieratic stretches the construct of style in the direction of more tangible infrastructure. At the same time, the hieratic specializes the style construct around control.

The classic example of the hieratic is in separate social formations committed to fighting, the military. Active fighting requires control over friend and foe alike. A combat exhibits style. Fighting requires unpredictable alignments and changes of neighborhood and cooperation; it requires constant respecification of information and of the interconnections of actions. Equivalence within a rank, with attention focused on invidious comparisons to other ranks, opens up connectivity within the rank to a much closer approximation of all the possibilities inherent in complete interconnection.

Common across a wide range, historically, regionally, and culturally, is finding segregated levels within a body of military, with formally distinct production tasks. Analysis of this example suggests that interchangeability, or structural equivalence of all within a level, is as important for getting military action as the hierarchic ordering between levels. There is more freedom of maneuver to string together coalitions, because of equivalence within a level, and thus more leverage for overall control, given strict precedence between levels.

A related but singular example is the Roman Catholic Church (cf. Greeley 1979). In common thought, the church's hieratic flavor is associated with quietude, but this mistakes the reality. Recognition and engrossment of partitions of events and of actors into absolutely distinct levels of purity, and power, tend to cut or atrophy the otherwise endless strings of interconnection within the concrete functioning of the church. Such truncation of chains of contingencies makes interventions more calculable. And this segregation makes all attempts to reach for control more visible, with the end result that only those from high up in levels, or from very far down, have legitimacy, are seen in the story-lines of all as consistent in their identities.

The obvious view is that hieratic form is asymmetric, unidirectional, from the top down. This is to mistake formalism in story-line for the underlying likelihoods given the concrete organization. A detailed study of ethnicity and revolts within the Nigerian military (Luckham 1971), for example, suggests that hieratic segmentation into a few structurally equivalent sets is also easily exploitable by insurgents from lower ranks. Numerous similar ethnic turbulences within that and other armies since then, in Africa and elsewhere, led sometimes by noncommissioned officers, confirm the suggestion. The arousal and conduct of such insurgence is not predicted simply by this, but the hieratic style in itself is exploitable symmetrically, exploitable from below as well as from above.

4.9.2. Committee Styles: New Guises for the Hieratic

Extreme ostentation has gone out of style; so in the current world the hieratic comes in new guises, but it yields the same impacts in getting action, even without gorgeous uniforms. "Committee lattices" is my designation for what ostensibly are organizations and actually are new story-lines in which the hieratic style can be embodied in today's world. Follow Vancil (1984) in his contrast of committee style in the governance of General Electric (GE) with that in the governance of International Business Machines (IBM) before the 1980s. One such committee may be described as council discipline (cf. Lazega study in chapter 3) or as arena discipline (cf. Gibson study) or as production interface, but the lattice of committees is a distinct emergent level.

IBM runs on the story-line of being a single business, and its management committees bring together functional specialties. Conflicts and disagreements within and between initial committees are not just inevitable but encouraged, as the vehicle for getting action. Action stirs first in flows of appeals in what turns out to be a hieratic structuring of committees into clusters by level. Getting action can come both via pruning the appeals as well as via developing them. The initiative is coming from below, much as in the Japanese management style of "ringi" (Yoshino 1968; Yoshino and Lifson 1988).

All managers wore shirts of the same color in IBM, just as Japanese managers differ little in dress, but the impress of the hieratic is of magic, and it is as easily coded by trifling differences in pay as by velvet over fustian on office furniture. One decisive point is that a few distinct levels of magic are the shelves into which all IBM committees are sorted both by themselves and by others. The second is that there are no unique individual identities, either of actors or of events, but rather a structurally equivalent set of magicians.

An important indicator is the development in IBM, as in many other large firms, of a collegial chief executive as committee. In IBM this has been a three-man chief executive office. The hieratic style is not an architecture, a set of rules or the like; rather the committee clustering system is a style; it is a flexible lattice of constraints and leads for making action possible.

It is not the committee in isolation but the arraying of committees that is crucial. The looseness of agenda, the flexibility of mobilizing issues and timing interests to which March has drawn our attention (March and Olsen 1976; Cohen and March 1974), depends on there being a flexible field of occasions for and meetings of and attendance at committees, who can also cite and call one another. By contrast, fully settled committees become opaque; perhaps each turns into a council discipline that blocks action. Unsettling committees requires not just conflicts, and jurisdictional and appeals interfaces for sustaining unsettling, but also some such longer-range influence as emerges with hieratic style.

4.9.3. Segmentary Style

These last committee variants of hieratic style have to be crossed with the initial analyses to obtain the sort of context in which instead a defensive, segmentary style has been evoked. Tribal regimes around kinship are at once hierarchic and yet loosely followed, as is seen in a range of classic treatises such as by Fortes (1945, 1949) on the Tallensi, Evans-Pritchard (1940) on the Nuer, and Hart and Pilling (1960) on the Tiwi. And even regimes around classificatory kinship also exhibit a segmentary fractionability in kin groupings that plays off the hierarchic (Spencer and Gillen 1927; Bearman 1997). In modern contexts, segmentary style is invoked similarly: see, for example, Star (1989) on early British brain science.

Agglomeration is the key to segmentary style in control, even if not in tribal or kinship contexts. Additional outreaches just accumulate, rather than get incorporated under the aegis of valuation ordering that has operational reality. So, segmentary control is defensive. Discussion goes around and around with developments recycling, not available to innovation.

4.9.4. Colonialisms, Old and New

There is an analogy between this hieratic lattice of committees in a business corporation and the style and format of British colonial rule, evidenced in prewar Burma (Furnivall 1948). "Natives" and British expatriates, specialists and generalists by background, were all mixed up together throughout a lattice of governance that was partly by courts and advisory councils and partly by district executives. The elite, the "fair-haired boys" in this as in the IBM example, could thereby mingle throughout layers and networks of the rest, enabling reaching through to an underlying population that could easily become very opaque. To be a generalist was the finest thing, in the British scheme, and its lattice of committees kept being regrown on structural equivalence lines of recruitment that dovetailed with the hieratic form of stratification emphasis.

Now consider parallels in style of controls to Dutch East Indies colonialism. Successful searching for control is prominent in both colonial situations, whereas it is difficult to find in functionally departmentalized governments or firms, as Chandler (1962) underlined. Dutch colonialism, in the East Indies, evolved a different form of committee system from the Burmese one. Yet the Dutch like the British system evinced a hieratic style (Furnivall 1948). Every manager in Burma was a magistrate, every manager in the Indies was an official: judge versus cop, that was the difference.

Both hieratic styles had emerged where small sets of outsiders, the colonialists, had to be reaching through if they were to maintain controls, much less get action, but the actions sought were different. Burma was to be directly productive, a sort of tributary economy. The Indies were conceived as a self-sustaining entity composed of innumerable productive sectors that could flourish in a context that made them transparent to the colonialists.

Next, a second example of an American company completes a balanced parallelism. General Electric, as laid out in Vancil (1979)[34] had a remote sector of general management, which, like Dutch colonialists, disdains hands-on production and its functional specializations; nevertheless, like the Dutch it uses a subtle lattice of committees to reach through to production interfaces. In General Electric, as apparently in the Indies, there is an elaborate cycling of draft strategy reports through committees over time that provides flexibility. Also, both administrations in historical fact were endemically changing their specific arrangements in "one last change that will really get it right." The hieratic style was reflected in the scope of autonomous time between meetings, for the importance of which consult Jacques (1956). It was also reflected in the dependent dovetailing of one layer of meetings on another. And finally, the hieratic was reflected in the use of diacritical symbolism of residence and office, dress and the like. The same held for Dutch colonialism. Dutch and British styles were nothing new, and there are other variants.

Roman imperialism operated through municipality, through a lattice crafted from preexisting committees, namely the notables of respective preexisting city-states (Garnsey and Saller 1987; Reid 1913). Republi-

[34] On GE, see the previous subsection, and one should also consult the Harvard Business School case studies done under his aegis that underlie Vancil's analysis.

can Rome actually forced and coaxed Italian tribes of all descriptions into the formation of cities (Stevenson 1939), and a hieratic style in lattice of cities and tributaries and provinces resulted. The state of Rome itself was a sort of general office from which Alfred Sloan of General Motors could have learned new wrinkles. This general office often tended toward hieratic lattices of committees that were conduits for reaching through (Eckstein 1987).

On a much smaller scale, the same style persists in many traditional American cities: Crain, Katz, and Rosenthal (1961, 1968) lay out civic contentions where invocation of a cascade of committees of higher and higher status is the only way that action was got. In other cities they studied, where hieratic layers could not be energized, paralysis stymied proposed action.[35]

Hieratic style can be episodic, and thus not be registered as long-lived lattices. Turn to the example of the War Industries Board. Cuff (1973) lays out the emergence of a shifting hieratic style of committee mobilization, in the eighteen months or so of America's leap into World War I with full industrial weight. Dupont, General Motors, GE, and the like do not figure prominently as actors. They figure through agents, persons drifting and popping in and out of the Washington venue for their industries, trade association, and commodity networks. There are literal committees, set up under the War Industries Board, with memberships, always at least dual between military procurement fiefdoms of long standing and variously defined opposite numbers from the civilian side. There was a public story-line, from Bernard Baruch, which prefigured the Tennessee Valley Administration story-line of David Lilienthal two decades later (Selznick 1955). This story-line of "grass roots" exactly avoided any mention of the hieratic style.

Later chapters will also bear on control style. Even in the examplar cases sketched earlier, style can seem a misnomer depending on period, locality, and so on, although an advantage of the term is the attention drawn to actual habits of interpretation in associated network population. This all bears especially on the colonialism examples, where ongoing life among the colonized can capture and distort the attention space of colonizers. When rigidity of cross-interaction grows, as it did more, for example, in India than in Burma (Parry 1971, p. 306), the ambience of control is no longer style. It is appropriate to turn now to the chapter on institutions with their rhetoric and organization.

---

[35] These actions were variously on school desegregation and on fluoridation.

FIVE

INSTITUTIONS AND RHETORICS

G OING to an appointment is an institution, sustained by a rhetoric of promptness played out in some public, large or small.[1] An institutional system shepherds social processes by channeling them, by configuring institutions through rhetorics in a way that proves self-sustaining. They draw heavily on structural equivalence as they invoke story-sets across networks. Blockmodels, introduced in chapter 2, can suggest architectures, blueprints for institutional systems. A given institutional system has selected only some among the very many homomorphisms which as analysts we can compute from blockmodels as being possible (Boyd 1991).

Kinship is the earliest exemplar and remains ubiquitous and important, but in this chapter most of the attention is paid to other realms.

Four broad sorts of institutional system will be laid out in turn, after I present some general theory about rhetorics. First, extensive treatment is given to careers, individually as institutions and also in systems. Stratification is then treated as a second sort of institutional system, followed by an extended account of the production economy as an institutional system of a third sort. Following that, tangible organizations are described as uniquely flexible templates that dovetail with, and evolve with, the other three sorts of system.

Institutions and rhetorics are akin to networks and stories, in that spaces of possibilities for the ordinary in life, of what will be taken for granted, derive from each pair. Rhetorics make institutions explicit just as stories make networks explicit. Rhetoric is the garb of a realm, much as story-set clothes type of tie. An institutional system has come to accommodate a wide range of disciplines and styles as well as networks within a realm, along with the particular institutions. They are gathered together with rhetorics that constitute that realm. And yet institutional systems also precede and influence, as well as build from, these constituents. Within each system, stories

---

[1] In social science usage, there are several connotations for the term *institution*: the broad architecture of functional areas (e.g., education, the arts, health, business as institutions); a special kind of organization infused by values (Selznick 1952, 1955); any social routine of behavior, such as a handshake; and so on. None of these alternatives is hostile to my usage, as will become apparent.

must continue to accompany local enclaves at the scale of disciplines and yet be configured so as to transpose across network populations and styles. The stories become mutually shared accounts when they muster through publics into rhetorics.

According to chapter 4, styles index profiles of tempo and of content in ongoing network processes. So styles report the interpretive tone and texture established in the dynamics of netdoms, as was also presented in chapter 1. Institutional systems, by contrast, concern longer-term cumulation into self-reproducing network arrays based on series of contingencies and collisions, whether anticipated or not.

Because chapter 4 has established that persons are separate from identities, I am free now to use conventional umbrella terms such as *actor* and *action*, along with *organization*. But underneath each realm, the channeling still focuses on switchings by identities among distinct netdoms. Deployments of rhetorics and styles enable the switchings, which can yield conventions as either practices or institutions.

I will draw here on subsequent chapters as well as on earlier ones. Most of these systems could not persist without renewals of actors and organizations that were not generated by the system itself. For example, the production economy must draw flows of workers and firms, not to mention changes in technical practices (e.g., Windeler and Sydow 2001). However, a career system does encompass its own demography.

In the following pages, I will elaborate around corporates and around realms, as guidance for action, and will offer examples of many scopes. Years ago, I proposed and analyzed an institutional system for culture at monograph length.[2] Here I put forward suggestions for doing more such studies, such as one focused on the production economy.

5.1. Origins and Contexts

An institutional system builds a realm among any number of gatherings among netdoms as corporates and disciplines, and also styles. Styles with their profiles of switchings come in various scopes. A single person can embody a style, which then covers the component identities of the person in his or her networks, as seen by certain others as well as oneself. After the fact, and thus not spread over time, the complexi-

---

[2] This earlier study is applied more widely in White 1993, chapter 4, which works with the 1993 edition of the original *Canvases and Careers* (White and White 1995), as well as with the 1991 translation into French by Bouillon, who provides expert appraisal in his preface.

ties of that personal life can be arrayed so as to fit some rhetoric. So a human person is spread out across different network populations, with any integration coming through institutions. The character of a person is induced through participating across several populations, though not as much among hunter-gatherers (Howell 1979; Rose 1960) as in more elaborated social formations.

Rhetoric for person invokes the fourth, the biographical, sense of identity given in chapter 1. This is identity as career, and I argue that it is this concept of person as career that channels switchings and thereby also creates person as style. On the other hand, changes of rhythm (of style) will put pressure on persons as rhetorics. "Practices" intervene in these dynamics.

Practices are usually implicit and capture how humans individually relate to their bodies and biophysical environment. But I also use the term, as Bourdieu did *habitus*, to discuss social habits, like the corporates in chapter 2 and turn-taking in talk as laid out by Gibson in chapter 3, which are not captured in explicit institution. Observers, whether within the given system or not, have their own practices: they develop pragmatics to construe meaning and action.[3]

Whether an institution is explicit or implicit, practices are the vehicles for enacting and reproducing it. Take an obvious example. The monarch as an institution depends on practices that have become so routinized that they are protocols: bows and other ways of addressing the monarch. Rhetorics such as those associated with etiquette provide guidance for participation in institutions that also helps to build them through persistent switchings. Rules of circulation during promenades at the Versailles court of the French monarchy are an example.

5.1.1. From Status into Contract?

Since at least Sir Henry Maine's *Ancient Law* (1861), a major theme across the social sciences has been modernization (cf. Inkeles 1991), recently turning into globalization (cf. Sassen 2006). This is just Maine's postulated universal evolution away from status—conceived as the nexus of reciprocal obligations enmeshing all persons and actions in traditional bonds ultimately derived from kinship; evolution toward contract—conceived as free-standing adults running around a cosmic beach playing some generalized tag in which coup is counted.[4]

---

[3] Seminal papers in practice theory are Bourdieu (1980) and Swidler (1986); Calhoun, LiPuma, and Postone (1993) and Breiger (2000) provide overview appraisals.

[4] The same issues bedevil evolutionary arguments about periods long predating our modernization, as in discussion of changes from moiety systems to cross-cousin marriage (Homans and Schneider 1955; Needham 1962; White 1963a). The issues are ones of universal analysis as much as historical periodization.

Inside each of Maine's adults is presupposed an apparatus of preferences, together with a hidden god enforcing the rules. As C. P. MacPherson has pointed out (1962), this contract theory of possessive individualism was believable only by the real social context of an emerging class, and so was contingent upon that context. More precisely, it was dependent, in the England of its genesis, upon the gentry as a fraction of a class unable to realize itself fully as the dominant formation.

Accounting for the putative trend from status to contract was the classical puzzle that, more than any other, generated sociological theory. It was in part an argument about identity, its sources and changes. Disentangling how order is created by competing agencies of control can yield understanding both of identity formation at the micro level and of macro-level trends. Generalization of identities is necessary to both enterprises. Discipline is one such generalization, rhetoric another. Each generates identities in the course of integrating disparate realms onto the same population. In so doing, it gains identity itself.

Analogous puzzles have continued being posed at smaller scales, in less global form and with the polarity interchanging. This has been true since Maine's time. The classical status-to-contract argument has been brought down to middle-range scope in organization-versus-market arguments. Recently, in the economic realm, the special form of the puzzle is "from hierarchy to market" (Williamson 1975), whereas a generation or two ago, it was the reverse, "from ownership to management" (Berle and Means 1932).

MacNeil (1978) reformulated the whole set of presuppositions about contract in his relational theory of contract, by intertwining them with aspects of status reciprocities. So, at middle-range scope, some theorists are arguing that the concepts of status and contract cannot be seen as unmixed poles; and others are arguing for contingency rather than unilinearity in movement between the two poles. Rational choice approaches deserve criticism exactly when they elide the decisive impact of context, which generates the very identities that rational choice takes as preset and unproblematic.

5.1.2. Contexts in Natural Science

An analogy from natural science can help us rethink the status-to-contract arguments. Consider a phase transition, which could be in patterns of electric-dipole order, or in antiferromagnetism. Transition from one phase to another is a radical disjunction, so this analogue is also instructive for the next section, which considers a radical disjunction in budgetary process.

Now focus on a homelier example of phases: take a liquid-to-solid transition (de Gennes 1979; Ma 1973; Ziman 1979). Temperature is important, analogous to how the larger context induces level of activity in a social example, because temperature calibrates the level of order and disorder. But the existence of phases, here liquid (Gray and Gubbins 1984) and solid, is a statement that "order and disorder" as a congeries of local arrangements must be referred to a wholistic context. This wholistic context, or phase, has a direct and overwhelming bearing on the topology of order, indeed the phase is defined by the topology. The analogy argues against the usual markets-to-hierarchies theorizing (Williamson 1975).

Transition from one wholistic context to another is a radical disjunction. Yet it must take some tangible form of intermediate behavior. Only in the past few decades has there emerged cogent observation of this, and also modeling of the process as distinct from mere endpoint thermodynamics. The transition is a system state of its own, although indeed typically it is narrowly bounded in terms of relevant parameters. Physical space, which heretofore seemed all-determining, loses its absolutely sharp character. The main line of theory, initiated by K. Wilson (1979), introduces a metrical measure of dimensionality ranging continuously—not discretely!—from at least one to four and more in various contexts. Spatial correlations almost disappear in the form of local orders.

Control and production, analogous to temperature and force-gradients, are the impetuses to social process. Both the social analogue to space and the analogue to molecule are emergent and negotiable; they are context and identity established by chance. But surely that is true of their physical analogues too.

The central point from this analogy is to think of contract as the phase transition itself, with "status" referred to the phase regimes on either one "side" or the other of the transitional regime. Contract is seen as exemplifying the switchings presented in chapter 1. Adam Smith himself never subscribed to naive notions of free atoms contracting at will in some abstract arenas, as his thought is commonly caricatured. But even the caricatures can be seen as real possibilities if hedged in sufficiently as being delicate, as being poised on a cusp of transition.

This cusp lies between immanent and contending wholistic contexts.[5] Yet another, wholly new, possibility emerges: the analogues to two different phases in physical material may coexist not in the narrowly circumscribed sense of phase transitions, but rather as two emergent and

---

[5] As in catastrophe models, for an overview of which see Fararo (1973).

negotiated contexts of possibility, which might co-occur. For that matter, these could be thought of as styles as much as institutional systems, since there will be stochastic signature in profiles of sensibility.

5.1.3. Situations, Stories, Networks, and Pronouns

Accountings of situations are sought by each identity for itself as well as vis-à-vis others, especially fellow members of some corporate (Davies and Harré 1990). Confusion about choosing and telling a story evokes guidance that comes in the form of sharing some set of simplified, stereotyped stories. There is a dual problematic here.

First, how does a situation come to be recognized? And then, how does the attention it garners become shaped? Mische (2007; Mische and White 1998) lucidly lays out the possibilities as captured in types of context for process within various realizations of publics. One could try modeling them in terms of game theory.[6]

The dual facet of the problematic focuses around network rather than around situations per se. Identities in structurally equivalent positions across a set of networks will tend to share stories for each of several types of tie. They will adapt their perception of a situation within those story-sets. That is, structurally equivalent identities are likely to share a set of mappings from story-sets across situations. The blockmodels discussed in chapter 2 are algorithms to search for possible rhetorics that can emerge out of social process in network population. Explicit interpretations may be ascribed in terms of roles in frames of positions, as for kinship. Story-sets in institutional settings mold the person.

The study of indefinite pronouns as indicators seems a promising approach (White and Mohr 2006). Indefinite pronouns too are couplers that mark ambiguity and thus wider interpretability, while at the same time they mark actors in deictic terms. Haspelmath (1997) is the guide to using this approach, which also relates to the use of discourse markers in oral stories as was laid out earlier in section 3.5.4 on Gibson's research.

---

[6] When most game theorists take on populations, they disdain network topology to focus on subtleties of strategic interaction between persons as entities taken for granted (Axelrod 1984; Bendor and Swistak 1991; J. M. Smith 1985). Boorman and Levitt (1980) take the opposite approach of folding strategic subtleties into robust response contingencies, in order to model how innovation can invade population by a network cascade process. Other game theorists (cf. survey by Riker 1982) turn toward very large but unstructured populations as in general equilibrium theory (Arrow and Hahn 1971; Scarf 1967, 1973). See also the section entitled "Entourages" in the previous chapter.

5.2. Rhetorics and Realms

Action and organization each derives from identity and control, yet each also presupposes the other, even while counteracting the other. The melding of action and organization induces theory from participants, as well as from observers. This is folk theory.

Rhetoric is theory for participants in institutions; it is folk theory in action. Rhetoric is an important building block of an institutional system. Common sense is the preeminent folk theory, which goes hand in glove with institutions of everyday life. Everyday life is the base realm, the realm that common sense inhabits. The term *common sense* reveals that rhetorics are jointly held, are shared, but we will see from cases in this and other chapters, that like styles, rhetorics also figure in dominations and exclusions.

Stories in sets define these network ties that can also support rhetorics across sets of persons. Some rhetorics point outside themselves toward a well-developed larger social context that supports styles, while rhetorics also themselves influence styles. Styles are supported by a certain context, and then they themselves shape rhetorics: so switching among netdoms shapes rhetorics, which justify these switchings. The larger context of a style may instead be a realm articulated in a control regime; we will return to this point in the next chapter.

One can compute within a network population, for example by blockmodeling, the recursive processes—the long loops of perceptions, together with control efforts and causation—which, along with contingency, bedevil analysis of a network population for its own members as well as for other observers. Then, as network populations overlap and interpenetrate, complexity increases still further.

Such computations point to and can identify further realms and rhetorics besides the everyday base. "Realm" is a metaphor like "level" and "dimension," but it is not basically spatial (although it is this too); it is basically social. Each realm with its rhetoric is grounded in some institutional system, which is the term corresponding to the pattern of recognition achieved in folk theory. Before developing this point for some particular sorts of realms, I will consider several general approaches next.

5.2.1. Luhmann's System Theoretical Approach

An interesting approach toward theorizing the evolution of institutional systems has been constructed over many years by the German sociologist Niklas Luhmann (1995, 1989). His theory's foundations are

(a) communication as the concatenating events that form social systems, together with (b) a second-order cybernetics perspective for these systems. The latter perspective refers to *autopoiesis*, meaning that the systems create themselves by observing themselves and their environment, using a certain code that allows them to disentangle their environment, which in turn allows for higher complexity in the systems.[7]

Luhmann's encompassing social theory arguably builds on narratives, which he defines as follows: "The communication—in the full sense of a unity of information, utterance and understanding, constantly controlled by understanding—that is incessantly stimulated forms islands of comprehensibility in a sea of meaningfully indicated possibilities, and these islands, as culture in the broadest sense, facilitate the initiation and ending of interaction" (Luhmann 1995, p. 417).

These islands of comprehensibility and their carriers allow for interaction to occur (overcoming the problem of double contingency, of who is making the first step in an interaction) and for specific meanings to evolve within a society. In my context, these islands of comprehensibility can be translated as the rhetorics of involvement[8] that facilitate the initiation and ending of the interaction. The further development of communication media then allows for higher complexity, as Luhmann explains:

> later above all the communication media of writing and printing cease to be fixed specifically to interaction and thus enable interaction and precisely thereby enable meaning specific differentiation within society. . . . One cannot dismantle the societal system into interaction systems. (Luhmann 1995, p. 417)

But Luhmann offers only thin descriptions of particular systems, as we will see in the next chapter.

Realm, like *rhetoric*, is an analytic construct that can apply at many scales. In Luhmann's theory, the realms such as law and science and business are themselves differentiated into further subsystems. There is some rhetoric in common across arts, but from my perspective the disjunctions between the arts are more striking, which might lead to questioning their clear positioning in a bigger subsystem. For example, American theatre can be seen as a realm of its own (see my illustration in White 1993, chap. 6).

---

[7] An interesting peculiarity of this approach is that human beings are excluded from social systems, but constitute its environment as physical and psychological systems. For a serious critique of the conception of the structural coupling of psychological systems and social systems, see Habermas 1975, pp. 426ff.

[8] These rhetorics of engagement are an important building block of the book on the development of national sports in America by Eric Leifer (1998).

Luhmann's portrayal is involute, with scarcely any mention of constructs concerning interaction, such as the networks that are foundational in my account (which Fuchs 2001a has attempted to graft onto Luhmann). I now turn to a theoretical framework that is non-Eurocentric, though it started from the opposed theoretical framework of Jürgen Habermas.

5.2.2. Effective Rhetorics from Hierarchies of Publics

Institutional systems can call upon rhetorics through some configuration of publics, often a nesting of publics.

In our current social science there are tendencies to bias other than personalism. In *Bonds of Civility* (2005), Eiko Ikegami exposes, to my mind, the Eurocentrism of Luhmann's functional subsystem view that was sketched earlier. Ikegami shows how the upper realm of Japanese society prior to modernity ignored and disdained civil life and kept what we would think of as middle-class and commercial and artistic fractions totally without law or state power. Then she skillfully weaves a picture of the evolution of a highly networked society quite below/outside what Luhmann would no doubt have thought of as the functional subsystems of state, law, and so on in Japan. Yet when one inspects modernity in Japan, it becomes clear that the below/outside aspect was indispensable in the emergence of the regime of modernity from the Meiji restoration onward. Ikegami is working on the specific constellations of aesthetic public spheres in medieval Japan, which contributed to the cultural specifics of modern Japan. In her formulation, publics and their possible hierarchical orderings have to be considered:

> The types, varieties and formats of publics in a society may be conditioned by the interrelationships among larger scale social networks. . . . The resulting interpublic relationships, often arranged in a strict hierarchical order, influence the contents and effect the social effectiveness of discourses . . . (Ikegami 2000, p. 1010). In short, it is not enough to recognize the multiplicity of publics, one must examine the dynamics of interrelationships of publics in the social field to understand the dynamics of emerging cultural properties. (p. 1012)

So publics might be understood also as accumulative spaces of practices and institutions, bound up in story-sets whose effect on society is determined by their positioning in the hierarchy of publics. Thus, unobserved dynamics as in the aesthetic publics of Japan, which created networks among all ranks of the Japanese society by providing different measures of status (artistic skills), might prove very influential in transition phases, when the hierarchy of publics changes. This masterful study points to the relation of a control regime and institutional systems. The Tokugawa control regime was built on vertical principles, "the organizational force that succeeded in reorganizing Japanese society along hierarchical lines was best represented by the samurai's vassalage organizations" (Ikegami 2005, p. 128).

The constraints imposed by the Tokugawa regime on prior important publics for the process of generating horizontal associations such as the sacred alliances of the "ikki," gave even greater importance to private artistic networks. Organizing most of the publics hierarchically, the regime insulated the practices of horizontal tie-creation established in the Middle Ages into the private artistic circles, which as a public had a very low position in the hierarchies of publics. At the same time, the "Tokugawa network revolution," the expansion of networks of trade, of the nation-state, and of commercial publishing, favored the extension of private aesthetic networks throughout the whole of Japan, a premise of the evolution of a proto-modern Japan. This public also allowed for the continuing importance of the politically unimportant emperor (p. 373) who again gained power through the Meiji restoration.

At the end of her book, Ikegami notes, "It is interesting to observe the development of ritual technologies in the Japanese aesthetic publics for creating and maintaining these publics in the face of challenges to sociability posed by political and economic pressures" (p. 384), which leads us to the role of rituals in publics and their importance for institutional systems.

5.2.3. Ritual as Calculus

Mary Douglas (1970) suggests that aspects of human bodily functions can stand for uncertain social contexts, which is to say for ambage in present terms. Douglas's argument has only bodily symbolism at work, but it yields a rhetoric that can fit the facts. Douglas's work argues the possibility of a symbolic calculus for unbundling and bundling of action in the same metrics across cultural as well as social patternings, for a calculus of trading ambage with ambiguity. Solutions to problems expressed in such a calculus are found in ritual.

There is also an opposite "take": ritual is specialized as a rhetoric in which a tight correlation of action in biophysical space-time is imposed. For example, in church liturgy there is exact prescription of times and location and movements.

Douglas distinguishes two social contexts, groups and grids, which translate roughly into the corporates and networks of chapter 2. Douglas takes her two contexts as total settings, each seen from the inside, for correlations, rather than as boundaries—the same approach as in blockmodels. Her first correlation translates into groups tending to exhibit high ambage and low ambiguity. This is a correlation from gamings through agencies that are played out in forming and reforming bundles of social connections. This "group" of Douglas's is an ideal type: it is homogeneous, it is the *Genossenschaft* of von Gierke: this group is comradeship with its intense ambage that plays as converse to minimized ambiguity in role and value—all with physical uncertainty bracketed and held constant.[9]

More generally, the moral evaluative components of rituals should not be allowed to obscure their great importance in sheer representation and cognitive explanation. Ritual expresses a calculus solution as a rhetoric. Fortes (1945) argues this for the tribal Tallensi society:

> Even a very simple cultural heritage or social organization may be composed of a large number of strands and elements whose interrelations make up a very elaborate pattern. . . . The core is the sacrifice. Personal feelings are of secondary importance. . . . At the level of social and political relations between clans . . . the social interests are more complex and diffuse . . . an organizing mechanism of a different order comes into play, the mechanism of ritual . . . so complex is the overlapping of fields of clanship . . . that the whole system might be compared to a piece of chain mail . . . the basic rule of interclan linkage is that spatial proximity is translated into terms of putative genealogical connection. Ritual collaboration and common ritual allegiances [external *bxcar* cult, Namoo cult, earth shrines, etc.] are indices of common interests and mechanisms of solidarity.

The "chain mail" of corporates overlapping is laid out quite literally for tribal members to learn. This is done by positioning and orderings at and among the unending succession of ritual gatherings, which also allow some play for change.[10] In modern times we develop some of the same capacities (Boltanski 1989).

Rhetoric is explicit, as in ritual; style is more implicit. Rhetoric is decoupled from stochastic contingency through its rigor of prescription in

---

[9] This ideal type is not restricted to small or simple settings. The classical polis is an illustration. In the words of von Gierke (1950): "The state appeared simply as *the* human association. All social ties were entirely derived from it. . . . The individual had ultimately no autonomous purpose" (p. 87). "No Roman corporation existed that had not first been recognized by Roman constitutional law as a political unit" (p. 117). As also in the Greek polis (Kitto 1958), the subtlety was in ambage and its yielding of policy by manipulation of gamings in social patternings. The polis, like the group of comrades, is insistently homogeneous in cultural terms so that there is little scope for ambiguity.

[10] In a fashion reminiscent of Mayer's Indian villages discussed in the next chapter.

story, but at the cost of blurring of network pattern in that context. Style, by contrast, works through and takes form in stochastic variation, at the cost of increased ambiguity in meanings and stories, but with enhanced similarities in network clusterings.

5.2.4. Disputes and Stories—Boltanski and Thévenot

Boltanski and Thévenot zoom in on some particular tie within a situation of dispute in order to examine the texts, whether in discourse or written, mobilized by each end, who also have an eye on some public (Boltanski and Thévenot 1999—summarizing work over a decade). The two authors focus on the syntactic and lexical cohesion within and across the texts over time. By so doing, they uncover a fascinating etiology around the justifications mobilized according to the critical capacities of the pair in the tie. Each justification takes shape into a plot played out among denouncer, victim, prosecutor, and jury.

But networks, I argue, resurface at once in Boltanski and Thevénot's central argument. The situation of dispute could have been triggered only within some public, and that emanates out of a tie's network, as we saw in chapter 2. Legitimacy is their criterion for denouement, and it amounts to coding as commonsense normalcy, a proper public. To describe the etiology, the analysts distribute justifications among six sorts of context called *cités*. These can be seen as distinctive sectors observed in the modern West among networks. Thus, *cités* are historical, like my examples of institutions or styles. And, indeed, recently Boltanski and Chiapello (2005) argued for a new, seventh *cité* as having become established since about 1960: I find it ironical that this is exactly a *cité* of networking seen by those authors as the latest fashion in management rhetoric, rather than as a foundation for all analysis, as in this book.

Boltanski and co-authors' contribution toward my project in this book is guidance on how to identify and specify stories, which I consider central for networks. I see those authors' deepest interest as focused on the insides of a tie, whereas mine is the ecology of ties between identities. Their emphasis on the critical capacity of actors parallels my search in chapter 7 for how one gets action. And their construct of "agents" resembles mine of identities. They too, like I did in chapter 2, derive much in terms of structural equivalence. They seek, as I do, story-sets that sustain instances of a type of tie in common as viable.

Boltanski and Thévenot are known for formulating the etiology of justifications in terms of orders of worth, to which I will return in the next chapter. Orders of worth are externalist, since they are what persons in a discussion can refer to as a legitimate way of reasoning, close to rhetorics. And orders of worth also comport with the valuation orders in this book that come as precedence orderings in network context.

5.2.5. Packaging Explanations

Stories within a network need not cause what is happening, but the package of stories is sufficient to account for what happens in an institutional system, if taken together with style to form a rhetoric. Actions may be erratic and zany under the usual pressures of contingency and chance from the physical as well as the social context, and also from the flukes of maneuvering for advantage. But the rhetoric that accounts for those actions, by invoking a fixed set of stories and the institutional arrangement thereof, induces the perception of regularity: that is its chief attribute, which supposes some mapping from rhetoric to institutional system.

Sets of stories are vital to maintaining as well as generating social networks among continuing actions at all levels.[11] Any of the general forms of explanation—stories or pragmatics or types of tie and story-sets—comes about through evolution. Evolution will always occur among packages that each contain multiple versions. There is some fit of each version to what happened, but what happened is also subject to contingency, control manipulations, and competing accounts. What eventuates are sets that can account after the fact for whatever happens. The set for identities was termed a *convention* earlier; *rhetorics* is the general term for sets of sets of explanations.

5.2.6. Emergence of Rhetorics

Rules of thumb are a primitive rhetoric. Rules of thumb (Simon 1945) come in packages, a simple form of the multiple stories that accompany embeddings into networks. But rules of thumb are very widely transposable across concrete social contexts and across role frames of interpretation. It is not an accident that rules of thumb are transmitted and vouched for along strings of interconnection. Rules of thumb have the property that they are unlikely to generate events; thus, they keep

---

[11] For methods of analysis, consult de Nooy (2006). For a fresh illustration turn to the evolution of a famous charity (Brilliant 1990): the initial purport of a medical foundation disappears as a new and simple cure appears through medical innovation. The standard story-set about treated cures and untreated disasters from syndrome x no longer holds. The foundation regroups by inventing a new story-set, a new rhetoric, again heartrending. One rhetoric is substituted for another with no major changes necessary in the behavior and ties of the foundation.

simpler the field of identities being rationalized. Consider ethnic minorities, for example. Ethnic minorities tend to be at a disadvantage in blocking action, but they can be at an advantage in getting action because their ties do not connect as densely into central groups. Thus, ethnic minority groups are less credulous of standard rules of thumb, which are transmitted along traditional strings.

Rhetorics can emerge along with stratification. Stratification is where valuations from molecular disciplines come together with networks of stories into larger, compelling formations of stochastic order, such as styles. Inequalities themselves are commonly by-products either of getting action, to which we turn in chapter 7, or of elaborate structures associated with blocking action, as we will see later in this chapter, section 5.5.1. Conversely, institutions and their rhetorics can in part be by-products of stratification (as in the caste and science template discussed in section 6.8 of the next chapter). They are by-products that, of course also must survive the evolution of that system.[12]

This by-product correlation with stratification helps to explain why, as we saw in chapter 4, it is so very hard to modify inequalities or the rhetorics associated with them. Planned repartition of rights and duties does invoke, and may induce, inequalities. But planned inequalities never are as large as inequalities that emerge as unplanned by-products. Inequalities are largest just at the disjunctions between social formations such as occur in liminal zones, discussed in section 3.7.3 (Turner 1974, 1969).

Put generally, an institution with its rhetoric is a robust abstraction from linguistic practices generated by the intersection of style and rhetoric as tendencies in networking networks of disciplines. Social sciences have emerged partly in this tradition of rhetorics. One classic rhetoric is the exclusive use of individualistic and dyadic concepts by people-changing organizations whose effectiveness depends essentially on the extreme wholism of a total institution (cf., e.g., Street, Vinter, and Perrow 1966, p. 73).

Rhetorics can also emerge as explicit articulations among concepts for use in control, as in formal organizations. These planned rhetorics are articulations that correlate across styles and publics. Such rhetoric evolves with a network of the control regimes to be discussed in the next chapter, so that rhetoric also, unlike its concrete messages, is not easy to change. It matters a good deal whether the extrapolation to perceived order comes down from higher or moves upward from

---

[12] There is some rhetoric in each field of scholarship, as a doctoral candidate facing comprehensive examinations should be able to testify. All these rhetorics are extraordinary languages that provide additional ways to conceal as they explain away social reality.

lower levels of embedding. Vichniac (1985), for example, draws an elegant contrast between British and French (metalworker) unions based on the respective realities perceived by lower- and by higher-level officialdom, and the resulting mismatch at any particular level.

5.2.7. Rhetorics, Disciplines, and Queues

A discipline and a rhetoric can come to characterize each other as a discipline embeds into a system. Stories are generated as explanations along with the embedding, and sets of explanations can shape practices as well as institutions that guide constituent identities. For example, take one of the interfaces presented in chapter 3. The same duality obtains up through larger formations, as we shall see for the production economy. Each of these rhetorics concerns just one species of discipline in one system, along with networks in the corresponding types of tie. So rhetorics, like styles, can come nested. Accountings of the cultural and the social thus play out together in a rhetoric, and are perceived by participants as framings.

Rhetorics appear in a great variety of other contexts and scopes. Queuings are rhetorics about how to service individual stochastic arrivals at a limited facility. Stocking algorithms, such as FIFO and LIFO (First In, First Out; Last In, First Out), are parallel rhetorics that institutions use for storing batches of arrivals to guarantee and smooth the flows to destinations. Both examples remind us that social organization also orients itself around objects and physical attributes of all sorts.

Queuing rhetorics are shaped by and around assumptions about the contexts of flows external to the particular facility and organization. Effective engineering shifts rhetoric toward a more accurate class of assumptions—the discipline of operations research arose around this task. Estimates are needed about impacts from extreme events such as breakdowns, which may be "natural" or a by-product of social organization, as when the right of preempting place in a queue is granted to some class of arrivals.[13]

5.3. Careers

The career of a person is an institution with rhetoric channeling across time. Careers get recognized only within an institutional system of

---

[13] White and Christie (1958) present and solve a stochastic model for "[q]ueuing with preemptive priority or with breakdown." Subsequently, Stephan (1958) presented a direct intuitive solution in terms of contingency chains.

careers. Rhetorics guide individuals' perceptions of possible futures as well as institutional characterizations of possible career trajectories and points of access.

Persons come into existence not singly but together, as by-products of, and set within, an envelope of control projects in network-population, as we saw in chapter 4. Yet, there are varied ways in which any given person may emerge and develop, ways worth studying. A person comes into recognition as a hybrid of ties with disciplines, a hybrid held together with stories. Any person is an uneasy balancing of disjunct identities that were triggered independently, which chapter 4 analyzed in terms of a profile across switchings.

Since a "person" is a continuing balancing act among distinct identities, often very disparate, no unilinear track of interpretation makes sense. The term *career* is misleading if it implies a unique track. But it does capture the idea that there can be some coherence over longer periods despite the switchings. Career as developed here is a construct that is applicable to other than personal actors, also. Career is constituted as rhetoric.

5.3.1. Development and Stories

Chapter 2 introduced stories as told about particular ties. And pressures toward sharing a discipline can themselves come as stories, in sets. But there is another basic constituent of storying: besides language and social spread there is time spread. Events strung together are a story. This is story as realized in time, just as ties realize story-sets in social space.

Meanings are not separable from structure, any more than social action is. A precursor to plots is the use of stories to frame the disciplines (presented in chapter 3) and the ties (chapter 2) over time. Stories do not cause social action, nor need they guide it. Rather, they account for it in much the way a certified public accountant gives account of the doings of a firm. Stories come as sets. Each story-set can account for a wide array of possible events, after the fact, in some range of social and ecological settings, to sustain a discipline or a tie and also a person.

There is nothing weird about being weird—it's normal. So our accustomed stories are just too tame to individually match reality, even of the everyday. Each "normal" story defining some "normal" path is itself a one-dimensional abstract not matching any real-life segment. It takes a whole set of stories to incorporate a segment of real life. It would take an abnormal, weird story to, by itself, describe a normal patch of an identity's existence. In this sense, our lives are all weird; it is the stories that are "normal."

Sets of stories are eminently practical tools rather than mere decoration. They are tools analogous to gears in mechanical machinery. That is, stories are ways to bridge between different scales. For example, by personifying a giant state or bureaucracy, an actor is enabled to conceive and maintain ties to such. Differences in scale make it all the more inevitable that stories come in a set able to accommodate to a given value whatever happens.

Dramas are another matter; dramas are stories that interlock and imply a discipline, imply embedding. It is appropriate to distinguish these dramas as a contrasting sort of rhetoric, call it vertical.[14] A longer story is harder to match to actual happenings. That match is important to the identities involved. But actual happenings are nearly unpredictable—even now, despite all our vaunted social science, we could not predict next week's social climate in some second grade classroom!

5.3.2. Story-Lines for Identities in the Fourth Sense

Given multiple stories available for ex post explanation, feedback is not tight from actual ravelings of networks among disciplines. Accountings are accepted whether or not the series of events would seem explicable to an outside observer. But this is possible only because story-lines organize the perceptions. Any particular story by itself would quickly get so far out of step with the ongoing situation as to be unusable.

A rhetoric can emerge in terms of story-lines. A story-line of stories is analogous to a path of ties; it is in a way an expansion of the path in words of that language. Each position generates at least one recurring path in a story-line as part of its continuing reproduction across distinct identities. Sets of stories become partitioned into story-lines able to accommodate whatever occurs with that position, in the reality of a stochastic, fluid context.

A calculus requires more specification of the intervening mechanisms for decoupling than was developed at the end of chapter 3. Indexing of one role by other coincident roles is what yields position. In this city, say, the citizen may be a member of the assembly, who is head of a family, who is a soldier. There, citizen may be a resident of the locality who participates in an economy. Decoupling is presupposed and must be enacted to make possible this identification of several identities as one position with several roles in distinct network populations. Story-lines build up out of such constrained stories. The

---

[14] For other social science usage of horizontal/vertical imagery, see, for example, Moore (1988) and Schwartz (1981).

time-frames are social times, which are constructed out of the application of story-lines. Hence, these times are multiple and not necessarily consistent (cf. general equilibrium models in Winship 1978).

Social time interweaves ex ante and ex post in ways that may not be available to the awareness of many or any of the conscious persons or other personal actors continually being regenerated in ongoing social patterns. Social time consists as much in switchbacks and other nonlinearities as it does in any linear sequence. Story-lines accommodate these irregularities of social time (cf. Ricoeur 1988). Story-lines can also be seen as rational expectations, in the modern phrase (Muth 1959; Hechter 1987), but only in a limited sense. Social time is as much a by-product as a shaper of social pattern, just as social space is a self-consistent field. So social times are by-products of story-lines. But physical realities of work also contribute to shape time and to shape population.

Story-lines must serve a number of contending identities. Story-lines survive in a matrix of contending control projects. There must be some correspondence between stories and the facts in physical space, and also the facts as may be seen by an observer in social space, but stories depend on each other as much as they depend on any other facts. So story-lines end up as a set from which is picked a parsimonious account that is consistent with control projects being pushed. Whatever comes to pass, and thus whatever process can be conceived, must be describable after the fact in terms of the story-lines.

Story-lines are explanation spread over time. And story-lines come at least in a pair. The members of a set form what mathematicians call a basis set. Each set of story-lines is a kind of orthonormal basis (Birkhoff and MacLane 1953) in terms of which to account for whatever observable comes along.[15] This is an accounting that does not itself lead to further shake-up of the events and actors already generated out of preceding mismatches. The pair (or more) that make up a story-line in some given context cover all possible outcomes, thus expressing the logic of the narrative (Scholes and Kellogg 1966).

Story-lines do constrain the accounting of process, constrain sifting into events as well as arrangements. Ambiguity is, then, the slippage between examples that have been articulated into a given story-line. This means that there are multiple descriptions available as plausible descriptions of process. Stories are paths both to the frames for, and to the by-products of, multiple levels of control. Each by-product is itself a resultant trace from interspersed movements of decoupling, playing off embeddings. Story-lines are devices accounting for this confusion,

---

[15] Price systems are in our day the best-known exemplars of such sets of story-lines—see, for example, Rapoport (1953) and Luhmann (1995).

before and after the fact; they do so as decouplers. Then there can be further slippage between articulations by different story-sets, when two or more are invoked as elements in a larger codification, a framing.

Story-lines intertwine structuralist with individualist viewpoints; they do so as decouplers. Collins's (1987) concept of ritual interaction chains appears to be similar to story-lines. So too does Goffman's frame (1974) concept. The story-lines approach also seems analogous to an approach taken on a much broader scale by Berman (1983): he has realities being dealt with in terms of parallel discourses of statute law, natural law, the common law, local customary law, merchant law, Roman law, equity, and so on.

Identities come from mismatches in contingencies and so perceive and try to control turbulence. An identity must have multiple possibilities from a story-line available so as to be able, ex post, to give accounts of whatever in fact is happening concretely. The constituent stories from a story-line must be shared.

Stories thus take form in social organization as distinctive sets over time, as well as in cross section for networks. These are packages of accounts that provide the multiple story-lines needed by a population of identities to situate themselves within the contradictory situations that gave rise to the identities. The identities include events as well as actors. Identities are shaped mutually so as to fit into sets of story-lines.[16] A person can be seen as a set of story-lines.

5.3.3. Positions and Plots and Events

Location of a particular identity rquires tracing how that identity came to embed in and be interlocked where it is. Position, therefore, gets elaborated into a historical statement. Position of an identity is its posture with respect to several disciplines and networks, and across levels. Position correlates with story-line, but requires several story-lines because of the reality of fluid, stochastic context.

To see persons, or organizations, chatting back and forth in everyday life is to see one primitive sort of plotting in operation. This is the framing of picaresque stories, stories about the concrete particulars of happenstance in a population, such that all actors stay within a stereotyped format. This is also stereotyped content, which would be for us,

[16] Story-lines as well as sets of stories should be correlated more explicitly with blockmodel applications. One such line of development is Abell (1987), another is Cicourel (1980), a third is Skvoretz, Fararo and Axten (1980); and see Breiger (1990), and more recently Grabher (2006).

in today's society, variously dealing with sports or children or discs as actors in the skits.

A plot decouples events in one role frame from events in other frames. Dually, events serve to decouple plots. The material for plots are story-lines. Plots deal in stock characters and scenes so that they can be transposed from one story-line to another. The combination of stock elements into a plot gives it an inner side that can furnish accoutrements for melding identities into further level as career.

One speaks of a plot when certain occasions always trigger one story-line from some given set of story-lines. Plot is built from a given set of story-lines. Plot accommodates positions, and yet plot can be transposed across a larger fluid context.

For example, movie-goers know the conventions in cowboy movies. The conventions work by relying on stereotyped positions for actors, call them positions or niches: greedy rancher, corrupt sheriff, heroic knight-errant, beleaguered family, and the like. And in a production market, complementary stories are used about niches for price leaders and the like, which also constitute a convention (see the earlier sections, and White 1981b). Stories can be understood by identities who are not themselves active in the convention and are also consumed by them.

5.3.4. Career System

The Rapoport-Granovetter tracing of connectivity (chapter 2) can be subsumed, in principle, in career analyses. And career analysis exhibits some similarity to blockmodels. Both are relativist, both can be couched in terms of structural equivalence. Also, both are concerned with specifying connectivity paths, the former in multiplex and the latter in multiple networks. So both can help analyze interactions among networks. But career does so at the cost of lumping together different aspects of relations within a given pair, as a multiplex tie. The contrast, in blockmodels, is to dissect ties into separate aspects and then treat each as a separate analytic network across the field of actors.

Careers, on micro and macro scales, generate envelopes in the perceptions of those involved. Careers are also the product of contingencies that can be described by envelopes of contingencies. These can and do embed persons across induced network populations, and do so through social interactions not heavily mediated by perception. Padgett (1990) has worked this out for careers of U.S. congressmen moving between committee assignments.

Envelopes are large-scale alternatives to disciplines in constraining joint action. These are whole venues rather than disciplines such as interfaces. So these envelopes provide a basis for rhetorics, in particular career as rhetoric.

An actor succeeds or not, and now rather than then, according to the actor's position; to specify that position requires rhetoric. Embeddings and their stories fix each position in its full sociocultural matrix. The whole of religion and of magic wrap around this (Durkheim 1915; Niebuhr 1959; Tillich 1963). So do modern descendants of religion: embedding is part of the realization side of the wishes encapsulated as justice (Zajac 1985). Rhetorics enable the evaluation of advancement in the past or future by an identity and surrounding identities, therefore serving as bases for future control efforts.

Career is a general concept applicable beyond persons, and beyond persons' positions. Terms in which actors perceive their social organization, and particular embodiments of those terms, also have careers. For example, the vacancies intervening between incumbencies can themselves be construed as entities having careers: for development of this theme, see the later discussion in this chapter and White (1970b), also Stewman and Konda (1983).

Consider budget construction as an example. Budget construction is also about the shaping of identities for social organizations that are themselves treated as actors. Budget construction is about the shaping of an interacting set of identities. Identities for leader disciplines require the promulgation of goals, that is, require kernels of interpretation from which successive strings of particular targets can be spun off in story-lines.

Stedry (1960) models the budgetary process in just such terms of aspiration level. Existing networks of contingencies and interrelations are hard to reshape to goals. These networks are reproduced among the actions of yet other disciplines that are closer to tangible production sequences, and which in a context of accounting take the form of projected budgets. Seams must be welded somehow across these independent shapings of identities as budget lines from above and from below.[17]

The disciplines each also presuppose some sort of time embedding, some memory. But in disciplines, there is neither the loose-jointedness of career, nor the decoupling of career and anti-career as played out

---

[17] Associativity (for which see also notes 19 and 23) in this welding process must be surprising. It matters very much whether the initial integration of disparate lines of interpretation is done first between B and O and then between the pair and L, or, on the contrary, the first reconciliation into a joint social form is done between L and B, and only then is an overall reconciliation attempted; all this without changing that the sequential order is L then B then O!

together. Within the arena discipline, complementarity of specialty being held constant presupposes long-term memory. Within the council discipline, the endless shifting balancing of coalitions exhibits short-term memory. The string architecture of kinship that often lies underneath the mobilizing discipline codes in long-term memory.[18] And commit interfaces generate embedded identities that are material to careers. But none of the disciplines are loose enough in construction to support or require such loose coupling as in careers.

Not only disciplines and budgets in place of persons, but also the ties that analysts use to code connections into networks, can have story-lines. A long time frame for a tie is partly unavoidable given its phenomenology. Even the most intimate connection is only enacted occasionally, so that a tie must always in part be a memory, a memory negotiated among parties in control struggles in that neighborhood.

The time frame for network ties is also the focus of much struggle for control, for discipline, and for standing. Field studies (Jacques 1956) have demonstrated systematic variation in the length of time before ties have to be reenacted. There is very high correlation from the length of time to acquiring official status and to leverage for actual control. Discretion over the spacing of reports, and thus autonomy, is a main focus of larger structures of control.

The time course of an agency-form can become reified, but it can also be enacted so variously that it is recognized as once more broken apart, as having a career. Take an example: the evolution of administrative formations through the medieval period of the English monarchy (Chrimes 1952). The wardrobe, the exchequer, the chamber, the council, all began as interfaces (using the present terminology), concerned with running a household on a royal scale, with feudal technology.[19] What the detailed historical record shows is the subsequent evolution, slow and painful, of these royal interfaces into what we recognize as today's instruments of administration with general and abstract fields of activity (van Doosselaere 2004).

The point is a double one: first, the form of a discipline itself—one of the species discussed in chapter 3—can split and evolve. Thus, that species throws up exemplars of new embeddings for specializations. Second, a particular discipline will be defined, for its constituent actors and for others, partly through its particular career.

---

[18] This guarantees the nonassociativity of mobilizing; Boyd (1991, pp. 8–9) gives a lucid prose discussion of associativity in network relations.

[19] No doubt each also had come as the later career of a yet more primitive interface in smaller households.

5.3.5. Contingency Chains

We have seen that careers are anticipations, or careers are retrospections. That leaves the question: What corresponds to career not *over* time but *at* a time? Vacancy chains do: see White (1970b) and Chase (1991). The importance of vacancy chains is appreciated best in systems of control that focus on careers, as we will see in chapter 7.

Objective, measurable traces of connections among disparate social spaces are needed, across both networks and populations. Such traces are best sought in changes and motion, for it is too easy to project some elaborate architecture into any static, cross-sectional view. The traces sought can be called contingency chains, of which careers are prime examples. A vacancy in a job decouples, and it too can move in a chain of decoupling among jobs at a given time.

I examined mobility in detail in the special case of large organizations where opportunity came in single-occupant jobs (White 1970b). It is clear that chains of moves by vacancies, not persons, were the causal dynamic in mobility there. Even when there were central authorities who, at least in principle, could direct moves, these had to fit into vacancy chains. And this was generalized to the much less restrictive case of the Federal Civil Service (Stewman and Konda 1983).

In addition, jobs fit into careers, whose manifest content is coupling over time and among identities hypothesized to evolve. But careers also exemplify decoupling. Career is meaningless if preordained; so where careers are perceived, flexibilities of decoupling exist as well.

Careers, like queues, become the occasion and context for control efforts, as persons emerge and try to achieve style. Story-lines, told around identities, are where stability and permanence and coherence can be found because they are sought there. They may be propounded and also enforced as careers in the building of networks, and of disciplines for production.

A career links disciplines that thereby may be mediated into yet another identity, and a career acquires uniqueness only in that way. Career as construct implies activism and some search for agency. Career is not merely a neutral measurement construct, although it is that too.

Think of tenures at given jobs as a sort of tie between job and person. Careers are made of tenures and so go beyond social space, and site networks in social time. Careers and blockmodels provide contrasting approaches to uncovering compoundings, that is, the equivalences and subtle interactions that must underlie identities as disciplines. Through blockmodels we can conjecture, from reports treated as a cross section in time, about the enormous pressures toward equivalence that must come from the endless cycling of transactions and signals along paths in networks. Career concepts and constructions pick up more on contingencies, and build upon overall subtleties in particular dyads.

Careers may be touted as objective reports of realities and realistic choices, but there must be much of both speculation and hindsight in that presentation. Rationality may be attempted in the career, as part of a broader search for control, but the very meaning of rationality depends on a structure across levels embracing many careers. Careers are actors time-extended in terms of contingencies; careers are perceived as such and embedded by others into a larger system.

5.3.6. Career and Anti-career

Anti-career goes along with career. An obverse of embedding is decoupling. When business consultant Jacques is showing the increase in unsupervised, unaccounted-for time span that comes with his higher position in business firms,[20] he is also showing a change in boundaries of career. At one end, a clerk who is under close programming of time, is enacting career on a micro-scale within daily activity. However, that same clerk may have no career horizon at all in the perspective of longer intervals with which we started. One can contrast micro-time career with macro-time anti-career.

Upper managers exhibit a rhythm opposite to clerks' rhythm. Life is picaresque on a daily, hourly scale as their binding in disciplines and identities calls forth erratic fire fighting following upon perceived contingencies.[21] But at the same time, these managers are always pressed to be endlessly shaping their possible changes in position over the longer intervals into structured sequences, into careers. Managers have careers on a macro-scale of time but anti-careers on a micro-scale.

Careers and anti-careers alike relate alternative identities to network contexts, to changing contingencies. They both presuppose and induce joint perceptions, which are of some complexity and which can only in part ever be realized in actual patterns. Spilerman (1977) offers systematic exposition of the stochastic envelope of such patterns. A career embeds identities from different chunks of time. So a career is partially analogous to a discipline, as well as careers constituting networks over time. Furthermore, careers—and in general, anticipated memories—induce multiple possible identities in their story-lines. Without careers, one imagines systems that could not contain beings whom we would

---

[20] That is, with high standing as confirmed by observed autonomy.

[21] This has been modeled formally by Radner (1975a, b), who demonstrates desirable efficiency properties.

recognize as people. Persons have unique identities thrust upon them like the beached litter of ongoing social processes and embeddings.[22]

5.3.7. Projecting Reality

Constructing meaning is vivid to actors in connection with their whole careers, not just with their initial selection of career paths. But their perceptions, colored by the agreed set of story-lines, may not correspond to ascertainable facts. This is not a mere convention of our era and locale.

In the tenth-century a.d. transition from T'ang to Sung dynasties, there was an important innovation in a tangible social mechanism of middle-range order (Whitney 1970). This innovation illustrates well the unusual importance for social ordering of time embeddings in all their multiplicity. Careers were implemented in the three functional sectors (civilian, financial, military) into which administrative activities were seen as divided. No doubt there had been a long prior period of merely factual sequences of distinct local positions held by particular persons; "careers" then came into existence as certain shifts became anticipated and consciously enacted. The significance of a later-held position is different according to whether it is merely a fact or is also the fulfillment of an anticipation: this is precisely the significance of career.

It does not follow that careers must interlock through networks or through levels of embedding. The formal positions in a sequence can,

---

[22] There is a further basic aspect of time cumulation in social process. It goes beyond the Markov property and its negation. It is yet another way to put, in more general terms, the career versus anti-career confrontation. One tends to assume associativity in any formal rendering of processes. That is, only time order counts—to know that the sequence of three events is L then B then O is to know the important aspect of ordering. But when the events occur in a process across a network of changing identities of actors spread among interfaces, the sequence aspect may be minor. In projects of control and joint production, efforts at shaping joint identity continue with great energy during, before, and after the "present." Bindings into one or another interface and embedding and story-line and envelope are the turf of contest. Nonassociativity in the mathematical sense (Kurosh 1965; Birkhoff and MacLane 1953) may result. That is, if B and O are wrestled together into a joint form that imposes its reality, the outcome of the sequence with L may be entirely different from the flows and other outcomes when it was L and B that were first bracketed together into a merged form. The letters L, B, O, suggest one family of examples, a famous wave of leveraged buyouts on Wall Street (see Eccles and Crane 1988). The most familiar field of examples around us are in accounting, the shaping of budgets and the "control" of expenditure. Zero-based budgets, policy budgets working down from goal figures to concrete program expenditures—these provide ready illustrations (Padgett 1981).

but need not, be identified within some cumulation of disciplines (e.g., embeddings of commit interfaces into an authority tree). Positions can also be defined by localities and other ad hoc designations. Careers can come about simply on a basis of concrete population.

Careers can be more than stereotyped particular sequences, or a choice between sets of subsequent stereotyped sequences. When the subsequent position cannot be predicted adequately just from knowledge of present position,[23] careers play a more formative role. Careers contribute by this formative role more to the embedding of levels into one another over time. The corresponding tracks of positions that are reported are therefore more varied.

"A good career," or vita in modern academic parlance, is more than just the quality of the particular job; it is the balance and diversity of the track as perceived contemporaneously. Non-Markovian careers give scope for control projects. These can be undertaken both by incumbents and by others interested in playing a hand. Contention can arise from different ascriptions of identity given a person's vita. The central dilemma could be whether such a vita is adequately matched to requirements or specializations of a certain institution, such as an academic department or governing board.

Since careers are as much perceptions as they are accomplished tracks, their scope of influence can be the greater. In the Sung period, it seems that triple the number of persons actually in any position regarded themselves, and were regarded, as eligible for and therefore participating in the system of careers. We can see the same phenomenon around us today in common use; this is the basis for our credentialing industries, schools of business and law and medicine as well as faculties of liberal arts for awarding degrees. Careers tie to the style of professionalism.

5.3.8. Demerits of Merit Systems

Take an extended example of recruitment into organizations, and how they interpenetrate style. Modern civil service recruitment in Britain, at its upper levels, in the 1880s was shaped by a major change in style to a "merit" system, the famous Northcliffe reforms (Kelsall 1955). This can be seen as a regression from career in the style sense back to an institution. Or it can be seen as the emergence of professionalism.

The ostensible core of the new system was an examination that was strenuously academic. The topic itself was sufficiently recondite to give a closed-corporate cast to candidacy: Classics (Greek and Roman)

---

[23] Careers are non-Markovian as probabilistic sequences (Feller 1968).

dominated in the early years when classics could be studied effectively, at the highest level, only at the elite universities, at Oxbridge. As Kelsall shows with great care, the style of examination, partly viva voce, as much as the content, made successful competition next to impossible for those not from the "right set."[24] Structural equivalence predominated here and shaded into closed corporation.

The earlier recruitment style had been much maligned as permitting a "spoils system" to operate and thereby often letting in unsuitable if not dishonorable candidates. This earlier system was very much a matter of networks. The Walpole era in the eighteenth century had made no pretense at a coherent civil service (Plumb 1967). Back then, recruitment had constituted a true spoils system.[25] By the mid-nineteenth century, the idea of coherent frames of paid offices in a bureaucratic mold was emerging, and the total number of positions was growing sharply. The result was pressure for episodic and ad hoc use of whatever network ties came to hand for recruitment. As Kelsall makes clear, and as he illustrates with vignettes, someone often got plumped into a civil service post in an arbitrary way through a tie that could have been quite casual.

It should be noted that some of the most creative and notable members of British government came out of these casual networks. The actual choice often was not lightly made: able men had an eye for the novice "clark" or tradesman's nephew who showed remarkable wit and energy. On the other hand, Kelsall conclusively demonstrates that class bias in selection was enormously greater under the new "reformed" mode of civil service recruitment. Stories did and do not jibe with the facts, as a blockmodel after adaptation might be able to show.

5.4. Stratification across Realms

Stratification induces native theories of orderings and their boundaries. Sociology itself can be seen as one such rhetoric. Yet at the same time, stratification is curiously elusive to explicit analysis, except in the extreme case of a social class system with explicit rules and enforcements.

This elusiveness should be juxtaposed with the intensity of phenomenological experiences of invidious distinctions and blighted chances. Social stratification manifests as invidious sensitivity from what initially, at micro level, are just the happenstances of opportunity

---

[24] It was, of course, possible, if one took aim early on, to achieve membership in the gatekeeping mechanism so that the ostensible fairness was not entirely bogus.

[25] Of the sort taken up under clientelism in the next chapter.

supplied by momentary positioning. It is not surprising that the early and best analyses of stratification (e.g., Svalastoga 1959; Hollingshead 1949) require tangible groundings in disciplines and ties and locales as well as persons. Stratification might be analyzed as a super-catnet (chapter 2) of profiles resulting from stochastic interactions within networks and disciplines.

Control struggles among identities do come to be constrained by the stasis of stratification. This stasis can consist in size distributions thrown up from specific and particular blocking patterns into which control interactions of identities settle down. One bias in particular obscures perceptions of stratification: only occasionally are the same story-sets that account for action in lower strata made available in high culture, as, for example, Rabelais did centuries ago (Bakhtin 1968) and the War on Poverty of the 1960s in the U.S. did for a few years in street murals (Cockcroft, Weber, and Cockcroft 1977). Conversely, high culture is made unavailable to lesser folk (DiMaggio 1992; Lynes 1954).

The central point is that stratification is an emergent patterning that cross-cuts the realms from all institutional systems. This point will next be highlighted by a study focused on human health.

5.4.1. Blocking Action

Choice being blocked by the stratification system is not a mere abstract notion; it impacts upon lives in the small and in the large. Misery and opportunity are both facets of blocking action; they are two sides of the same hard social die. Misery can be articulated as it becomes an aspect of a style. And opportunity knocks only in a rhetoric, as a signal to one position concerning other positions.

Mobility is often studied as the movements of actors, but this omits the other face, of what opportunities exist to attract and enable mobility. To understand how mobility changes lives, one has to examine and tally chains of contingency and understand their interdependencies. I develop this further later in sections on careers.

Stratification as blocking action supplies the phenomenological basis for an empirical argument by Bruce Link and Jo Phelan and coworkers about how pervasive the impact of socioeconomic status is on mortality rates.

Medicine and epidemiology currently dominate the study of the strong association between socioeconomic status and mortality. Socioeconomic status typically is viewed as a causally irrelevant "confounding" variable or as a less critical variable marking only the beginning of a causal chain in which intervening risk factors are given prominence. Yet the association between socioeconomic status and mortality has persisted despite radical changes in the diseases and risk factors that are presumed to explain it. This suggests that the effect of socioeconomic status on mortality essentially cannot be understood by reductive explanations that focus on current mechanisms. . . . Socioeconomic disparities endure despite changing mechanisms because socioeconomic status embodies an array of resources such as money, knowledge, prestige, power and beneficial social connections that protect health no matter what mechanisms are relevant at any given time. (Phelan et al. 2004, p. 265)

What style does is exactly override particular tangible mechanisms in reproducing a sensibility. The research team goes on to test its claim:

The following prediction from the theory: For less preventable causes of death (for which we know little about prevention or treatment), socioeconomic status will be less strongly associated with mortality. . . . We tested the hypothesis with . . . 370,930 respondents followed for mortality for nine years. (Phelan et al. 2004, p. 265)

Confirmation was strong and uniform across subpopulations of various sorts, with as much as a 1 percent gap in cumulative survival, both as between strata (judged by educational attainment) and as between high and low preventability causes.

5.5. Production Economy as Institutional System

What we recognize as our "production economy" has been built by trial and error in historical process rather than according to a cultural blueprint. In the past twenty years, partial replays of this process have been under way in production systems in Eastern Europe (e.g., Stark and Bruszt 1998) and in Asia (e.g., Feenstra and Hamilton 2006). How the institutions of such systems channel and coordinate the underlying switchings of netdoms is enormously complex, not easy to uncover, but I can offer sketches.

In our own economy, the institutions of such systems cluster around terms for deliveries of production in networks among firms, which are the principal actors. Rhetorics get activated on multiple levels. Our present system operates across an array of production markets, but this builds out of earlier systems that concatenated agency and occasion. In such "putting-out systems," profiles of repetitive transactions get cumulated, as we shall see. Sequences in payment for delivery are the switchings being channeled. These putting-out systems evolved from networks of traditional work groups.

5.5.1. Prior Evolution

Udy (1959), in his study of tribal work groups, uncovered a general truth (Udy 1970): material production is limited mainly by the ubiquity of control projects among actors concerned with their mutual standings rather than with production per se. This suggests decoupling as an antidote. Decoupling was recognized early as essential to control in production; for example, for the factory insides of manufacturing by the engineer R. W. Shepard (1953).[26] Much the same argument can be made for Asia (Feenstra and Hamilton 2006).

Social forms such as the discipline species detailed in chapter 3 are emergent designs that can ease decoupling in building a putting-out system. Decoupling is recognizable within all varieties of markets and market systems. Their institutions in price-setting can build in decoupling with embedding in flow transactions. We have seen this with the commercial network systems already described in section 4.2 (and to be taken up again in section 6.9).

Lawrence Stone (1965, chap. 6) supplies an account of work arrangements on the largest scale known during just the intermediate European centuries in which the all-encompassing history which we now take for granted was coming into existence (cf. also Anderson 1974; Braudel 1982). It was a context where, especially at the scope of noble estates considered by Stone, decoupling mechanisms were new and raw, more visible and transparent.

The apparent paradox was that to free production for effectiveness, one introduced decouplings of one manor from another, one form of husbandry from another, even decoupling of one accounting language and format from another, in order to achieve some control and some choice in operation, exactly because there was some separability and accountability.

> This intellectual and technological revolution—for it was no less—meant that by the beginning of the seventeenth century it was at last possible for the lord of many manors to keep a close check upon his agents and his agents upon the tenants. (Stone 1965, p. 311)

There are parallel accounts, such as Chrimes (1952) and Roseveare (1973), for the parallel and earlier seizure of control in production by the state in England. Each of these occurred via new forms of decoupling and devolution, so that the painful awkwardness of each step makes it easier to trace and to understand the resolution of the paradox.

---

[26] This was followed up by economists Fuss and McFadden (1978), but their formalist adaptation seems to miss his central phenomenology.

5.5.2. Origins of Putting-Out Systems

The putting-out system enabled (actually later in Britain than on the Continent) regular flows of product not just embedded in and through the operation of manors (Bythell 1978; Kriedte, Medick, and Shlumbohm 1981; Lachmann 1987; Najemy 1982).

Markets come under a new light in such system. Systems of exchange markets spanning large distances come in between. Such a system is complex; it is both a means of embedding and coupling and a means of decoupling. A prior transition from barter to monetary transactions was a necessary precursor to long-distance trade and to putting-out networks. New forms of decoupling were made possible because new forms of embedding had been evolving. Neither of these transformations is a matter for a particular market; instead each presupposes, and only emerged with, new rhetorics of business relations that went beyond patronage and agency.

There are two developments to trace.

Speculative gyrations are one possibility, an extreme form of decoupling. Speculation becomes endemic and exploitation is achieved thereby. Speculation can decouple production from use and yet at the same time guide in structuring exchange networks. Speculative moves sketch the routes later followed by emerging putting-out systems. Rationality seems a sideshow, since speculation is far more concerned with timings and interaction than with considerations of optimality and the other apparatus of formal rationality.

The second development is reinforcement from parallel rhetorics, without which the complex channelings of markets might not get established. Putting-out systems are the form taken in production of goods by the same sort of projects of control that led to what was called venality and corruption in state administration contexts, discussed later in this chapter, in 5.7. Each may be seen as lowering efficiency; at the same time, each can be seen as increasing exploitation. Many stories are possible and are used in these networks. There is no neutral ground in actual social organization that permits meaningful measures of efficiency that could differentiate it from exploitation. Exploitation itself can be seen in terms of interacting projects for control amid numerous passive social actors. These concepts are relative and social rather than absolute and technical.

Unless input-output coupling for supplies to local sites becomes established, local disciplines will not reproduce, and there is no settling in of production.[27] And it is a lemma that specialization always signals

---

[27] In Florence and other Italian cities of the early Renaissance, production of cloth induced networks for "putting-out" aspects of producing a product, each of which aspects could itself become established as the product of a separate market (e.g., Lachmann and

corporatist efforts at embedding to escape projects of control. Putting-out and venal systems are less specialized than bureaucracies became as they grew common, but that is not just a matter of architecture. They are processes that exemplify decoupling and introduce stylistic elaboration. Decoupling is an active process that cannot be frozen into a form but is always playing against existing embeddings.

5.5.3. Embeddings into Production Markets

Our modes of discourse take the parallelism between firms and persons for granted, personalizing firms as actors; so can network analysis. The present analysis traces back to the work of Bott (1957) and other anthropologists on traditional sorts of personal embeddings in networks of affective ties. Embedding in a kinship system results from each actor not only knowing entailments and warranties as to further relational roles, but also being known to have that knowledge. By analogy, the firm may become subject to, and be known to be subject to, the hegemonic pressure exerted by the others engaged in the continuing reproduction of a distinct identity as market. So there is also a decoupling for firms from the original underlying networks. No longer need warranties and entailments approve or embargo particular further ties across the downstream market interface. The social discipline over member firms by market profile, itself built from networks, can be strong enough to substitute for these habits and particularistic injunctions (an alternative is taken up in the next subsection, 5.5.4).

Firms may embed into a production market for an industry, following the template laid out earlier in section 3.3 as interface discipline. The industry takes on a life of its own as a distinct actor, a separate identity, only by gaining general recognition of its siting. There is some leeway as to exactly which firms and industries transact with each other in a given period. But a pervasive polarity of upstream versus downstream survives this decoupling. This remains true even for markets at the edges dealing in raw materials or with consumer purchasing.

How do markets, in turn, fit among other markets? Production markets are constituted only through embedding into networks, but this embedding is more general than the standard current definition, which was provided by Granovetter (1985). It is not that persons are not in-

---

Petterson 1988). There were similar developments into *verlager* and *kaufman* systems (Kriedte, Medick, and Shlumbohm 1981), in the hinterlands of medieval networks of German cities, as early entrepreneurs "put out" raw materials and/or tools to cottagers and then "marketed" the resulting production, which they collected. And the process was elaborated further in subsequent periods and locales (e.g., Bythell 1978).

volved. The point is that the patterns of action can, in some contexts, come to be interpretable as, and taken as, emanating from actors on a second level. Now let us reapply that point, with *market* replacing *firm* as the second level.

Formulas for embedding firms in a market define niches in a first sense. Here niche is one of a set, as niche for one producer within the rivalry profile established in some market. But this notion of a representative firm and its niche suggests the further notion of niche applied to a market as a whole, when it is taken as an actor on a level with other markets. Call this niche-2. Such a market is itself embedded within networks in ways that at the same time constrain the actions of firms. Such a market is an actor on a distinct level.

The market connections can be seen as a network-2, a more abstract sort of social space, which is a by-product of greater freedom of connection together with less freedom of valuation. I develop this approach in parts 2–4 of my 2002 monograph *Markets from Networks*. There is a transmutation of hitherto entailed ties into market parameters. The market is in effect projecting a new, more abstract sort of tie. Warranty and entailment on the level below are thereby abrogated, as to addressee if not interpretive content.

A public subculture of rhetorics can build across actors at both levels within a particular sector of markets, even though commitments and decisions remain tied into catenations and compoundings of particular ties. (For elaboration, see Chiffoleau et al. 2003). The rhetoric recognizes, and personalizes, actors of different levels while at the same time providing customs of switching from the calculus for one to the calculus for another.[28] Participants in the various markets act as if they were embedded in a curious web of cocoons among markets (see Tilly 1996 for an analogous term).

5.5.4. Industrial Districts

The institutional system of production was portrayed in successively more abstract forms, in the previous subsection, appealing to the panoply of distinct social forms drawn from all chapters of this book. One could instead cut back to the basis in network analysis (put forth in chapter 2) and attempt to describe institutional patterns more concretely, and with at least as much emphasis on their shaping through history.

---

[28] Cf. White (1995); Mische and White (1998). For examples of tracing this sort of evolutionary history for structural equivalence in networks, see Anheier, Gerhards, and Romo (1995), Baker (1990), Boyd (1991), Breiger (1991), Faulkner (1983), Giuffre (1999), Pattison (1993).

Figure 5.1: Complex supplier-buyer networks among thousands of distinct firms within one industrial district in Tokyo (Nakano and White 2006)

The latter approach was taken by Nakano and White (2006) in a detailed study of complex supplier-buyer networks among thousands of distinct firms within one industrial district in Tokyo. Figure 5.1 is a portrayal of their findings (somewhat simplified, for just 947 firms not at the bottom).

Control is Nakano and White's preeminent theme, signaled by the ties all being in fact asymmetric ties, in what they see as a pattern of control by an elite of production firms closer to the ultimate consumers. These are also generally larger firms and with better technical and financial resources; they have better information on commercial conditions, but not the specialized skills and practices of the layers of suppliers and subcontractors shown beneath them. Rather than elaborated theory, Nakano and White depend on extensive computation by network algorithms to portray how this institutional system works.

The buildup into overlapping pyramids vertically follows from the absence of any cycles. The spreading out of firms on a given approximate level across the pyramids is an artifact: the algorithm pretends that firms are spread out by springs between them. Such springs might in principle be coded from the extent to which firms share dependency ties to the same forms on higher levels. I would favor seeking data to support modeling of such clusters in terms of the disciplines as discussed in chapter 3: some combination of interfaces with councils; but the task is formidable. I also think the dynamics over a period for some set of firms could be captured as one of the styles discussed in chapter 4. But without such additional data and analysis, a figure such as 5.1 is prima facie some representation of an institutional system, which is at core the reenactment of strings of ties and networks as habitual. Whatever the analytic approach, confirmation requires probing the discourse and rhetorics observable in, and about, the industrial system.

It may be that the Nakano and White approach is particularly apt for Asian economies. But they argue that somewhat the same results may be found with the industrial districts in Italy where notions of alternative network firms first came to prominence. Rather than emphasize possibilities of greater autonomy and flexibility as in Piore and Sabel (1984), Nakano and White argue for increased domination by an elite coterie of firms; they think this has possibly been enhanced by recent growth in very expensive technologies of communication and production that become monopolized by the elite.

5.5.5. Decoupling and Phenomenology

Decoupling concerns dependencies. Dependencies express themselves in ties. The expectations from which any market profile is constructed can be seen alternatively as resulting from ties and at the same time as reproducing ties. Decoupling is the process aspect of establishing and thus embedding a new sort of identity, compounded from firms but risen to a distinct level. Among previous analysts of embedding, Granovetter (1985) slights the decoupling aspect, but not Burt (1992a) and not Evans (1995).

Different possibilities of arraying markets imply that markets are also concerned in decoupling. Decoupling is signaled by the seeming paradox in the asymmetry between the view from downstream up along a tie in contrast with the view from upstream down along the same tie. So far, an industry is shown as a set of producer firms that has transaction ties to specific other economic actors upstream, but with guidance from a joint market profile that overrides specific ties downstream. This is a profile sustained vis-à-vis some generalized "other," consisting in a cumulation of unspecified counterpart actors downstream. It emerges as the envelope from struggles by those becoming members of this particular profile, rather than of such profiles for other industries. The struggles are governed by a perceived schedule, a market profile from which derives a set of terms of trade across the specific processors that proves sustainable in the given context.

On the habitual side, by hypothesis, individual producers are ordinarily dealing with, and focus on, their ties to diverse other individual firms rather than paying attention to whole industries. There will be some tension from their alters, the other ends of the ties, being oriented toward rivalry with producers parallel in their own market rather than toward particular transactions with particular alters in that downstream market. Exactly the same account applies for a market in upstream mode, the difference being that the habitual side is identified with downstream rather than upstream.

How can ties decoupled when viewed from upstream be habitual when viewed from downstream, and vice versa? A narrative account is suggested by previous chapters. Much of the time, producer firms can be running on automatic pilot, filling and placing a variety of customary orders with other firms again and again. These orders will be at some habitual terms of volume, price, and service, which no doubt got established in some earlier market context. However, some firms may court or force changes, or new actors may appear, perhaps from abroad, or technology may twitch, or the environment shift. A nightmare of conjectural variations can emerge in which a producer imagines what some set of others, and self, may do in response to various changes in the responses conjectured for some given actors. This is fertile soil for the social construction, or reactivation, of some joint profile offering common guidance. Such profile presupposes positioning with respect to other markets. It may be a new positioning.

Some broader interpretive framing that encompasses both polarities must be manifested. The continuing joint reproduction of a market profile binds producers such that their ensemble becomes treated by themselves and others as a player. This player is a molecule in which constituent firms are bound as atoms. Yet also, this is a player with an identity, a player that participants and observers alike speak of as taking action, and which guides interpretations. Embedding is defined in and by this process. Each production market is thus also a folk theory that reproduces itself out of the continuing perceptions and actions of all participants in a market. The market is an actor with a different ontology from firms, whose actions are clearly on a different level.

Pressure on the robustness of any relation being coded as a tie may come when the other end also perceives itself as in a rivalry profile of its own that subsumes the origin end of the tie. That is, what might appear symmetric cannot be symmetric because of the differences in the concrete embeddings. Neither end of the tie focuses on it as a relation; both ends are concerned instead with their places in their own rivalry profile. The strain is greater than if just one end of the ties is anchored in a market rivalry profile.

Thus, the likelihood of disruption is predicted to be greater for a tie whose two ends face one another from distinct profiles. Consider, for example, production streams in the computer sector. The likelihood of disruption is higher, for example, when component manufacturers orient downstream toward PC vendors while these same vendors are orienting upstream toward their suppliers as the problematic, the profile side.[29]

In contrast, disruption is less likely when a tie, and also connecting ties in a chain, are passing through a sequence of profiles of the same orientation: either all upstream or else all downstream. This suggests there is friction in juxtaposing upstream vis-à-vis downstream mode (perhaps even more than in switching between the two modes). By this argument, either of two pure extremes may be much more likely than any one of the endless other variant stackings possible. Overall, the pure downstream stacking would be more likely in a deflationary period and the pure upstream stacking in an inflationary period.

The key issue of the dynamics from which an interface can emerge is when and where the representative firm's flows come to be perceived together as an overall commitment, rather than as merely some collection of rivulets. In the downstream orientation, delivery rivulets get chunked together as a commitment. In the upstream orientation, it instead is the rivulets of procurements that somehow must come to be perceived together as overall commitments by the peer producers as they eye one another. In either case, asymmetry is seen to be basic to the relations.

5.5.6. The Reverse Side

Attention has been focused on the profile of a market, the profile that as an interface in that direction protects the producers from Knightian uncertainty. It is time to give more sustained and explicit attention to the other side of the market. Whether the orientation of the given market is upstream or downstream, there is a back side.

On the one hand, transactions in this unproblematic direction are construed as taking place in continuing ties according to habitual terms of trade. In a habitual tie, say, to an upstream supplier firm, prices paid to them will tend to stay the same no matter what the volume: there is some attention to deviation, so that sanctions could come into play against deviation from habitual. This defines the processor as a price-taker.

One might say that producers within the given industry do not pay enough attention along this unproblematic direction. But this back side

---

[29] Still to be explored for each such case is which of the two facing profiles is more subject to disruption.

of the industry reflects the whole network evolution—and not just particular habitual transactions—through which that processor market came into place along with other markets.

Producers are assumed to be price-takers in that direction because bounded rationality, in the form of habitual decision rules, ensures reluctance to try to focus in both directions. Transactions of these producers with firms in some particular other industry may well be seen not only as habitual but also as too small in comparison with their totals in that direction to seem worth strategizing, worth fussing over. These producers may not perceive possibilities to exploit variation in pricing between producers of quite similar product varieties in that other industry. In the problematic direction, on the other hand, especially when faced with some disruptions in habitual sales or procurement transactions, processors are impelled to look away from those particular ties and instead derive guidance from perceptions arrived at jointly.

Thus, decoupling is a subtle process in which a given market distances itself from any particular ties with particular other markets. Even if the previous ties of a producer are retained, those habitual partners are decoupled from the market interface. That is, any such habitual ties are decoupled from the setting of the next period's production commitments made with guidance from the market profile, the interface. How does this come about? Common membership in a market by firms does derive from similarities in what ties they have had with all the other sets (markets) in the evolving partition into markets, and not upon their being connected with specific other firms as such.

5.5.7. On the Fringes

It is because of these decoupling phenomena that analysis with the model can accommodate auxiliary forms such as professional service markets, along with mainline production industries, and also industries on the fringe, such as mining.

Much the same internal mechanism functions whether transactions for a particular market occur near middles or near ends in tangible chains of procurements and supply among firms. According to the sociologic of decoupling brought out here, each production market operates as a role structure of firms that is embedded among other such markets, but with room enough also for agency. Decoupling leaves room for exercising options jointly (which in the model is represented by an arbitrary "historical" constant). It also leaves room for options exercised severally on firms through investment. That leads to patterns of financial binding between firms across markets.

Sites near boundaries between markets and the surrounding social context are the ultimate sinks and sources for a given economy, as reported, say, in an input-output network (e.g., Carter 1967). The consumer edge, where it is devolution of downstream market, is taken up in the literature on distribution chains for all sorts of products. Such devolution processes are treated very little in microeconomic theory proper (but see Porter 1976; Katz 1988; Perry 1989).

It is devolution at the other, supplier, edge that has been the focus of most research in recent decades, if one counts only research that gives some attention to implications for theory. This research is particularly concerned with subcontracting in various guises.[30]

With decoupling, the context need not extend either up- or downstream beyond the core tripartite distinction of roles as procurement, transformation, and sale. That is why one would be justified in using the more general label of processor market. A processor market does not just transfer ownership, as does an exchange market. It is steward to a line of business through the agency of its member processors.

Consider enactment of decoupling for a processor market. For example, department stores will stock shoes, but so will independent shoe stores carrying wide arrays of brands. So too will shoe stores with ties, as well as TV and Web shopper services tied to warehousing and/or to the Walmarts of big-time retailing. Each producer instead eyes its peers, fellow members of that market, in construing the terms of trade.

It is the phenomenon of decoupling that argues against believing in a planar and singular network among industries such as suggested by the imagery of the input-output school (Leontief 1966; Carter 1967, 1976). There is no need to reify a production economy in terms of a singular input-output network. Such relaxing of perspective better accommodates the diversity of observed markets, which obtains notwithstanding the fact that these have been devised and evolved in interpretive cultures with considerable overlaps and borrowings that reach beyond immediate siting.

Markets grouped in a sector by business convention will tend to be in nearby positions in networks of flows. Network locations may, like similarities in technology, be what, through distinctive history of production and routing, transmute mere sets of markets into market sectors. A further level may emerge, beyond the scope of the present model.

---

[30] See, for example, Eccles (1981a) on construction; Uzzi (1996), Lachmann and Petterson (1988), and Lazerson (1995) on textiles; and Romo and Schwartz (1995) on manufacturing. Also see Hamilton, Zeile, and Kim (1990) and Yoshino and Lifson (1988) for analyses of Asian firm-market systems where subcontracting seems central if not predominant.

Allegiances of firms to their respective markets reflect the degree of structural equivalence within existing networks of procurement and supply relations. So structural equivalence will guarantee some similarity in situations encountered over time. Nesting and overlap of perceptions may accord with some distribution of attributes correlated with region as well as technology, but in any case, perceptions, are from their evolution, in accord with structural equivalence in the networks of the production economy. Nesting and overlap are important, since a particular sector may well have a recognizable subculture but yet share varied key, generalizable aspects with various other sectors.

Processes of decoupling and embedding supplant birth and death of particular actors as foci. Demography is not the point. Decoupling is essential to the paradoxical duality of markets and firms as being both embedded in tangible networks among concrete actors, yet simultaneously being actors with scripts for relations that are transposable and readily interpreted.

5.6. Organizations

Organizations usually have names and some familiar rhetoric about their makeup, whether supermarket, little league, equipment supplier, or federal agency. Let us denote those cases that have an explicit table of organization as "formal organizations."

Formal organizations were patterned on early bureaucracies. Corruption and venality were built into bureaucracy, and early systems of venality coupled the beginnings of salary systems through careers. The larger context and occasion for this venality was a decentralized arrangement for raising capital; corruption was, from a larger perspective, just a more informal route to the same end.

Early bureaucracy was a new style whose chief effect was to loosen earlier rhetorics, as is seen most clearly in this early format of explicit corruption. So at first, bureaucracy cut through blocking action in a path of breathtaking decoupling, even to the point of noncomparability. But bureaucracy settled into a rhetoric that aided blocking even those actions it was set up to support.

The formal organizations of our own era are most commonly related to work. But formal organization is a special template that enables disparate realms, whether of governments or of nonprofits or business, to establish interpretive connection, as we will see in the next chapter. For example, a business firm as a corporatist regime integrates a set of interpretive specialties, say, engineering and sales and accounting, each a network population, but the efforts at control are shaped, and deflected, by members' acceptance of a table of organization as the style guiding them all. But such a hieratic style must be supported by legitimating rhetorics either externally sited—as in rhetorics of "corporate social responsibility" or internally occurring, as in assertions of a charismatic leader's vision.

So in this aspect, formal organization is a style. Common adherence to a formal organization among any set of actors can engender careers as personal rhetorics guided by the organization. Formal organizations synthesize styles that can adapt and regulate meanings via a new type of tie. These are ties of authority that are explicitly public and serve to bridge separate interpretive frames, which are being brought into some coherence quite aside from their connection to work. But formal organization also does the opposite, which avoids blocking action just as in stratification. Paul DiMaggio comments (personal communication, August 13, 1991): "Working social structures require a mix of bounded solidity and hazy obfuscation (so that the secret of the system is never so entirely revealed to the participants as to block all action)."

Formal organization is, in the abstract, a transposable set of directions about the interlocking of premises for making choices. But in its insistence on boundary, formal organization becomes a native theory, a rhetoric that argues for, but goes beyond, models of disciplines and other universals. Organizations are supposedly stable structures of rules, positions, and the like. Or in March and Simon's (1958) more sophisticated formulation, they are delegated sets of stable premises for deciding. As we all can see, but few of us learn, the only sure thing, in fact, is that forms and rules and slots all change. Ambage and ambiguity trade off in a setting of uncertainty flows. Manipulations should not be conceived at personal levels only. Important manipulation comes to be about the changes (March and Olsen 1976), and a cycle of changes and switches becomes the steady state, even if unrecognized.

One may argue that some formal organizations function as "inside-out markets." The common image of markets is as sites where rigid social actors such as organizations can achieve accommodation and yet also as sites that yield coherence of interpretation. But formal organization as style can be the flexible negotiating ground to reconcile the rigidities of established markets. A publicly enacted organization is better able than most observed markets to supply ties by arbitrary fiat! So a single organization can provide bridges among incomparable strings of actors out in the social seas of urban life. The trade federation (Levy 1944) and the regulatory agency (Libecap 1978) both operate in that way. Each can be visualized as a common forum serving markets in much the way that exchange markets are visualized as serving to bridge and regulate firms.

Formal organization as a complete reality mixes hostility formats—such as authority trees that cumulate spans of control as interface disciplines—with corporatist binding through other disciplines, with this mix both overcoming and producing blockage of action. Today, formal organization is the commonest venue, into which older forms often are repackaged. But to say this is to say little; any stereotyped story-line for organization conceals that there is as much diversity as for the other common modern term, *market*.

5.6.1. Imitation and Fad

Many investigators have been pointing to the emergence of flattened hierarchies, decentralized organization, dating back to the vogue of "matrix organization" in the West and of Sogo Soshai and Just-in-time in the East. David Stark (2006) generalizes this tendency as the emergence of "heterarchical" organization, arguing that it is as much a matter of integrating distinct sorts of values as of administrative arrangements. Scott Lash (2002) expresses the point in terms of the hegemony of communication, a sort of applied version of Luhmann's theoretical edifice.

Yet there is a history of endless proclamations of new days in organization. Perhaps the current trend is another fad, enabled by a tendency to parallelism between organizations. A key doctrine of the new institutionalism in organization theory is isomorphism in relations (DiMaggio 1992; DiMaggio and Powell 1983).

I turn to a study by Shin-Kap Han, which examines such practices over time and across levels. He finds neither extreme dominant. His abstract says it best:

In an earlier study on the audit services market, I [Han 1995] showed that an individual client firm's likelihood of imitation in auditor selection systematically varied along with its relative position among competing peers within the industry. This paper extends that finding to aggregate industry level by shifting the analytic focus from within-industry to between-industry variation. The data on 2,254 auditor-client pairs across 45 manufacturing industries in the U.S. are examined to specify the social structural conditions under which the firms are more, or less, likely to produce the outcome of isomorphism. In general, the more hierarchically stratified an industry, the more likely it is to have a highly homogeneous practice among the firms within it. *Inequality leads to and exacts behavioral homogeneity.* There is, however, a threshold in the relationship between the aggregate homogeneity and the industry structure. When the disparity between the top and middle tiers is too large, the social reference process breaks down and the level of homogeneity declines. This industry level finding complements the earlier firm-level finding and empirically substantiates the mechanism of mimetic isomorphism, further elaborating the theory. (Han 2000, emphasis supplied)

5.7. Evolution of Rhetorics: Venality versus Corruption

The formation of rhetorics out of joint perceptions has an evolutionary logic, as does the converse (formation of joint perceptions out of rhetorics). Objectively odd but strongly held beliefs can result. For example, there is a strong prejudice against venality in our society. This seems an accidental by-product of an evolutionary course, a feudal assessment. Venality simply states that there is a payment flow to an actor in some discipline or more complex social formation, which is not calibrated to participation in that formation. Bribery is certainly a case, but it is only a special case. Any salary is to some approximation an example of venality, with only the details varying, say, between a research professor's salary for "teaching" and a general executive's salary for "planning."

Corruption and venality can take on social forms not keyed to market systems (Mousnier 1971; Swart 1949). They epitomize style, but at the same time can be characterized in the more abstracted form of rhetoric. Note, then, that they are a solution to the search for decoupling from social embeddings. The stigma attached to them is to be expected, since their basis is exactly interference with accepted functioning of social embeddings.

Let us examine venality versus corruption. The difference is whether those in a given setting account for the unbundling and bundling by cultural rules, or whether instead they do so by the patterning of social connections. So we come again to the calculus of ambiguity and ambage introduced in chapters 2 and 3.

Consider an example of this same trade-off at greater scope. Inviolable tradition, rigid in the way perhaps found only in church liturgy today (Thompson 1961), always goes with arbitrary, capricious decision-making in specific matters. The Ottoman bureaucracy was an extreme example of this theorem:

> The tendency toward a kind of bureaucratic formalism . . . and restriction of initiative appear at the top-most levels of the ruling class, just as among the clerks of the scribal bureaus . . . the routines of the office confirm that scribal functions tended to be conceived solely in terms of document-producing procedures. . . . The discretional use of power by those in highest positions had as a necessary concomitant the servility, in practical as well

as formal jural senses of those who worked in their shadow. The decline of the empire surely compounded both this problem and the bureaucratic formalism. For the progressive loss of control by the central administration over the provinces created a discontinuity between the document-producing processes of the central offices and the world outside. (Findley 1980, p. 90, pp. 223–36)

Troeltsch's dissection of Christian church formations (in von Gierke, 1950) suggests how important the translation between ambage and ambiguity is in even the oldest social formations. Troeltsch is puzzled that it is the ecclesiastical church, fully rationalized in Thomism, that encourages heroic and extravagant deeds, sainthood, whereas sects, despite Gospel commitment to radical individualism, do not. The calculus of ambiguity and ambage suggests an explanation.

The ecclesiastical church greatly reduces ambiguity, but it attempts to do so for a differentiated set of roles and positions, which yields an inevitable increase in ambage. This increase in ambage measures increased arbitrariness as seen in actual social patterns of relations. The resulting social tension can be eased by denying social fellowship, by instead insisting on an extreme pursuit of rules vis-à-vis the hypostatized residual actor, who is the summation of contextual uncertainty.

By contrast, the sect is von Gierke's *Genossenschaft* (1953). In the sect, fellowship is carried to a radical extreme in which ambage is minimal. But this is so only so long as all are in step, time after time, in beliefs. And then the ambiguity can be unlimited.

These arguments on the ambage/ambiguity trade-off resemble those of several recent theorists of culture. For example, William Connolly wonders:

> [are] unconscious contrivances of social control . . . a political response to the disaffection many manifest from the roles assigned to them? . . . Foucault's texts seek to document the multiple ways in which modern attempts to liberate sexuality, madness and criminality from arbitrary and repressive controls entangle the self in a web of more insidious controls . . . they enclose the objects of treatment in a web of "insidious leniencies.". . . The conventionalization of social life renders it more susceptible to imperatives of authoritative coordination and those subject to that coordination more resistant to its claims. (1987, pp. viii, 91, 127)

The obvious quality of engagement does not vitiate the implied insight.

Turn, finally, to a contrast between two exemplars of social architecture, the English versus the Chinese countrysides in their interpenetration of class with lineage (Bearman 1993; Dibble 1965; Hsiao 1960). The contrast can be formulated in the respective trade-offs between ambage and ambiguity levels. In England, daughters and younger sons do not generate or bind lineages; so socioeconomic status of particular families is clear whereas the abstract outlines of class are fuzzy. In China, lineages are agglomerated into a huge clan with the same patronymic so that standing of particular families is buried in an overall repute, which however permits, and fits, sharply defined class and status in the abstract. The ratio of ambage over ambiguity is much higher for the English countryside. The differing trade-offs are the trace in that countryside of endemic struggles over control.

5.7.1. Smith on Triestians versus Istrians

Over several years, Tammy Smith (2006) followed, on the ground and in archives, the evolution of competing narratives of identity in Istria, a region with more than a century of difficult relations between those who identified as Italian and those who identified as Slavs. Trieste, the large city there, saw several changes of governing regime. There was contention between the former Yugoslavia and Italy, before and after World War II. There were flows of displaced persons, before and after the war. Italians displaced from the province into Trieste, which came under Italian rule, were resentful and developed a supporting narrative of hardship and superiority. Slavs were subordinated in Trieste, but in the province were assertive of a narrative opposed to the Italians.

Smith then followed a subplot about relations among Istrians who migrated to New York City. She reports on how this ethnically mixed group overcame persisting conflict through changes in their original identity narratives (Smith 2006). These original narratives can be parsed as two rhetorics correlated with the two styles that the two groups inhabited. Living in New York emerged as being a new style that came to be shared so that boundaries and identities were muted in a new rhetoric.

5.8. Disjunctions in Rhetorics of Smooth Control

Social change can also come in radical, disjunctive mode. As Vilfredo Pareto points out,

> Human societies have a very strong tendency to impart a certain rigidity to any new social organization and to crystallize themselves in any new form. Hence it often happens that the passage from one form to another is not by continuous movement but by leaps and jerks . . . for example, in language, in law. (Pareto 1935, p. 160)

Such disjunction can indeed be entailed in a rhetoric of smooth control. Let us examine in some detail a major example. The rhetoric of organization is an obfuscation in government as much as in business. Levels mount up dizzyingly in the U.S. federal government, the scope of which is huge no matter how tallied; so Washington, D.C. should be a challenge for any theory that claims that self-similarity permits the same analytic devices to function at various levels. An obvious focus in government—for contending efforts at control, stratagems of decoupling, and efforts at reproduction—is the construction of the federal budget, and much of the process has already been modeled successfully by Padgett (1980a, 1980b, 1981).

Padgett's key ideas fit well with the theoretical approach laid out in this book.[31] He portrays all constituent processes, whether routine reproduction or episodic control, as stochastic processes. Sufficient decoupling into subprocesses is assumed that historical dependencies (in mathematical terms, non-Markovian features) are not needed within particular subprocesses. There is an initial wave of relatively predictable claims for budget resources called up from operational programs within units, within departments or subdepartments.

The main action is in cutting down these initial requests. According to Padgett's analysis, a dual hierarchy emerges, centered around the Office of Management and Budget (OMB). Within the federal government, OMB's organization parallels, like an inspector general, the higher levels in all operational departments. The latter tend to freeze up and be incapable of conceiving further cuts in their own programs as, over time, they become enmeshed in the blocking style of self-reproducing social organization. Cuttings, as a result, follow a complex interactive pattern between dual authorities, as well as vis-à-vis operative units. In Padgett's words, from the last of his series of analyses:

> Thus macro fiscal targets, derived on grounds having little to do with detailed programmatic priorities, tip the lower-level bureaucratic politics "balance of power" between organizations and among institutional levels. (1981, p. 121)

It is the OMB that can be likened to a semi-periphery, as between presidency and operational departments, as well as being in a dual hierarchy as seen from lower units.

Padgett's approach was to model from the grounding of actual program cuts and additions, for individual programs. He traced through the detailed archives of budget changes, both within the departments and within OMB. The departments and the OMB can be seen together as the dual hierarchy of authority through which a presidential elite exerts control pressure downward.

---

[31] Padgett and I jointly taught a seminar on complex organization in the early 1980s, and we considered collaborating on a book such as this one.

Padgett's key was to follow each single cut and confrontation in a series for a given unit program. It is this grounding that permits us to analyze even such a huge system as a congeries of interfaces that has evolved into an institution. The federal budgetary process brings together into a common concrete organization an enormous variety of role frames with their story sets and story-lines.

5.8.1. Padgett's Stochastic Model

Two radically different processes are at work in shaping the huge accretion of requests into a budget, according to Padgett's model. One is serial judgment, in which program authorities and departmental superiors both consider, in turn, various substantive bases for cutting, or enlarging, a program request. The other is selective attention, in which the dual hierarchy chooses what individual program requests, at what stage in serial judgment, to examine for pruning or drastic cuts. This strategic program of cuts is the key part of shaping the total, as well as the profile, of programs, and later of whole departmental budgets, to a policy. The policy may or may not realize ostensible presidential goals, depending on competence and attention balances (Padgett 1980b).

Padgett successfully models the first process by negative exponential distributions. Here averages reflect the degree of process controllability allowed by "the environment." The immediate conduits expressing the environment are legal and like constraints from Congress (a tertiary hierarchy).

Sequential attention, the second process, consists of deciding when serial judgment is to be invoked. Padgett models it as the columns of cuts, within a matrix of cuts by programs, which sum over time into a Poisson distribution of cuts for programs. The Poisson is the form into which cumulate the constituent distributions, each separately of negative exponential form. These are commit interfaces, the disciplines where it is the shapes that determine the processes, with the means reflecting accidents of environment.

Regime and rhetoric and style are not inconsistent with gaming and manipulation, but on the contrary build on and presuppose them. Each stochastic process in Padgett's model can also be seen as modeling a tangible series of perceptions, and of gamed counter-perceptions. The perceptions are socially constructed ones generated by disciplines. Whereas at the unit program level, the disciplines are interfaces, at the departmental level they appear to be mobilize disciplines, and at that level also the OMB dual hierarchy disciplines are select arenas.

Padgett's search for the distributional form that accommodates the observed distributions of cuts is thus a search for the generative principle of the process. The stochastic process is a mapping of very complex and various perception formations into an outcome that balances different control effects in the guise of different sources of uncertainty. Padgett brings it all together into a striking new insight into the process.

His principal finding is that there are, indeed there must be, occasional catastrophic budget cuts, including dissolutions of programs, because of the ways in which the dialectic of control with reproduction is structured within this regime. The programs, even at the finest recognized gradation, are themselves rhetoric devices in terms of which to recognize events and identities. A regime is a self-reproducing balance of control efforts from perspectives that are not mutually comparable with each other, much less with other institutions. A control process that cuts across and reaches into disparate rhetorics must generate occasional jagged, erratic cuts.

Most program units are incrementalist in their initial requests. At an even further disaggregation into locales, these requests, innocuous at the national scope with which Padgett's model starts, may prove to be generated variously in select or mobilize disciplines. Further control would require further decoupling, as is well realized by Congress members and other program supporters who devise couplings and embeddings, as in the "entitlement" provisions. This is especially apparent when it comes to successive exposures to cuts, and, given an exposure, the considerations of how much of a cut to make on that particular go-round. Programs not coupled into other programs are the prime turf for cutting by a strategy that is openly independent of programmatic considerations, which is a second-order fiscal strategy.

5.8.2. Comparing Budget Stories

The conventional ex post story about budgets has usually concerned aggregation, which, until Padgett, was the apparently logical and unavoidable way to construe the shaping of budgets. Padgett's model, in contrast, operationalizes control problems from a self-similar theory, the point of view of middle-range order: according to it, the results are more a matter of horizontal essays at agency, and at decoupling programs from their ostensible aggregate housings.

Embedding to a higher level, of new identities functioning in a different network of refashioned identities, can occur without any substantive aggregation whatever. And conversely, formal aggregation into larger partitions need have no impact on level of operation, on being perceived and perceiving in terms of more sophistication. Program units never touched by fights and confusions may have no standing whatever, no identities to generate bases and directions of action. Identities rear up out of frictions along networks of productions and events, whether or not these are being shaped by disciplines.

To put together disciplines into some stratification process is to build a tower of Babel. From an external observer's viewpoint, generality can be obtained only by a framework that is loose and flexible enough to accommodate concatenations of partly consistent schemes. Padgett's stochastic model of the U.S. federal budget's construction can be seen as an apt description. This stochastic model makes sense for observers of what is going on when numerous and diverse disciplines are competing and being put together into unified streams of claimants for flows of resources.

The other school of budget models (Wildavsky 1975) has urged that only the outside envelope of budgets be examined. From the incremental changes thus attended to, they argue that inertia is the main "dynamic" in the accommodation of disparate organization units, the accommodation that is the substance of budgeting. No stochastic elements need be introduced.

But Padgett has demonstrated very much better fits using his models. His models also conform better to the accounts of participants, and furthermore they provide bases for predicting secular changes. Above all, Padgett's models predict occasional dramatic shifts in allocations, which indeed are the crux of the real historical process observed.

Another model parallel to Padgett's, but for the private business economy, can be found in Burt (1983). Unlike Padgett, Burt did not have access to inside documents, in this case, documents for sequences of market share and profits across industries and firms. So Burt infers dependencies and contingencies from a black-box analysis that predicts to the variation across firms and industries in rates of return. Burt bases these predictions upon measures of the range of alternatives in sourcing and the range in selling. These ranges can be construed as measures of feasible decoupling and therefore of likely control and autonomy.

One could draw for industry a stochastic analogue to Padgett's analysis. Congress and the other government presences operate so disjointly that the parallel to government from the market economy may be worth drawing. Padgett's and Burt's aggregation paradoxes are solved at about the same scale, in government and business, respectively.

The next chapter takes a general look at how regimes are built that try to avoid revolution from rhetoric.

SIX

REGIMES OF CONTROL

A REGIME generates control over the controls always being attempted by identities. It does so as a by-product of continuing commitments to valuation within a realm, set in contrast with another realm, or other realms. A control regime can thus develop when one realm is in conflict with another. These regimes are akin to, but generalize beyond, the three disciplines of chapter 3. The valuation order of a discipline can be derived from, as well as built into, some control regime, yet it is of more restricted scope than in realms. Furthermore, control regimes can be interlocked, as in the political parties example described later, whereas disciplines are disjoint. Control regime is enabling, like identity and discipline, whereas an institutional system orchestrates explanations, as does network. This chapter lays out theory for control regimes, along with a number of empirical studies.

Each of the three species of discipline was described in chapter 3 as a template, each with myriad realizations. Templates for control regimes, however, are more varied, correlating with the number and kinds of realms invoked. To give an example: Democratic and Republican parties in present-day America are control regimes in conflict. Liberalism and conservatism are rhetorics for their two realms that clothe institutionalized differences of the parties. In an earlier era of political bossism, each party may have been an involute regime whose realm contrasts just with the everyday world in general.

Styles as well as disciplines can be seen as prototypes for control regimes. Both resemble control regimes in providing the framing for identities struggling around to get joint action. Institutions channel into realms the underlying switchings of netdoms, while a control regime manifests a template/blueprint by which these switchings get coordinated. As a template that shepherds social actions, a control regime is a constraining discourse. Narrative must be evoked and reinforced that establishes a contrast of values that is binding. The configuration in the template inhibits deviations. Hence, analysis of control regimes yields blocking action as a major theme in this chapter, accompanied by embeddings and decouplings galore—whereas chapter 7 will feature the paradoxes of getting fresh action.

A prototype can be drawn from the section entitled "Households, Family, and Gender" in chapter 2: patriarchy is a control regime, common around the world, which is visible on the scale of household; commitment to gender precedence interacts with commitments to family council and to household work, to stabilize an interlocking nexus of domination.

Each network for a type of tie draws reinforcement in stories through higher-level organization in control regimes, as well as institutional systems; by contrast, in chapter 4 it was multiplex networks that were invoked by style. So theory for regime can also be grounded in analytics around uncertainty that were introduced with networks in chapter 2. An identity seeks control in any of its dyads, and control of control becomes the issue already at the level of reproducing a triad of dyads from a network. In such a relationship, there will always be an unequal balance of resources and information. A control regime might emerge from a triadic relationship where each participant exerts controlling forces in struggling for new actions.

Any example of a regime is some deposit of accretive and evolutionary processes, some with intentional components, whose pattern, in self-reproducing, maintains a historical particularity. And a given regime can be found at different scales, nested variously in other regimes. Irregularity-based identities call forth and propose alternate frames of interpretation, putative realms, which become known across actors. When personality exhibits some consistency of ends within the person, it resembles a control regime. Distinctive persons are a product as much as a cause of diverse overlays of different interpretive frames in generating a regime.

It is not possible to derive a regime from first principles, just as it is beyond current powers of observation and analysis to identify, much less to test for, all the regimes able to reproduce themselves. Historically reproduced control regimes can be found, for example, along lines of social cleavage. Lipset and Rokkan (1967) considered that these cleavages developed variously during the time of nation building and industrial takeoff, between labor force and capital, country and city, church and state.

It has to be noticed that when any larger social formation begins to emerge, control efforts proliferate, which makes discernment of the regime more difficult. Since one often finds only scrappy empirical manifestations, Weber's method of formulating ideal types of elaborately articulated architectures seems appropriate. I will deploy it later for regimes of corporatism, clientelism, and professionalism.

Before doing that, however, I will address theory of mobilization around value through narrative. That is followed by an example, using a study from chapter 4, and then by a discussion of evolution. Next, attention shifts to further theorizing about values, which illuminates dual hierarchy regimes. Then I cycle back to control regimes that induce involution of constituent realms, as in Luhmann's and Bourdieu's theories of law and of art. This construal as a functional subsystem is also extended to aspects of the economy.

Finally, after the three Weberian types comes a famous example of changes in regime around William the Conqueror that mix together bits of the preceding types. This will prove a prototype for regimes on more sophisticated templates that adjoins style and institution. In the next to last section, I take up caste and science, applications apparently so remote from one another, and argue that in those cases, distinct skins cover very much the same template. The last section traces the evolution of commerce regimes, yielding a different parsing of template. A general conjecture is supported from evidence about the commercial template.

6.1. Mobilizations around Values

Mobilizations around values build with narrative that goes beyond the story-set of chapter 2. Narrative acts in development of a regime much as DNA does in bodily development. Accounts by multiple sources, strung together over time around a value, yield a narrative of events, and this narrative sustains regime at a higher level across two or more realms.

It is characteristic of three regimes discussed later—professionalism, clientelism and corporatism—that they mobilize multiple events within only one of the three disciplines. In each respective regime, instances become embedded by narrative according to a general value, being invoked in contrast to the surrounding realm of everyday life. However, in this chapter, after some theory, I also dissect one particular regime of feudalism that crossbreeds from these three that stick with single discipline. And in the later theory section, I sketch a regime with a dual hierarchy, which mobilizes around countervailing values, as between the realm of church and the realm of state.

But regimes do not impose linear local status orderings like those in disciplines. There is not the same intimate correlation of social array with interpretive dimension. Very diverse mechanisms prove able to sustain narrative around value contrast, and thereby constrain deviation. There is not a limitation to a fixed number or kind of species of control regime.

A regime splits off realms, each a section of reality in which a special dimension determines the character of every individual operation belonging to it. This contrasts with liminality, introduced at the end of chapter 3. The latter operates as an overriding conflation of realms into a special public as compendium,[1] as unioning of realms that mark institutional systems.

Style disdains distinctions of realm, whereas discipline is embedded into a realm, but style can also be directly adjoined and embedded in control regime alongside realms. I would emphasize here the difference between a control regime and the institutional system from chapter 5 in regard to their genesis. On the one hand, institutional system is about inclusion; it draws all sorts of actors into its realm as it emerges, including styles. On the other hand, regime mobilizes around contrast between realms.

6.1.1. Narrative around Value Contrast

Accountings of social actions as regimes presuppose values that are common across social networks. Yet story-sets evolve and reproduce in a matrix of contending control projects. Values fuel these unending conflicts for control among distinct actors, whether individual or composite, which indeed are channeling and affirming the values in the course of reaching some equilibrium despite duplicity and contention. Stories end up as a set from which mobilization builds a parsimonious account, a narrative that invokes a value but is not inconsistent with control projects being actively pushed. Whatever comes to pass, and thus whatever can be conceived, must be describable after the fact in terms of a set of stories, the convention in which a value is expressed. The resulting set serves both to express and to conceal the conflicts and the orientations in that context. It characterizes a type of tie.

Identities interact with each other as they mobilize around values. The endless stories being invoked and applied in control projects obscure how in fact larger formations are being constituted out of disciplines as well as networks. The singular valuation order that braces a discipline branches upon devolution into values that no longer map tightly to a structure of discipline. Story becomes story-set, which accumulates around a value contrast with another realm, and a correlated contrast in types of tie.

Thus, as identities provide accounts for and of themselves, they jointly generate the device of values out of valuations from disciplines, and marked by distinction in type of tie. The meanings of values are to be inferred as much from the social architecture as vice versa. Values extract that aspect of valuation orderings in discipline that can be com-

---

[1] It is the antipodes of public as formed in ancient Athens, which is realm for the political control regime of Athens.

mon across a broader setting. The settings vary in their boundaries and in the contextual impacts they exert.

A control regime is thus seen to draw upon story-sets from networks, and valuation orders from disciplines, and to generalize them into value that gets contrasted with another realm. It seems to me that much this same perspective is offered by other analysts.

Take two examples. First, this assessment by Foucault, at a scope beyond any particular regime:

> Each society has its regime of truth, its "general politics of truth": that is, the types of discourse which it accepts and makes function as true; the mechanisms and instances which enable one to distinguish true and false statements, the means by which each is sanctioned; the techniques and procedures accorded value in the acquisition of truth; the status of those who are charged with saying what counts as true . . . we cannot raise the banner of truth against our own regime . . . there is no common measure between the impositions of the one and those of the other . . . each regime is identified entirely with its imposed truth. (Foucault 1980, p. 131)

These truths can be understood here as a way a story has to be told, its underlying grammar of right and wrong, its embedding in story-sets, where at the same time this way of storytelling is enforced by sanctions and reinforced by tests.

In 1977 Foucault expressed these ideas somewhat differently:

> Truth isn't outside power or lacking in power: . . . Truth is a thing of this world: it is produced only by virtue of multiple forms of constraint. And it induces regular effects of power. [To him,] "Truth" is to be understood as a system of ordered procedures for the production, regulation, distribution, circulation, and operation of statements. "Truth" is linked in a circular relation with systems of power that produce and sustain it, and to effects of power which it induces and which it extends—a "regime" of truth. This regime is not merely ideological or superstructural; it was a condition of the formation and development of capitalism. And it is this same regime which, subject to certain modifications, operates in the socialist countries. (Foucault 2000, pp. 131–32)

However, although Foucault's discussion about a "regime" of truth translates into a cognate of my control regime approach, there seems little place for mobilizing by identities within his anonymous discursive practices that account for order within the regime.

Therefore, in order to discuss order within a regime, I turn to Luc Boltanski and Laurent Thévenot. Over the past twenty-five years, Boltanski and Thévenot have issued a series of publications on justifications invoked in disputes; these were introduced in chapter 5. Their focus, in both fieldwork and literature searches, was on situations that arise in ordinary living. Their central point is that people argue not only about facts but also about what "order of worth" is proper to invoke to justify oneself in that dispute. To call on such "order," I argue, is to invoke a realm for a control regime.

I first quote from Boltanski and Thévenot's overall summary paper in English.

> We shall now give a short description of these common worlds, pointing out for each of them: first, the diverse underlying principles of order as extracted from the classical texts; and second, the beings (persons or things) which inhabit these worlds as they are depicted in the corresponding practical guides . . . we focused on six worlds. We suppose that these worlds are sufficient to describe justifications performed in the majority of ordinary situations. But this number is not, of course, a magic alone. These worlds are historical constructions and some of them are less and less able to ground people's justifications whereas other ones are emerging. (Boltanski and Thévenot 1999, p. 369)

Boltanski and Thévenot offer a variety of detailed mechanisms that can contribute to mutual support of overlap between realms.. However, I argue that each of these orders comes into existence as an underpinning in realm for a control regime, regimes that get reflected in the classical texts. What I have called switchings between netdoms, in chapter 1, Boltanski and Thévenot portray as endemic in ordinary living. But they also point to a different sort of switching. A dispute often brings switching in what order of worth is used for the justification. This is what we should expect, wrestlings in and with the control regime; I will return to that in chapter 7.

A third example of an analyst with a compatible perspective is Luhmann, whose work was introduced in the previous chapter, in section 5.3.1. That source will be developed at more length later, in sections 6.3.1 and 6.3.2.

* 6.1.2. Control Regime around Narrative

[In each chapter, with a section marked with an asterisk, I point out how the studies there can also be seen from other perspectives. These commerce and trade examples are also taken up, more than casually, in the prologue and in sections 3.1.1 and 4.1.4.]

Can rhetorics characterize and thereby induce a whole realm? For example the "world of business" or "world of law," to which we turn in two sections hence, or the realm of motherhood? Eric Leifer shows the answer is yes for each of four realms in U.S. professional sports. *Making the Majors* (1998) is his long-term, large-scale account. He first shows that the key to establishing a professional sport in this country (baseball, basketball, football, ice hockey) is in the grounding of a rhetoric of involvement by spectators. This is partly manifested in rules of play that prove transparent and even-handed. But these get established only if and when a control regime coalesces around a narrative sustaining the realm in which the rhetoric can persist.

Narrative, like story, ceaselessly substitutes meaning for the straightforward copy of sequence of events recounted (Maines 1993). The interaction and switching of identities across different realms in a regime needs to be accounted for, and narrative can do so. The rhetorics of involvement in Leifer's sports, for example, provide to an identity, as it enters, a narrative of spectatorship. That identity can assume an insider's view and passionately follow the events, taking sides, yet also switching repeatedly. The presupposed knowledge translates into and enables telling a narrative.

So new rhetorics do accompany joint creations of yet more complex social reality, including whole control regimes, for which these rhetorics provide matrices of supple explanation. For example, we can assign the rhetorics of the charity switch described early in the previous chapter to the particular realm invoked by the regime of foundations that witness values of charity. Thus, formation of a rhetoric can depend on the correlative emergence of a larger context. But narrative remains essential in control regime.

Now, for a second example, turn back to chapter 4, to the emergent style in the nineteenth century given in *Market Sentiments*. The novel sensibility there depended for its creation and continuance on special narratives that were sustained by a well-planned regime centered on *Godey's Lady's Book*. This magazine was at the core of the style of women's living that was evolving in mid-nineteenth-century America (Nelson 2004). Godey both observed and sought to shape this style. The *Lady's Book* also presented a whole class of rhetorics for realms that included manuals of good manners.

In Nelson's words:

> After 1830, *Godey's Lady's Book* became one of the most influential sources of advice about behavior in the marketplace. Chapter 3 demonstrates how Louis A. Godey capitalized on the reading audience trained by religious tracts and earlier magazines to create the first commercially successful magazine. . . . Its wide circulation demonstrates how sentimental ideas that originated in eastern cities circulated throughout other areas of the

country. Also the editors and contributors to *Godey's* produced a wide range of additional novels, essays, advice books, cookbooks, and other kinds of popular manuals that added to and elaborated on the ideas expressed in the magazine. (*Market Sentiments,* pp. 17–18)

I point out that the energizing focus in common was realization of a new realm. But which control regime has been installed then? The reader can take on that question as well as an exploration of regime for the *Protecting Soldiers and Mothers* book that was presented as parallel to *Market Sentiments.*

6.1.3. Types of Tie

When data allow, control regime is understood best from analysis of a set of types-of-tie that are being kept distinct exactly in the mobilization matrix of narratives around values in the distinct realms. The most extensive and thorough data archive that I know of is the one built for Renaissance Florence by John Padgett and collaborators (from which I shall quote further in the final chapter). They set the scene as follows:

[N]ew economic and political relations that cut across and through Florence's segmentary social structure inherited from its medieval past, without however destroying that traditional base. The fact that these newer social relations cross-cut the older cliquish social base was crucial to their economic consequences . . . turned the Florentine multiple-network economic ensemble into a "small world" (Milgram 1967; Watts 1999) of easy and fluid access to capital liquidity through numerous and redundant routes (Moody and White 2003). (Padgett and McLean 2006b, p. 38)

Padgett and McLean's own focus, as we see in the next chapter, was on genesis and innovation. Those authors' judgment concerning types of tie is clear-cut:

[I]t is crucial for the dynamic reproduction of any hybridization of traditional with modern that newer networks be distinct types of networks, not isomorphic in topology with older segmentary kinship. We showed above through business letters that "modern" and "traditional" were fused at the level of interactional practice in Renaissance Florence. At the macro level of network topology being discussed here, however, historically layered organizing principles were kept cross-sectionally distinct through embedding partnership systems in marriage and social class, which cross-cut segmentary kinship and neighborhood. (Ibid.)

This latter configuration has already been shown, in my first chapter, in figure 1.1. Padgett and McLean reiterate in emphatic terms:

To put the same point another way, differentiation of networks into distinct types of tie is important to the stable reproduction of hybrid ensem-
bles, because this keeps multiple social logics in synergistic tension rather
than permitting one to implode into the other (cf. White 1992, pp. 87–89).
(Ibid.)

And they explicitly draw a contrast to institutional system much as I
portray in section 5.7.1.:

We would generalize further that failure to enforce cross-cut among multiple networks is one reason why social embeddedness often degenerates
into pits of corruption, quite different from the outcome here, Florentine
clientage and favoritism notwithstanding. (Ibid.)

In section 6.3.4 I will continue this excerpt with regard to the impact
on credit as a mechanism.

6.1.4. Evolution of Control Regimes

The sources of larger views of explicit social order beyond rhetorics
seem clear. A regime like professionalism, for example, to be discussed
in a later section, involves structuring discourse to concern social networks and disciplines and institutions, as much as to act within them.
Styles and institutional systems alike are open-ended and can be extrapolated beyond present local disciplines and networks. We call the
product, which can combine styles around rhetoric, and which might
be expressed in a native statement, a *regime* when it constrains reproduction, rather than just expressing what it is.

Analysts seek to predict movements within a regime, whether they
be changes of identities, criticisms, or opinions. The endless stories
being invoked and applied in control projects slow attempts to sort out
and analyze what is going on. But analysts trace contingencies in the
story-sets and disciplines, and they also look for a balance, which need
not be reflected in any one of the stories current in the realms of a
regime. Change in values derives from fault lines in social patterns
thrown up by turmoil, such as social movements, wars, or revolutions.

Social formation must sustain and regenerate itself from within itself, but each such process is shaped by context. The wholistic context
has as tangible an impact on the process as do direct local forces, which
can be fully accounted for only within its hegemony. A regime may
offer native theory for middle-range order. *Middle-range* is a relative
term. It is the smallest scope, in time and in actions, for self-reproducing formations. It is also the largest scope that yields interpretable accounts in stories that do not require reference to unobservables, such

as the evaluation, judgments, and preferences that are unsaid or uninformed in social interactions.

These last three chapters deal with social formation that is of larger scope than a tournament and of longer duration than Mardi Gras. This is formation that is not at an extreme of ambage or ambiguity and which is thus less simple to describe and theorize than tournament or Mardi Gras. Computations of decoupling are required in the calculus for trade-offs among ambage, ambiguity, and contingency. As attention shifts to this larger scale, analysis requires more explicit attention to de/coupling—just as we become more attentive to decoupling when, in ordinary life, we move from conversation, with its instinctive decouplings, to arranging agendas with their strategic de/couplings.

Only pervasive de/coupling can permit formations that encompass many disciplines and networks and much history, which is to say, can permit regimes. A regime builds in conflict but achieves some flexibility and some potential for the exercise of control. Conflict can be set as a dual face to solidarity, the two together offering both decoupling and integration with a control regime. Bring to mind for Europe the powerful rhetoric of "the working class" versus "capitalist exploitation" that marked a control regime of the Left, with Socialist or Social Democratic parties and unions at the fore. The contrasting realms of an overarching control regime have been the "horizontal" milieu of workers before and after industrial work, as contrasted with the realm of "capitalist production," in which subordination under the rules was enforced (thus vertically structured).

6.2. Theories of Values

Conventional usage differentiates value facets central in social process, called values proper or ends, from peripheral value-facets, called attitudes. Values do appear also in styles and in rhetorics. But a regime is mobilized around values through social interactions that prevent as well as generate new actions. With the economy, for example, it is business value calibrated in money.

As values mediate between stories, control regimes split out realms. Developing a soothing nostrum is a chief concern, but nostrums also provide materials for effective switching. Multiple descriptions are available to serve as a plausible description of the course of some value in a situation. And goals are a device that bridges contradictions, goals stereotyped in terms of values. So values are a peculiar hybrid between socially programmed reproduction of regime, on the one hand, and idiosyncratic actions by identities on the other. Identities are sharing stories, no one of which corresponds to actual habituses that any one of them is in, but which together form a sufficient base for constructing accountings that can be shared. Sets of stories intertwine structuralist with individualist viewpoints; they do so as decouplers.

6.2.1. Regime, Decoupling, and Accounts

A regime is an ongoing accomplishment, dependent on decoupling. The simultaneous existence of a set of stories concerning any hunk of social reality is a necessity because the sheer plasticity and chaos of actual events cannot otherwise be accommodated, by either native or observer. And yet, an overall narrative must be sustained.

Embedding and control are the most difficult issues involved with studying regimes, where many paradoxes impose themselves at the same time. Identities and events are used in new ways as the original performances become embedded in further levels or later reen-actments.[2] Control is being sought by some persons, and at some un-predictable times, and this overlays the emergence of identities. Em-bedding and control are especially tricky when they interact with the concrete space of geography and the like, in buffering conflict or bro-kering dependencies or local jurisdiction.[3] Uncertainty remains a key indicator because it reflects the impact from meshing into the environ-ing biophysical world.

Actors, whether as persons or compounds, are embedded in seas of accounts and are generating accounts constantly. Participants are in-sisting upon accounting schemes consistent with the perspectives they variously bring. Each of such schemes has some accountability, reports some piece of sense about what is ongoing. And each such scheme has to take some account of some of the others. One example, Axelrod's tracing of the Munich talks can be generalized to the growth and fur-nishing of social spaces for political worlds more generally. Forment (1989a, b) has the right line in his talk of political discourse as rhetoric interacting with power to the effect of generating social spaces and times out of events and story-lines. He has demonstrated how this came about over centuries across Latin America and for shorter peri-ods in specific regions of a country.

There are difficulties about coverage, recording, biases, and reliabili-ties, in making observations, but these are ordinary difficulties of workmanship. The real problem is validity of the observations. Some

---

[2] See Griswold's monograph (1986) on how repeated revivals of Renaissance plays changed in the course of centuries.

[3] On the former, see Chay and Ross (1986); Crozier and Thoenig (1976); Eccles (1981c); Porter (1976); Schwartzman (1989); Tarrow (1977); and on the latter Ashford (1982).

even argue that there is no reliability in the accounts available in and from social formations, just because many participants are caught up in strategies in interacting with others. However, there is no such thing as pure behaviorist observation. Observers, as well as participants, cannot avoid dependence on "native" frames and accounts. The accounts being in multiple frames merely show recognition, within styles and regimes alike, that social action is sometimes strategic, in terms variously of how to put out an image, interpret the context, as well as generate actions that can lead to intended outcomes.

Distortions of accounts by self-interest are but one niggle, perhaps a minor and modernist niggle, in the problem of observation, as to the distinction actor/observer. Frameworks for accounts are thrown up universally and diversely within social formations wherever observed. And there are multiple accounts, as in the story-sets of chapter 2 and rhetorics of chapter 5. Leach (1954) offers a particularly vivid parsing of this sad truth for the would-be scientific observer.

6.2.2. Values and Contexts

Social organization becomes the deposit of previous interventions in social organization. This also applies to the genesis of generalized values, each being reestablished as the collation of story-sets from merger between network populations and over time. Since values are important common elements across sets of stories, values are couplers of stories. But stories can also assert values. This clears the ground for the predominant role for values, with particularities submerged. Each exemplar regime below calls on value disentangled from particularities. One generalized value traces back through discipline valuations to presumed ultimate dominance ordering. And each regime can be recast around some pair of general values, one regarding dominance and one regarding inclusivity.

Earlier theoretical perspectives were typically focused on values abstracted from their context in social organization. For example, Talcott Parsons, in his efforts toward a general theory of social action, pushed for transposability and separability of values so that the ultimate ends of different means-ends chains could constitute an abstract system. Thus, for Parsons, ultimate ends can be cultural facets of coherent social action across a society.[4]

---

[4] "Culture is . . . transmissible from personality to personality by learning and from social system to social system by diffusion. This is because culture is constituted by 'ways of orienting and acting,' these ways being 'embodied in' meaningful symbols . . . which are the postulated controlling entities . . . unlike need-dispositions and role-expectations, [symbols] are not internal to the systems whose orientation they control . . . they have external 'objective' embodiments" (Parsons and Shils 1951, chap. 3, part 2). What

By contrast, Erving Goffman (1955, 1963, 1967, 1971, 1974) denied this transposability in his push for local phenomenological truth: viz., a "backstage" where reality and valuation of even the simplest social acts must be negotiated afresh, endlessly.[5] He seeks to induce style as well as value out of everyday minutiae of social organization.[6] This reminds us that scientific discourse is subject, like any other discourse, to the variability with context upon which Ricoeur (1988) insisted.

It was Parsons who was following tradition as he sought to strip values out of forms of social organization. Yet values used as the foundation in many means-ends schemas of analysis (notably in Parsons 1937) were themselves extracted from the intersections of story-sets, which in turn derived from valuations spread across different tangible disciplines. It seems to me that what Parsons misses is the fundamental split between institutional systems and control regimes.

Eisenstadt and Lemarchand (1981) return us to one of the principal sources for sociology on values, Max Weber: "*Wirtschaftsethik* is, in a sense, a 'code,' a general 'formal orientation,' a 'deeper structure,' which programs or regulates the actual concrete social organization" (p. 172). In the present work, the reverse direction is traveled instead, from concrete organization to whatever values there be. Others, such as DiMaggio (1987), Habermas (1975), March and Olsen (1976, 1989), and Merton (1968), also push for explanation of value only in interaction with tangible organization.

Either way, a value is made recognizable across different locales and periods by symbols and their use in social action. This is supported by Michael Schudson when he claims that

> culture is not a set of ideas imposed but a set of ideas and symbols available for use. Individuals select the meanings they need for particular purposes and occasion from the limited but nonetheless varied cultural

---

had made Parsons's first book (1937) so stunning was its supersession of Pareto's synthesis, which was a synthesis of an abstract logico-experimental model of society with a biological/sentimental model. Pareto had relegated economics to a subordinate role, as unable to shed light on the general ends, the values, that drove and determined the whole means-ends schema of economics. Parsons argued, against Pareto's retreat to instinctual biology of the emotions, for a direct sociological interlocking of general ends into a web of values that was exactly *The Structure of Social Action*. Parsons's approach was a bold vision for linking society to individual by observable cultural fiat.

[5] For one overview of the phenomenological position, which situates Goffman with Sachs and Garfinkel, see Rawls (1989). For appreciation and critique of Goffman, see Burns (1991).

[6] Even though Goffman seems concerned only with the evanescent, a principle of self-similarity suggests there should be similar stylistic regularities in large and ponderous institutions.

menus a given society provides. In this view, culture is a resource for social use more than a structure to limit social action. (Schudson 1989, p.
155; and cf. Swidler 1986)

Nevertheless, because symbols are "polysemic" and contain various
purposes, ambiguity in communication and interpretation may arise.

6.2.3. Packaging and Parsons

In the formation of a regime, values operate in packages. Lessons in
white lies of tact and adaptability go along with lectures on honesty,
and together they form a value set for living in institutional context.
In one regime, tact will predominate with honesty secondary, whereas
another regime will have tact as a shadow to honesty.[7]

As an example, take values in science research in today's American
academy. Originality (a variant of scope) is the preeminent value, with
its complement and obverse in scientists' thinking and talk, the value
of truth (a variant of purity) being the shadow value.[8]

No unique package, no single set of values is ordained. For example,
priority and precision is another common pair of values, alongside
truth and originality, through which to analyze stories of research
within the discourse of a scientific specialty. From one regime to another, one may code a different set of values. But instead the same set
may obtain, with the shift being in relative frequencies of use, within
the given set. The shift then occurs in how given values are mapped
onto sorts of interaction, and in how actors sequence among the set in
giving an accounting of action.[9]

At the level of "honesty" and "prudence" there is a whole package
of values that can be operationally distinguished but which may collapse into one in subjects' appreciations. That was the approach of Tal-

---

[7] Until some proper calculus has been developed for analysis of narrative—perhaps
along some such lines as Abell's (1987)—metaphor and intuition will have to serve. Linguistic theory of poetics (Culler 1975, pp. 197, 202, 227; Jakobson 1990, pp. 130–31) points
toward some discriminations, as of metonymy from metaphor according to voice—discourse versus narrative—and theme, character, genre, and so on.

[8] See the discussion in chapter 7 of Cozzens's (1989) case study.

[9] Take a topical example. U.N. ambassador John Burton, or earlier Senator Jesse Helms
of North Carolina, operated within a set of values that you hold, too. A set of values
comes with a scene, and the national political scene, the realm that you and Burton both
attend to, is huge, but it is also abstracted and limited to attitudes and accompanying
ties as expressed in public media among entities and actions which themselves become
defined as being public. It is the ambassador's priority, sequencing and frequency in use,
as well as his concrete mappings from values to social actors, that distinguish him from
your hold on values.

cott Parsons, who invoked highly abstract and universal values that were not socially anchored. In Parsons's pattern variables from later work, the honesty package would presumably be reduced to particularist, universalist: cf. Brownstein (1982).

Distinctions within a set of values should be correlated with concrete social context, so that the package in its concrete correlation is a moving target of analysis. Take an example from a different discourse, Bob Dylan's adoption in 1965 of electric instruments, which then were adopted by many others. Within the preexisting (corporatist) regime of folk music, a general value—"genuine" hands-on music from and for the people—was no doubt violated by the shift of instrument. Indeed, there was a ruckus if not a schism. But among the active members of a world, operative values concern much more specific matters than such an abstraction. The change to electric instruments violated some but not others of a set of specific values, so that one could encompass the shift, cognitively, with rather small adjustments in the values set. The shift also at the same time would be impacting social relations, and in particular relations among performers, and between them and new sorts of technicians, all of which would be reflected in shifts in specific values. Actors, like observers, are as much reading values out of accomplished actions as they are apprehending values as freestanding guides.

There is one commonality between the abstract, floating approach of theorists akin to Parsons, and what I have just argued. Both imply and induce a public or other realm as their siting.

6.2.4. Dual Hierarchy, as between Church and State

After having elaborated on both values and an alternative to functionalism, and before laying out the three Weberian ideal types of corporatism, clientelism, and professionalism, let us turn our attention to regimes that emerge out of bipolar social formations.

A regime can emerge in and from control struggles between two social formations that build contrasting interpretive realms that embed dual social formations. A prototype is the dual hierarchy of church and state seen in medieval Europe. Church and state each supplies a contrasting realm to the other. I will draw an example from the tension between the Roman state and the emerging Christian church to illustrate the dual hierarchy as avenues for control.

In medieval times, dual regimes emerged as a European substitute for the Roman emperor grew in stature, and so too did the newly empowered head of the church. In the fifth century c.e., Saint Augustine wrote, in the *City of God*, that people should give to the emperor what is the emperor's and to God what is God's. The specific relation of the emperor and pope was often fraught: e.g., the walk to Canossa by the German emperor after he had been excommunicated by the church; the besieging of the Italian popes by the German emperors, along with the French counter-popes in the fourteenth and fifteenth centuries.

There was tension between their two contrasting narratives of supreme value, which played out between their hierarchies all up and down levels. The internal splittings on one side of the hierarchy were responsive to those on the other. Take Cardinal Richelieu besieging La Rochelle and thereby, the French king and the cardinals. As regional magnates extracted more power from the king, so a veritable torrent of new monasteries was founded, setting up local economic as well as political autonomies in the church. As feudal levy and militia gave way to a paid professional army, so too did preaching orders develop within the church.

The papacy showed endless ingenuity in use of dual hierarchy. First the religious orders helped penetrate diocesan and parochial obscurantism; then mendicant orders penetrated both to reach the lay publics. At some subsequent time, a particular new order is set up as the backbone of reform, only to be superseded by yet another, or by a reinvigoration of a particular specialism among the ordinary clergy.

The Reformation from the sixteenth century is viewed as a split from papal power, notably in Germany and in Great Britain, but it was in counterpoint with a correlative splitting away of national states from the Holy Roman Empire. Each of the dual realms claimed supremacy for, and in, its distinctive value, and correlative material advantage. Neither side could walk out on the duality, since such control regime endlessly generated corrections to such attempts.

Dual hierarchies come to be perceived by those who see subtleties as affording them helpful avenues to overall projects of control. A dual hierarchy makes several devices available for this: the collegium of bishops, for example, is a device of the hieratic style that makes it easier to penetrate through an equivalence set to a wide diversity of networks.[10] From a horizontal viewpoint, the collegium can be a resonance structure for bringing together local tendencies into sufficient correspondence so that events can be defined across and among them, and thence actions induced. The inspector general corps as a function of an army exemplifies still another device, having a chain of agents that reaches into all levels of another bureaucracy, with these agents being bundled together and set apart.

---

[10] As spelled out in chapter 4.

6.2.5. Pillarization

One can see dual hierarchy as bringing together different but complementary values, along with interests, in establishing a control regime. This process can work across more than two realms of hierarchy. A colorful and instructive example of regime with multiple parallel hierarchies can be traced back to the mid-century period of *Verzuiling*, or pillarization, in the Netherlands (Lijphart 1968; Bank 1981; Van Schendelen and Jackson 1987).

The origins of pillarization, *Verzuiling*, show its focus on meaning woven into blocking action and energized along strings of concrete ties. The following excerpt points to the fall of the *Verzuiling*, and it suggests that many came, over time, to see only opacity and clientelism (see the clientelist section that follows). But the history is clear when Van Schendelen and Jackson find that this pillarized system of consociational politics essentially disappeared. When pillarized welfare organizations had encountered financial problems, the state took over and installed regulations that restrict pillarization. Consequently, new social groups as well as modern-minded firms were established and requested depillarization from the state.

It is a fact that control regimes can best be observed in transition, in struggle and change. In addition, Bank defines, "*Verzuiling* [as] widely credited with 'having brought stability to a society which is otherwise divided by contradictions and antagonisms' between the Protestants, the Catholics, and the Socialists, who have in turn withdrawn from a society dominated by liberal values" (Bank 1981).

Another expert, Windmuller (1969), emphasizes the subsequent labor explosions that became compressed into yet another, socialist, pillar, leading to the full-blown pillarization system in the First World War, with full-blown narrative justification.

These three historical depictions suggest that such a plural society is held together by a grand coalition of the leaders of the significant segments, which can be seen as distinct subcultures around distinct meanings. These separations of meanings in fact greatly strengthen the tangible networks of favor and obligation that serve to freeze up the social formation. Such networks are energized exactly through strings of interconnections across the elites of different pillars, who, by their own public definitions, can have no meanings in common!

The three control regimes that will be discussed in the following sections exemplify the translation of discipline values to regimes of control and are to be understood as Weberian ideal types.

6.3. Functional Subsystems

Functional systems have long been a staple in sociological theories, with subsystems used in specification of realms and allied constructs. The theorist who has given this the most sustained attention is Niklas Luhmann, so we begin with his views, together with an application.

6.3.1. Luhmann's General Formulation

Luhmann develops his approach focusing on form, where a form, something that can be distinguished, creates an inside (system)—outside (environment) distinction and develops its own differentiation of inside and outside on and on in itself (further subsystems). His thesis is that the principle of functional differentiation has, since the sixteenth century, restructured the European and later on the World Society along several functional subsystems (as so far specified: education, economy, religion, science, politics, and mass media), none of which gains a dominant position in modernity (earlier in history, e.g., in European feudalism, stratification and center-periphery had been the dominant differentiating principles). These functional subsystems structure communication within their realms along overarching binary codes, such as true/untrue (science), payment/nonpayment (economy), and so forth; they observe the other subsystems and their relations to themselves and might couple structurally, which is the case when self-creating systems mutually depend on each other (as applies for social and psychological systems).

Narratives are, for Luhmann, the forces that allow for the formation of expectations that abate the complexity of interactions; the development of forms of communication influences the further differentiation of society. In his theory, this differentiation into hegemonic realms of subsystems, whose communication codes are untranslatable into the codes of the other subsystems, leads to greater independence and greater dependence at the same time. The communication systems don't need the other systems in order to perform their chains of communication; on the other hand, these subsystems form their mutual environment and are thus able to irritate each other (as, e.g., when the malfunctioning of the economy spills over into the political realm of discontented voters).

What Luhmann is keying into, I think, is the magical aspect, the awesome aspect of regimes like law and art and economy. We speak of the modern world here, but it offers echoes of the taboo known in earlier eras (cf. White and Erikson 2005). One cue is the hush that comes with the sacred.

In contrast to Luhmann's theory, my approach accounts for the separation of realms from out of the switching of identities among different netdoms.[11] To understand his opposing argument fully, one would need to survey Luhmann's whole massive apparatus of theory, with its rich commentary and wry personal illustrations (e.g., p. 420, found between the prior excerpts). Previously, I have built my own view of *realm* as mobilization in narrative around values in an explicit social context of particular types of tie.

Luhmann's evolutionary system-theoretical account, focusing on self-differentiating forms, provides a narrative of historical development, in which the differentiating subsystems require alignments of the rhetorics that justified the prior structuring of the society (e.g., during the shift from the stratified noble society in Europe to a functionally differentiated society). In his theory, rhetorics might represent realities that no longer hold. For example, in modernity in the law system, a rhetoric remained that equated the good and the right, left over from a time when the political system was ruled by a king who, as the divine ruler, was embedded in a rhetoric of doing the right and the good. The realignment of those values might take violent clashes, which disprove the unity of the good moral intentions and the right actions as, for example, in the French Revolution (Luhmann 1986, p. 92), which delegitimizes this rhetoric and allows for greater ambiguity in the final telos of the law.

Luhmann's conclusion about independence of the different subsystems might hinder any theorizing over macro-control regimes in modernity, as stratification, for example, had become a mere by-product of functional differentiation to him. On the other hand, in his last lectures in 1993 in Bielefeld, Luhmann theorized about the possibility of inclusion/exclusion as being the metacode of his subsystems of modernity, where the exclusion from one subsystem (as from politics by not having a passport) might lead to the exclusion from all other subsystems (Luhmann 2005, p. 81). On the other hand, he suggested that the dominant subsystem at a given time might be the one that is the most defunct, as it irritates all the others.

---

[11] An interesting phenomenon that my concept of style may illuminate is that this switching might have impacts on the psychological systems (which Luhmann has as the environment of his social system) and thus might provoke irritations in the subsystems, something one might imagine along the lines of language.

Nevertheless, despite the beauty of the theoretical construction, his large-scale functionalist view of societal development, which is also evolutionist, might obscure actual developments on the historical ground.[12] Thus, for our middle-range approach, Luhmann's proposal needs to be specified concretely.

6.3.2. Luhmann's Law

Whatever else a legal system is, it does invoke and involve organization. But within Luhmann's principal monograph (2004) on law, it is only in chapter 7, when treating the courts, that Luhmann moves in this direction.

> The operative closure of the system and its detachment from any direct participation in the environment corresponds to the internal necessity to have to decide. . . . Contracts need not be concluded and statutes need not be passed . . . but courts have to decide every case submitted to them. . . . Therefore it is necessary to replace the model of hierarchy with the concept of the differentiation between center and periphery. (2004, pp. 281, 284, 292)

This brings us to a central realization: Luhmann nowhere admits, much less invokes, a middle-range order in between a (doubly contingent) relation and the system. He explicitly declined to deal with organization as he points out in note 1, p. 600, to chapter 10 of his magnum opus:

> 1. We leave out of consideration here a third mode of forming social systems, which cannot be reduced either to society or to interaction, namely *organizations*, because it is not as universally relevant as a *difference*. . . . On the next level, that of concretizing the theory, one would perhaps need to distinguish . . . and develop separate theories for each type. (Luhmann 1995)

Instead, "[r]eturn to the premise that communication is rendered asymmetrical as action. Social systems are communication systems, but, via selective synthesis of communication, they construct an interpretation 'of' communication as action and thereby describe themselves as action systems" (Luhmann 1995, p. 469).

Courts are merely in the background here. Luhmann's general characterization of the function of law does seem apt here:

> Abstractly, law deals with the social costs of the time binding of expectations. Concretely, law deals with the function of the stabilization of norma-

---

[12] A fact Luhmann acknowledges when differentiating himself from historians by his interest in a theory of societal evolution.

tive expectations. . . . Law makes it possible to know which expectations
will meet with social approval . . . one can take on the disappointments of
everyday life with a higher degree of composure; at least one knows that
one will not be discredited for one's expectations. One can afford a higher
degree of uncertain confidence or even of mistrust . . . this means that one
can live in a more complex society in which personal or interaction mechanisms to secure trust no longer suffice. (Luhmann 2004. pp. 147–48)

Luhmann is tracing here the effect a differentiated law system has on
a functionally differentiated society. It permits one to handle a higher
degree of complexity.

But later he takes this to an extreme that clashes with the view even
of realist Lazega: "The differentiation of the legal system cannot be
achieved without the decomposition of social ties, obligations, and
expectations of help" (Luhmann 2004, p. 271). One might wonder if
this total disentangling actually took place or if it is more theoretical
in nature.

In contrast, here is the conclusion of sociologist Neil Fligstein and
colleague on the basis of a comprehensive review of the literature on
"Law and Corporate Governance":

How do social and legal arrangements affect firms, markets and economic
growth? . . . The literature now agrees that there is variation in systems of
corporate governance across societies and that most of this difference reflects national political, social and cultural trajectories that have created
and continuously shaped the laws. (Fligstein and Choo 2005, p. 62)

And it also becomes clear, later on the same page in Luhmann, that he
is not even attempting to portray the actual evolution of a rhetoric:

This example supports our theoretical assumption that the evolution of
autopoietic systems is more a test of how much room autopoeisis frees up
for the formation of complex orders, than of adjusting the system to a
given environment. . . . It may suffice here just to introduce the hypothesis:
it is not economic efficiency but complexity that is the intervening variable
that translates evolutionary structural changes into adjustments within
the system. (Luhmann 2004)

Luhmann's massive *Law as a Social System* (2004) contains little beyond generalities, and no particular legal rhetoric, aside from repeated invocation of Roman law. And there are weaknesses even at
this general level. Whatever else a legal system is, it surely embodies
some sort of rationality, and I argued in chapter 4 that rationality
emerges as, and so is best comprehended as, a style, with rhetoric
being post hoc. And whatever else a legal system is, it induces and

invokes disciplined, tightly constrained language. Thus, a more historical investigation is required.

The term *control regime* attempts, with critical association onto Luhmann's subsystems, to define the specific channeling of action. Thus, the term focuses more on the specific programming for the application of his "codes" of realms, rather than on the codes themselves. In his book *Ecological Communication* (1989), makes a distinction between the binary code and the programming, the latter containing the conditions and procedures by which one of the two binary codes is applied to the occurring events (i.e., criteria for applying the code), and which provides the communication system with the opportunity to react to irritation by its environment (see Luhmann 1989, pp. 90ff.).

This focus also allows us to see specific control regimes on smaller scales than functional subsystems and especially to consider the interdependencies of subsystems that lead to the emergence of new control regimes. For example, consider the emergence of the rhetoric of "Corporate Social Responsibility" in recent decades. One might argue for several firms that rhetoric becomes a part of their program for deciding the profitability of their investment decisions. Negative action in this respect might irritate the mass media, generating information that is broadcast, and thereby irritating psychological systems on whose participation the firm depends for its survival. This change of the program is an indicator of the emergence of a new, "green" control regime, something that in Boltanski and Thévenot's terms (1999) might be identified as a "green order of worth."

6.3.3. Bourdieu's Art

The issue with Luhmann in his treatment of law remains: from which actual historic development does that rhetoric originate? Let us contrast Luhmann's treatment with that of his great French contemporary, Pierre Bourdieu, in his incisive work, *The Rules of Art* (1996a). That work is, in my present terms, a study of a rhetoric. But the subtitle, *Genesis and Structure of the Literary Field*, seems to call for treatment back in my chapter 4, as a style. What I will argue, using Bourdieu's own words, is that *field* instead maps into realm.

Note that Bourdieu begins with as emphatic an endorsement concerning the on/off distinctness of a rhetoric for art as Luhmann gave for law:

> The collective belief in the game (*illusio*) and in the sacred value of its stakes is simultaneously the precondition and the product of the very functioning of the game; it is fundamental to the power of consecration,

permitting consecrated artists to constitute certain products as *sacred* objects. . . . The collective labour which goes to produce this belief . . . the
innumerable acts of credit which are exchanged among all the agents . . .
with group exhibitions or prefaces by which consecrated authors consecrate the younger ones, who consecrate them in return as masters or heads
of schools; between artists and patrons or collectors; between artists and
critics, and in particular avant-garde critics. . . . It would be foolish to
search for an ultimate guarantor or guarantee . . . outside of the network
of relations of exchange through which it is both produced and circulates.
(Bourdieu 1996a, p. 230)

He goes on to specify his "field" in terms not unlike mine regarding
"realm:"

The field is a network of objective relations . . . between positions—for example the position corresponding to a genre like the novel . . . or the position locating a review, a salon, or a circle as the gathering place of a group
of producers. . . . To different *positions* . . . correspond homologous *position-
takings*, including literary or artistic works, obviously, but also political
acts and discourses. . . . In the phase of equilibrium, the *space of positions*
tends to govern *the space of position-taking.* (p. 231)

For commentary and assessment, see Calhoun, LiPuma, and Postone
(1993).

6.3.4. Economy as Functional Subsystem

Despite my earlier critiques, Luhmann's theory can help clarify the
general argument made in this book. In the previous chapter, I developed an account of the production economy as an institutional system
for a realm. But we can also envision economy as a control regime for
a distinctive realm, which is to say as a functional subsystem in Luhmann's terminology. I argue that Luhmann's functional subsystems
can go along with White's institutional systems to yield a control regime here.[13]

The multiple-network account of Florence given earlier goes on to
cite fiscal consequences as the hallmark of emerging capitalism:

---

[13] Matthias Thiemann, an exegete of Luhmann, phrases it thus: institutional systems
form the realms for control regimes. They provide the code, whose applications are determined by the forces constituting the control regime. This finds its condensations in
the programs.

Why then was credit so powerful in Renaissance Florence? Our bottom-line answer is that credit functioned multivocally in many practical do-mains at once. . . . Because of these inter-domain functional spillovers, in-duced structurally by cross-cutting social networks, credit was good for business, good for sociality, and good for politics all at once. (Padgett and McLean 2006b, p. 41)

What about larger stages? Managements of large business firms in a sector—or even across a whole economy—cluster and imitate and thus offer an example of regime (Fligstein 1990, 2001; Burt 1992a) in which disciplines, networks, styles, and rhetorics are orchestrated across busi-ness realm.

Mintz and Schwartz (1985) argued for the emergence of the hege-mony of banking institutions in American business. "We apply the con-cept of hegemony to this arrangement because it produces domination of policy without strategic control. The influence exercised by financials operates mainly through the elimination or creation of options for other institutions, that is, by altering the profiles of constraint" (p. 40).

One of these constraints, imposed by the financial sector acting in consortiums and enacted through lending relations, is the refusal to finance destructive (cutthroat) competition (p. 111). Furthermore, di-rect and indirect interlocks of financial and industrial firms were iden-tified as providing "the mechanism for the circulation of general infor-mation about investment policy and opportunity, for informed speculation about capital flows, and for promulgating the variety of values and norms that constitute a corporate culture based on financial hegemony" (p. 183).[14]

Fligstein (1990) instead argued that not the varieties of business in-terlocks as Mintz and Schwartz would have it, but rather the "concep-tions of control" as developed and upheld by the dominant power group ("subunit power base") within incumbent firms in their organi-zational field, are structuring business behavior. Delineating three his-torically dominant conceptions of control (manufacturing, sales and marketing, finance), he argues: "This progression does not imply, how-ever, that one conception of control caused the emergence of its succes-sor. New conceptions of control evolved out of key interactions among firms and between firms and the state" (p. 16).

This historical inquiry of the emergence of control regimes from at-tempts of American firms (read *identities*) to control their organiza-

---

[14] With respect to the financial development of the last twenty-five years, this concep-tion might have become historically outdated, as more and different sources of capital have developed. That might ask for a new inquiry into the relationship between financial and industrial capital.

tional realms (read *environment*) along the lines of price and profit stability by copying successful competitors, is an erudite application of the mutual observance of market actors that I also use in modeling (e.g., White 2002).

Most interesting, probably, is the claim of changed valuation orderings of ascending new elites in the firms that shape a new understanding of the firm in their environment, and that promised new profitable paths to growth. As it is illustrated in Fligstein's argument, entrepreneurs formulated new strategies of finance and accounting that were not shaped by the necessities of production or the desire for profit, "[but] they focused on the corporation as a collection of assets that could and should be manipulated to increase short run profits" (p. 226). Therefore, the conception of control of the finance system, in this case, was established by the agents' concepts and perception of finance and evaluations of their strategies.

This is an example of how economic rhetorics can come in a stochastic environment too fluid to sustain rational choice, but fluid enough to induce it and to sustain individual persons in the modern sense. A whole new layer of interpretation can be superposed—as is done in some microeconomic theory—upon an economy actually grown out of a putting-out system but which needs, in the present, sufficient social software to continue running, as shown in the previous chapter.

There (chapter 5) I traced various institutional systems of production economy, with more emphasis on the explanation of reproducibility than on control. I relied on the work of Udy in tracing the putting-out system of economy. The main argument to which Udy built (1970), however, was that history provided an accidental concatenation of various windows of opportunity sufficient to define a new system of industrial capitalism, all of a piece. And also that this system is no abstraction: henceforward, it is undefinable except as a unique and all-encompassing context.

Nevertheless, if capitalism is seen thus as one control regime, then it means that the variables of coding, profitability (profitable/nonprofitable) and property (property/nonproperty), become the encompassing driving principles. In allusion to Marx, we might say: if it is true that the foundation for the claims to the product produced in the common action of identities is property rights in the means of production, then these property rights must be defended so that the self-reproducing system of capitalism can go on, resting on the private initiative of the entrepreneur.

On the other hand, the profit nexus disentangles commercial decisions from moralistic considerations and is an overarching force that constrains and channels the attempts for control by identities. This disentanglement is a trend Luhmann observed for all subsystems. In this respect, the reader should be reminded of Luhmann's thought about the threat of exclusion from one subsystem, as it might lead to the exclusion from all.

Economy today embraces more than an institutional system of production. It emerges in establishing further the fiscal realm of capitalism. Perspective shifts from the rhetorics of tangible production to mobilization around overriding value, around capital and its fiscal flows in counterpoint with flows of goods and services. I have developed this theme at length in chapter 12 of the book on markets (White 2002) used in the previous chapter.

6.4. Corporatist

The most common form of regime may well be corporatist. Corporatism is a control regime that serves as a blueprint or template by which work activities and division of labor are managed. It can be seen as the induction and defense of rightful meaning around right value. Corporatism is especially concerned with particular claims and rights about relations of agency. Corporatism is articulated by constellations of social bodies that, in fact, produce the claims, rather than the reverse. These are claims regarding three-party transactions, at minimum, which are being made to a fourth, supererogatory and embedding party.

Corporatism explicitly organizes around values. For example, the *Standestaat* that preceded modern states across Europe for centuries drew resiliency from its expressive focus in value commitments, notably varieties of honor for aristocrats and holiness for clergy (Duby 1980; Poggi 1978). So corporatist abuts dual hierarchy, treated earlier, in subsection 6.2.4.

Any nascent regime may, in coming to reproduce itself around values, flesh out into still other network populations. Many of the examples used in this section will be historical from periods when the construct of corporatism was explicitly recognized, with an acumen from which we can benefit.

Corporatist regime builds from a soup of disciplines in which events and issues are generated plentifully, and in which arena disciplines are rare among the three species. As identities are selected into groups, discussed as corporates in chapters 2 and 5, actions become routinized as connections among them, so that continually re-forming teams of complementarities is not a theme. Attention is directed to explicit corporate boundaries and positive identities, so that paradoxically there is suppression of many possible ties bridging distinct network populations.

6.4.1. Corporatism as Blockage

Many popularizations of corporatism (e.g., cf. Lehmbruch and Schmitter 1982) have been misled. They have been misled by the insistent rationalizations that are the very stuff of corporatism. They have been misled into thinking of corporatism as something grand and different, even esoteric.

This is nonsense. Corporatism is a common, everyday affair. As a regime routinizes old actions, it also blocks actions. Corporatism is a system that organizes exactly around an assertion of specific meanings—as rights and immunities, which are for explicitly operationalized sets and nestings of actors. Corporatism exists, therefore, at all scopes and in all contexts.[15] It is to the end of sustaining these meanings that fresh action—that is, innovations inconsistent with the prevailing rhetoric—gets blocked. Correlatively, an underlying importance of corporatist regime is that it makes comparable, and in so doing brings together, otherwise disparate and unrelated clusters and network populations.

Corporatist regime is sufficient to block getting action, yet is not free to exhibit its own low overhead. Its narrative becomes so persuasive that onlookers come to mistake its intentions for tangible actuality. Constraining the possibilities of agency by setting stable premises for deciding, is as common in the economy as in government. For example, the illustration used by Fine and Harris on entrepreneurship was a striking characteristic of England when it was the prototype of industrialization; but so, even then, was blocking:

> The banking system that was constructed (by 1914) put the banks in a position where they acted as a block against the external forces that were necessary for industry's growth, and it has been the structure of the system rather than the attitudes and choices of bankers that has been at the root of the problem. . . . The banks have met industry's demand for credit all too comfortably, and, as a result, have developed a special relation with industry which has given them a blocking role . . . regulated their lending

[15] The Old Testament is the Bible of corporatism. The Ph.D. comprehensive exam is a text for corporatism. Corporatism is around you all the time, a stalwart of blocking action on every scale from boys' gangs to college departments and to bureaus within businesses. And, of course, we find it in the endless lattices of law courts and tribunals.

by a set of negative rules designed to minimize the damage that could be done if a loan failed. (Fine and Harris, 1985, pp. 124, 130)

6.4.2. Work

Corporatism, one may argue, is the social elaboration of physical production that emerges in a larger scope, when different groups of individuals (identities) participate and manage the distribution and reorganization of their activities. In other words, corporatism is the template that shepherds and routinizes production activities.

Networks of disciplines do not build themselves from a concern with ecology. In shaping yet further structures of importance, it is control projects that continue to compete, and they only peripherally attend to the effectiveness of physical productions. Each network, as well as each discipline depends crucially on the social context, which is supplied in large part by themselves as populations.

Work activities can induce each other and thereby temporarily outline a material population. But social life is about actors' importance within social settings; so work settings are not shaped primarily to achieve effective joint operations on physical settings. As Udy (1959, 1970) early said explicitly, and demonstrated empirically, production in the ordinary sense of practical work is difficult to reconcile with the universal tendencies to elaboration and to embedding that come with the ongoing processes of social structuring. Udy worked out his argument from an extensive cross-cultural canvass of detailed forms of hunting, gathering, agriculture, and craft, as well as manufacturing and other contexts for work.

Succession is one major exemplification of this tension between work and the social. Performance in a work team can be seen as dependent on succession, day by day, to tasks of work. And the same issue recurs at larger scopes and periods. Solutions of social equations of balance are what deliver the successors and thereby impinge on technical equations of physical production.

Udy's theorem is that the longer and more fully developed the social context of production, the less effective and efficient the work process: hunting and gathering, he argues, dominates settled agriculture in efficiency, but not in social elaboration. In his study, corporate realm deposits around work as a kernel, in a context of tribal and ethnic overlay.

6.4.3. Consensus in City-States

The regime of corporatism is proclaimed as well as exemplified by the guild systems of medieval and Renaissance cities. These illustrate that corporatism asserts stories about itself as interrelated boundaries. Guild systems and their cities are small and clearly demarcated, so all interconnections can be traced. Corporatism is defensive, and thus one might expect each corporatist regime to have some counterpart. This counterpart would have its own constituent corporates; it would be a counterpart corporatism shadowy in reality and ill-perceived by outsiders.[16] Consider a case:

Renaissance Florence is a city-state with highly articulate elites and extensive archives, which have been studied intensively; and so one can examine whether or not special transparency was achieved there. Najemy (1982), who has sifted a great array of detailed studies to draw a portrait of this polity, summarizes it through a theory of consensus. Paradoxically, consensus is not the product or even the goal of this corporatist formation. Rather, Najemy makes clear that consensus is the urgent outer face of elite control that must stay in shadows, given the brilliant light of consensus. Strings of dependency must abound in corporatism, and indeed in other regimes too, just because the obscure, real struggle is over control of such strings. Control by corporates is counter to the reality lying beneath the consensus hegemony.

Now, return to the preceding discussion about blocking action: the following sections are examples of how corporatism prevents new actions in various different ways. Take a preview of the first example, the Fronde, where the initial focus is on a group of royal officials, which served as the "parliament" and was in charge of the enforcement of law and royal absolutism in medieval France. The Fronde illustrates a corporatist control regime for the French kings such that its members asserted certified meanings to legal and administration principles in order to block rebellious actions. At the same time, the Fronde also mobilized the French cultural and political values that were embedded in the legal and administration principles. In this example, one can see that control is exerted and constructed by meanings around rules.

6.4.4. The Fronde

Corporatist regimes are not confined to cute little city-states. Nor, despite the narrative of values, need it be a pacific system. Consider a particular counterexample. When an irresistible social force meets an immovable social frame, paradoxes result. Such an encounter was *The Revolt of the Judges: The Parlement of Paris and the Fronde, 1643–1652*

---

[16] The concept is familiar from Simon, Smithburg, and Thompson (1950) and has been developed further by DiMaggio and Powell (1983).

(Moote 1971).[17] Earlier periods in France, as throughout Europe, had seen governments differentiate and evolve into largely corporatist forms (Major 1960), such as the *Standestaat* of central Europe (Poggi 1978) already mentioned. A mosaic of collegial representations, a veritable tiling of the floor of state administration, came into recognition. Always there were rights and privileges to be asserted for repeated recognition by a higher authority itself brought into being in part by urgent desires precisely for definitive recognition of turfs. These desires were expressed not just by one variety of discipline, not even a whole species for partition into interests and claims, but rather by an apparently endless spawning of still further subclaims and refinements and imitations.[18]

The *irresistible force* against which the Fronde operated was the absolutist state of late medieval France, an unprecedented device, of the dual hierarchy and hieratic manipulation discussed earlier, which was bypassing and smothering the *Standestaat* (Lachmann 1987; Anderson 1974). The *immovable body* was the skein of legal corporations, the parlements. This skein was triggered into stonewalling against royal invasion of their claims during a confusion of war and peripheral rural revolt.

The great paradox of the Fronde was the fact that a body of royal officials dedicated to the enforcement of law and the principle of royal absolutism—the narrative story-lines of parlements—could rebel against the king's administration. The singular article is inapt: even "the" Parlement of Paris was, in fact, a complex of ten chambers that might only rarely meet together in plenary sessions. And this core complex itself was meaningful only because, and in that, it was part of a formal network of other regional, local, and specialized parlements. This network combined law with registration and legislation, to express it in the modern idiom.

This Parlement lattice itself was resilient to being rooted out because it was contraposed to other lattices[19] that were more directly fiscal in operation. But all and each of these lattices were intent upon operationalizing meaning for its turfs and its members. This was the case as against even a "sun king"—who in their halls was invoked only to

---

[17] This early example is selected from among accounts of government corporatism because it identifies explicit and tangible mechanism, whereas typical modern accounts (e.g., Schmitter 1975; but see Lehmbruch and Schmitter 1982) primarily concern ideologies divorced from explicit social mechanism.

[18] On Spain as a parallel example, see Carr (1966), and on Poland, see Anderson (1974).

[19] Of *tresoriers* and *elus*; on the social science use of the term *lattice*, see, for example, Mische and Pattison (2000), Pattison and Breiger (2002), and Mohr and Duqenne (1997).

preside over their magisterial concordance of rights with rites. In the larger context:

> The powers which the Frondeurs claimed, and which were at cross-purposes with one another, were all defined in relation to the monarch and therefore limited the extent to which they could undermine royal power since it ultimately took down their claims as well (which is evidenced by peasant rebellions which erupted in the wake of the Parlementaires' Frondes). (Lachmann, personal communication in 2006, based on Lachmann [2000, pp. 127–31] and Beik [1985])

The Fronde gained "eventness," identity, just by the failure of Parlement to notice, as it were, to register, absolutist decrees. Was registration a mere formality? No, registration was the assignment of meaning by a pinnacle of a lattice of mutually recognized corporations whose own identities came from certifying meanings, which is to say from creating meanings. These corporations' historical (and etymological) origins always were to block action through asserting meaning.

These meanings were primarily and originally tangible. As meanings, they were socially operational; they were rights and immunities and the like. It was a late trick of the absolutist era, dressed up as a liberation and also as an enlightenment, to conceive and assert meanings so abstract as to have little social content.[20] There cannot be any self-evident corporate body to assert and define an abstract right.

> Absolutist arguments had no effect on the parlementarians, who simply countered with legal measures which forced the regent to make further concessions. ... Any Royal legislation to enact their reforms (increase taxes in war crisis) then had to go through each court separately ... (yielding) a many-sided scramble for redress of diverse grievances and a legal nightmare ... at lower government levels petty bureaus had first to submit reforms to sovereign tribunals—provincial and national—and often lengthy appeals for and against from officials. There were provincial parliamentary Frondes in the making, but the real revolt of the judges in the provinces got under way only when the Parlement of Paris forced the regent to send legislation for the consideration of these local corporations. (Moote 1971, pp. 136, 140, 145, 150)

In the example of the Fronde, we become the observer of a defensive act of a corporatist regime versus an autocracy that attempts to redefine the law by the will of the sovereign. It was only special circumstances—a regency of notable ineptness, confused war mobilizations,

---

[20] Just so did earlier Greek philosophy emerge in the age of tyrants, though it was the public relations of the occasional and momentary republican forms that impressed itself upon the later world as the character of the age.

and the like—that made corporatist institutions limpid to the observer and analyst. And also not every culture has the lucidity and consistency that the French show even when running amok. But the corporatist regime whose bones are laid so clear in the Fronde example is no esoteric flower confined to France, or to the great, or to one era.

Before I move on to the discussion of another control regime, I briefly summarize how corporatism generates new meanings through resource allocation and management of activities.

6.5. Clientelist

As corporatism illustrates the emergence of new meanings through daily activities, I claim that clientelism builds up a regime upon a relation of exchange between unequals, a tie that can be understood by itself, without direct coupling to a next tie in a string of patronage. The dyad tie itself is what is carefully crafted in clientelism, even though the meanings built up around it invariably argue the cascading of loyalty along chains. The coupling needs an obverse side. Decouplings are and must be effected—decouplings from the past of relations and from the ecology of concrete surroundings.

A similar dialectic of decoupling recurs across all levels of scope and focus, from localities on up. It is for this reason that clientelism as a construct is so fluid as to bring endless complaints from analysts that it obscures distinctions.[21] Clientelism tends to be slighted, perhaps because of familiarity. It is by no means limited to small casts on small stages. The underlying assumption for clientelism is that parties entering an exchange relationship have unequal resources. Therefore, clientelism relies on a stratification system that centers on the information and resources exchanged between persons and their ties. We will see that it can be set off against professional regime, as well as variants deriving from the corporatist regime just described.

During its original Roman manifestation, clientelism became adapted to structuring international relations across the complex field of cities and provinces and empires and kingdoms and other flotsam of the early Mediterranean. Badian (1958) argues:

> The year 146 b.c. sees the end of proper international relations and proper international law. . . . Henceforth all allies—free or federati—are clients, in the sense that their rights and obligations are in practice independent of law and treaties and are entirely defined and interpreted by Rome. (p. 105)

---

[21] I argue that another problem is confounding of regimes with rhetorics and styles in much existing theoretical analysis.

This is Rome as concretized in particular senatorial families and with senators as patrons. From the Roman case one can learn general regularities. For example, multiple "ownership" is what makes any patronage system "go," as when, in the case of American academia, several older figures attribute the merits of any particular younger figure to their own efforts—teaching, tutelage, favors, and evaluations.

Clientelism is not limited to huge social formations, but also applies in small and subtle group interaction, such as a patronage network. I will draw on Perry Anderson's study of a patronage network in the emergence of an absolute state. As Perry Anderson points out (1974, p. 49), grandee houses infiltrated the state apparatus with parasitic clientages of lesser nobles. Thus, they formed rival patronage networks. Patronage could penetrate downward as well. Focus here on the structural possibility for patrons to use story-sets to their advantage. Accumulation of favors which, if not respected, should disqualify the person as a client, ensures that the power position of the patron induces a certain notion of truthful, of appropriate behavior.

Some theorists are almost incensed by what they see as the inability of theorizing about clientelism to recover clean-cut regimes. For example, Higgins concedes that descriptive categories, such as "action-sets," "quasi-groups," "social networks," "factions," and, of course, patron-client and patron-broker-client relations, aggregate social relations within a social structure; but he argues that, the consequence of such abstract aggregation is the failure to capture the evenness and unevenness within the totality (Clapham 1982). Here we see the analyst obsessed with imposing meaning as also characterizes blocking action generally! But I sympathize with his demand for channeling action into one framework through efforts in one theoretical direction, as opposed to just one descriptive study after another. The intention of *Identity and Control* is, after all, similar, except that Clapham misses the depth and intricacy required for such "one" theoretical direction to prove at all adequate.

There is a tension between the stringing aspect of clientelist dependency over against the focus of blocking action upon meaning, and the tension is exacerbated under clientelism. This is because clientelism does not make widespread use of style. In particular, clientelism does not ever generate issues, which are the event analogues of style. In the soup of clientelism one will not find interfaces.

6.5.1. Blocking Action

What is similar between clientelism and corporatism is blocking action. The initial stages in forming clientelist regime are vulnerable because of the lack of explicit interlocking between dyads.

There are large social formations that arguably are entirely clientel-ist, at all scopes. Then once clientelist ties are established, new actions are blocked by the routinized interaction subsisting in each tie. Hausa city-states (Smith 1975) such as Kano, Katsina, Daura, Gobir, and Zau-zau, which were contemporaneous with Medici Florence, had a reper-toire of what can be called craft guilds along with tensions with sur-rounding agricultural holdings that seem parallel to those of many of the contemporaneous Italian city states. Smith argues elsewhere that the basic bond was clientship:

> Every free man regardless of his social or ethnic origin through the con-tract systems of *chapka* (allegiance) and *barantaka* found his place and his protection secured. . . . The ruler used this competition (for formal offices) to award title to lineages that lacked proper hereditary claims and thus reinforced monarchical power through the parallel system of client pa-tronage. (in Griffeth and Thomas 1981)

This is also reminiscent of the absolutist French scene, but in Africa there does not appear to have been the lattice of corporatist jurisdic-tional bodies seen there, or even the simpler lattice in Florence.

Thailand offers a special example: "[U]nlike the situation in many other societies where patronage is seen as something opposed to the structure of the system even if it does 'oil the wheels,' in Thailand it is analyzed as being an integral part of the system" (Kemp 1982). This is a highly complex society and yet one with an absence of corporate groups. Especially and above all, there is no sense for structural equiv-alence in Thai society:

> Any relationship is between unequals and the recognition of this fact is an integral and emphasized part of Thai culture . . . there are no kinship groups in Thai society . . . a lack of role differentiation between political, economic and other types of activity. . . . Thailand can be seen as a chang-ing population of entourages, the entourage joining unequal individuals in a highly personalized manner in a relation that lasts for only as long as it is mutually beneficial.

From all these examples of clientelism, it is clear that the dependent variable should be seen as immobility, as blocking action. Reports on all of them—Mexico, Hausa, Thai, and others—insist on blockage. An equally common report, not surprisingly, is of a preoccupation with meanings, a preoccupation that is beyond any proportion to actual op-eration and accomplishment. Poggi argues both facets:

> By addressing all political energies and aspirations towards the pursuit of private advantage; by validating others' privileges in so far as one hopes to draw from them some petty favour toward oneself; by fragmenting and

dispersing solidarities; . . . clientelism can at best conserve and reproduce the environment which generates it. Its "molecular" aspect, its ability to personalize, to make proximate and frequent the search for political protection and influence, is part of its deceptions, and as such it should be treated with diffidence or deprecated . . . it must be the task of political practice *to render* clientelism again vestigial and interstitial. (Poggi 1983)

6.5.2. Semi-periphery in World System

Clientelism is not limited to individuals in an exchange relationship. This control regime also applies to nation-states that are in production-exchange relationship. For example, world system theory (Wallerstein 1974, 1980) can be construed to center on the distinctions and interconnections of semi-periphery with core and periphery. This theory can be seen as a claim that the present architecture of the world, taken in the large, is clientelist regime. The clientelist relation in the world system yields exploitation of the periphery, which is alleged to be beneficial to the periphery through allowing them to build up capital stock. The semi-periphery is the client of the core, and itself is the patron for the periphery. Center on production and exchange, and let the physical space scale be maximal. The system of control is reduced somewhat arbitrarily to only three strata.

The semi-periphery is where decoupling mechanisms become concentrated from the cumulation over time of attempts at control in many realms. Wallerstein construed semi-periphery at a macro level, as whole national economies that fit as brokers between the two main positions that he conceives: exploitative center and exploited periphery nations. The awkward hyphenation of the term *semi-periphery* aptly suggests its awkward standing: as a structural locus that however is defined by a process goal of decoupling, a goal that is exactly about subverting embedding. Wallerstein's account of a "world system" reads easier, once the semi-periphery is understood in these relativist terms, rather than as some fixed and specifiable role or technical function, or as a halfway house.

The doublet position of the semi-periphery fuels a special form of clientelism: there is need for a disarticulation of the clientelist relation to the core in order to establish a patron relation to the periphery. And this can allow one to explain the different levels that clientelist regime can embrace.

Schwartzman (1989), in her account of Portugal, gives the most explicit analysis extant of the mechanism of semi-periphery. Her formulation is that semi-periphery, as a position within a system, must also imply "disarticulation" internally within the semi-periphery. What this semi-periphery does, viewed as a unit, is triage writ large (see chapter 4). This triaging is a complement to responsibility being taken from above, and more specifically it governs the aspect of timing. This and the structural aspect are in tension, and that is why there must be the disarticulation.

Structural change in the world system is deflected and blocked by the emergence and consolidation of this tier of the semi-periphery. A semi-periphery unit permits and arranges just some changes in ordinary flows. The presence of the semi-periphery does allow for "policy initiatives," from below, i.e., the periphery, as well as from above, from core standing. Guilarte lays out the brokerage pattern in flows (1990) in an empirical study of semi-periphery in world political context. And there are many other exemplars of the semi-periphery mechanism that can be abstracted from Schwartzman's account.

The key is that the moves for decoupling, played against embeddings in the ongoing crossings of projects for control, tend to cluster in parallel locales. Consider, for example, Hsiao's account of a nineteenth-century Chinese context (1960, p. 506): "Retired functionaries, expectant officials, and degree-holding scholars far outnumbered officials in active government service." And it was these figures, supernumeraries in a formal context, who were the actual avenue of control, as gentry resident amid a massive rural population.

6.5.3. Nesting

Clientelism has issues of respect, of the following of certain codes of conduct, of rules of reciprocity, as we know, for example, from the Mafia. And one can expect to find council disciplines, for example, among barons understood as a semi-periphery important for clientelism. But without much in the way of disciplines and issues, and with few identities, clientelist "gels" exhibit larger-scale ordering in ways quite other than those for corporatist regime. There is a nesting of clientelism, a nesting into larger formation. But the nesting is derived from the context of other ties rather than from explicit three-and-more body chains of interconnections.

Consider, for example, the clientage ties of early Irish society, which have often been interpreted in mainly symbolic terms. Nerys Patterson shows how very practical and material these ties really were, and also how separatist. Yet she goes on to show how they were sustained and reproduced because of an intercalation of flows at different levels (but here clientage ties nest into clientage ties, which thus forms a larger formation):

The contract of free clientship was thus conditioned by and secondary to the relationship between lord and base-client. The terms of free clientship were sustainable by the free client only because he had reserves of cattle vested in base clients that he could draw on in a crisis. In the relationship between overlord and free client the overlord skimmed off some of the free client's profits that were generated by the base-clients' direct output, and their indirect contribution to the free client's productivity by permitting the latter to specialize in stock keeping. In return the lower-level lord received short-term injections of additional stock and was assured of the political support of other members of the cattle-lending class in maintaining control of base-clients. This class solidarity took the form of direct political alliance, and of the jural privileges accorded to members of the nobility by the jurists and genealogists. (Patterson 1980, p. 60)

Tribal contexts have been referenced earlier,[22] and clientelist ties can be found there. But tribes may be misleadingly simple exemplars. It is exactly because in tribes there are presumably fewer levels of embedding and decoupling—as well as fewer stories about, and intertwinings of, control projects—that we feel intuitively such direct access to anthropologists' accounts. No one in a tribe would or could write either this book, or the anthropologist's account. Likely it is that we overconceptualize accounts of tribes. Any one set of concepts may be mappable into tribal reality, but perhaps that is so only because a tribe condenses what in more complex contexts we are forced to see as really distinct.

Instead we expound an example from early Europe and draw general lessons on type of tie induced from such complex tapestries. Examining a case with written records will help open up distinctions among roles and position made on the ground.

6.6. Professional

The professionalism style introduced in chapter 4 intertwines with rhetorics across tangible base in networks and disciplines on the way to shaping a regime around a value. Jurisdiction is the obsession of professions, as part of a focus of concern upon meaning. It is a struggle to shape as well as allot a structured order of legitimate interpretations.[23] Professionalism always orients to and thus generates a succes-

---

[22] For example, see excerpts from Fortes on the Tallensi in the section of chapter 3 on the council discipline.

[23] In the strict mathematical sense, this ordering is a partial order; cf. Birkhoff and MacLane (1953).

sion of depths of interpretation, as the texture of jurisdiction, a texture reflected in social organization as well as in ideas. The style is willing, but the social flesh is disorderly and unmalleable, so there is never, in fact, a tidy rhetoric of nesting and depth.

The system of professions, to use Abbott's term (1988), induces a distinctive style primarily as the outcome of control struggles in a context of increasing specialization of role structure in a given population. One indication is the extent to which professions, as recognized in the contemporary United States, form a single lattice or tree of cultural domination and subordination.[24] By contrast, jurisdiction in the guild fights of corporatism is but a jostling for agreed partition.

Events are a form of identity compatible with jurisdiction, and they can fit with professionalism. But the antipode of jurisdiction process is mobilization process. Although mobilizer disciplines will always be part of any actual social formation, the impetus of professionalism contradicts mobilizing. Mobilization is bottom-up, whereas jurisdiction is top-down. So in a professional regime the incidence of mobilizer disciplines is lower.

The term *professionalism* has modern connotations, but the professional style is as historical as clientelism. Before monotheism, social formations especially imbued with religious interests exhibited the nested jurisdictional tendencies of professionalism. Priests and shamans and the like tended toward professionalist distinctions, in contradistinction from magicians and the like who fit variously into guild institution and corporatism (cf. Stark and Bainbridge 1979). Monotheist religions, after coming to be used to permeate social formations, can also spin off sufficient distinctions of sacerdotal standing to undergird professionalism as style. Tellenbach (1946) spells out this process among Roman Catholic clergy and other orders during the Gregorian revolution (and see Berman 1983, chap. 2).

The elaboration of canon law was one aspect of this professionalization of Catholics into complex partial orders of sacerdotal standing and expertise; the elaboration was parallel to spelling out theologies of different depths. Control projects are intertwined with professional as a style. Deference is extended to experts in ever deeper layers in the centripetal process of ideation within professionalism (Abbott 1981). But

---

[24] The Brzezinski and Huntington survey (1964) argues that professionalism was the style of Soviet communist leadership. Professionalism could be the style of a whole society, rather than just the accoutrements of specialists. Simirenko (1982) went further, and argued this extreme view in his title *The Professionalization of Soviet Society*. Whether for a society or for middle-range formations, professionalism is a style that inhibits innovation.

the deeper layers are also but reserves to strengthen efforts of control over those in outermost circles. The Reformation was a reaction to this professionalization of the Church (Oberman 1981).

6.6.1. Ripostes

Control efforts induce counters as well as parallels and refinements. The priestly hands always find themselves being sheathed in secular gloves, though further along in development the secular sheathing itself perforce has to find professional garb. Secular legal systems may emerge in part out of some such confrontations, as in turn laws build into a realm for a supporting subsystem. This yields a control regime with differentiated and concentric layers of interpreters. The sheathing process reemerges: a striking illustration is the commercialization of American law as argued by Horwitz (1977).

Defensive power is a major concern of modern professions, within a social formation of organizations (Johnson 1972; Sarfatti-Larsen 1977). A not unexpected counterpoint to professional style is a Utopian plan for total authority and control, such as, for example, Veblen described for the beginnings of technocracy. This is not confined to religion as venue, nor to older times. This Utopian moment of professionalist style proved (Bailes 1978) to have as wide a resonance in the USSR as in the United States, the two contexts in which engineering has provided a basis for extensive professionalist claims.

Engineering has since lapsed into a corporatist guild mold. Between corporatism and professionalism there is not a clear divide. Neither has nor can have some unique architecture; each is a historically contingent configuration. They are similar in blocking fresh action.

As Abbott (1988) has made clear, the developments of professionalization should be seen and can best be interpreted as part of an unfolding and sheathing of the very many sorts of professions with their many demarcations and competing inner layers of interpretation, sheathing into a regime, or rather a set of regimes. As in other regimes, whether corporatism or clientelism, authority osmoses through any putative spectator. Authority oozes into and out of any one profession in an Abbott "system" to extents shaped by the overall pattern of struggles for jurisdictions.

Abbott is himself ambivalent about using *system* but chooses it over *structure* because of its connotation of boundedness (Abbott 1988, p. 343, note 8), also seen in Luhmann. My term *control regime*, by contrast, eschews boundedness and yet, still like Luhmann, works with codetermination between realms.

6.7. Norman Feudalism

Before I move on to the discussion of movements and evolvement of control regimes, I will point out that regimes do not remain constant nor are formed through a static process. Once a regime has emerged, it is constantly experiencing forces of confrontation and transformation. Because control regimes are not static states, they will switch from one regime to another through interaction. I will draw on stories of Norman feudalism to illustrate the switchings between regimes.

The shock of the conquest of England was both so large and so long-lived that detailed stories are still known about patterns of interlock in relations among individuals, which proved to set the tone of how the relations evolved subsequently into a control regime. Stenton's (1965) historical analysis points out that the relationship between lord and man in pre—Norman Conquest England was as common as it was in France. This relationship was only one element in a social order that was essentially based on hereditary status. However, Stenton finds that this social order based on hereditary status had become the basis of a new type of society organized specifically for war in France, and "no process of evolution could have bridged the gap" (Stenton 1932, p. 217). This sounds like a switch from a more corporate to a more clientelist sort of regime.

6.7.1 Kinship Gangs

The Norman Conquest was sudden, though not unexpected, in 1066 (Searle 1988); and for decades afterward, William the Conqueror and his French barons were all too aware that Danes could pull the same turnover on them. The essential point is that one can hope to see the bare bones best, the networks and disciplines in raw, unmediated form, during the turbulent period. The replacement of Anglo-Saxon by Norman was abrupt and by conscious intervention. Searle (1988, pp. 238–29) is vivid on the consciously exploitative nature of Norman society and its takeover of England. Networks of kinship gangs made up the Norman polity. The Norman invaders acted to set up an exploitation network of networks akin to but more flexible than the one sketched earlier for a putting-out economy. In modern idiom, the Capone gang moved to add Detroit to Chicago as its turf. Kings start as gangsters.

Nonetheless, the conquest was limited in much the same way as is a merger-and-acquisition takeover of a big corporation by outside capital today. The point of takeover is to exploit even further the broad reaches of the existing structure with no more change than is necessary beyond throwing out the existing barons to bring in your own. As quickly as possible, new stories and meanings and identities are to be woven from speculations and gamings and control crossings, but this is not itself happening very quickly, given the scale and the shock; so for a while participants and observers appear freer to perceive. And for a while there will be less of the actual embeddings into hierarchies of smoothly operating interfaces that are bound up with the stories and gamings.

6.7.2 Shift of Rhetoric

A shift of rhetoric may signal a switching between control regimes. Here, I will draw on the case of the Norman Conquest to illustrate how corporatist regime shifts to a more clientelist institution. As mentioned earlier in Stenton's depiction, the distinctions of personal status were more firmly drawn in Anglo-Saxon society, which run throughout Old English society, than those of the succeeding feudal order (Stenton 1932, p. 5). However,

> [t]he Norman settlers in England could not maintain the clear social distinctions with which they had once been familiar. They were a miscellaneous multitude. ... [p. 27][T]he fundamental distinction between Frenchmen and Englishmen overrode all the matters of detail in which the custom of one French province differed from that of another. ... [p. 29][T]he whole elaborate system of knight-service in England could be traced to the conditions which the Conqueror had imposed on his leading followers. (Stenton 1932, p. 3)

It was exactly that the conquerors could, and were vulnerable enough to, enforce much crisper definitions. And these were centered on military service, which in the technical conditions meant expert personal service under arms and with support sustained via a grant of land actively farmed. The tie was to be so well defined that it generated automatic indirect ties.

That is, the king, and presumably magnates in their turn, asserted a claim to the allegiance of undertenants overriding the claims of any intermediate lord (Ibid., pp. 113, 11). Conversely, although one man may well hold land of many lords, in *ligius*, the central feudal relation, he is bound directly to a particular one, of whom he holds his normal residence and whose contingent he must join if the host is called (Ibid., p. 30). The term *knight* that eventually became the norm was itself Anglo-Saxon, showing that network ties in the new raw situation were being baldly redefined using all constituent material.

Interaction among the corporate and the string modes of perceiving and building social space emerged early in this rude conquest, and indeed each always, in any social context, shapes the other. Never did the conqueror or successors grant compact lordships; rather, lands even of the greatest barons were scattered widely, dispersed among the "fees" of other lords. At the same time that this inhibited forming new corporates of possible opposition, it also reinforced the long-standing corporate compound of the thegns whose lands were handed over as integral units.

As integral to dependency as the compounding of ties was the linking together as corporate of the men who held the constituent feofs of an estate. Peasant tenants with various forms of claims on the lands also had rights of consultation. Courts of a variety of forms were the most precisely defined instances of this conflation of corporate with network forms, but justice was seen as so localized, both in the chains of infeudation and the determination by local experts on local corporate custom, that it is anachronistic to draw a sharp line between court and council of advice (Ibid., pp. 91, 42, 67).

The ideas of social standing melded network positions in particular into more general corporate standings as "[t]he reputation of a feudal lord in the world of his day, his influence in the king's court, and his standing in his own country largely turned on the number and quality of the enfeoffed knights who were bound to him by service" (Ibid., p. 60). In this case, networks of ties become rigorously separated from corporate forms only in a very distinct line of development, that of *ministerials*. There were landless knights—roughnecks and layabouts in the terms of a later era—who proliferated in years of troubles and private wars. But there came to be built into this society officers, *dapifers* or *seneschals*, with definite duties of administration not related to war, not episodic, and not of right connected to courts and councils. Social standing and corporate form were largely erased for them. They are precursors to positions, which prefigure formal organizations.

However, social standing and authority derived from it, was not univocally set by location in the network of feudal dependencies, important though that was. "Many (lords or larger manors) held larger fees than the lesser among the king's barons held of him, and as a class they were men of the same social standing. And the word baron denoted a man's place in society without reference to the position which he happened to hold in the tenurial scale" (Ibid., p. 98). As a result, the Norman Conquest marked a shift from more corporate to more clientelist regime.

6.8. A Common Template for Caste and Science

After I have discussed the ideal types of control regime, I will bring in applications of these templates. I will take up simultaneously two more control regimes, one around caste and one around science. The intriguing point is that I claim these two are based on the same template for control regime, which counterbalances rhetoric with style. These regimes extend to demography, to control over the turnover of persons. Like the career institutional systems of the previous chapter, then, they extend and close feedback loops over time.

Go on to note that style may precede and influence an institutional system, or the reverse. Or, more likely, one encounters some partial overlap of style with system across processes in some tangible network population at a given period. When such overlap sustains the reproduction of the overlap, the joint configuration is what I have called the template of a control regime. A style is involute. A style is its own context. Yet willy-nilly, style here supplies the template a contrast in value that gives impetus to the rhetorics of that institutional system.

A crucial test is robustness, whether the joint configuration survives contingent eruptions. And the more disparate are the contexts of the examples, the more disparate the bombardments by contingencies that are testing robustness. So finding multiple and distant realizations of the given template is prima facie evidence for an institutional system. That institutional system is, of course, also embedded in a broader context, commonsense public, so that it is itself a control regime, nested within the template of overall regime.

Here, the two realizations are from maximally distant contexts: on the one hand, caste and kinship in village India, which, on the other hand, will be paralleled by departments of and research in science in American academia. The template plays localities, as a space for disciplines, against network configuration across localities.

6.8.1. Caste and Kinship across Villages

Despite the forces of confrontation and transformation, control regime may also remain stable over time. In the following two sections, I will draw cases from the Indian caste system and academic disciplines as the regime of corporatism that survives from pressures of foreign invasion and internal conflicts.

The specific referent for caste here is the institution observed among central Indian villages and mapped out in networks of behavior and perception by Mayer (1960). Within the village caste rhetoric, it is caste ideology to which professional style is analogy. The layering of purity as professional ideology can be imagined parallel to the tangible layering between castes in public social interaction. Meaning is asserted and even calibrated, in direct coordination with strings of ties to be recognized and asserted. Professional jurisdiction is not a monovalent matter of tasks; nor is jurisdiction within a system embracing caste, which ramifies into kin and marital networks across regions, and into ideas beyond religion. And jurisdiction permeates within castes: "[M]y central theme [is] that the caste is ordered internally by the same principles which govern relations between castes" (p. 6 in Parry 1979).[25]

Accounts of Indian caste in general (Dumont 1986) emphasize the value placed on ritual purity and the strict demarcation of bounds for corporateness. A curious topology underlies and justifies both emphases, within the ongoing networks of kinship across villages. This topology very much depends on how networks weave together corporate structures of purity. The topology can be tagged as a metonymy, specifically a synecdoche: "the smaller contains the larger."

Mayer's account (1960) of a field of villages in central India is used here. Purity is operationalized with extreme explicitness as practices in villages. There is a ranked series of substances whose passing from one to another grouping permits precise imputation of purity, of sociocultural standing. The groups ranked are local and constitute a partition of all family units within a given village into specific caste groupings. Rankings of each caste can be imputed from observed transactions, especially those on public occasions as in religious feasts and weddings. Party food, cooked in butter, comes at one extreme: it can be offered to any caste including the highest. Then comes ordinary food, not refined enough to be offered to higher castes. And then raw food comes still lower (counter to our custom at cocktail parties!), and on down through smoking pipes, and drinking water. At bottom are garbage and feces, in principle offerable only to untouchables.[26]

The village is the site of primary economic activity, farming and artisanry. Caste matters do not tie directly to most of this ecological activity. Nor do struggles over ownership, over improvement and change in property, which lie largely outside the scope of the village.

Through marriage, kinship cuts across villages. The unit of intimacy is the subset within a village caste that have married into a like subset of an analogous caste in another village, or rather the many such intermarrying sets across a number of villages in the region. Call this the

---

[25] He is a follower and developer of Mayer and Dumont.

[26] Explicit network modeling of such caste interaction data can be found in Marriott (1968).

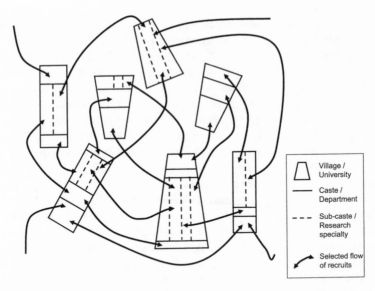

Figure 6.1: Village caste and university science. Only seven villages/universities are shown.

subcaste, a network construction hopping across the region. It is a *sub-caste* because within any particular village, the persons in the given affinal network are only a subset of the several clusters of blood relatives that make up the whole caste in that village.

Figure 6.1 lays out this institutional system as networks across a field of villages containing caste disciplines, whose subunits are the nodes of the networks. Paradoxically, the subcaste is larger than the caste. The reality is that inheritance and marriage, the engines of major change, lie within the subcaste and outside the village. There is both village exogamy and caste endogamy. The corporate reality of a subcaste interlinked through affinal ties across a whole region, this intimate corporateness is broader than the only caste unit that is actually embodied, that of the village. Indeed, the subcaste may be comparable to the whole village in size.

Only the subcaste has explicit organization, a council and like agency for regulating caste affairs. Wealth flows along subcaste lines, through marriage and inheritance, as do innovations, material and other. There are only the thinnest threads of purity calibration that can be spun out by the Brahman "priests," themselves scattered as local caste units in villages.

Some mobility can take place without disturbing perceptions of purity value. It is the mobility not of individual persons but of whole subcastes moving to new villages. They can do so because there are more distinct castes in the region than can ever be found together on the ground of a particular village. The Brahman argues primarily in terms of the four broad varnas of their scriptures; so a subcaste new to the village can appear and argue for a location in purity rank within that village in the only way that matters, getting the appropriate exchanges going.

Looking at Mayer's photos of separate caste groups hunkered down in separate locales at feasts, one spots the institutions and can almost supply the rhetorics, story-sets used to account for and tidy up the value ranking by purity. Not amenable to photograph, but equally central, are the sprawling networks of kinship bonding across other villages that sustain and reproduce the system. A separate set of institutions and rhetoric is embedded in these ties among subcaste segments across villages. The caste illustration is a vivid one that is easy to recognize in transposed dress in other institutional contexts. The subcaste requires a broader canvas, and my claim is that it constitutes itself as a style.

Caste as it evolved across villages on the central Indian plain interlocks in a dual structure, a template that will be brought out by showing how to transpose it to a patterning of science across American universities. In both caste and university guises, this institutional system is long-lived and of great scope, encompassing hundreds and more villages and universities. With caste, change in either structure or production is generally thought to be precluded, whereas in its other dress as academic science, the system is generally thought to encourage change.

Both control regimes have proved to give stability, redressing local changes and disturbances. The caste system may well have evolved as all that could survive the unending invasions of nomads and other gangsters that repeatedly spread out across the plain. The American university system is also very effective at enabling mobility and so readjustment despite surface rhetoric.

6.8.2. Tribal Regimes in Academia

Shin-Kap Han (2003) marshals complete national data for a seven-year period on thousands of first hires of their newly minted Ph.D.s by hundreds of U.S. university departments. His "tribes" are, of course, academic disciplines, such that each discipline possesses its template and blueprints of conducting research, training students, producing publications, and pushing the field forward. Han provides us with an illustration of how a corporatist regime survives through internal forces within the regime generated through network ties.

Employing blockmodeling analysis, Han combines systemwide with triad analyses to argue the existence and nature of a control regime in each of seven disciplines. Much of his punch comes from exploiting the differences, once an overall similarity is established, between the regimes for economics, English, history, mathematics, political science, psychology, and sociology. The analysis also shows clear similarities of exchange relations between departments in each given discipline.

Most of the relations are, of course, asymmetric given the concentration of Ph.D. production among a smallish core of departments (and possibly also the draining off of many new Ph.D.s into nonuniversity careers). For sociology, there are fifty departments in the core, who, while hiring from each other, send Ph.D.s to a set of four other blocks, containing altogether 120 departments, and also to a huge residual block of nearly 400 departments that send essentially no new hires. The four in-between blocks are in a pecking order, shown by each block sending to all the blocks below it (and, of course, to the residual block). This overall feeder network pattern is prima facie evidence of a control regime, tied to academic careers. *Cui bono?* Why do certain networks in the 50 top departments sustain it? Well, getting one's own Ph.D. students into a top university department requires our taking also from other top-fifty universities. This is the control regime that is built upon the institution (analogous to a caste), with networks of overlapping researchers as a disturbance term, vortexes of identities who generate surplus from using these institutions in a certain way, to which we return later.

The core in each of the seven cases ranks higher than other blocks.[27] A given core is by no means homogeneous, and the extent of internal hierarchization varies across disciplines. By the measure of centrality index, the economics core, for example, is more homogeneous than the sociology core as to hierarchization. Han goes on to report strong tendencies of cores toward breaking up into factions, defined as cohesive internally and structurally equivalent externally. Only in the core for economics are all the top prestige departments concentrated in just one of the factions.

To get at systemwide differences among the seven disciplines, as well as confirm and amplify these cohesion results just for the cores, Han turns to the MAN triad inventory modeling previously discussed

---

[27] Evidence for validity comes from comparison with established national rankings of departments by prestige, in *U.S. News & World Report*, and in the National Research Council ranking by scholarly quality of faculty.

in chapter 2. There is only one type of tie, so he digs for differences by contrasting configurations of symmetry/asymmetry in all the triads in this multiplex tie for an academic discipline. He emphasizes two parameters that measure tendencies across all sixteen types of triad in the inventories: transitivity, designated by the Greek letter ô (tau), which reflects hierarchy, and as contrast cyclicity, C, which reflects instead tendency toward generalized exchange, solidarity. Psychology and sociology are low both on ô and on C, whereas economics and mathematics are high both on ô and on C. English is high on ô but low on C.

The implication of these variables is that there are substantial positive correlations of these rankings both with ô and with C, indicating that these measures reflecting hierarchy and cohesion both do point toward prestige in the external world. Moreover, the two measures correlate with the extent to which an external ranking stays stable over the 1990s. Altogether, the case is strong for academic departments fitting to a control regime from its footprint on their career patterning.

6.8.3. The Template

Here I will go over much the same ground, but now in more abstract terms. A general value—call it purity—is operationalized in the strongest kind of social ordering, a ranking close to the full linear ordering of the mathematician. The institutional face is prescriptions and proscriptions on interactions. But this ordering is confined operationally to a small locality, a geographic one defined by mundane activities. Linear ordering enforces itself only through transitivities in chains of behavior that cannot be monitored on a large scale. So it is an ordering not of individual actors but only for recognized clusters. The institutions and rhetorics apply to this prescription within and proscriptions between.

Recruitment of new members is not from within the locality itself but instead follows institutions holding between localities, and yet cluster loyalty is central for these as well as for the everyday institutions. Early recruitments from other localities are interpreted as being from clusters there that are comparable.

Intuition tells us that although cluster more than locality guides everyday action, identity will lodge with the subcluster. Both intimacy and repute will stay with the set of subclusters. Yet a subcluster network, in fact, sprawls out across localities—without, however, interfering with behaviors whose patterns are sufficient to enforce purity. This is the pattern of self-balancing dynamics for the template as a larger social formation, a control regime.

Any examples of this template will tend to be pluralist in value terms, affording parallel sets of story and interpretation. Such values have localized facets, which are used for ex post accountings. For a century, purity in caste, like analogous valuations in other climes, had hypnotized observers into treating the social formations of caste on a macro scale as automatic by-products of a few values writ large.

With a new generation of anthropologists who were alerted to networks as analytic and phenomenological bases of social topography, values came to be seen as by-products from social pattern, from institutional system, rather than as exogenous cause. And it became clear that particular values from a known package were tied together and mapped very differently in the sprawl of networks from locality layering.

Now, sociologists of science have been bringing to bear this same new perspective of networks, and their results can be mapped into the same template as village caste! This is detailed in the next section. On some matters, one will argue for common predictions. All realizations of this template exhibit social formations that are peculiarly resistant to attempts at external control. This follows from rumination on the illustrations, as well as from the template considered in the abstract— a balanced and stable yet decentralized skeleton.

Caste is argued (Ghurye 1957; Hocart 1950) to be the resilient formation that has survived repeated waves of external invaders. Defensive or blocking action in the larger sense is the genesis of caste as social organization. The inner circles of recondite validation for caste do center on Brahmin priests—priests who make no claim to economic or political predominance. Successive waves of external marauders common in these Indian regions are offered no obvious social foci through which to control and exploit, as opposed to plunder the population.

The structuring of academic research science can be argued to be a parallel reaction against the emerging dominance of American universities by autocratic presidents in the early 1900s. It is not particular values as abstract symbols that accomplish this; rather, it is a template that embeds value facets operationally into a certain sort of balanced formation that is hard to unwind bit by bit.

6.8.4. American Academic Science

So the second illustration of this template, from an utterly different discourse, is academic science as a social formation in the United States. Academic science in the form of university departments is every bit as resistant to innovation as caste systems. When a genuine innovation comes along in academic science, there seem to be two likely fates.

Either it is expelled to industrial application, as Charles Townes's laser seems to have been. Or it is encapsulated within departments and spun out into what is, in social organization, a new network: this seems to have been the fate in the 1950s of the new biophysics of Delbruck and the Committee on Mathematical Biophysics as well as of Watson and Crick's molecular biology, and it was also occurring with the new physics of matter, to mention only three unquestionably major innovations.

The social organization of a science as an institutional system is reflected in how existing theories combine with or reject any new theory entertained in that science. There proves to be a close parallel to caste in the organization of American academic science. For village read *university*, and for village caste group read *department in a university*. Purity becomes prestige, itself a stand-in for degree of ultimate truth. Sub-caste translates into specialty, which is at the heart of science as research, as generator of originality. With this translation, the earlier statements on Mayer's village caste system can be carried over into the social setup of American academic science.[28]

A pecking order for scientific disciplines is operationalized only among departments within the particular university, physics or mathematics often being top and sociology near bottom.[29] (See Han's more general analysis of academic tribes earlier in the chapter.) Degree of scientific purity may be attributed to this order. Ritual pervades this scene, whereas action and excitement and intimacy grow along research networks spreading outside the given university.

Sprawling networks of collaboration and intimacy in actual research reach across the nation on specific subjects. Specialties are concretized in them. For specialty as subcaste, read *style*, in this case *invisible college* (Crane 1972).

Seen from outside within its university, a given department has meaning and indeed coherence. The meaning comes within and expresses a hierarchy of purity and accomplishment, which can vary from one to another university. The hierarchy is enforced by deference behaviors in committee meetings and luncheon interchanges. It is also expressed and enforced in larger and more solemn ceremonials, at

---

[28] It may be that the following dissection carries through as well to the humanities, with whose organization I am less familiar. Better analogues to the humanities, as well as to professional schools and the like, may be the ethnic enclaves that crosscut villages and castes in a region like Mayer's.

[29] This pecking order varies a little between universities. Sociology, for example, is higher at the University of Arizona or the University of North Carolina than in Ivy League schools.

which symbolic capital can be exchanged like any other.[30] Contents of interchanges can be typed analogously to the discriminations from high to low in the material exchanges among castes within a village, and there is a parallel range of meeting contexts within a village.

Seen from its inside, a university department of science, analogous to a village caste, is a shambles of unrelated specialties. Different collections of specialties will make up that discipline's departments in various universities. And universities differ in their exact menus of departments. All this is parallel to the caste/village/subcaste formation. A specialty spreading across scores of departments is typically much larger than a given university department—just as a given subcaste spreading into scores of villages has more members than are in that caste in a given village: see figure 6.1 again.[31]

Each specialty is the prime world of motivation for its working scientists. And when recruitment of new (faculty) members to the given department comes up, it is recruitment largely along invisible-college networks of specialties active in that department and competing with each other. Just so do marriages and children get formed through networks within a subcaste quite separate from the other subcastes, which together in the eyes of that village make up the weavers (or the blacksmiths or whatever) as a single caste entity. One specialty is linked to its departmental counterparts in other universities in a different way than another specialty, which is another reason why they tend to operate separately and independently within their own department. Again, there is a parallel to Mayer's descriptions for subcastes.

6.8.5. Effectiveness and Efficiency Applications

As a preliminary to full topological measurement, a control regime can be coded in terms of discipline species. This coding, by my present hypothesis, should be the same for science, or other exemplar of this template, as it is for caste.

Operation of caste distinctions within a given village is that of arenas oriented by purity as value. By definition, the medium that codes exchange (here as *pacca* and *kacca* foods and so on) is stylized. Concrete contents of exchanges, amounts and so on, are arbitrary, subject to ne-

---

[30] Consider, for example, the Feast of Grades meetings annual in arts and sciences faculties, at which higher honors for graduating students are negotiated and solemnized. One might speculate that in the university, as in the village, these local ceremonials absorb energies and distract attention from flows of main action and resources through corporative networks.

[31] Even the numbers are quite comparable, for sizes of units and subunits and spread of networks.

gotiation in arena discipline. On the other hand, kinship organization is in the council species, adapted to mobilizing.

What is missing is the interface species, which is the discipline distinctive for effective material production. This is not to say that material production, here farming, is not key to the whole life of Indian villages. Farming does go on, in parallel exactly to the third aspect of the template, the locality aspect that defines villages but is marginal. Thus, production is divorced from the main control regime. In academic science the analogue is instruction of students, also divorced from the control regime of science.

The Indian caste system may prove to be, upon close agronomic investigation, an efficient one for farming. Our intuition on efficiency may be better for the academic science embodiment. Here too there is total divorce between social form and the actual accomplishment of the material task, which now is instruction of students. Teaching in the American university system[32] is efficient exactly because it is divorced from the main concerns and ties of the professors, which revolve around science research.

The important point for production efficiency—as we have learned from Udy's (1970) analysis—is exactly that there be low correlation to social organization, that there be divorce. The normal outcome of social organization is blocking action and thus inefficient production. Hence, to establish a segregation of social from productive organization is a major achievement in the Taylorian sense. What it takes is an architecture in which values and processes from diverse species of discipline balance off. In this system, the balancing mechanism is summed up by "smaller is larger" (i.e., subcaste is bigger than caste).[33]

The other face of the coin is that the caste institution may prove ineffective in its principal social concerns of shepherding wealth within familial lines as well as purity within caste. Analogously, the European professoriate is principally concerned with and oriented around teaching, at which it thereby is inefficient, whereas in the past it was famously effective in what is now its sideline or hobby, research.

---

[32] Most of the professors in which are scientists.

[33] To go beyond such ad hoc and qualitative assessment, an ambage-versus-ambiguity calculus is required. Unlike in the tournament/liminality extremes described at the beginning of the chapter, there is extensive substructure. In particular, trade-offs are among three interpenetrating formations so that qualitative assessment is difficult and unreliable. Contingency levels vary among these three, as well as within each, and it seems to me that it is these variations that will account for the different functioning of the caste and the science exemplars in ambage/ambiguity trade-offs. The sorts of computations required are of complexity like those in Jasso's (1991 and see 1990) application of relative justice theory to medieval monastic contexts.

Whereas the current American academic science system may be more effective than present European ones in the essentially social yet recondite task of establishing scientific realities.

6.8.6. Control Applications

The Norman regime, whose multiple networks we dissected earlier, could be seen as a third exemplar of this caste-science system, along with various other regimes that have been called feudal (Coulborn 1956). In feudal situations, it could be that the network aspect, here vassal ties especially, could structure the local cells, with the strata ranked on purity, here noble rank, being spread widely.

Feudal cases suggest focusing on control properties instead of production. There is no analogue to the Udy theorem on production as guide. This caste-science regime has sufficiently complex structure that its processes may change drastically with apparently minor shifts in parameter—say, the average number of caste ranks in a village, and its variability.

The numbers of subcastes within village caste groups, and the number of the latter within a village, seem about the same as the corresponding numbers for American science, as mentioned previously. What seems entirely different is the average overlap between locales—villages and universities, respectively—in which ranked local groups (castes and departments) are present. This difference seems to correlate to a difference in control properties.

Different universities have far higher overlap in their menu of departments than do villages in their menus of castes. American universities have higher levels of central control, one guesses, than do Indian villages. This suggests a conjecture of exactly academic relevance.

During a major retrenchment in the American university system, there would be what in business is called downsizing. One likely component would be elimination of whole departments. There are two possibilities: first, university presidents clamber on the same bandwagon, as business CEOs do (Chandler 1969; Fligstein 1985), and choose the same academic disciplines to eliminate. Second, presidents react to or analyze primarily local context and history to choose sacrificial goats. The conjecture is that if the local adaptation predominates, presidential control in universities will weaken. The reasoning is that diverse local choice will move the academic parameters closer to the caste parameters and thus to lower central control.[34]

---

[34] Such a conjecture made without benefit of a calculus is at risk because there is no way to allow for interaction with other possible changes. Exogenous (federal and business) financial support of science research may decline more or less than the number of

6.9. Template Evolution for Trading Regimes

Before I end this chapter, I will point out that control regime is also characterized by style. Instead of rendering template at smaller scale in terms of disciplines, as earlier, now try to construe template as made up of style juxtaposed to institutional realm. The focus is now on overall pattern of interanimation between style and institutional system through a stochastic process of endemic switching. One can construe this as mobilization around values to yield the realm of perception for that regime. For example, caste and science also seem eligible for this construal, with, respectively, kinship and science research networks as the style side that is being juxtaposed with some hierarchic institution. I will make the case that each of these two studies does sustain a cross-sectional view of regime such as led to the caste and science template discussed earlier.

6.9.1. Style and Institution Reciprocally Embed

Embedding has been introduced between a higher and a lower level, accompanied by paradoxes of decoupling for identities on each level. I now extend this to argue for a reciprocal form of embedding, at the same level, between two distinct formations in process, namely between style and institution. Style and institution reciprocally embed to form a template for control regime. This can be seen as the programming of switching among functional subsystems regarding certain decisions. This reciprocal embedding is accompanied by paradoxes of decoupling for both sides.

The trading network of the East India Company came into being as style, as was laid out in the first section of chapter 4. This style, in stochastic dynamics of routing and voyaging, resulted in great growth in trade, but this was accompanied by endless switchings of priorities with the other realm with which it embedded reciprocally, the side of the East Indies Company as complex organization. But the trading network realm also came to be an institutional system. Chronic switchings of action between these two sides, style and institution, bound them, made them mutually embedded, and yet this was accompanied by recurrent paradoxes of perception and interpretation.

---

professors. The different contingency flows implied could override the impact of changes in overlap across universities in departments. Such override could come through a change in the number of specialties within a department (subcastes within village caste). Once again, it becomes clear that a calculus applied to reliable measurement is a necessary guide even to qualitative conclusions on sheer direction.

A main focus of Erikson's was the selection/continuance of ports, out of the very large number spread from Madagascar across India and Southeast Asia. Erikson first examined the institutional side, where the system of investment among investors was inadequate and scattered as the capital was tied to groups of voyages (Erikson 2006, p. 47). It was not until 1685 that a pool of permanent capital was established in order to keep up the permanent settlements. Erikson displays the spread of ports among eight ideal types (p. 56) according to degree of commercial sophistication, obviously of great importance for the EIC management, but also according to degree of decentralization (e.g., autonomy from local rulers). And the EIC management itself was six thousand miles and up to a year distant from both market information and reports from their employees, so that they enjoyed much de facto autonomy.

This employee side was very distinct, with most employees, and especially captains, trading privately beyond their official brief. Multiple opportunities for multiple traders, produced by decentralized access to port markets, are what they sought. Erikson finds that the disjunct Eastern trade regions were connected by private traders engaging in trading in the countryside, buying goods in one port and selling them in others, on the one hand. On the other hand, "EIC directed voyages left England for ports where English factors waited with goods for return shipment. EIC trade was driven by access to decentralized institutions in the East. Centralized trade in ports closed off opportunities to the employees of the EIC" (Erikson 2006, p. 87).

However, this decentralized access to port markets yielded opportunities for illegitimate profits, such as corruption, smuggling, and free riding. Officers and crew often illegally supplemented their allotment in order to smuggle additional goods into England. According to Erikson, "[S]muggling and corruption are best seen as opportunistic trimming, reducing company profit but not seriously impacting the dynamics of trade" (2006, p. 160). Nevertheless, the private trade of the captains was very important to the organization of EIC trade network. Private trading relied on information gathered by the firm and the institution in expanding the network. Therefore, ports that were integrated through small exploratory voyages played an important role in the EIC trade network. Information about prices, goods, and political conditions flow through ports (Erikson 2006, p. 148).

In this case, the style, in stochastic dynamics of routing and voyaging, resulted in great growth in trade, but this was accompanied by endless switchings between opportunistic behaviors and of priorities with the EIC complex organization side with which it embedded reciprocally.

In comparison, Van Doosselaere (2006) also offers a wealth of evidence of interpenetrations by switchings between commercial style and elite institution. With Genoa, the institution accompanying the style initially was of feudal origin, the commune of Genoa. The trading style in his description is that opportunistic behavior was the norm, in which investors selected travelers who were ready to take the sea. Therefore, as the investors provide the travelers access to cash or goods, the travelers could not take the opportunities to travel for granted. Van Doosselaere's vision of the institutional system is that the Genoese social organization was the foundation of the traditional land-based feudal economy and the reciprocal bond of its social and military organization (2006, p. 42). Thus, both sea travel and war came early to characterize Genoa. The traditional feudal elite controlled both military and public policy, using public taxes as well as kinship alliances to maintain itself in leadership through the almost constant warfare of that period around the Mediterranean.

The key point is that very early on, these traditional leaders of Genoa not only joined but also took leadership in the growing *commenda* trade, which was the Mediterranean controlled by a few large operators, "each surrounded by clients who were only indirectly connected to each other." Moreover, "the exclusive character of feudal clientelism permeated not only social organization as whole but also the commercial network as well" (pp. 151–52). In comparison, as we found for the EIC case, the rapidly fluctuating and growing opportunistic sea trade, organized here through *commenda* partnerships, as a style lay cheek by jowl with traditional commune as institution, many of whose leaders avidly pursued trade profits.

6.9.2. Regime Evolution toward Capitalism through Style Feedback with Institution

The claim has been that style and institution each stabilized the other in constituting a regime, much as I argued for caste and science. Now I enlarge the scope and offer a conjecture, backed with case evidence, that they can also coax each other down a course of secular change. That is indeed the paradox from the reciprocal embedding in these cases. Through the lens of Erikson and Van Doosselaere's depiction of the EIC trade and the commune of Genoa, I argue that the switchings of templates, such as corporatist and clientelist regimes, slowly bring about the emergence of a new template.

In Erikson's study, as the EIC trade network became increasingly cohesive in time, it evolved into a stable infrastructure with features of capitalism. She points out that "[m]alfeasant captains built on and elaborated the stable infrastructure of the EIC, bridging the regional clusters that the EIC had earlier reproduced. . . . The unintended consequences of the EIC's loss of control created the characteristic features of capitalism, well-connected buyers and sellers" (2006, p. 163).

Consequently, the cumulating development brought to the renewal of trading network, which involves bureaucratization and organization of the trading networks, gave rise to the modern era and the emergence of global markets. and Bearman (2006) find that during the evolution of the trading network,

> [w]e identify the dynamics underlying structural cohesion of an emergent global trade network in the East, tracing its production to a loss of control that multiplies external contacts, thereby securing strady supply streams and lowering prices through communication across markets. Central components of this argument include the possibility of persistent localism through bureaucratic processes (Bearman 1991; Savage, Stovel, and Bearman 2001) and the importance of organizational flexibility in uncertain environments. (White, Godart, and Corona 2007; Piore and Sabel 1984; Weick 1976)

The innovative information traveled across well-connected traders. The decentralization of the EIC trade and organization among the private traders produced innovative information about trading routes, goods, and prices, which became the important features for modern economic structure (Erikson and Bearman 2006).

In the case of Genoa, Van Doosselaere (2006) provides a more explicit tracing of the evolution for much the same template. The remarkable point is that the evolution can be read out of just changes in the kind of transaction generated. Earlier, and in chapter 4, I referred only to *commendas*, the equity contracts between partners chosen ad hoc. These were indeed predominant through the first few generations, but then credit relations supervened, and later came in insurance contracts. Each shift in contractual form corresponded to a change in correlation between institution and style. These shifts were gradual.

Indeed, Van Doosselaere is able to specify quantitatively a change in this correlation even within the data on *commendas*. He computes for each period a measure of centralization and another of connectivity, which reflect the two major dimensions of action. His figure 2.22 graphs the continuous changes, over the 150 years after 1160, in the average values of these indices. Even with just *commenda* ties, one sees a striking decline in centralization, combined with some decline in connectedness, which, however, goes back to a high value by 1300. This suggests decline in influence of the commune bigwigs.

However, the more important point is the changes in partner selection that open the channels for information exchange. Van Doosselaere finds that the partner selection process offers a better understanding of how the early medieval long-distance commercial organization was being replaced by the involvement of the community as a whole in the mid-thirteenth century. More specifically, he illustrates that

> [o]ne of the reasons why the *commenda* network developed into its particular architecture was the irregular availability of a given partner, both because of uncertainty as to each venture's duration, and because of an irregular cash flow for both travelers and investors. As a contrast, credit contracts fostered more regular transactions and concerned more experienced traders. The movement of people and funds follows a pattern allowing for embryonic strategic planning and the formation of clusters of regular associates. Aside from the earlier period, when merchants from northern Europe and from other Italian towns had not yet formed the bases of the first routinized mercantile network in Genoa, the credit network architecture was relatively stable. Thus it is not by the pattern of change of the network's construction that the emergence of the Genoese mercantile group can be explained. Rather, it is the study of the social make-up dynamic of the credit participants that reveals the mechanism that gave rise to the Renaissance mercantile oligarchy. (pp. 212–13)

Furthermore, Van Doosselaere then turned from social status to occupational distinctions and separately measures for artisans, for merchants, and for professionals the changing curve of homophily for that occupation. For the first two there is a gradual rise that tracks with the rise in connectedness.

> The increasing use of occupational categories as a salient characteristic for partner selection by artisans can be considered to be both constitutive as well as a result of economic factors . . . the records show a disintermediation in the trade network. (p. 163)

Changes for merchants will be better understood from within the second major class of data, on credit networks. Loans and other grants of credit became increasingly important and then predominant, it would seem, according to just the three forms of credit subject to notaries (table 3.1, p. 175).[35] He finds that "[t]hese credit-based instruments associated with long-distance trade formed an institutional framework for routinized traders" (p. 196).

---

[35] Although these do not include the growing number of letters of credit—note 256, p. 185.

The payoff begins with two graphs over time that, separately for combined nonmerchant occupational groups (artisans and professionals), trace the share in the long-distance trade network from *commendas* and the share from credit. His figure 3.2 shows that throughout the 150 years, and increasingly at the end, the *commenda* share is larger. Then turn to the proportion of ties involving aristocrats: for *commendas* this peaks at 50 percent around 1250, whereas for credit ties an initial low of 20 percent rises uniformly to 60 percent, twice as large as for *commendas*. Detailed analyses then establish that partner selection settled into a pattern in which an elite that now combined populares and aristocrats traded stably with each other.

Finally comes the third class of ties, of insurance, which grew in relative importance, primarily toward the end. Two facts get established. These ties are not profitable; instead they are a break-even affair. And they are found primarily within the same elite as found from credit ties. Van Doosselaere goes on to group the entire network of insurance ties according to a partition along familial clan lines. His blockmodel turns up a core-periphery pattern: the top 26 clans as core have high density; the other 146 clans are grouped as a periphery with almost zero insurance ties with each other, and only moderate tie density both to and from the core.

Such is the extensive evidence for a gradual but profound change over 150 years in results from the reciprocal embedding between commercial style and city institutions in Genoa. The general conjecture is that although at a given time a template portrays the reciprocal embedding between style and institution as the basis of stability, the template also channels impulses to change. The latter are the topic of chapter 3.

Note that this conjecture on the evolution of regime modifies the conjecture offered late in chapter 4 that styles must mate to change. Here too the style is seen as the interweaving of social with cultural sides, but so must be the institution, since it, like style, builds from netdoms. And here I argue that the reciprocal embedding with institution can enable change in style—but now coordinate with change in institution.

In conclusion, much more specification of this conjecture is needed, as to where and how it seems likely to apply. There is an enormous range of possibilities for template along with realm to be explored. Some existing studies may supply the sort of evidence required, as well as the immense detail—by no means have I portrayed all the evidence furnished even just by Erikson and Van Doosselaere in their studies.

SEVEN

GETTING ACTION

SOCIAL LIFE shows two faces. On one side is the challenge of blocking larger waves from the endless upsets and contingencies that are inseparable from living. From this blockage comes some sense of coherence among everyone, as well as some continuity for some locales. This is known as solving the problem of order. This has been the face examined in the chapters thus far, a view of the interaction of organization and action.

The other face cuts open the Sargasso Sea of social obligation and context to achieve openness sufficient for getting action. Any changes must originate from countering the inertia endemic in social organization, that is, change comes from fresh action curing blockage. Action is fresh when it overcomes the inherent lethargy of social life; it's an accomplishment. That is what the chapter lays out: How to get there? How to *get* action?

Structure and fresh action each presupposes the other, while countering it. To understand one side in social process, one has to account for it in relation to the other, as from the vantage point of identity and control. Yet in any particular moment, social and cultural aspects are inextricably intertwined. Previous chapters traced how the dynamics of identities seeking control yield control patterns at various levels, as the outcome. But such patterns are subject to evasions, avoidances, and exploitations in continuing action by and through identities. Chapter 4, for example, shows how the hieratic style can open a way to obscure and break up the endless recurrences into an inertia of blocking action that are endemic in social organization, in either up or down direction. And chapter 6, in exploring for regimes that yield control over control, had to work from a presumption that violation of such regimes was endemic. Now this chapter illuminates how identities seek and achieve control over control, by sidetracking, breaking through existing control patterns, manifested in common sense. Fresh action derives from fresh control, challenging previous control while, nonetheless, seeking new blockage. Paradoxes abound.[1]

---

[1] DiMaggio (1982) offers parallel dissection and diagnosis. He too insists on the necessity of intertwining social and cultural moments in analysis. He too is lucid on institutional analysis while pointing to control regime and fresh action with his brilliant account of the founding of the Museum of Modern Art (MOMA).

The first section of this chapter hints at tangible clues about effective mobilizing, taking account of these paradoxes; the last section unfolds a general vision using the metaphor of annealing. In-between, one section establishes four general claims about getting fresh action, followed by a section on general management, and preceded by analytic accounts of intervention and of agency for control. Penultimate sections analyze seemingly inescapable escapes from control.

7.1. Mobilizing

Even as control interactions come to seem determinate, to be part of some order, fresh control presupposes indeterminacies, some breaking of connections hitherto perceived between contingencies. Such indeterminacies are the results and signs of decouplings as by-products of actions, both physical and social, in processes that extend across space as well as time.

7.1.1. Decoupling

A queue for taxis at an airport illustrates decoupling, by abbreviating interactions among passengers and drivers to a focus in a single portal with its queue. Customers are decoupled from each other, as are drivers, in aid of matchings. If there is a queue supervisor, the simple decoupling based on a fixed rule may become triage, with much consideration of which parties might go in the same taxi, of emergency needs, and so on. A more complex example is triage in a hospital admitting room, which generalizes these stochastic aspects of decoupling, as was sketched in chapter 4 on styles.

A habit of saving from current income illustrates decoupling over time. In saving, conceded rights that are forgone now may become activated later, but at a time not stipulated. Saving is, like other decoupling, also influenced by what goes on with other identities, as well as by larger patterns not perceived by any of the identities. Some sort of panic could ensue from failures in such decoupling (cf. Coleman 1990, p. 903).

Decoupling provides the lubrication that permits self-similarity of social organization across scopes and levels. Decoupling makes it possible for levels of social organization, such as cities and organizations and families, to mix and blur into some inhomogeneous gel. Decoupling explains how it is that the same social formula can recur on different scales.

Failure—that is, the social recognition and construction of breakdowns—may entail an extreme form of decoupling, thus offering a fresh social start. Failure thus permits and stipulates a sharp ending to what seemed locked in by social pressure.

Decoupling is always affected by dynamics of other identities. It is the network context, as social process, that predetermines the kind of decouplings that occur. This insight also points to options for achieving fresh control. Consider an illustration from the complicated setting of an industrial firm. Joseph Bower (1986) studied control efforts moving up and down among management levels, all high enough not to be constrained by production routines. Their contentions clustered around projects of capital investment, many for the development of new products and processes:

> If one wishes to explain after the fact precisely why and when a project developed the way it did, situational elements are likely to be critical to the explanation. In the specifics, events tend to dominate patterns—which in passing is why history tends to be anecdotal. But, for the manager interested in influencing outcomes it is also clear that with one exception he should focus attention on the patterns. *It is structural context that determined how the events of importance were perceived. Where the context seemed to be designed to serve strategic needs, events lost their disorienting impact. . . .* Where traditional financial technique focuses attention on individual project plans separate from the businesses they are meant to serve, severe distortions in focus and timing can result. (Bower 1970, pp. 277, 279. Emphasis supplied.)

It is sophisticated design of context that yielded decoupling across chains of events that otherwise seemed preemptive.

The internal arrangements of any particular firm are pressured by those of other firms. One avenue of pressure is the markets in which various firms seek to find niches. The menu of actions thus reflects fashion among peers, but seeking control implies actions that are original at least in their timing. Bower avoids concepts that presuppose fixed systems and that stipulate that management structures are realistic and effective. His "context" is a residual term that includes the kind of specification for social organization developed in this book. Bower insists on the reality of decouplings that vitiate strategic plannings, such that emphasis shifts to the network context that shapes perceptions of events.

7.1.2. Getting Action

Social organization is just the perceivable traces left from contentions for control in social action, so that efforts at fresh action are already discounted in such social organization as survives to be observed. Interventions may yield new sediments, thrown up by the continuous dialectic of identity and control.[2] Yet it is true, as will be shown throughout the chapter, that getting action can, but need not, yield reconstruction of pattern.

There has to be a peculiar flavor to "principles" for intervening in social organization, for getting action. There may be elites, circles of "movers and shakers," who may jointly go about maneuvering the future. Possibly they have special location and abilities that yield insights to them about integrating both openings and shuttings in social life, but maybe not: see, for example, Bonilla (1970, pp. 92, 99–100, 104, and 112–13). Getting action requires maneuvering choice by indirection to obtain intervention. Getting action can make use of prolepsis; that is, getting action may proceed by inveigling others to take an anachronistic view of the future. Either way, proleptics is for them an art of paradox.[3]

Attempts at fresh control may initiate at any level. But in each case, getting action itself is preconditioned by modes of blockage peculiar to each level. Thus, interventions have to deal with disciplines and their cumulations through networks. Disciplines suppress or transform some contingencies, but disciplines also, in the process of emerging, enlarge the spaces of possible social action. Each new discipline helps to generate occasions for novel control efforts, which can be less subject to counteraction and thus yield fresh action.

Intervention happens also in rhetorics and styles, which tend in different ways to also block fresh action. Rhetorics and styles elaborate and sustain meanings through reenactments. Getting action thus has to take account of meanings, and to rely upon them; but the principal task is to stay ahead of and strip away meaning. Hence, getting action becomes a higher-order project, playing off disciplines and their embeddings into still further levels of networks and styles, making use of decoupling.

A similar point is made by an economist who specializes in game theory:

Strategic decoupling is also in evidence when money is used to decentralize the organizational decision process . . . devices such as overhead per-

---

[2] With different vantage points, Bourdieu (1977, 1980 [1990]) and Giddens (1984) too point out such temporality in structure.

[3] Emirbayer and Mische (1998) further discuss such projective dimensions of agency. Bourdieu (1984, 2000) also sketches how the perception of time and the use of it hinge on position in social space: the sense of being able to dispose of one's own time and the sense of the capacity of planning ahead of time are characteristic for upper (middle) classes. On this view, it would be a vertically relative high social position that figured as a precondition for using time strategically for maneuvers.

centages, and department budgets. . . . Money, the decoupler, smoothes away many of the difficulties that arise in dealing simultaneously with several independently motivated sources of strategic decision. . . . Chamberlin represented a mathematical step backward from the clarity and precision of Cournot, but a considerable step forward in modeling and economic insight concerning competition among the few. . . . The natural way to imbed oligopolistic competitions into a closed economy is to invent money and markets. (Shubik 1984a, pp. 10, 50, 162)

Style, and insights by particular persons are also important, as Weber (e.g., 1978) insisted in his account of charismatic leadership. Within a larger regime, specific position can affect getting action. For example, a final appeals court can be distinguished from lower appeals courts—and each can be distinguished from courts of primary jurisdiction—just through their leverage for fresh action (Shapiro 1980). Another example is how venture capitalist circles may quite consciously manipulate the careers of large firms and even entire industries through apparently neutral changes in money markets.

Getting action may be either more or less cumulative within a given period, and may be on either a larger or a smaller scale than in the routines of disciplines or rhetorics or styles, and it can invade them as well as evade them. Annealing will be developed as a metaphor for this, near the chapter's end. Annealing sets its own boundaries. Also at chapter's end we will trace how getting action for a whole regime can, but need not, generate new pattern, new organization.

Getting things done, getting choice given control becomes, on any scale, a self-contradictory and bizarre problem when one goes beyond the surface stories that suffice for routine reproduction. Getting action and control require ingenuities of decoupling and agency that crosscut the stories of disciplines as well as rhetorics and styles and the regimes into which they may cumulate. Having anything to do—being subject to routine and responsibility—may interfere with getting action. Sticking to preset boundaries in social time or space also interferes with getting action. So getting action may be indirect and delayed. More direct and timely efforts are better described as control.[4]

---

[4] The ambiguity of the term *control* becomes understandable. Chapter 1 already signaled this with the excerpt from Chanowitz and Langer (1980) and the end of chapter 2 related control in my sense to system theory and engineering. Now turn to linguistics for further guidance. Control is, of course, a noun, but this book focuses on control as verb. Even that is ambiguous: is control used as a transitive or as an intransitive verb? That depends on perspective, and linguistics teaches us that the predominant perspective shaping a language can shift over time. Exactly that seems to be happening in English with many verbs, including control. M.A.K. Halliday, in his magisterial portrayal of the grammar of English (1994, p. 163), tells us of a massive shift in recent centuries

Whereas control and getting action both can set off at any level, the ways that perceptions form, partly rooted in physiology, remain such as to sustain self-similarity across levels. It is for this reason that stories can operate as gears, as transcribers between actors and action on different levels as they maneuver for control. Failure and other forms of decoupling make up the lubricant that permits self-similarity. Style is a positive mechanism for self-similarity across levels.

Multiplicity in social organization is the key to getting action, with stories serving only as mediators. Analysis should be universal, or self-similar, so that the same terms and analyses apply at various scopes.[5]

To convey all this requires the wide variety of cases from all scopes that I will canvas later. Next comes the first case study, brief but even so, touching on all chapters. Then I will examine control over control, beginning at the smallest scale, within the single pair-tie, and moving on to disciplines, then styles, and then rhetorics, examined at some length. After that the chapter will cycle back through much the same issues, but making larger claims illustrated by a variety of studies with larger scope.

7.1.3. Mobilizing for Truth

A detailed case study of conflict over innovation analyzes the use of story-sets amid struggles for control that centered on the creation of an event, a discovery, as an affirmation of values. This particular illustrates the emergence of distinct types of tie and their subsequent spread as networks, all as a by-product of ongoing struggles between identities at several levels. Originality and honesty are asserted ubiquitously in science. The study, by Susan Cozzens (1989), dissected a controversy over a multiple discovery in neural pharmacology. In her study, four research groups are struggling for recognition as initiators, and many other groups and isolates are comprised of interested bystanders and contributors. Stories of honesty and of originality are being negotiated in interaction with one another, through various agencies in a complex field across styles and rhetorics.

Multiple networks—of collaboration, of training and sponsorship, of gossip, of friendship and the like—figure as sources as well as products of prestige standings. These standings appear as scientific pecking or-

---

such that more and more of the twenty thousand or so principal verbs exhibit as both transitive and intransitive because of a shift to focus on cause instead of object.

[5] For similar arguments on self-similarity, restricted to a macro scale, see Ashley (1980); Bergesen, Fernandez, and Sahoo (1987); and Caporaso (1989).

ders in specific subfields surrounding neural pharmacology, and more general status-layering, personal and institutional.

Mass-media news conferences were one sort of agency and arena used, but the focus remained on the consensus of fellow experts. Another agency was through brokering and conciliating senior scientists. All these control struggles melded into activations and adjustments of network and standing among the four different working groups as they vied for recognition as co-discoverers.

Dual to all this is the semantic negotiation of concepts and perceptions in rhetorics. These negotiations proceeded along struggles over whether there is an "it" to be discovered, and over the bounds and shape for this "it"—the "opiate receptor." The ordinary terminology of *priority* and *originality* dissolved in confusion amid the bewildering struggles and claims. Participants manufactured, as convenient, new criteria of connection and information. For this scene, scientific values did not operate as universal guides transposable as stories.

The civil rights movement across American black communities is on a completely different scale, but many of the analytic issues are similar. Polletta (2005) provides insight into how stories and story-sets got formulated and passed on in new ways that proved to cumulate impacts. And McAdam (1988) emphasizes the role of social networks: in this example, values of equality and antidiscrimination are intertwined and even sharpened as the civil rights movement moved forward; stories were rendered around formal and informal organizations and social networks that contributed to the momentum of the movement. The values of social and racial equality as well as antidiscrimination of the civil rights movement were mobilized and woven into the social fabric of movement organization. In his words: "Activism depends on more than idealism. . . . There must also exist formal organizations or informal social networks that structure and sustain collective action. The volunteers were not appreciably more committed to Freedom Summer than the 'no-shows' among the college students initially recruited; so that it was position in mobilization networks that tipped who actually came, rather than intensity of individual beliefs in Civil Rights values" (p. 237).

7.1.4. Mische on Brazil; Walder on China

I briefly sketch an account by Mische (2007) of a mobilization for impeachment of the president of Brazil, an account based on nearly two decades of fieldwork and study and modeling and writing. Her study is grounded in a relational approach to social action that focuses on the fluid, interactive, contingent (yet structured) character of social process, which is more akin to a conversation or dialogue than to a set of isolated actions. Let us turn to her words, from her chapter 1:

> The experiences of young Brazilian activists like Barreto reflect a more general paradox of newly democratic public arenas: as actors create new forums for public participation and dialogue, they also create spaces for the pursuit of particularistic and contending projects. These emerging "publics" quickly become "partisan publics" as actors jockey. . . . Publics, which I define as *interactionally constructed spaces in which actors temporarily suspend at least some aspects of their identities and involvements in order to generate the possibility of provisionally equalized and synchronized relationships.* . . . The process by which such efforts succeed and fail—and the implication of these processes for the robustness and vitality of post-authoritarian public arenas—is the central puzzle of the study.

And from her chapter 2:

> While some aspects of style come from the cultural logic of the institutional sector (e.g., church groups vs. political parties vs. business organization), subtle but important differences arise from the relational challenges that come from the multiple affiliations of members. Attention to affiliation profiles can help us to understand intra-sectoral differences. For example the student activists of the Worker's Party . . . are embedded in a wider range of popular, church-based, NGO, and labor organizations (in addition to their student participation), while the Communist Party youth stayed more focused on student and socialist organizing. This relative dispersion vs. focus of relations clearly differentiated the communicative practices of these partisan activists.

Mische evokes rivalries among her student activists that parallel what Andrew Walder finds out about the Red Guard movement of 1966–1968 in China. Here is his own abstract:

> Theories about political movements typically posit models of actor choice that contain untested static assumptions about content. Short-run changes in these contexts—induced by rapid shifts in the properties of political institutions—can alter choices and actors' interests, rapidly transforming the political landscape. China's Red Guard Movement of 1966–68 is a case in point. A generation of scholarship has attributed its violent factionalism to the opposed interests of different status groups. New evidence about the origins of the movement in Beijing's universities indicates that to the contrary, factions emerged when activists in similar structural positions made opposed choices in ambiguous contexts. Activists subsequently mobilized to defend earlier choices, binding them to antagonistic factions. Rapid shifts in the contexts for political choice can

alter prior connections between social positions and interests, generating new motives and novel identities. Close attention to these contextual mechanisms can yield novel accounts of the nature and origins of political movements. (Walder 2006, p. 710)

7.1.5. Intimacy and the Leifer Tie

Identities can appear in person or as event. Regardless of their packaging, when they are continuously reshaped in contentious accountings of the contexts of their coming together, they are Leifer ties. These comings together occur within networks under impetuses of control efforts and pressures of production. Stories are the form taken by these accountings, stories as everyday framings.

Control is sought in, and thereby it loosens, all formations. The smallest formation is the pair, which nonetheless sustains subtle processes when both in the pair relation are actively contending for control. Intimacy grows from subtle gaming interactions between a pair of identities; it can also be found in larger settings such as entourages (chapter 4). Strategy and ambiguity underpin the intimate, and they must be used to sustain action flows in delicate balance in order for identities to be maintained in such ties. Leifer (1991a) has developed a theory for such a tie of maximum intensity. Leifer's fundamental point is that unending gaming and speculation is a constituent of any tie significant to both its actors and to onlookers, which is to say a tie that is contributing to active processes both inside itself and in larger structures. Just as intimacy can be sustained in large scale, as style, so intensity can be sustained in small scale, as when it joins with intimacy in a love tie.

Leifer terms this a theory of local action, but as will become clear, it can as well be termed robust action. Robust action comes from unraveling of, but is a sophisticated replacement for, the dominance ordering that would override any particular tie within a discipline mechanism. The initial example used in Leifer's work was tournament chess.

Tournaments provide an unusually transparent structure and process for observing pairs as encounters. Leifer ties are subtle ties, constituted by skilled players locked in positional balance. Accounts heard about the ongoing relation between players in actual play are vague, but Leifer shows that players of tournament quality are, as persons, aware of and sustain ambiguity in their play.[6]

---

[6] Through careful dissection of samples of games and tournaments to support his interpretation of the extensive chess literature.

Robust action is just that which permits gaming and speculation to continue, which prevents anyone from seeing clearly an outcome that would end the social tie. Ongoing relations lack the sharpness of a conceded game. The transparency of chess, tournament chess, as a social context makes apparent the cost of robust or local action. In good chess, the better the game, the more likely a draw. Leifer's work demonstrates that clear goals can inhibit establishing identities.

Tournament chess allows insight into processes of establishing pairs and the identities deriving from these pairs, because tournaments are coordinated to yield public and reliable rankings of players across national populations. The long-established context of tournament chess thereby has been worked out to minimize differences between players in a game. Thus, only pairs thought likely to sustain a tie of robust action are encouraged. In addition, great care is taken about what population of pairs to form, what network of encounters to arrange. The arrangement is to ensure a clear spread of ranking, and thus it increases the number and distinctness of identities.[7]

It seems a paradox. Robust social action, and identities as by-products, presuppose a veil over intermediate goals that may be driving play in a game. Furthermore, robust action is likely to negate the ostensible end goal, which is a victory, an assignment of asymmetry. The better established the identity of a player (that is, the higher his scores in the meticulously computed rankings of the chess world), the more his actions avoid events, which is to say striking losses or gains.

Leifer's ingenious dissection of chess playing among experts can be extended to a wide gamut of strategic interaction. Chess skill—and, by analogy, strategic social skill in general—consists exactly in keeping the state of interaction hard to assess through making very many possible evolutions continue to seem possible. Any such tie is stable only through being ambivalent and ambiguous at any particular instant and in any tangible action. A set of such ties can embed into a team, or into an identity, exactly because purposes and standings are unclear. Leifer both establishes and solves the paradox of such a tie, the conundrum of achieving comparability through attempted inequality.[8]

---

[7] This can be analyzed further in terms of the disciplines of chapter 3. Leifer has gone on (1991b) to study long stretches of outcomes from professional sports team encounters, and uncovers a variety of larger regimes and styles: see also Mizruchi (1991).

[8] Romantic love is another extreme case of Leifer tie. It is extreme, first, on intensity—but no more so than are competitive ties between chess masters. But here the conundrum is achieving inequality through the attempt at utter equality. The defining characteristic of romantic love is that it is not embedded in everyday networks; it comes "out of the blue," socially. Thus romantic love need not concern sexual attractions, either hetero- or homosexual. Some bolt-from-the-blue relations have always been found, even in tribal contexts. Where we think of Jane Austen and ceremonial combat, Germanic tribes

7.2. Intervention for Control

Control is achieved only across levels. Levels are not just an analytic convenience of aggregation, but by-products of the turf war between getting action and blocking action. New levels of social structure emerge from, and only from, interventions for control. Coercion and the like, by contrast, exist on the same level. Control, reaching across levels, presupposes embeddings for disciplines.

Events and identities variously embed action in further levels of the creation of still further identities. Skilled chess players come into existence out of the blatant discrepancies in play with other players initially just chosen at random: in short, through events that later come to be reported as striking. Thereafter, the skilled identity continues functioning by avoiding the very mismatches that gave rise to it.

The identity is now embedded in a different level, almost a disjunct world where expertness is the agreed basis, to be demonstrated by avoidance of what can be seen by outsiders to be action. This illustrates how mismatches and multiplicities that generate identities are in turn themselves regenerated. Events become important as the medium in which already established actor-identities interact, fill out stories, and possibly lead to still further embeddings. As they are regenerated, stories adjust to changing ties.

7.2.1. Intervention through Disciplines

A network population is a stew of disciplines. A network evolves, like disciplines themselves, under the social pressure of contending efforts at control. These efforts play out over time in physical space, geographically, and also under pressures of material production, of work—that is, subject to ecological pressures.

Disciplines become the main site for focused efforts at control within the networks that make up social space. Production—social and material—comes out of disciplines and relies on specialization. Production by disciplines is always at the same time reproduction, that is, renewed implementation of some known social form. Specializations of three kinds index, by dependence, differentiation and involution, how each of the three disciplines embeds into context. Effective search for control views a discipline from the context into which its production is being embedded.

---

thought of blood brothers in physical combat. Recognition of conquests by an interested circle, often a corporate, was the focus in chivalrous troubadours.

Disciplines are locally overawing expressions of social control, but within a population there is no simple mapping of discrete form onto discrete effect. For example, a council discipline is a prime way to embed action and make it effective, and yet it also is a species of discipline with which to obfuscate action. Which effect predominates depends upon "context," upon the environing networks of disciplines. But context is more than a static cross section of environment; context includes those processes of forgetting and of historical referent that are always being invoked in various crisscrossing projects of control.[9]

Search for control must act upon disciplines and thus must somehow express or put them together within new contexts or in new exemplars. Sometimes a new variety will be created for one of the three species of discipline. A new choice may be found, say, from upstream for interface, in the embedding that is present with all disciplines.

For interfaces, however, a new choice more commonly is found with embedding from the downstream side. That corresponds to the numerator of the embedding ratios, as discussed in chapter 3. These embedding ratios are, of course, extreme abstractions from direct description of a discipline in context. Each ratio is only a matter of tendencies. The analogy in visual perception would be the gradients of illumination thrown off by texture and pattern in a curving surface of the three-dimensional field outside the eye. But these embedding ratios are important abstractions; they index which forms of specialization can reproduce in that context and point toward possible intervention for fresh control. Where, and how, there are the most openings for fresh control may also suggest the most likely routes for evolution of more complex social formations.

Control is achieved across levels. And only disciplines generate and provide the endogenous social energy without which control is merely a facade. Disciplines develop through spreading out into networks in which each tie is a balance of gamings for control. Stories are always being spun into ties, and then whole sets of stories emerge, which can keep up with whatever happens. And it is this process that leaves the opportunity for fresh control attempts. Here indeed is a paradox: whatever happens can be normalized through stories, which thus are resistant to change, and yet the new stories thereby yield openings for change through fresh control attempts.

[9] Lily Ross Taylor (1949) lays out this latter for contending senatorial factions during a period in the late history of the Roman Republic over two millennia ago: such basics of action in social organization do not change with period or with scale or with cultural realm or with strata. The values invoked to color action change, but not the species of discipline involved.

Control efforts are attempted across levels resulting from embedding. The idea of levels comes with embedding. Levels build up in social formations as by-products of interacting control struggles. Actors on presumably different levels can relate directly through control projects. Yet social spaces are not tidy layerings. "Actor" can be anything from a multinational giant firm to a Goffmanesque creature of the brief encounter. And whatever it is, this actor will be viewed differently for styles and for rhetorics.

7.2.2. Style and Control

The playground networks used as illustrations in the first two chapters imply, and also presuppose, some larger social environment. Control must build from others' ties. Results of control cumulate beyond networks to weave varieties of locality into larger social formations, regimes that prove their robustness by persisting. Style in control can characterize such larger social formations and guide efforts at getting action by personal actors.

Efforts to control other actors consist in unpredictable action.[10] Identities are the source of social action and thus of seeking control, including control of social action. Identities are the only source of intentional efforts, which is to say of potentially un-routine action. These efforts contribute to uncertainties until they are interlocked in social formations by interaction with other such efforts.

Gaining control cuts across and mixes up self-reproducing social organization, and hence does the same with meaning and its reproduction. Meaning is simply another face to blocking action through obtaining coherence in social organization. In one sense, therefore, there can be no particular type of organization associated with additional control. Nevertheless, there are styles conducive to shaking up for fresh control, as will appear in two examples developed in the next section.

Styles can embrace sibling identities that project from much the same physical creatures, but which are nonetheless distinct. Styles thereby decouple between network populations that overlap in physical space. These multiple populations come into existence only with and through the induction and construction of new and specifically social space-times. Styles, in short, loosen regime and open it for fresh control.

---

[10] This is developed further in this chapter at the level of pair-ties in the earlier section on Leifer ties, and with respect to game theory.

Getting control at any time tends to lay a social track of tangible organization, as it requires some mixing of disciplines and embeddings across networks—and as efforts at blocking control begin coterminous with the laying of tracks. Control is endemic at all scopes and levels. Distinctive styles of control regarding blocking action among regimes can be observed. And yet control plays as large a part in getting action as in blocking action.

7.3. Agency for Control

Agency resulting from control has been a principal theme so far, agency as a by-product of gaining footing. First, identities and simple social organization derived from agency, and eventually led to persons as agents between populations in complex social organization. Now the principal theme becomes agency for control, with identities striving for control in and of their context, as social process. This corresponds to the rhetoric for control as consciously motivated action. The term *agency* can apply at any scale from triad on; but agency for control operates mostly at the level of institutions.

Attempts at fresh control must aim to sidetrack the blockage of action inherent in social organization. Whereas decision-making structures figure as devices for enforcing custom, scalar organizations serve as devices for resisting change. Hegemony seems to rest on stasis, whether or not authority speaks of change. These are implications of the analysis so far.

Although blocking action is an endemic project, as common for the high and mighty as for challengers, fatalism need not follow. On the one hand, it is true that within any regime, following any style or profile, attempts at control tend to counteract one another and thus to engender new disciplines instead of fresh control; the same applies even within a tie. Yet, on the other hand, such control efforts that lead to blockage of action can turn into an important initial leverage for somebody's managing, by yet further impulse for control, to generate some action that could not be anticipated. Control for fresh action can be achieved, and even to some degree can be routinized, within various styles and regimes and for various rhetorics.

Think of the new theme raised here as a contrast with the previous chapters, which all concerned tendencies of action to freeze into a regime or other social organization, thereby denying innovation, blocking action. In contrast with that stasis, there are ways of using agency to upend regime and initiate fresh action in the course of seeking control.

Agency may be kept immediate—for example, in the study of Italian city-states:

> The real state, the state felt all around one in the form of potent commissions or as a source of income (via speculation on the Monte), existed in the corporate and individual holder. . . . Nothing in the Florentine constitution emphasized the principle of indirect representation. . . . The contact with power was direct, immediate, sensory. (Martines 1968, pp. 391–92)

The evolution of social organization generally occurs as turnover of control in agency. Such agency can be captured along a vertical axis that distinguishes between two positions of principal and agent, together with levels of embedding regarding the five senses of identity as defined in chapter 1. Hence from a principal's perspective, agency is confined to the third and fourth senses of identity, whereas from an agent's perspective, it concerns mainly the second but also the third. When some set of agents captures control, when agents wrest control away from their principals, the correspondences shift: the agents tend to move into identities of the third sense, whereas the principals are being put back on the interpretive shelf in being confined to the fourth sense.

7.3.1. Mechanisms

Agency may loosen up mobilization, so that agency can operate by delegation. That is, agency can apply through a direct tie, a tie that can be inserted arbitrarily so far as the otherwise existing network context knows. The extreme special case of agency is the *shaliach*, the Old Testament term for one who is but a shadow, or plenipotentiary agent, designed solely to carry out the implications of another's identity for concrete action. Agency in general turns discipline mechanisms away from a primary focus on network context, to taking identity as important and as transposable. It often works through institutions.

Joint perceptions of networks require articulation, just as perceptions for disciplines do. Identities are aware of the connections coded as ties in a network, and they are even aware of some of the topological parameters that are the scientific motivation for introducing networks. For example, actors have a sense of whether they are sociometric stars and of how connected-in they are. Actors also may sense how inbred their space is, how "weak" the ties are in Granovetter's sense (1973).

Once identities are established—and by hypothesis, where and when this appears is chancy and erratic—not only do ties spin out from their nodes, but identities may also perceive and activate ties among other nodes, especially as part of their control projects. Types of tie can become differentiated and coordinated with story-lines at the phenomenological level, along with issues and interests.

An example is the adaptation of clientelist ties for individual Romans to use in binding larger corporate actors (Badian 1958; Garnsey and Saller 1987). Or story-lines can be differentiated on the basis of types of ties. As examples, take the ways the Roman republic built up military leadership doctrine by cobbling together existing sorts of relationships from other institutions (Suolahti 1955). For instance, the Senate delegated military authority in various forms to senators and others as generals for a great variety of campaigns (Eckstein 1987).

Even the simplest exemplar of agency, on the smallest scale, presupposes settings both for events and for actors. Mismatches can be shifted from one setting to another, but not eliminated.

Agency shades down from more complex maneuverings and interpretations to binary imperatives, all of which deal with meanings as much as with social patternings. Agency generates both perception and analysis, and it can express a duality between event and actor. Agency can be linked to actors, by their intentions, but also to events, which entails an analytic duality. Control comes from interaction of agencies.

7.3.2. Agenda for Agency

An agenda denotes the outcome of more or less conscious shaping of issues and interests by projects of control, within rhetorical forms. Agenda also describes the sequence of issue-interest pairings agreed upon for a specific meeting.[11] Agency as control by agenda is necessarily intertwined with particular agents, goals, and social organizational context, however conceptualized. It is the specific context that provides the essential constructs, such as "power" and "authority," and their particular discrimination.

Consider an example. The Medici recognized a vulnerability that had crept into their corporatist city-state. To all appearances, this corporatist regime had locked in the social formation of Florence in the early Renaissance. Taking for given the corporatism that existed amid all but the lowest strata, the few score of leading families had come to perceive control as only a matter of factions among themselves as an

---

[11] Exotic examples are helpful in bringing out the formation and effects of agenda. It is, after all, easier to discern the role of an agenda when the observer has no personal investment in the content of interests and issues. Then a result is to decrease the degree of exoticness perceived! And this process helps us to be as clear-eyed as March is about agendas in our own time and context (Cohen and March 1974; March and Olsen 1976).

elite, with merely some mirroring to control as a show among guilds and lower-level corporate forms.

Then came Cosimo de Medici to consciously spin down strings of patronage, systematically cutting across the range of banking and business and social and kinship activities that he himself and his associates engaged in (Padgett and Ansell 1993; De Roover 1966). The factionalized style of patron-client politics took over nearly in a flash and then proved to be stable. After all, it was but a resuscitation of the sort of party politics that Lily Ross Taylor pinned down as central to the late republic of Rome (Taylor 1949; and see Syme 1968).

Through agency, events can be framed via agenda into issues; but also actors can be framed into interests.[12] In many tribal contexts (Fortes 1949; Evans-Pritchard 1940; Hart and Pilling 1960), the emphasis is reversed: issues are imputed in order to achieve coherent strings of actors by interests. And, from an advanced society, accounts of Thai society and government, in the provinces as well as the capital, offer another and extreme example of issues being concocted to generate coherence among interests:

> Heavy reliance on oral, therefore secret, communications for much of the real business of government combined with a proliferation of paper work designed to maintain appearances . . . little or no serious attention is given to documents by overworked higher officials [p. 319]. Inadequate scheduling of time leads to alternate periods of under-occupation and furies of last minute work [p. 113]. Over-centralization is a vain hope, a groundless aspiration and pretence, masking the actual dispersal and localization of control . . . the formalism effect [p. 282]. All the conspicuous doors cannot move, and egress must be sought through moving panels controlled by hidden buttons. (Riggs 1964, p. 7)

The fascination of the "club" groups that Barth (1965) describes among the tribal Swat Pathans is that they appear to be an intermediate case where issues and interests are being imputed and perceived more on the same footing (Skvoretz and Conviser 1971), so that agendas are more complex. Events concatenate into issues, and actors into interests and factions, by social negotiation. There is an active, manipulative aspect to the resulting mechanisms. Cumulation of ties is a substantive

---

[12] These framings are an activist alternative to their being seen as part of the regular operations of styles and rhetorics in regimes among networks of networks from the preceding chapters. Issues and interests are not attributes, not passive categories of perception by persons; instead they are by-products of efforts at control. They come out of projects of control, often through agencies, as these interact into larger dynamics through cumulation and specialization in a population of networks.

social process of its own, rather than being a matter of sheer stipulation from the sequence of ties in some representation of a network.

Consider how cumulated agency can occur. Interests are socially imputed to actors in such a way as to reduce ambage in social organization, to make it less ambagious. That is the process of story-lines. Also, issues are imputed to events in such a way as to minimize ambiguity of interpretation. That is the process of rhetoric. But one imputation tends to interfere with the other in actual contexts of networks among disciplines.[13] Construction of an agenda deals with implications of this interference. It requires considering more complex, three-body interactions in real time.[14]

Agency calculus is the computation of trade-offs, among ambage and ambiguity and contingency, to suggest fresh ways to gain control. Agency calculus needs to be developed for specific disciplines and their combinations; and it must be framed by context. Barth's classic study (1965) of men's clubs as political systems in a mountain valley is one example of council and interface combinations. A second is Prince's descriptions (1974) of putting together Broadway productions. The two examples differ in size and in institutional background, and so presumably also on locations in index space. How disciplines would mesh depends on the specific context. Barth's examples of wheeling and dealing over dependencies and land rights would, one supposes, be at intermediate levels. And Harold Prince's matchings are at low levels. But each combination would require the kind of treatment of context that is given in Barth's monograph to identify a population. And each situation is articulated in terms of values.

One of the varieties of mediation discipline is the extreme of zero differentiation ratio; autocracies can be described that way. When autocracies occur embedded in the upper caste in the valley of Barth's study, his mediation disciplines can be seen as approximating that extreme ratio. Prince's meditation discipline, by contrast, is among sets whose differentiation is to be seen as very high, viewed from the outside. The War Industries Board examples of mediation discipline that I give near this chapter's end, however, cluster around an intermediate ratio of differentiation; the presence of the military assures that outcome.[15]

---

[13] The extreme form of *shaliach*, of plenipotentiary agency, cuts ambage toward zero but with no limit on ambiguity (White 1985). In another extreme, with agency extended as into surgeon or investment banker, ambage is high and ambiguity low (Johnson 1972; Johnson 1983; Eccles and Crane 1988).

[14] This is fleshed out in the case studies in Riker (1982).

[15] In much the same way, presence of East Tennessee mountain Republicans assure that V. O. Key's "one-and-a-half party" system obtains in that Southern political regime (Eccles and White 1986b).

7.4. Four General Claims and Three Angles

Getting action will override particular species of discipline and particular regime, rhetoric, and particular style, and will tend to mix together contexts. That is the **first general claim**. Rhetorics and styles variously interlock network populations made up of discipline species; and regimes are concrete whereas styles are floating anchors of frames of interpretation by story. Getting action, by contrast, tends to invoke and bring about generality, which crosscuts all specializations. Getting action is not some new form of specialization. Specializations are ineluctable because they are the dynamics of discipline production, but getting fresh patterns of action requires cutting across and overriding both specializations and larger social organization.

Consider an illustration of this first general claim. In educational systems there is a general tendency for actors to opt for training that is "more general" than is suitable for them—for example, training in law or other information-based field as opposed to specific manual arts. One aspect of this tendency is a realistic perception that the more general and abstract training is, the more likely it will fit with getting action and hence with surviving through changes of opportunity. There are counterexamples, such as the extreme specialization within former Soviet education, which may tend to prove the rule.

Another example is the growth of engineering as a learned profession. Industrial production, both with and without advanced machinery, had tended to be subject to control or at least veto by numerous groups of craftsmen who shared skills and were permanently committed to their respective specialties. Engineers were in part a deliberate creation by owners, a new form of generalization of the particular skills of craftsmen actually engaged in production. The production disciplines, and the craftsmen communities of role and position, were all crosscut thereby, though not destroyed. Owners sought to get action.

Getting action must invoke changing concrete patterns, attaining new varieties and combinations of discipline and role and position, and such changing must continue, always. This is the **second general claim.** The illustrations must deal with getting action that continues over periods of time. This claim suggests how it is that control must be a two-edged concept: control may be realized by stopping change and thus blocking action, as well as by getting action via changing and mixing specializations, roles, and the like. Likewise, decoupling, which pairs with control, is two-valued: decoupling can be as central in blocking action as in getting action.

An example will best illustrate that it is change in more than content of organized arrangements that gets action:

> The change in [Athen's system], when it came, was sharp and sudden, following the overthrow of the tyranny in 510 with Spartan help and a two-year civil war which ensued; and the architect of the new type of government was Cleisthenes, a member of the noble family of the Alcaemonids. Cleisthenes was no theorist, and he seems to have become a democrat virtually by accident, turning to the common people when he urgently needed their support in the confused struggle to fill the vacuum left by the deposed tyrant, Hippia the son of Peisistratus. . . . Having committed himself to a major innovation, Cleisthenes with his advisers, whoever they may have been, created the institutions which they thought their new objective required, retaining what they could, but not hesitating to demolish and to invent boldly and radically. (Finley 1977, p. 76)

This example at the same time illustrates the first general claim, that getting action always involves crosscutting existing specializations.[16]

What getting action does generate unfailingly is inequality: this is the **third general claim**, which is also illustrated by the previous example. This claim may explain why interpretations of society as diverse as Marxism and functionalism give so much attention to systems of stratification. This third claim implies, however, that these other approaches have gone at the study of stratification wrongly. There are not classes cleanly differentiated by relations to the means of production, nor strata rationally arrayed according to worth of their occupations. On the contrary: one cannot establish stratification criteria once and for all objectively, as these are principally in flux and themselves the outcome of processes of getting action; while inequality remains, the underlying criteria may get altered in social process, as part of control projects.

The central point about inequality is exactly that it is the only systematic regularity one can adduce from the continuing operation of

---

[16] The example also illustrates a practical limitation in my exposition. Only historically prominent and otherwise famous or significant instances of action are well enough known to enough readers for brief exposition to be effective (if still not sufficient). I have been and will continue to cite studies without substantial description in hopes that the source monographs will be consulted. But even these studies tend to concentrate on larger scale and more prominent examples such as feudal England (Lachmann 1985) and Soviet Russia (Urban 1987)—or at least on the prominent as judged within the horizons of that world, say, of highland New Guinea (Strathern 1971). Yet built into my whole approach is the claim that the same sort of generalities apply to getting and blocking action across very diverse scopes, at various levels of the complex cumulations and concatenations of embeddings of disciplines, across various forms of specializations and identities in networks.

getting action, considered as an observable drive that is widely present, with quite varied and changing sources within social spaces. Inequality is the by-product of attempts to get action and gain control: inequality, the most pervasive idiom of blocking action, is the cumulative product of attempts to get action. The implication is that stratification is the inevitable direction taken as regimes become increasingly removed from ecological constraint. Stratification is the destination, at least the interim destination, of the purely social evolving under pressures of getting action.

Getting action, or for that matter control, is not reserved for designated "positions," say elites of some sort. On the contrary, any particular designated position is by that very character likely to become part of blocking action, and thus also of getting action. This is the **fourth general claim**.

This fourth claim suggests differentiating three distinct angles from which fresh action can be attempted. I will lay these out in turn. Afterward comes an extended example of getting action at a national scale in which all the claims and angles can be seen in play; and the fourth claim is then tied in with an analogy that applies, usually, at the level of person, in suicide.

7.4.1. Reaching Through

"Reaching through" is a main strategy for the conundrum of getting action. Reaching through to other levels and neighborhoods, ones other than those of the disciplines of current routine social action—reaching through to gain control cannot be pinned down as occurring in one discipline species, say the interface.

The argument has been that beyond a particular scope or level of discipline embedded in a network of identities, beyond that immediate scope and context of production and action, there is an endless variety of nestings, concatenations, aggregations. The physical analogies urged from the beginning have been to minerals, gels, glasses, and other forms intricately historied and packed. It is only in the clusters of story-lines evolved in some society that apparently regular macrostructures have appeared.

Generally, "reaching through" can thus not be a technical term. "Reaching through" instead is a phenomenological term about strategic efforts to get action and control *through*, rather than *despite*, these complex deposits of social organization; and also despite the orderly stories invoked by participants. Neither reaching down, nor reaching up, is as likely to be theorized or even explicitly perceived, and so strategic effort is less likely to get summoned. I argue that it was the student leaders, on which the Mische mobilization study (2007) focused, who strategized explicitly and mostly about other factions on the same level, even though an impeachment mobilization, taken overall, by definition involves reaching up.

Reaching through is a matter of occasion and process as much as of structuration. Crisis is always associated both as cause and as product with reaching through. Crisis is as much a labelling to help make action possible, as it is a report forced into the perceptions of disparate actors and events by configurations of network contingencies. Crisis regimes are the subject of studies presented later in the chapter. Reaching through is as much selectivity, as it is persevering through multiple connections.

Whether vertical or lateral, reaching through social organization can be facilitated by kinds of formal organization whose prime story-line is exactly preventing violations of orderly authority! Turn to the unique case of getting action given by British entrepreneurship. Bythell argues (1978, p. 198) that the putting-out system, the informal network style in which English manufacturing had evolved, discussed in chapter 6, remained attractive "in industries with a more stable pattern of demand, or with only modest and irregular growth over long periods." Whereas dramatic growths in demand for some particular items over a period of a year or two "force some entrepreneurs towards technical innovation and new forms of organization."

Mergers and acquisitions (M&A) in the present setting of Western industry can be argued to be similar covers for the introduction of shake-ups and disorders. M&A is reaching through on a more extensive scale than is easy to effectuate within a context defined as a continuing single formal organization. This fits with surveys such as done by Salter and Weinhold (1979, pp. 4, 27), who report that good diversification deals occur suddenly rather than being planned and smooth, and the goodness can be explained only in terms of huge variances in returns on equity. Or take a particular case, normal in its bizarreness: American Express's adventures:

> An odyssey of corporate decision making that would destroy Roger Morley's career, make James Robinson's, and culminate months after the debacle of (attempted acquisition of) McGraw-Hill with the celebrated acquisition of the brokerage house of Shearson Loeb Rhoades—an acquisition that appeared a daring masterstroke, but which, in reality, came as the result of miscalculations, opportunity and just plain luck, an acquisition no one at Amexco would have dreamed of or wanted when the process began in 1977. (Grossman 1987)

Another prime illustration of reaching through by M&A can be found in the Eccles and Crane account (1988) of changes in the U.S. investment banking industry. The predominant relation in earlier decades between an issuer of equity and an investment banker was an analogy to the family doctor. The same few people within the bank were the long-term trusted advisers of company management, with friends among directors and executives. These few nurtured the impression of their being the expert and informed guides to a dangerous and weird universe of capital—the source of which was decoupled from the advice relation, in the hands of more routine officialdom within the bank that serviced investment trusts of all sorts. Control was thereby achieved over the client corporation, almost complete control except for the very largest handful of corporations daring and large enough to be sophisticated in a context set up to deal only with trusting naiveté.

This traditional agency relation eventually became cozy and profitable—to the agent. The reversal of control into the hands of the agent is, after all, an old story, begun by "factors" of commodities, which likewise eased into exclusivity with client (Schwartz 1976). However, this was not getting action; on the contrary, the context was one of protection and guardedness just as with the family doctor. "Doing deals" emerged as a kind of virus breaking up this peace, the febrile atmosphere of not wanting to miss one of the endlessly possible new sorts of financing. Why stick with the family doctor when there is available a street full of glittering specialists thinking of new ways of reslicing reality to sell it yet again?

At the same time, the buyer side became integrated into a troika network, binding issuer companies together with a range of specialists within investment banks. This was reaching through with a vengeance. Action was being gotten so obsessively there was never even time to worry about organization charts or to cultivate trust. Why cultivate trust when glamour would trump you anyway?

Structural equivalence is the underlying guide in this recasting, and not just in the search for parallel agents and the search for equivalent targets for nostrums. Structural equivalence underpinned the successive banking nostrums, the successive waves of new ways to partition and reassign ownership and debt. Stringing had been the core of the old agency. And now the agents corporately, and their shifting kaleidoscope of self-defined experts individually, were being harshly stratified by success defined along "show biz" lines (Faulkner 1983). Timing becomes all—a week late with an idea, and it is dead.

Acquisitions and mergers assume, induce, and impose stratification by revaluations made unusually abruptly. At the same time, these revaluations intend to, and do, generalize across the large-scale special-izations indexed by industry and market.

7.4.2. Reaching Down

An earlier example of reaching down was the Padgett and Ansell ac-count of the Medici strategy. More examples will be helpful. The triage seen in a hospital emergency room (see chapter 4) is a prototype for reaching down at a much larger scale. Getting action can never be any sort of universal; it is always a particular moment of, and interlude in, ongoing social life. Without selectivity, even a moment of getting ac-tion disappears. Triage can be seen as the timely reaching through of disciplines, in layers or levels, in order to get action.

Reaching down to get action is not some mechanical predictable matter. An entrepreneur combining ownership and control to elide a level is getting action, but so is the same entrepreneur bringing in trou-bleshooting in various staff guises in order to scan and sample in test-ing for where a crisis is appearing or can be coaxed into existence. Identities would never have been triggered in the first place if there were no uncertainties, no contingencies. Once formed, they encounter other identities, and each defines further contingencies for the others, eventuating in the full panoply of ambage and ambiguity in addition.

Eliding levels helps to reach down through. British entrepreneurs of the previous century must be regarded as paragons of getting action. They showed tenacity throughout the nineteenth century in marrying together ownership and management as completely as in the Indus-trial Revolution itself:

> Entrepreneurs with exceedingly little technical knowledge were prepared to risk large sums of money in manufacturing ventures and . . . to build a factory the size of which was determined not by rational calculations . . . but by the capital available for investment . . . and the maximum output the entrepreneur thought he could obtain. (Payne 1974, p. 32)

This is getting action, not blocking action. Nor were these entrepre-neurs settling into quietude through family descent:

> In 1830, of the 135 firms in Leeds engaged in the sale and manufacture of woolens, worsteds and blankets, for example, a long-established industry in the industrial city, only twenty-one houses had partners who could pro-vide a direct link with those in 1782, only fifty years before. But this small scope under direct entrepreneurship made outreach limited: they could not engage in vigorous selling effort in world markets by means of a sala-ried force of commercial travelers. (Payne 1974)

Reaching down is seen as a positive opportunity for action in that it allows for the continued outreach to wider and changing scopes, which is indispensable to continuing to get action.

Lateral relations as such are irregular, just as is reaching down through vertical layers, according to Sayles (1979, p. 81). They are irregular because they interfere with routines, require iteration, are ambiguous: "Management thus becomes in large part a process of working interfaces. . . . Rough-and-tumble reality with its stops and starts and many cross-interrelationships and bargains thus seems disorderly and political" (pp. 90–92).

At very different scopes and in very different institutional contexts, one can recognize similar strategies in reaching down through, in order to untie knots in congealed structures. Compare Gorbachev in the USSR of 1988 with Alfred Sloan in the staggering General Motors of the 1920s. Gorbachev's industrial reform calls for an expanded role for managers of industrial associations and enterprises, and a steep decline in the role of economic and administrative bureaucracies in day-to-day supervision of managers' activities. Gorbachev's plan did not envisage an increase in the direct responsibilities of the (Communist Party) "apparat," which however would still expect to guide industry's transition to the new methods of planning and management (we return to this example at more length later).

The parallel is striking to Sloan's reaching through the complexly specialized federation of the old General Motors, which was a haphazard throwing together of a host of diverse industrial entities through merger and acquisition. Sloan reached for a new, removed formation of general managers in a central office. In both situations, the control structure of routine information flows was supposed to and did become more abstract, and yet actual accounts show that eruptions of central agency into concrete enactments of production became much more common, while still unpredictable (Hopwood 1978). In both cases, the newly abstract central oversight came to be housed in an apparatus (*nomenklatura* and general office, respectively) that focused on and decided personnel moves at all levels whence elite careers may emerge (Bialer 1987, p. 77; Chandler 1969, chap. 3; Sloan 1963).

Forms of state terror had characterized versions of reaching through the Soviet economy in earlier decades, and they had substantial effect. The analogue in General Motors lay in economic terror, in bankruptcies and destroyed positions. Reaching through is not painless or neat; as in simpler forms of control, the only real fuel for reaching through is from excitation of grievances and fractures in the motivations of existing networks, identities, and disciplines embedded through many levels.

The moral is that autocracies induce structural equivalence. Both Gorbachev and Sloan rely on structural equivalence effects from their pulling up selected personnel to be in central, generalizing offices, whose idiom is the flexibility of being able to operate effectively across diverse units. Both faced some tension between this accomplishment of generality, on the one hand, and orientation to change, technical and social, on the other.

Innovation is not the same as getting action, and requires some stable embodiment of social support, some structure that allows the obsessive degrees of specialization that always attend successful technical innovation. It is hard to read through layers of obfuscation to check if the same is true of innovations in social organization, but it seems likely. Nevertheless, streams of innovation are necessary for keeping alive the option of getting action, as much as they are for their ostensible missions to yield better fits to technical and competitive environments. Identities of both events and actors are reshaped and re-created more when there is a flux of innovations, and it is such reshaping that provides the material for getting action. In the sphere of events, to reach through is to invoke and create local history in hopes of getting non-Markovian impact on the inevitably stochastic process that is unfolding.

Issues and interests are engendered out of events and actors whose identities are being shaped among contending efforts at agency. Getting action must continue to break up the hardening crust of issues and interests that is congealing continually to block action. Let us turn back to General Motors' early evolution. In 1913, the regime of the banker Storrow was seeking to block action in a scramble to bring coherence to a business then understood only by its creator-entrepreneur, Durant. General Motors was centralized into three offices by this regime. One of these was purchasing, an apparently logical choice, since half the product valuation was in purchased parts. The other two departments were changed when Durant regained control for a few years, and then, when Sloan was brought in from his own Hyatt Bearings to run the whole operation, purchasing fell back into organizational insignificance. Control was needed over disciplines to purchasers, not the ones to suppliers, since the former were still inchoate aggregates where action could not be gotten.[17]

Consider in parallel the earlier evolution of Soviet industrial reforms before Gorbachev. Here too events were induced and issues thereby generated because they were necessary for getting action, for reaching

---

[17] Burt (1983) has developed and exploited this logic in his analyses of current American industry.

through impacted layers. But here too, earlier reforms, creating regional decentralizations, proved arbitrary, unrelated to the actual balances of ambiguity and ambage in the architecture of agencies that had been built up (cf. Granick 1967, 1972).

7.4.3. Reaching Up

There are special features to getting action when oneself and one's collaborators are not perceived as already the high and mighty. The study by Mische discussed earlier is one example over a short period. Also, V. I. Lenin is credible as an expert on reaching up, through a complex social fabric, to get action on a large scale (Lenin 1966 [1902]). On a similar scale, first- and second-century church fathers are also credible (von Campenhausen 1955; Dix 1947).

Lenin speaks for specialization; this apparently is the opposite of my claim that generalists are the path to action:

> Lack of specialization is one of our most serious technical defects. . . . The smaller each separate "operation" in our common cause will be, the more people we shall find capable of carrying out such operations (people, who, in the majority of cases, are not capable of becoming professional revolutionaries), the more difficult will it be for the police to <oqauote>catch" all the "detail" workers . . . in order in breaking up functions to avoid breaking up the movement, and in order to imbue those who carry out these minute functions with the conviction that their work is necessary and important . . . it is necessary to have a strong organization of tried revolutionaries. (Lenin 1902, part D: in 1976)

But Lenin goes on to link to elite and hieratic themes:

> Specialization necessarily presupposes centralization, and in its turn imperatively calls for it. . . . [It is] our duty to assist every capable worker to become a *professional* agitator, organizer, propagandist . . . he is encouraged to widen the field of his activity, to spread it from one factory to the whole of his trade, from one locality to the whole country . . . his outlook becomes wider, his knowledge increases, he observes the prominent political leaders from other localities and other parties, he is striving to rise to their level.

Then he connects back to the special problems of reaching up:

> We must arrange that he be maintained by the Party, that he may in due time go underground . . . otherwise . . . he will not be able to stay in the fight against the gendarmes for at least a few years . . . *all distinctions as between workers and intellectuals*, and certainly distinctions of trade and

professions, must be obliterated . . . of people whose profession is that of revolutionary.

Reachings-up need not be on such a scale, and they need not wear political or economic dress. Changes in art forms appear to come about more often from reaching up than do politically or administratively garbed changes. Reaching up can also originate from intermediate locations in a complex formation.

Consider P. Kuhn's account of Chinese gentry's response to the Taiping rebellion in the nineteenth century (P. A. Kuhn 1970). The Taiping itself was rationalized by a syncretism of Western religion with Chinese secret society. And the Taiping itself acted much as a reaching-down operation elsewhere would do. The Taiping could be seen either as Nazi forerunners or as descendants of the astonishing Swiss peasant-city alliance that established its independence (Brady 1985).

The gentry were embedded throughout China's provinces, yet they tied into the city network of empire by the shifting minority actually in office, from the larger pool certified to having passed the classics exams. The gentry waited and waited for the Taiping to be suppressed. But it was an empire in the last throes of involuteness through blocking action. Dual hierarchies pervaded the system; there were whole parallel sets of armies. On paper there was a rationalistic registration and surveillance system down through a village headman level that paralleled the informal local-notable networks of the gentry. The dynasty, like the Taiping usurpers, were from ethnic fringes disdained by the main Han.

Kuhn pieces out many threads of mobilization for defense and counterattack induced among dispersed gentry in desperation as the Taiping tide spread up the river valleys into core provinces. It is a bewildering kaleidoscope of crossing projects of control. And it is a classic account of social process at the middle range of order that is, arguably, the only one possible of tangible realization on the ground. Action is gotten by astute juxtapositions of disciplines and skeins of social formations that normally served to block action.

The Charles Tilly school of social science has engendered a whole literature (see Tilly 1978 for review) on contentious gatherings, what used to be called riots, informed and stimulated by earlier dissection of the mechanics of riots (Milgram 1977; Granovetter and Soong 1983). These studies bring out the rationality of riots, the ways and extent to which they get action, reach through from below. There is plenty of room below, but never any absolute bottom in social fact.

Tilly's accounts of Western European riots can be juxtaposed to Kuhn's tracing of gentry countermobilization to the Taiping (1970). Abstracted from cultural overlays and scale, the essential similarities of gaining action by reaching up become clear: events have to be generated and polished as identities so that issues can be forged. Hand in hand, new identities of actors are disgorged in the turbulence of mobilizing action. Structural equivalence is and has to be the key, to an even greater extent than in reaching down. Generality is achieved in the organizers, the initiators who become central not to just one but to many facets of events of mobilization. Generalization is sought also across the events. In Europe often it was bread, the price of bread, which could serve as the generic event.

7.4.4. Glasnost versus Career System

Careers can be active counters in efforts at change and continuity in regime. Careers appear to have multiplier effects, to trigger and be triggered by other chains of contingency. In doing so, careers can induce boundaries of populations as a perceptual overlay (Stewman 1976, 1988) from a career system. This can be seen, for example, in the dissolution of the USSR regime around glasnost (Baker 1982; Urban 1987). A fresh explanation for this case can be suggested in terms of career systems as boundaries.

Career is anticipated memory. When the time is short, career shades into the present and memory that contains the present. Career systems can then verge on being pure institutions rather than sophisticated overlays among style and institution. Careers, both as anticipation and as observed tracks, couch into concrete networks; thus, careers crosscut the ostensible specializations that divide up, or rather attempt to divide up, actual social organization into coherent abstractions. In our time and place, one way to see this is by recognizing how much careers are bound up with committees, systems of which are presently the common way to bridge concretely specialties that, in the abstract, are incommensurable.

Glasnost decoupling is, in the first instance, a shift in the expectations of the relatively small numbers—thousands rather than hundreds of thousands—of high-level social engineers. These are the professionals, discussed by Simirenko (1982), who had kept reproducing the hegemony of the regime. Their engineering of vast collocations of networks and levels are based upon an intricate but rather clear-cut structuring of disciplines among themselves (Granick 1967, 1972, 1975). A key to any binding together of this upper control apparatus is the panoply of careers that this population of high-level (but not elite) actors has come to expect. It is a corporative ensemble that they expect.

Let me pause to point out that this Soviet Russian example is not unique; there are parallels, such as in the early move for economic liberalization in Mexico (Herredia 1989). In the two countries, there were parallel attempts to reduce centralization and government participation in flows of goods and services—parallel despite the great differences between the larger societies. Each regime was in serious trouble, which on the surface looked like effects from some sort of turbulence from below, as constraints and coercive disciplines began to be loosened. Government career systems were crucial for the playing out of attempts at fresh action. As long as the career panoply below remains unchanged, elites may rely upon mutual competition for perceived, complex career possibilities to keep individual social engineers isolated vis-à-vis the elites, just as was so in the Sung dynasty.

In the pre-glasnost period, the USSR had a system of personnel placement, the *nomenklatura*, which explicitly concretizes this Sung prototype, and there are informal parallels in the Mexican main party of that era, the PRI (see Herredia 1989). But glasnost came to suggest the simultaneous dissolution of a large chunk of the panoply of careers that were anticipated by the social engineers. Their identities, and their control projects nourished in endless professional gossip, are to be disrupted, not just for one or the other but for all at once.

Their identities had been accounted around story-lines concerned with broad political issues. These were the envelopes of endless concrete fixings of particular anomalies by these same high-level social technicians. Some will perceive their career crisis more explicitly than others, and this will spread through the endless gossiping.

Some sense of alienation must have mounted among this group whose task is precisely to be reducing alienation in others. Yet their story-lines do not encourage explicit discussion of the career disruptions. Instead, one would expect, and did start to see, the appearance of dissident splinter groups, factions public or not, whose ostensible causes will be highly diverse and variable. They may even appear to be an intensification of exactly the glasnost process that is the real irritant. This somewhat speculative example also serves to suggest that careers, whether of individuals or of disciplines, cannot be discussed fully except in the context of networks of other careers involved in the larger social setting. One can argue that the attempt at fresh action in glasnost lost out to career system.

7.4.5. Suicide as Envelope

To explore persons and events simultaneously, turn to suicides as a unique combination of person and event that is designed to erase identities and end story.[18] Suicide is a personal speculation about context insofar as no rhetorics are deemed available or adequate to guide future control efforts. This is failure as involution in contrast to glasnost.

Suicide comes when the set of stories available fail to account for how disciplines are woven together in this person. Suicide is rare, for sets of stories have evolved over time to give maximal flexibility as well as robust rhetorics to subsume identities in institutional contexts. Priests are rarely caught short in explaining things, and other persons can imitate that skill.

As judged by identities participating in the disciplines producing skilled action, the higher the skill stratum, the less clear-cut the events. But such high-skill stratum in turn is embedded in, indeed is materially dependent upon, a larger world of inexpert playing. So events must be regenerated so as to sustain the interest of the larger world as umbilical cord to needed resources. Not only wins and losses but also definite strategies and ploys are required. Rankings in particular tournaments as events themselves become assertions of identities rather than identities inducted out of contradictions. Case in point: Chess players avoid suicide.

Suicide is the identity disembedding. An external stochastic trigger may signal some perturbation that is overwhelmingly disruptive to the identity's embedding, but often none is evident. Durkheim (1997 [1897]) pioneered systematic study of suicide, and some of his arguments carry over here. Persons in common patterns of disciplines with the others are less likely to be focuses of mismatches that generate identity, without which suicide will not be conceived. But such homogenized contexts are not going to generate the intensity of rules—from crossing story-lines only evoked by mismatch and inconsistency—to which Durkheim attributes an "altruistic" suicide (Bearman 1991).

Suicide can generally be seen as an event generated as a means of filling in and making effective an identity. Events of suicide must be construed in terms of the contingent network in which they are embedded. Stories among events and actors are further developed so as to accommodate the contingencies and mismatches that are their origins. Suicide provides a resolution of mismatch through a story centered on termination of identity.

Suicide can be seen as a meld of reaching through, reaching down, and reaching up. And it can be seen at all scales. Widen the previous

---

[18] Stories apply as readily with other scopes, such as tribes, nations, age sets, clans, cities, markets (e.g., Cornell 1988; Deutsch 1953; Eisenstadt 1956; Fortes 1945; Grabher and Ibert 2006; Schama 1987; Waley 1969; White 1981a). And the suicide construct can apply there as well.

perspective on glasnost to include the entire Union of Soviet Socialist Republics. Is it not the case that the USSR committed suicide, unable to sustain its identity?

When social formations are dissected into disciplines and networks, rather than into reified groups of actors, many of the anomalies in Durkheim's theory of suicide are reduced. There will remain others, since human suicide is also in part a phenomenon of a different theoretical venue, of organism as part of biophysical space and its ecology. It may make more sense for social research to look at more purely social analogues and antinomies, such as the creation and destruction of actors through manumission and enslavement (Patterson 1982).

7.5. General Management

Getting action implies continuing to change and expand but also to contract and to otherwise elide efforts at coherence, which is to say, to evade efforts at blocking action as they come along in the name of ex post stories. Management consultants in the United States come to this same judgment. Consider this injunction:

> The good manager can function effectively only in an environment of continual change. . . . Only with many changes in the works can the manager discover new combinations of opportunities and open up new corridors of comparative indifference. . . . In the day-to-day operation of a going concern, they find the milieu to maneuver and conceptualize. (Wrapp 1983, pp. 491, 496)

The amazing swathe of sorts and examples of organizations we perceive around us should be interpreted as shells from previous getting-of-action. These shells block action. There are a huge number of organizations, many inactive, a sort of new fossil record for social forms. An active population of organizations compounds style with institution to sustain routine, for justifying not getting action. Getting action always does continue to some extent, and it manages to have organizations, like other actors, involved. Those getting action are also perforce making use of organizations, but usually only parts and aspects of what the common story says to be the organization are activated.

7.5.1. Eisenhower Style

Dwight Eisenhower's initial months as president provide an analogue to the War Industries Board treated later, but one explicitly concerned only with policy, not with production. National security policy had settled into containment in the cold war; Eisenhower and Dulles had campaigned in part on a theme of rollback, on seizing initiative from the "Communist world." After the fact, it became clear that Eisenhower had no belief in any such change. But there was a vast array of officials and politicals actors out there that needed some kind of policy-nesting if blocking action were not to remove any presidential initiative entirely (Greenstein 1982). This is consistent with the hieratic style described in chapter 4.

Declassified security documents now permit us to infer a masterly hieratic strategy on Eisenhower's part (Solarium 1988). He convened a large and mixed set of dignitaries of security, in and/or out of political or official offices, into an intensive, total-institution setting for one month. A conference was factored out into three parallel committees, ranked by magical powers, though not formal status. One was for yes to the campaign promises, one for no, and one for maybe.

These committees for scenarios, or hypothetical policies, became a lattice. During later joint sessions and discussions, the foolhardiness, by their own respective standards, of the change policies were borne in on each committee by the others, and on each member by the hieratic structure of consideration. Once again a set of committees permitted a shake-up of ongoing production and expertise, and led to an outcome structured more by the sociologic of the committee assignments and contrasts than by explicit intellectual contents.

7.5.2. Western Businesses

Now let us narrow the focus to Western business of the recent past. As other sociologists have argued (Coleman 1973, 1990; Laumann and Knoke 1987), this is distinctively a world in which organizations are common and central as actors (cf. Burt 1978a for measurement). These populations of organizations are a new phenomenon not duplicated in other complex social contexts.

"General manager" is used to designate those expected to cut through organization style to get action in this world. "Administrator," in contrast, can designate orchestration of blocking styles. We should be able to find some recognition of each, and of the basic distinction between them, in the classic modern literature on business management.

An early dean of the Harvard Business School, Wallace Donham, expressed both sides well without being conscious of the contradiction between them (1952). Himself a former chief executive officer who had gotten action, Donham emphasizes situations and questions that involve both policy and action. He argues that this joint conception would be peculiarly difficult (p. 9), but in his words, "consciously or unconsciously it is the subject matter around which the lives of all our leading men in the world of affairs revolve." This is what was termed general management earlier when quotes from Wrapp and others showed it to be an endlessly unpredictable practice of dealing with contingencies to achieve action.

Yet he goes on:

> Ours is a professional school . . . business administration should be treated as a profession depending, to the same extent as other professions, on developing and constantly improving an intellectual framework the implications of which can be studied and taught . . . [including] acceptance of responsibility by each member of the group to the group as a whole . . . [with] special standards . . . of the relation of the whole group [of administrators] to the society. . . . Social change, which follows technological change, disintegrates the social group upon which our factories must depend . . . the difficulties of management increase almost geometrically. (Donham 1952, pp. 16, 34)

The modern organization is confusing, and its ostensible management is conflicted, because several styles are being lumped, and combined into an institution across populations of organizations.

One can conjecture that business organizations are primarily concerned with blocking action. Sets of stories elaborate these organizations, claim boundaries and integrality for them, argue jurisdiction and spell out chains of influence. These stories are all aspects of striving for meaning. This striving can be observed to block action. Exactly by codifying what is to be done, into skeins of the allowable in sequence, and of the assignable in tie, the effect of formal organization is to block fresh action.

Blocking action is not the opposite of getting action, and it does not mean the mere absence of efforts at control. Blocking action achieves continuance of some social formation with some degree of coherence. Blocking action is induced, and sometimes motivated, in projects to maintain some coherence and some effectiveness of production.

In a sea of recurrent but uncoordinated disciplines for production, the pressures for blocking action are enormous. Inconsistent story-lines are packaged in order to account for the events and actors whose identities are generated thereby. That process was argued earlier to be universal. What is not universal is the growth in density of production and action over time, and the cumulation of networks of disciplines into organizations.

Thirty years ago, "Management in the 1980s" was the topic for predictions by two respected social scientists in American business schools; they provided a follow-up in 1989 in the *Harvard Business Re-*

view. They took a very professionalist line: conceptualizing and measuring information would provide the growing core of management as a discipline. They say:

> Within ten years . . . a digital computer will be the world's chess champion. . . . We expect top management to become more abstract . . . and correspondingly less directly involved in the making of routine decisions . . . many middle management jobs may change in a manner reminiscent of (but faster than) the transition from shoemaker to stitcher, from old-time craftsman to today's hourly worker. As we have drawn an organizational class line between the hourly worker and the foreman, we may expect a new line to be drawn heavily, though jaggedly, between "top management" and "middle management." . . . There will be many fewer middle managers . . . depersonalization of relationships within management and the greater distance between people at different levels. (Leavitt and Whisler 1958)

In this statement, they mimic the professionalist style yet also build in corporatist assumptions. The Utopian technocrat tone is there, professionalist, yet there also is awkward recognition of clientelism and corporatism: "The committors' . . . role of approving or vetoing decisions may be forced increasingly to have the top men operate as a committee, which would mean that the precise individual locus of decision may become even more obscure than it is today."

Their central substantive prediction, and its derivation, are what is wrong. They predict recentralization, with top managers having a bigger percentage of "creative functions," and much more structured jobs for middle management. "Decentralization has, after all, been largely negatively motivated. Top managers have backed into it because they have been unable to keep up with size and technology." Nonsense. Top managers embraced decentralization to enhance control and ease getting action (Eccles and White 1986a, 1988), and those tasks remain as urgent to them as ever.

7.5.3. Rhetorics of Organization

Problems of modern organization bedevil administration, and induce increasingly elaborate educational processes for management, because, under a cloak of technical rationality, they combine tensions from several quite different styles of coping by blocking change around meaning. Up to three quite different rhetorics of meaning are floating around in the soup of organizational disciplines. Administrators know this intuitively, however much they may be irritated by it. There are patron-client strings, there is a nascent ordering of purity or depth of expertise, and there are jealous partitions into corporatist turfs of differential registration. Administrators are trying to maintain coherence, but across different systems of rhetoric; general management is there to keep breaking up coherences and getting action, and is aided by multiple coherences.[19]

In parallel, the business firm administered well will not be in but rather out of any wave of change. This is so of DuPont in America as chronicled by Alfred Chandler [1962] 1969. One Western nation is as apt an illustration as another. This also applies to ICI in England, so well chronicled by a succession of astute historians (Reader 1975; Pettigrew 1985). And period per se is not crucial. For the end period of Dutch hegemony, which Kossman (1971, p. 157) describes, merchants and industrialists grew so much less in size and wealth than those in banking because, perhaps, the former were reduced to administration, whereas the latter had plenty of chance at broad interventions, at general management. This was in the context of an economy of forms that had evolved from clientelist and professional roots over a long period.

From all this there follows a proposition that general management will be easier where administration is harder, and the reverse. The rationale is clear, though measurement and operationalization are not. General management, getting action through the complex web of disciplines—whose groupings into designations as this or that organization are the coin of maneuvering rather than neutral facts—is easier the more complex the mixture of styles of blocking. By contrast, administration is more difficult with three styles together than when it deals with some fairly pure clientelist, or professionalized style—or corporatist system.

7.6. Regimes in Crisis

Agency has to be traced through measurements capable of showing changes in both ambage and ambiguity. Agencies are both ambagious and ambiguous in their weavings together of interests and issues via actors, events, and delegation. Retrospective measures can be derived from episodes that are important enough to generate many contemporaneous accounts and intense investigation.

For example, fifty years after the Great War, Cuff (1973) traced that war's emergency mobilization process. The initial system was dichoto-

---

[19] The same argument can be made and illustrated from the government realm. To quote Ashford (1982, p. 20), "As political and administrative hierarchies become less effective, national government turns toward spending and investment controls."

mized between private and public, with clear rules and high ambage. Then it was overlaid with a novel set of rules that were then quickly reduced to nullity: agency was invoked to maintain unchanged existing systems in the face of proposed delegations.

These defenses were the interfaces of purchasing by the military. They were manned not only by military officers but also by experienced civilian bureaucrats and tough-minded members of Congress, notably Senator McKellar of Tennessee. McKellar,[20] for example, successfully sponsored a rider amendment that put the businessmen on the embedded committees at legal risk when offering recommendations (that often verged on inducements).

Business immediately spun further network interconnections and remobilized along preexisting ties. So business reappears in yet another dual structure of committees. That is, there was a second embedding. The recently created chambers of commerce, seeking distinction beyond their localist origins, were pressed into service to set up committees more openly appointed and explicitly representative of the respective trades and industries. These committees became the official interfaces to the War Industries Board (WIB) from the respective military purchasing agencies—the latter still advised by much the same elite committees as before.

Bailey (1984) was much quicker, indeed contemporaneous, with measurement for his account of the New York City bankruptcy crisis. And he deals with a different sort of case from Cuff's: a case of striking change in a system conceded to be a mix of pluralist and bureaucratic, one with high ambiguity and low ambage. The change was overridden by a set of rules that was defined with striking clarity. Operationalization of the rules in cash flows resulted in a system with low ambiguity and considerable increase in ambage of social patternings—measured across both the pluralist politics and the functionally departmentalized bureaucracy.

In crisis regimes, networks decouple and committees embed. A crisis regime is one where by common agreement a rapid transition is sought through rearranging an existing complex that is, at least for the moment, not viable. Two examples will flesh this out.

The Great War produced an unparalleled expansion of the state in the United States. . . . An administrative army marched into Washington. . . . Networks of agencies spanned the nation and cut deeply downward

---

[20] Who later, during the Tennessee Valley Authority (TVA) era, showed the same disdain for songs of organic unity and innocent corporatist cooperation from David Lilienthal (Selznick 1955).

through the country's social structure. . . . This book is about . . . the War
Industries Board . . . established at the end of July 1917, almost four
months after America entered the war, it was the outgrowth of a number
of earlier, less satisfactory arrangements. (Cuff 1973, p. 1)

With these words begins what should apparently be a straightforward
tale of cumulation, one that in fact unravels midway: "The WIB and
its administrative program were a bundle of paradoxes where decentralization vied with centralization, competition with combination, individualism with integration, freedom with coercion" (p. 149).

Underneath seas of rhetoric, the basic plot line is conflicts between
established military purchasing agencies and businesses newly come
to Washington. These businesses embed themselves in a succession of
committee forms—mediation disciplines in present terms—and thus
gain a kind of control, albeit one contingent among competitors, over
a new bonanza customer, the military. Thus, the businessmen, particularly the industrialists, used networks, or more exactly the filling out
and further growth of networks, to pick apart the defenses against
their assumption of control.

Cuff misses the point of how control is achieved by a sort of jujitsu,
by using the strong forces of existing structures against themselves,
via reliance on second-order efforts among networks and committees
themselves to decouple diverse projects and inconsistent ends, all to
the aim of control.

Cuff himself summarizes earlier (p. 165): "[T]he WIB's commodity
sections are less a victory for WIB mediation disciplines than one result
of a successful fight waged by military institutions to maintain a wide
area of discretion for themselves in the face of bureaucratic invasions
by emergency agencies." The same processes of decoupling and embedding are played out again and again in idioms of competing committee systems and network engendering, played for different projects
which then interact and cumulate toward still other and more indirect
control results.

Was President Wilson the one who gained from this complex process? Cuff sees it differently:

> Until he appointed Baruch to the WIB chairmanship and enlarged the
> tools of priority planning, President Wilson exercised a meaningful con-
> trol over the whole process. But once he officially delegated his authority
> to Baruch and the WIB in March, he assumed an essentially passive role
> in the policy area, for he remained true to his habit of relying upon the
> judgment and actions of trusted lieutenants. (p. 192)

A parallel conclusion results for the more recent crisis regime, in the New York City 1975 bankruptcy crisis, in regard to which Robert Bailey (1984) argues: "The fact is, however, that the powers of the mayor have been reinforced as a result of the financial crisis . . . his legal powers have been circumscribed, his political powers enhanced . . . the financial controls imposed by these statutes . . . shed new light on management systems as political resources within the political process" (p. 139).

Bailey also supplies a cogent definition of regime consistent with the preceding one: "[R]ecurring and sustained values, norms, decision rules and authority structures . . . the general matrix of regularized expectations within the limits of which political actions are usually considered authoritative" (p. 9). Mayor Beame was a hapless and transparent mayor. Unlike the enigmatic President Wilson, Beame was bereft of insight and active agency for grasping the control engendered by the crisis shift in regime.

On its face, the WIB crisis regime and the New York City regime faced utterly different problems. The core of the New York City crisis was financial in the tangible sense of cash flows: the private money markets, normally invisible in and to the city polity, suddenly refused to continue funding. These markets thereby set off the creation of MAC and EFCB and other acronymic authorities able by statute to reset policy with the operational goal of starting flows from ostensibly private money markets. In the case of the WIB, by contrast, money flows were the least of the problems.

Underneath, however, both crises rested upon interaction among dual organizational systems of policy and action brought into close interplay for the first time. The crisis in each case takes the mode of successive embeddings in systems of committees—largely arena disciplines in our analytic terms—which were cut across by decouplings of ongoing structures. The mechanism attempted on each dual side was penetration by networks of mediation disciplines.

Networks decouple, committees embed. This formula runs opposite to the previous, classical contrast in which inertial status fixed by networks of traditional ties was set off against crisp change possible in contractual arenas, of which committees can be a modern embodiment. The new formula cannot be a fixed or pure truth any more than the old one could be. Social arrangements endlessly respin themselves in counterpoint to whatever the existing arrangements and competitive control projects are.

Crisis regimes show starkly that control is about the sheer existence of arenas in which to recognize the sheer existence of issues hitherto nullified by hegemonic perspective. Just as networks and committees are but one tangible form in which decoupling and embedding processes can materialize, so financial flows are only one form of signal.

7.6.1. Forms of Duality

In 1950, Simon, Smithburg, and Thompson (p. 294) introduced the everyday counterpart to the duality that sets off the crisis regimes. They speak of "counterpart units" as inevitable defensive formations by organizations being subjected to control (from "higher" or from the "center"), control in the guise of specialized or professional advice by overhead units. In New York, the city bureaucracy, organized by authority or by agency, has now feverishly built up defensive expertise in cash-flow finance to counter dissection by computerized intervention networks. But World War I ended just as the War Industries Board was becoming sufficiently ensconced so as to induce counterpart units within the military contracting agencies.

Control is a matter of pattern and process engendered as a potential by decoupling and embeddings among social formations. Events were much more important identities in the New York City crisis network than for the War Industries Board. But delegation of active agency was exhibited in both regimes.

The same tendencies hold on a smaller scale at a humbler level. One sign of reaching through by dual hierarchy is a flip in tasks between the segregated pillars. Heclo (1969) and Crozier and Thoening (1976) and Ashford (1982), from different perspectives for different countries, settle on a formulation of change in local government. In Heclo's formulation (p. 18), the official has become the policy maker and the councillor carries out routine administration.

The venerable conundrums of staff and line can quickly be disentangled as a variant of dual hierarchy. Various staff departments, of course, do have much of the magic of authority, despite formal disavowal, as seen in operational terms in behavior subject to disputes. MacMahon, Millett, and Ogden (1941) are especially lucid on this reality in their account of the creation of the Works Progress Administration during the Depression. The difference is that collegiality, assumed in hieratic style, is not enhanced at higher levels, but on the contrary decreased, so that in order to get action, other random and often media-mediated reaching through must be forthcoming.

On a comparable scale, large business firms are sites for dual hierarchies of new sorts. These go beyond the staff-line dualities that have been established long enough to lose effectiveness as contexts for reaching through. Eccles and White (1988) identify one version: corporations are split into self-contained divisions that each operate in a different market, jousting for a niche with a set of other corporations' divisions. A curious situation: markets are here functioning like hieratic levels or committees in a managerial control scheme of dual hierarchy. A chief executive office, individual or collective, has dual paths to reach through: either the market discipline context, or the conventional financial control context of the home corporation. Many of these messy dual hierarchy situations also have horizontal spread into servile elites.

7.6.2. Catholic and Communist as Structuralist

The structuralist conjecture is exemplified as pure organization by Wallerstein's world system theory (1980), in which our entire world becomes the successive unfolding of a unique system. It is also illustrated by Lévi-Strauss's theory (1969) of marriage alliances in which the whole social organization of a tribe plays out within one of a few overall structuralist schemes of balancing among splits and alliances.[21]

Genesis is always the problem with the structuralist conjecture in pure form: by what staggeringly unlikely concatenation of constituents could some such marvelously singular system of integration come into being? The timing metric is interaction exposures, not physical seconds, but under no reckoning is the metric comparable to actual evolutionary scales. This structuralist conjecture is best reformulated as one that concerns style rather than complete system.

The hieratic style, introduced at the end of chapter 4, is in fact one version of the structuralist conjecture. It does make an observable difference whether the overall configuration is constrained in hieratic fashion, a difference that should vary with some measure of violation of the structure. This difference is part of the impetus from many identities to push the configuration toward hieratic form. Yet one must expect exaggeration of the hieratic form as it appears in the story-line. And the hieratic is usually a middling affair, which at a period stretches over some, but only some, neighborhoods.

It was Gregory VII in the twelfth century who had the possibility of showing, and who in fact did show, most dramatically in Western history, the action potential of the hieratic style. The program of this former German monk reflected a dual hierarchy within the church between monastic orders and regular clergy. And Gregory VII induced the same duality with the outside secular powers, and so this is our first example of dual hierarchy.

---

[21] See Culler's (1975) analogous conjectures about literature.

> Prior to the late eleventh century ecclesiastical jurisdiction in the broad
> sense of legislative and administrative as well as judicial competence . . .
> lacked precise boundaries. . . . It was the Papal Revolution, with its libera-
> tion of the clergy from the laity and its emphases upon the separation of
> the spiritual from the secular that made it both necessary and possible to
> place more or less clear limits upon, and hence to systematize, ecclesiasti-
> cal jurisdiction. (Berman 1983, p. 221)

Gregory VII saw the potential for getting action and control that was latent in the hieratic. There was a structure of separate orders or estates in social organization, and of regulations and laws and doctrine that were parallels in cultural guise. To some extent, Europe-wide jurisdiction had already stumbled into being, but had not been taken at face value until Gregory made this an explicit and daring innovation. The many hieratic clusters within formal hierarchies and territorial organization demonstrated a degree of resonance to Gregory that was out of all proportion to the resonance that secular rulers obtained.

Gregory was indeed the first in Europe to see how to, and did in fact, create an absolutist state on hieratic style. He was thus able to reach through in a way not comparable from the secular side. And this was scale-invariant: bishop, pastor, and monastery head each could invoke hieratic clustering in reaching through bewildering strings of commitments and localizations.

The investiture controversy between emperor and pope was the preeminent issue of an era, a classic mobilization of ongoing interface productions into events. An issue emerged from what had been only forms of words. The obverse of this was the suppression of identity formation among actors. Striking individuality of clerics, and flaunting of kinship with and dependency upon secular elites, was dampened. Canon law became more prominent, and it was built up around events (Berman 1983).

Soviet Communist governments have been strikingly similar to the Catholic Church in the underlying architecture of control (Brzezinski and Huntington 1964). Both presuppose corporatist polities. The party was shaped in hieratic style, with successive layers of purity. Within each layer, offices and committees were treated as pools of interchangeability. In addition, the party was also a second government parallel to state hierarchies of offices. Schurmann (1968) lays this out as applying to the China of the 1950s, with the additional double vision induced by attention to preceding USSR practices. The importance of network context may be reflected in the greater success in the Chinese exemplar.

Like the early church, the Russian Soviet formation emerged initially out of a city-based movement, outside the established order of story-lines, but bound into the loosely coupled ties of urban situations. "Red versus expert" is like "clergy versus laity," and even more like regular clergy versus religious. Purity stories provide access for strings of connections reaching through large formations by skipping between hieratic clusters.

Purges in hieratic settings are said to eliminate heresies. Since at least the time of the Donatist heresy against St. Augustine, it has been clear that, on its cultural face, the side of the heretics may well be the orthodox side (Newman 1876; Willis 1950). The important point is that heresies are defined *after* the social organization shifts that make them necessary. Heresies are the type-case of forming issues out of events in reconciling troubles over identities of actors.

Schisms, in church (Gill 1959, 1964; Williams 1981) or party or government, are a converse. Schisms are mobilization into interests as part of reconciling divergent identities of process, of events. More generally, failing style, strategy must be created and continually renewed to deal afresh with the problematic of control.

7.6.3 Servile Elite

Attempts at control and getting action can themselves interact and cumulate into important changes in social organization, especially at elite levels. An elite is a heavily interconnected set of actors whose identities are so pronounced that all obfuscations about interests are suppressed. Thereby issues are suppressed as well. An elite is a particular social formation, not segregated in network from a broader population, a formation that is structured so as to get action among the broader set in part by being socially immunized against blocking processes endemic to social organization.

A servile elite is an elite induced and shaped from recruits arbitrarily introduced to a network, and so manipulable at least initially, but with the flexible social structuring common to spontaneous elites. The recruits' own networks of origin are diverse and dispersed. Reaching through for control is as much a horizontal problem of bridging sheer numbers of neighborhoods in social space as it is of bridging embedded levels and cumulated rankings, together with their stories.

The clear sign of a servile elite is the appearance of a distinction between public and private, in the meaning-accounting schemes. Elites proper have no need of such:

> In the eleventh century the key position in Italian society came to be held
> by the class immediately below that of the greatest landowners. Of varied

origins, these men were gradually caught up into the knightly class. . . .
In 1037 the Milanese *vavassores* (sub-vassals) after a long and bitter struggle finally obtained from the Emperor Conrad II security in the tenure of
their benefices and freedom to appeal to the emperor . . . in effect abol-
ished the feudal dependence of the vavassores on the capitanii (tenants-
in-chief) and had wider and more lasting effects in Italian society. . . . It
consolidated the various ranks of the feudal hierarchy into a single legal
class. (Hyde 1973, p. 28)

This managerial class crosscut the network of Italian city communes,
making possible the functioning of "national" factions such as Guelphs
and Ghibbelines.

More extreme versions of servile elites appear, for example, in the
managerial revolution of Berle and Means (1932), in which ownership
was separated from control in bringing firms public. The same variant
is identifiable in Germany centuries before, contemporaneous with the
Italian developments:

In Germany the lack of close feudal ties forced all lords, the king among
them, to turn to the servile classes for such administrative officers and for
armed knights; and so in Germany there rose a class of *ministeriales*. . . .
They seem to have been employed in the first place by the great churches
. . . because bishops and abbots were loath to enfeoff their lands to free
vassals, against the performance of such duties, for fear lest their property
might be appropriated. . . . And German kings, especially with Henry IV,
soon use them to run kingdoms . . . developed a ministerial administrative
class. (Barraclough 1946, p. 80)

During the investiture contest with the pope, the *ministeriales* were able
to throw off personal bondage, which became accounted as a differentiation into the ranks of the aristocracy. This was the same period that
saw the rise of the fantastic map of German local particularism, held
together only by the crosscutting of this servile elite.

A servile elite commonly co-occurs with dual hierarchy. The Italian
pattern of servile elite can be found everywhere and everywhen. Japan
is not so different:

In the twelfth century the ruling families failed to give social recognition
and security of tenure to the "Intermediate elite" in the countryside. Some
members of this group who came from the bureaucratic families of the
center, had served as tax collectors, and opted to stay; others were descendants of pre-seventh-century landowning families who had commended
their land to the bureaucratic families but remained in possession . . . together, . . . and entrenched, indispensable managerial class, partly literate
and always accustomed to wielding arms. . . . In 1180 a rising of this
class—a managerial revolution in the strictest sense—took place under the

leadership of Minamoto no Yorimoto. Its success led to the establishment of a warrior government or bakufu in Kamakura which made the Kyoto government subservient. ... This Kyoto Kamakura dyarchy continued until 1333. (Steenstrup 1987, p. 73)

What is lost over time by intervention in dual hierarchies, because of the hardening that results, may be made up by greater horizontal reach through the servile elite that comes to crosscut the pillar headings. The Prussian civil service as described by Rosenberg (1958) was in itself a hieratic formation in which, however, resistance to arbitrarily injected new officials kept them segregated and so responsive to royal authority. As in any real example, the principle of dual hierarchy was reused again and again, often with an issue crafted out of events within the existing hieratic to extenuate the introduction of another specialism.

7.6.4. Temperatures of Colonialism

Quite another formulation of the calculus of regimes is possible, one analogous to a thermodynamics (De Boer and Uhlenbeck 1962; cf. Leifer and White 1986). Most of both the preceding accounts was devoted to the particular ripostes of gamings and counter-gamings that were the particular paths by which the results came about in that crisis. Direct cumulation of and prediction from the outcomes of gamings has proved exceedingly difficult, even under simplified trial conditions without crises, and despite a wide variety of approaches (Axelrod 1984). Instead, a better path may be to create specifications of feasible regimes, made up of networks of disciplines, which can result from such detailed dynamics. I have taken this approach in two previous monographs: White (1963a), where I derived what architectures of classificatory kinship are feasible; and then recently (White 2002), where I laid out in a parameter plane where markets are feasible. Using this approach, one relies on measures of decoupling and embedding processes that reflect the net aggregated results from gamings.

Two sorts of "temperatures," or disorders, ambage and ambiguity, are to be estimated as averages or correlations across a system. The right illustrative case is one where the levels and kinds of disorder are generally agreed upon, there is no concealment of them, and where one finds a long time-series of relatively undisturbed observation. Colonial administration is a natural candidate for this new formulation.

For this, we can return to Furnivall's major comparative study used in chapter 4 that compared the Dutch Indies to Burma, over a century or more preceding World War II. He focuses on the institutions and styles of rule at concrete middle range, disdaining changing ideological fashions.

Our fathers and grandfathers . . . the generation of the Ethical leaders who aspired to build a brave new world in 1900 . . . put forward similar pretensions [to those] in Java at the onset of the great depression of the thirties. They in turn succeeded the Liberals who had thought to introduce a golden age in 1870 on the principle of freedom. The Liberals condemned, as rooted in unrighteousness, the systems by which Van den Bosch had expected to restore prosperity to a country ruined by the reforms that Raffles, a generation earlier, had claimed would bestow liberty and welfare. (Furnivall 1948, p. 281)

What is striking is how persistent through all these changing ideological climates the styles of middle-range order were. Also persistent were their contrasting balancings of uncertainties. Furnivall summarizes in a sentence:

On the Dutch system even the European officials are policemen, agents of policy; on the British system even native officials tend to become magistrates and judges, servants of the law. . . . Burma represents in its purest form a system of direct rule. In Java, on the contrary . . . the purest type of indirect rule [prevails]. In both countries there has evolved a social structure comprising distinct racial sections with an elaborate western superstructure. (Furnivall 1948, p. 229)

Ambiguity and ambage interchange roles between the contrasting forms of indirect and direct rule in Burma and Indonesia. In Indonesia:

Indirect rule through a local chieftain is the simplest and cheapest way by which . . . land and labour can be provided most readily by the local ruler, governing his people on traditional lines, and there tends to evolve a dual system of administration, half western and half tropical. (p. 276)

Onto a preexisting patrimonial traditional system, with low ambiguity and high ambage, is grafted a dual system of particularistic, policing control without explicit new rules, but with explicit new partition by race. Race becomes a new set of rules conflicting with the preexisting ones, and this is in balance with the reduction of ambage through reinforced punitive controls.

Burma was different.

There is indeed hardly anything in common between the character and functions of the civil servants of the two countries. In Burma there is one service divided into three grades, there are no Europeans in the lowest grade but even the highest grade is open to natives. . . . In Java, instead of a single service, there are two separate services, one European and one native, each with its own functions, and in neither service does any officer perform either of the two main functions of the civil servant in Burma.

There is a separate judicial service and a separate treasury service. . . . The European civil servant has magisterial or judicial powers, and no adminis- trative responsibilities of any kind. . . . [H]is function is to watch over and help the native civil servants . . . [who] are not servants of the law but officers of police or policy. (p. 237)

In Burmese colonial practice, an explicit layer of rules was superposed on secular native culture—and the more elaborated monastic aspect of governance suppressed—to yield much higher ambiguity despite attempts at interleaving the rules, like the races, of administrators.

In both colonialisms the element of getting fresh action, of control as we define it, remains despite seeming permanence of regime be- cause of the explicit exploitation. The briefest of Japanese incursions later managed to dissolve both systems.

7.7. Annealing from Switching

Successive waves of reform as strategy, as in the preceding examples, can be reinterpreted not as some detailed scheme of rational action pre- dictable in its course, but rather as annealing, intentional but indirect and opportunistic. *Annealing* is a term from metallurgy. To anneal is to heat and thus shake up the mineral inside, hard but more or less at random, and then to cool and encourage resumption of normality with attendant hopes that the new formation will have more desirable prop- erties. A mineral is a complicated mess with crystal bits and gels twisted together in historically unique configurations. Social forma- tions of institutions, classes, and the like seem analogous.

Temperatures of colonialism suggest annealing when they rise high. Popular rebellion is another prototype for annealing, one that can be accomplished in many forms. Annealing need not always depend upon privileged location for its instigators. Annealing is an important prototype for gaining control to get action. Annealing disrupted is counter-control, is blocking action.

Envelopes from contingencies describe the effective boundaries of a social mineral. Such population envelopes (discussed in chapter 4) decouple, passively or via explicit perception, which is the reason these envelopes can trigger and be used in action projects. Padgett offers a vivid example from his studies of Renaissance Florence:

At the level of historical evolution, the article (Padgett and Ansell 1993) analyzed how the social-network ligaments of both contending political parties were emerged out of and were shaped by class revolt and war, which were events 60 and 10 years before, inscribed in sedimentary Florentine social structure. In general, robust-action fusion of contradictory multiple networks, laid down in history, was the dynamic mechanism generating the emergence of political centralization in this historically important episode. (Padgett, research summary typescript of 2007)

This is getting action conceived on a population base, rather than control concerned with disciplines, identities, and embedding. Such action cannot be targeted, cannot be focused as implied by the usual connotations of the term *control* in ordinary discourse. Annealing is the proper metaphor for action attempts on a population basis (Leifer and White 1988), for such generalized control.

In social as in metallurgical settings, annealing may need to be repeated a wearying number of times for substantial improvements to show up out of the throw of the dice. The social agency is not as cut-and-dried as heating: it may be media floods of information, or inflationary fiscal flows, or a new cohort, or a split in an existing age grade (cf. studies of the Galla: Prins 1953). The social analogue of heating is not singular, but in any form must, like heating, consume some resources and requires some coupling to another larger population.

Cooling down may be less automatic in the social case. The distinctive fact of social organization is that, at any level and scope of population, there can be independent control attempts not predictable from routine analysis. We can conjecture that it is easier to smother such other projects during an increased level of activity than it is to dampen them once freshly exacerbated. Social annealing is less controllable than the metallurgical variety, itself notoriously unreliable without extensive repetition. Agency is therefore more problematic and important in the social analogue of annealing. The annealing metaphor should be restricted to where the agency concerns population rather than disciplines and the like.

A principal agent for annealing action may be surrounded by an entourage. The entourage are the hangers-on who account for viscosity in flows of control action, which serves to cool down much more reliably than to activate the principal. Hull (1982) details the development of such an entourage around Kaiser Wilhelm. It obfuscated but did not suppress his erratic ways, which short-circuited attempts at control that might have aborted World War I. There have been parallel accounts of a Hitler entourage.

Changing or shifting some regime, discussed toward the end of the last chapter, is the weightiest kind of task for annealers. Hardest to verify is annealing on the largest scale. Gorbachev's actions in the USSR through 1988 were analyzed earlier. One can now see that in the end, Gorbachev did not prove to be an annealer—perhaps not by choice, but by the exigencies of his situation. Ex ante coding is difficult.

Short of enormously detailed surveys, or a rare revolutionary period, it is hard to measure some regime such as caste with enough conviction to be sure about the when and what of a change. One needs a
study with explicit reports of intent for annealing. And it makes sense
to look for some cultural product in a visible interpretive genre, to use
as a signature for the regime. To qualify as annealing there must be
evidence about intentional agency. The evidence is extensive and clear
in the rock 'n' roll case described toward the end of chapter 4, and
summarized later. Among the many important (musical) "agents" per
se, there were one or two "disc jockeys" who proved to have great
insight to function as annealers. I end the chapter by drawing up a
general lemma on change of style.

The previous chapter dealt with changes in several control regimes,
some of which might proved to have resulted from annealing or other
forms of getting action, if enough detail were available. American academic science might seem a likely place to look, but I was drawing on
Han's cross-sectional analysis from a huge data set. I now take up two
studies that each exactly did concentrate on really close-up scrutiny.

7.7.1. Fluctuation of Pension Fund Management in Britain

We now turn to a long-term assessment of changes, indeed reversals,
of regime, drawing on an ethnography by an observer who, along with
his father, was a longtime participant in a finance regime.

First he sketches the setup:

> The pension fund manager's agency derives from his position at the apex
> of two chains of agency relationships. The first group of principals is the
> shareholders in the sponsoring firm. The agents of shareholders are the
> management of the company, and in the particular context of the pension
> fund the Finance director. The PFM is the agent of the FD. . . . The second
> group of principals is the membership of the pension fund. Their agents
> are the trustees of the pension fund. The agent of the trustees is, again,
> the PFM. . . . The provision of security to the members comes at the cost
> of higher employer contributions and lower sponsoring firm profitability.
> The PFM mediates between these opposing parties. Ambiguity is essential
> to the PFM's ability to suspend the reality of conflict between these two
> parties. . . . This relational model of agency contrasts with accounts that
> focus on the two-way principal/agent relationship and on information
> asymmetry. (Avrahampour 2007, pp. 2–3)

Then turn to the history. The ambiance here reminds me of the "strong-
culture bureaucracy" defined by DiMaggio (1992, D in table 4–1) in an
overview paper that is discussed further in chapter 8 in this book.

In the 1930s and 1940s shareholders delegated agency to the Chief Accountant (the precursor of the FD) and members delegated agency to the board of trustees. The role of PFM had yet to be created. . . . In assessing contribution rates the actuary considered the actions taken by the sponsoring firm in managing its relationship with the membership of the pension fund. . . . The valuation of the pension fund focused on guarantees provided by the sponsor. There was an actuarial preference for fixed income investment by the pension fund. Simultaneously, hostility marked the relationship between these two principals as they attempted to resolve resource allocation conflicts. Elaborate protection mechanisms were sought . . . solvency and interest guarantees by the sponsor, the hiring of separate auditors by the sponsor and the pension fund, use of insurance to hedge mortality risk and equal representation of members on trustee boards.

The first switch of orientation is associated with the emergence of the role of the PFM in the 1950s . . . the PFM was largely autonomous of the management accounting metrics and control processes of the sponsor. The sponsor's contribution rate was determined in negotiations between the PFM and the actuary who had discretion in valuing the pension fund. . . . The elaborate protection mechanisms of the 1930s . . . were dismantled. . . . Control rested with the PFM.

The PFM's autonomy was then eroded. . . . The first stage is the introduction of performance measurement of fund management firms in the 1970s. This introduced a market based methodology for valuing assets but not liabilities. . . . The specialization of the PFM is reduced as he is made comparable to other fund managers. Control now passes from the PFM to the FD and the board of trustees. The FD has sufficient transparency to measure the performance of the PFMs but there is insufficient transparency by the investors to monitor the FD. The PFM, shareholders and members orient towards the FD.

Finally (financial) Reporting Standard 17 introduced between 2001 and 2005, conducted performance measures of firms sponsoring pension funds and shifted control back to the owners in the sponsoring company and the members of the pension fund. The valuation of assets and liabilities is conducted on a market basis and discretionary practices relating to valuation by the FD and the PFM are eliminated. Actors orient again towards the owners of the sponsoring firm and the members of the pension fund. Despite massive technological change and the fact that at this point the financial economic conception drives the valuation and risk management of pension funds, there is a return to the contention that characterized the 1930s and the re-emergence of protection mechanisms that were used at that time to resolve conflict. . . . The four protection mechanisms used to provide assurance to members regarding the security of their benefits and

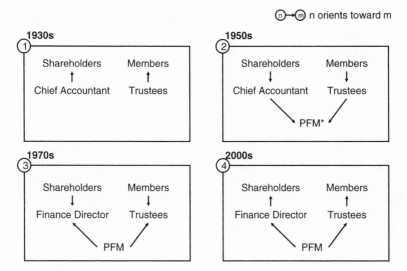

Figure 7.1: Changing orientation of actors toward the shifting locus of control.
Note: * PFM: Pension Fund Manager. Source: Avrahampour (2007).

> to safeguard the profitability of the sponsoring firm are those that are at
> the forefront of recent developments in the governance and investment of
> pension funds. (Avrahampour 2007, pp. 6–8)

Then Avrahampour explicates detailed mechanisms of these shifts in
locus of control by application of the present theory. With the performance measures came the emergence of rivalry profiles of advisory
firms, resembling the discussions in chapters 4 and 5. Switches are between restricted and generalized exchange. He goes on to show analogies with kinship systems and industrial markets, as well as feudalism,
taken up in the previous chapter.

And Avrahampour draws explicit parallels with the treatment of
U.S. investment banking by Eccles and Crane, given in the "Reaching
Through" section earlier; clearly, Avrahampour is making a contribution to the growing literature on financial sociology. Perhaps the earliest urging toward that new direction was issued by John Padgett
(1981), with a focus on fiscal practices of the state. Avrahampour's
study also fits with the section of chapter 6 on regimes of accountancy.

And he argues that dual hierarchy, discussed in the previous chapter, was a general mechanism of control throughout. Figure 7.1 captures the changing orientation of actors toward the shifting locus of
control. Thus, in his thesis, regimes are the result of the interaction be-

tween financial standard setting bodies and firms sponsoring pension funds. It seems to me that a strong case can be made in that situation for repeated bouts of getting action through annealing.

7.7.2. Bang-Bang Control betwixt Firm and Market

In *The New Old Economy* (2005), Josh Whitford reports his extensive field research on industrial restructuring, with principal focus on Wisconsin but also some comparison with other areas, notably the Italian districts made famous by Piore and Sabel (1984). Whitford interleaved many periods of intensive reconsideration of theoretical framings (e.g., Whitford 2002) with his intensive years of investigation across many districts and with many organizational systems.

His principal empirical findings, in his own words:

> The decentralization of production thus means that landing a branch plant does not have as large an impact on a state's economy as it would have in years past, whereas efforts to maintain the competences of existing component manufacturers can pay off more than they used to [p. 133]. . . . Contradictory and often failed efforts by Original Equipment Manufacturers (OEM) and suppliers to build more collaborative relationships are not so much a steady transition as they are the result of a complex but stable mix of hedging strategies. (Whitford 2005, pp. 158–59)

"Contested collaboration" is the construct Whitford, with colleagues, has now introduced to capture what he sees as most distinctive in the new stirrings in industrial organization (Whitford, Simmons, and Helper 2006). One can see it as analogous to crude bang-bang engineering controls (discussed in the next chapter). They conclude:

> With our qualitative data, we are able to show that interviewers identify complexes of practices as characteristic of one or the other underlying logics of relational action, yet report that it can nonetheless be difficult to know which is in play at any given moment. This raises important questions. . . . Our point has simply been that "impurities" in the application of these logics are themselves structured by the interplay of relations within and between firms. This results in a distribution . . . that is, to paraphrase Powell, neither collaborative nor arms-length, nor a mongrel hybrid of the two . . . our claim is that a contested logic of relational practice emerges when mutually sustaining ambiguities enter into processes of interest formation and definition. The radical decentralization of production has increased interdependencies between organizations, leading to a "fuzzing" of organizational boundaries in ways that make it matter much more than it had previously that organizations are not unitary actors. The

interplay of relations across organizations now increasingly affects and is affected by factional and interdepartmental struggles within organization, which may in turn result in deeply ambiguous signals to suppliers, who in turn hedge their own collaboration and reproduce contestation within customer firms as to the actual feasibility of a collaborative logic of action. We thus render contested relations as a distinctive logic.

Perhaps Whitford or Avrahampour, or both, offer witness to what may be the emergence of a distinctive new level of control regime.

*7.7.3. A Lemma on Change of Style

[In each chapter, with a section marked with an asterisk, I point out how the studies there can also be seen from other perspectives. These examples of style change are also taken up, more than casually, in sections 4.3.2, 4.8.2, and 4.8.3.]

Ennis's dissection of rock 'n' roll, laid out earlier in chapter 4, supports a lemma: a major new style can be created in a two-step process. First, some two (or more) of the existing styles must be mobilized through the institutions supporting them into an intensive program of hybrid examples, which come from a temporarily hybrid institution. This implies merging social carriers (creators, performers, critics, and the like) who are previously mutually specialized. Second, the reaction to the melding and to the new direction must become so intense as to cauterize the initial mixture. That is, the initially separate institutions again fall apart. This can leave the incipient new wave to sustain itself—or fail—as a separate style and institution.

This is a lemma worth exploring in other cultural venues. The earlier study of change of regime in the French painting world, from academy machine to dealer-critic system (White and White 1995), fits the Ennis paradigm well. There a single person, Durand-Ruel, who created a new sort of dealer role, was essential. Durand-Ruel had the exploratory and experimental approach of an annealer. In addition, Baxandall (1980) traces a major impetus to German sculpture in the early Renaissance, in which a new high style went hand in hand with the emergence of a new crossbreed of previous commercial and guild institutions. He traces lines compatible with the lemma, though across a dispersed field of small cities rather than for a primate ecology like that of French culture.

Many significant changes in science, called advances, appear to follow the Ennis paradigm of change. Here, the annealing agents are conscious of their agency and indeed insistent on credit (but see Merton

1985). The Ennis lemma appears to be a useful specification of Kuhn's argument (1970) about paradigm shift in science.

The great treatise by Spencer and Gillen (1927) on cultural-social evolution among a swathe of Aborigine tribes (at a period before their disintegration) can also be parsed in much the same way as Ennis dissects change in the pop music world. The populations respectively involved are even comparable in size and in focus on artistic aspects of life.

Early developments of Christianity as a missionary yet rooted gospel within our own civilization can also be modeled similarly (White 1991), on at least two levels: a newly invented Judaism overlaid for a while with nascent Christianity in its Jerusalem mode (Segal 1986); a Pauline missionary church and theology struggled across the Roman imperium with the Jerusalem mode (von Campenhausen 1955 [1969]; Dix 1947). The Catholic Church was the new institution resulting, and the religion of the church fathers was the new style.

Regimes and associated genres and their possible changes come in many scales. The Puritan strand of English history, without which the United States would not have come to be, provides two contrasting examples. Both are of abortive changes and are examples from periods that are neither too familiar nor too remote in idiom to be accessible.

Here is one assessment:

> History, indeed, has a further warning for the advocates of the "historic episcopate" divorced from "theories" as an administrative solution of troublesome dogmatic differences. . . . The treatment of the Puritans by the English episcopate from the reign of Elizabeth onwards must be sorrowfully admitted to have been as stupid as it was Erastian and wicked, whatever the provocation of factiousness on the other side. (Dix 1947, pp. 302–5)

Here is an assessment of a related struggle across the Atlantic:

> In *The Anglican Episcopate,* Professor Cross concerned himself with the history of an abortive institution and with a detailed analysis of the pamphlet literature for and against American bishops. . . . [Subsequent discoveries] now enable us to describe the backstage manoeuvres of individuals and organizations, which were unknown to Arthur Cross. . . . This contest was, in truth, far more than the customary religious strife: it was a *Kulturkampf* between the dissenting bodies—already well entrenched in New England . . . —and the Church of England—few in numbers, new, aspiring, and contriving. The Anglicans aimed at nothing less than the complete reordering of American Society . . . in a great struggle for power which ceased only with American independence. For eighty-five years . . . (Bridenbaugh 1962, pp. ix, xix)

Here we see the same riddle about the relations of control to rhetoric and style. The two cases are nicely converse as to churchly dominance, despite sharing exactly the same clash of styles. Neither exhibits accomplished change, and yet both fit the preconditions of the lemma. Change can come only through effective superposition, followed by hostility of each toward their cross product, which may but need not then spin off as separate. There was no effective annealing here.

But we have not yet justified designation as the lemma. Return to the Lazega law firm example we have been carrying through many chapters. There, tangible reality calls on all the aspects, all the perspectives from different chapters. The lemma is applicable to all. Styles mate to change, as do disciplines and rhetorics.

Let a theologian have the last words, since in them Tillich captures the heart of this lemma:

> But dynamics is held in a polar interdependence with form. Self-creation of life is always creation of form . . . there is a moment of "chaos" between the old and the new form . . . the creation of a new social entity or a new artistic style. The chaotic element which appears here is already manifest in the creation myths . . . creation and chaos belong to each other . . . echoed in the symbolic descriptions of the divine life, of its abysmal depth, of its character as burning fire, of its suffering over and with the creatures, and of its destructive wrath. . . . Destruction can be described as the prevalence of elements of chaos over against the pole of form in the dynamics of life. . . . Disintegration takes place within a centered unity; destruction can occur only in the encounter of centered unity with centered unity. (Tillich 1963, p. 50)

EIGHT

OVERVIEW AND CONTEXTS

HOW DOES the approach of this book differ from existing analyses of social process? I start this overview with that question. Then I develop how contexts and contextualizing are central to all the previous chapters. Following that, I sketch the gist of each of the chapters, and point to some alternative angles, after which I return to linguistics, as in the prologue. The central third of this overview deals with operationalizing my approach through explicit modeling. The chapter ends with two sections of further musings about context.

8.1. Triggers from Interlocking Contexts

8.1.1. A Fundamental Question and Four Answers

In asking how my approach in this book differs from prior analyses of social process, I recognize that the difference lies in a challenge. Here is the challenge, a possible foundational issue, in three formats: Where is the self? Where is consciousness? Who is doing all this thinking? I have excluded the self and consciousness from my account as rigorously as I could manage. My goal is a foundation for sociology that does not depend upon them. One obvious cost is some loss of reflexivity, in that the author himself escapes notice.

Many of the experts on whom I draw are skeptical of my claim. For example, Ann Mische, a longtime collaborator, from whose work I drew excerpts for chapter 7, is insistent on bringing consciousness back in, along with flesh and blood people. Here, from her chapter 2, are additional excerpts that pose this challenge:

> However, I argue that the styles of communication that appear in movement encounters . . . grow out of negotiation between the multiple forms of identity and involvement in play within an organization or event. . . . I am particularly interested in the role of individuals with experience in more than one kind of institutional milieu. . . . Such actors must develop what Neil Fligstein calls "social skill": the ability to mediate between different conceptions of identity and interest in order to generate consensus in a complex field . . . which he usefully defines as "situations where organized groups or actors gather and frame their actions vis-à-vis one another."

By *pragmatics*, I mean the ways in which people and collectivities situated within the push and pull of a field survey its problems and possibilities, formulate potential responses, and attempt to translate those responses into actions. . . . By *performances*, I mean the ways in which people communicatively enact multiple sets of relations in social encounters as they respond to--and attempt to intervene in--the challenges they confront in their day-to-day interactions. . . . As pragmatist philosophers such as Mead and Dewey argue, it is precisely such challenges that lead people to develop the reflexive processes that allow them to intervene in and shape the world around them (Mische 2007).

My rejoinder is fourfold. First, person *is* included. Chapter 4 argues at some length for person, in our everyday sense, being a style. But person as style is more a by-product than a generator of social process.

My second rejoinder is to claim that my theorization is compatible with a number of powerful studies of consciousness. I note particularly the tome by James Livingston (1994) on the impact of a new consciousness pattern across a century of American history. And the work of Wallace Chafe (1994) on consciousness, which crosscuts experimental psychology with literary analysis, is so compatible that I will use it in working on the planned extension of the present approach to the social construction of languages.

Third, Ann Mische's own project generalizes better in my impersonal framing. I place my brief account of her project in chapter 7 because mobilizing to get fresh action was exactly her trope. Yet her joint work with Philippa Pattison (2000) is what established a strong measurement frame, along lattice-theoretic lines that were pioneered by Thévenot and by Mohr and Duqenne (1997). And these lattice results can also be pointed toward exploration of the evolution, on a continuing basis, of new institutional systems and/or of control regimes. This is surely a more fundamental direction than study of a particular mobilization. This suggests that reversion to personalization tends to cripple theory by enmeshing it in endless detail.

My fourth rejoinder deepens the third. Accounting for language is an indispensable foundation for the social construction project. I have begun laying out efforts at such accounting, and what is clear is that personalization is a dead end there.

8.1.2. Context

Context is crucial in this explanation I have developed for social life as middle-range order. An identity triggers in its search for footing. Footing is reproduced in the context of nearby searches by other identi-

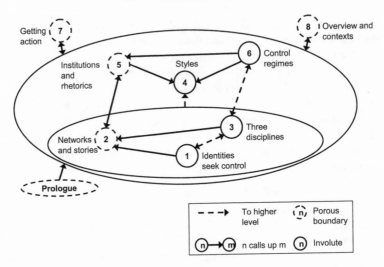

Figure 8.1: *Identity and Control*—Graph of chapters and conceptual guide

ties. Social spaces and times thereby are constituted in interlockings of locales, initially through continuing ties between identities. The resulting networks in part reflect the course of daily life in its minutiae. But social networks also embody long-lasting kinship and work relations so that order spreads to and across locales more remote in social time and space. This includes jumps to a higher level of identities that are embedded in discipline of work or institution of kinship.

Such embeddings are also necessarily, and paradoxically, decouplings from accountings at lower level. So positions in social spacetimes seldom map into geography and chronometry. Instead, context requires the multiple perspectives laid out in preceding chapters, which do not scale but rather each presupposes and requires the others. Chapters 3 and 5 showed an example of how interface discipline came into force only as its relational nexus downstream sustained a style (chapter 4).

Figure 8.1 diagrams the conceptual interlockings among the seven chapters. An arrow from a chapter goes to the chapter invoked, as for example chapter 6 invokes chapter 5, and also chapter 4--neither of which presupposes, much less invokes, its control regimes. In contrast, chapters 6 and 3 presuppose each other. The circle around a chapter number is solid when its constructs are relatively introverted, but is dashed otherwise, as with chapter 2 on networks. The central chapter, 4 on styles, is not only involute but also only receives arrows and does not send any. Moreover, the first three chapters are taken grouped together because they all invoke chapter 4. Similarly, the first six chapters taken as a whole invoke, and are invoked by, chapter 7 on Getting Action, as well as this concluding chapter.

Cultural cannot be disentangled from *social*: on the contrary, they intertwine in all perspectives, from netdom switchings in chapter 1 to regime control or overturn in chapters 6 and 7. That point underlies the finding that dispersions, measures of spread, as opposed to averages, are crucial. Identities reproduce formations by sustaining differences and frictions among them, as opposed to collation by some arbiter, supposed as being independent and external.

That point also shows that observing is both involute and multiplex; it is a paradoxical problem rather than a straightforward tool (Kontopolous 1993). Communications, and signaling more generally, are aspects of social structure/process rather than a matter of independent cognitions. All this reasoning was pioneered by Luhmann (e.g., 1995). All aspects of language, not just discourse, are to be accounted for as an integral part of the analysis (I plan to outline this in my next monograph).

Meanings make sense only as indexical expressions of context (Duranti and Goodwin 1992; Hanks 1990, 1993; Silverstein 1998). In the words of Shanon (1990): meaning seems, therefore, not to be selected by context, but rather to be generated in it. And networks are known to shape the way we think (Krackhardt 1987), which is conditional (Traugott 1986).

8.1.3. Contextualizing

Contextualizing contexts is central. These chapters develop distinctive ways to portray and analyze sociocultural structure and process. And in each, focus is paired with perspective to call up the appropriate context there. But in order to understand and portray ongoing social life, the external analyst or observer must extend this further and allow for several, or even all, of these perspectives of hers.

Figure 8.1 can help with this search for contexture, for the weaving together of separate strands of argument and structure into a veridical whole. And chapter 7 goes still further, supplying tangible examples of getting action, of going beyond control as induced and tamed variously according to the six earlier perspectives. Note again that "society" is our mirage, a convenient shortcut rather than a usable contextualization.

I intend this work as a useful framing for studies, providing theories with which to probe, not as the basis for some universal theory. Indeed, this approach embraces the historical, many of the insights being gleaned from historians' works. It need not be seen as a paradox that my approach is also stochastic, most notably in chapters 1, 4, and 7.

Accounts of social action must bring out the recursion built into any self-reproduction of social formations.[1] The scale of size is open, and also this self-reproduction can refer to a time scale of decades or months as well as hours or seasons, or indeed, seconds.[2] Self-reproduction was axiomatic for the middle chapter, styles, but other chapters must specify it with the aid of embeddings and decouplings.

With institutional systems and control regimes, chapters 5 and 6, recursion comes to depend on and call forth interpretive realms that are distinct, and within which social processes are oriented around taken-for-granted values. Such realms may be figured against the ground of a contrasting realm, which may be implicit, just a part of everyday life, or may be an explicit dual. One regime that was introduced, church and state, builds dual realms.

Styles generalize and frame types of tie and story-lines, and so they encompass several levels of embedding and rhetoric, whereas a regime includes explicit native identification of how style articulates to rhetoric, with associated decouplings, just as story-sets go with the endless struggle to sustain the viability of one and another network. So styles come to be perceived in sets sufficient to maintain the viability of a regime or of an institutional system through a trade-off between ambage and ambiguity.

Following a sketch of chapter contents, much of this chapter will be organized around context. But first we look briefly at how contextualizing can become radical transformation.

8.1.4. Invention of Organization

Some new forms of organization may emerge only from radical disjunction. Take the much-studied Renaissance Florence. In the words of John Padgett (2007):

> I demonstrated that this highly consequential organizational invention in business was the unintended consequence of political cooptation in the repressive aftermath of the Ciompi revolt. . . . Organizational emergence in this case was not a single good idea that spread. It was the simultaneous-invention corollary of a system-wide tipping in the structure of Florentine elites, produced by class revolt. In particular, global rewiring of biographical-mobility wirings across multiple Florentine social networks led

---

[1] Skvoretz and Fararo (1995), Skvoretz, Fararo, and Axten (1980), and Carley (1986) are sociological pioneers of modeling in this vein, which was opened by Newell and Simon (1972).

[2] Cf. Krauss and Bricker (1967) on effects upon conversation of delay in vocal transmission.

to the emergence of oligarchic Renaissance-style elites, based on marriage and patronage, out of factional medieval-style guilds, based on patrilineage and guild. This deep social-network transformation in the elite structure of the city ramified in many directions at once--economic, political, and artistic--thereby linking the many inventions observed in Renaissance Florence (and Renaissance Italy more broadly) into a synergistic, feedback system. (John Padgett, from Research summary to his Department of Political Science, University of Chicago, January 2007)

8.1.5. Sketch of Chapters

I devote more space to the first two chapters, which lay the groundwork.

In **Chapter 1**, social life gets realized via discourse evoked in and across particular relations that network together around some topics. Relations get constituted among **identities,** which each sprang out of a search for footing among and **control** over other identities amid perceived chaos. **Meaning** emerges, in my construal, through **switchings** among ensuing patterns.

Discourse thus frames itself in local **netdoms**, each of which for a stretch of time melds an array of relations within a domain of topics. When this array is completely filled, with common-denominator domain, that netdom serves as a **public**. **Footing** can come from just one relation, as between mother and infant, but one relation comes to implicate or be implicated by other relations among their common topics as a larger netdom. So footing can also be into a public.

Upon occasion the set of stories for a network gets reweighted as it switches into and/or comes out of a public. A playground for a neighborhood or school is illustrative, with its shifting skein of little publics and netdoms. Just go and observe kids stringing together in, and shouting about, various games of tag and chase, with others hanging out together around a fountain or swing.

Identities perceive other, as well as their own, netdoms and publics. So, one discursive process can impinge on another discursive process. And various happenings concern also relations involving physical locations and things, which calls for enlarged specification of **context**. Contingencies and constraints can chain to one another; so social processes are **stochastic** both overall and in detail. Theory seeks tidy structures as well as processes, but the empirical studies sketched in the later chapters make clear the sway of heterogeneity and surprise; those chapters tried to accommodate such sway within the theory via participants' perceptions.

Social processes accrue and align into their spaces and times according to structural equivalence across mutual positionings; designate this as **streq**. This streq depends on the absence as much as the presence of overlaps in relations and topics and sequences, so that any one closeness depends on closeness elsewhere and whenever, in some one of multitudinous possible outcomes from searches, such as discussed in chapter 2. The public is a special case, and if all its relations are asymmetric, implications tend to be transitive so that those identities array in linear order, an internal pecking order that is also seen from elsewhere as a special public.

Furthermore, identity and control processes are recursive and can yield distinct **levels**, as when some special public emerges out of clashes among identities as being an identity in itself, an early example being the pecking order.

Chapter 2 traces the growth of **networks** around **stories,** which, as they are catalyzed in switchings among netdoms, come to **mark** particular relations as **ties**. Out of netdoms from a particular domain comes a network in a particular **type of tie**. Network form varies with the type of tie, but searches for paths of connection can overlay all networks into an overall **multiplex** network. These searches find profiles of lengths across, as well as enclaves within, a fuzzy world of network. The results inform studies of diffusion.

As the network evolves through situations, a **set of stories** comes, over time, to characterize that type of tie. Some stories may be negative, and most will be specialized, with the matching of any one story to a tie changing over time. Some median story in the set will come to characterize that type of tie for participants. At each netdom switching, participants can reweight their expectations about these matchings in some Bayesian fashion. A network with its story-set filters perceptions of participants.

Contrasts between multiple networks reflect and can suggest emergent clusterings of relations and participants into everyday roles through the application of streq, as in blockmodeling.

As to the rest . . . Publics can be seen as special netdoms, and yet they also ground evolutions of the three sorts of disciplined cooperation that I discriminate in chapter 3. Getting joint tasks done tends to settle into one of three **disciplines**, each evolving with and around a distinctive **valuation order** out of some public. Each discipline is observably able to reproduce itself in ongoing process for some range of contexts.

Thereafter, networks from chapter 2 are folded into the chapter 4 analysis of process and **sensibility** at a higher level across a larger scope—in **style,** which also folds in disciplines. Flows of switchings characterize meanings in styles. Then chapter 5 enlarges on earlier chapters' attention to impacts from **folk theory**, including participants' own theorizing, via **rhetorics** and **institutional systems**. Chapter 6 focuses on the structural tensions around values across parallel structures that support **regimes** of control. It describes several large types of regimes common in history that each has reconstituted itself through thick and thin. Yet any social formation whatever, complex or not, tends to settle into blocking action over time. Getting action, as much as getting control, is thus a general problem.

Control continues as a focus in chapter 7, which examines the paradoxes of getting action and achieving agency amid all these mutually constraining processes and structures and levels.

8.1.6. Other Angles

This book aims to aid tangible analyses and research rather than just argue for some self-sufficient perspective on the social world. Analytic focus, not scope or level or domain, is what has distinguished each of these chapters. For example, identities within some discipline may all themselves be huge organizations. And although I expect to code the largest systems as regimes, regimes may also appear within various styles or disciplines, and so on. Tangible application is thus all bound up with recognition of the context for that social system, and that requires the careful exposition to which the second half of this chapter is devoted.

The reality frame implied by the way I present this analysis is troubling, however. We can see the centrality of boundaries as ideas and facts in folk accounts of social life. But a certain tidiness, a sense of order and regularity in social process is being generated as a by-product of my chapter structure, and this is, for better or worse, just not true. If one thinks metaphorically of social life as music, then:

> we have chapter 4 on styles as the aspect of rhythm,
> with chapter 6 on regimes as the aspect of counterpoint, perhaps,
> and chapter 5 on rhetorics being the melody, and so on:
> perhaps network stories are then musical notes,
> and disciplines are major chords.

This metaphor is meant to convey a sense of social life as affairs of messy interpenetrations and switchings and embeddings and decouplings.

Also there is some implication of a fixed sequence in chapters. But one could switch chapters 2 and 3, since, although tasks undoubtedly draw on networks, it is also the case that a distinct type of network may root in one or another of the disciplines. In fact, there is no irreversibility in movement from one form, level, and scope of social organization to another (Luhmann 1995).

In addition, there is, in the examples given earlier of successful control or manipulation, an unfortunate implication of inevitability. The material of control is social relations. Control in social context must simultaneously see to reproducing reliable responses while also having to track context just like an engineering system does, and all the while searching for openings for change. There is no inevitability. Each of the many examples of rhetorics and styles given earlier is also an ensemble of potential paths through to fresh control, but also potentially, to lock-step or devolution.

Overall, the argument is qualitative, although some sections also draw on quantitative and mathematical material (but without technical detail and its symbolism). Figure 8.1 already offered a schematic diagram of interrelations among concepts in this theory. Fittings across scores of published studies support its plausibility. Most calibrations with particular other theories have been kept to notes and the front matter.

I seek to identify particular findings that can be robust across contexts and thus earn title as lemma or theorem. Without these, the theory remains an interpretive framework yielding ad hoc description. Other interpretive frameworks can, in any case, challenge and supplement this theory. In particular, history and ecology also aim for such wide coverage.

This reinforces the use of style as a general concept in chapter 4. I use findings that, like many grammatical features, extrapolate across overarching master languages, such as the English that so heavily shapes what claims I make, and how I make them. Sublanguages are the fulcrum of discourse processes, and I seek findings that extrapolate across them too. Later chapters, 6 on regimes and 5 on rhetorics, go beyond discourse proper to invoke written language, where literary analysis, such as analysis of indirect free speech, supplements the linguistics of discourse.

Outcomes of interest need not directly revolve around meaning from switching as here construed, but even psychological profiles, epidemics of illness, and so on get realized only through social forms such as I have laid out. That is my claim.

8.1.7. Language Thresholds

Network populations build among disciplines, which presuppose a set of valuations that mediate their embeddings. Identities make use of valuations to maneuver--but, of course, they can do so effectively only as other actors at least know what they are signaling. And this implies at least a language of practice, a parole, in which a set of valuations gets expressed across some more-or-less definite population.

But language appears only when there are multiple populations. Language presupposes interaction among distinct network populations; so language is a cumulative by-product of boundaries and switchings (Bakhtin 1981; Holm 1988). And language deals especially with events over time (Hopper 1995). Niklas Luhmann had language central in how time and structure constitute each other (1995, chapter 8). And the encyclopedic linguist M.A.K. Halliday, posits time as the central concern of grammar (1994, chapters 3–7).

Kinship is the conscious-theory facet of the emergence of languages. They may begin as disjunct secret codes across an isolated tribe (Dixon 1972), but evolve into broadly continuous idioms across sweeps of interrelated peoples (Bradfield 1973). Kinship is the first matrix of valuations; then comes social class (Hawking 1977).

Bring this argument up to contemporary times. Stories are joint creations that evolve slowly and so only among social groupings that are self-reproducing. But stories are too flexible and numerous around us to be generated in one small setting. We cannot conceive of stories hat are purely local, tied just to one network or discipline. Other levels of stories are always implicit in any that we observe, with language as the limiting larger scope (Hawkins 1983; Kratchovil 1968).

So language is coordinate to processes that lead to stories and to types of tie being discerned and factored out as separate patterns, networks. Only the human species elaborates ties in stories. Social accountings ground social networks in a somehow-ordered heap of stories, only some of whose constituents map into biophysical space. The generation and spread of these accountings presuppose social contexts able to support language as structuring.

Thus it is that language presupposes not just a population, but interacting populations. Language is the integration of distinct functional dialects (Culler 1975). Such integration comes only from control struggles across wide fronts of interaction with other like populations (Hodge and Kress 1993; Lodge 1993). No language was ever known whose speakers were not keenly aware of distinct other languages, known to be languages. In short, language comes in only with metalanguage (Gal 1979).

Language builds with multifaceted persons, and with multiple populations, and their reproductions as social formation, in styles and rhetorics and the regimes of chapters 6. Combinatorics suggests an underlying impetus for language. Combinatorial counts of possible social patterns are astronomical. Over enough time, styles settle out, and thence language is induced as setting for rhetorics.

We can make the same argument in more concrete terms. Control struggles proliferate out into, and generate, multiple settings (Briggs and Baumann 1992; Brown and Levinson 1987; Cicourel 1991; Haiman 1978). Stories in language are accompaniments induced as the scope of interaction grows beyond some threshold (Forgas 1985). The evidence seems clear that this magic number is around one thousand. According to the records of anthropology, at that size social formations can reproduce across a range of activities, and correlatively a language can establish itself. This is the size of the smallest self-subsisting tribe and also of the smallest language group observed.[3]

In a literally isolate tribe, the number of kin and production and social ceremonial formations might be low enough, and their intercalation simple enough, to be described as just one population. There would be separate overlapping networks, but not necessarily further embeddings. And perhaps language might not have emerged fully; rhetorics might have been adumbrated.[4]

But any image of a neatly separate population with its own language is misleading. Tribal languages appear in a nested roll of parallel and similar and variational language (Dixon and Blake 1983). Each is in some use across a geographic region; each draws on neighbors as resources. There is not a need and occasion and goad for language until some such scope as one thousand actors is reached, interconnected across different settings, but usually the chain of mutually comprehensible languages goes further. In such settings, each network becomes the site of struggles for control that cannot be settled neatly because they spill over into other settings, other populations.

8.2. Modeling around Context

Tangible application is my goal. Each particular application necessarily is context dependent. But context appears in many guises. A microcosm of these guises appears in chapter 3. There, as earlier in chapter 1, one sees identities emerging, being constituted out of some continuing larger context.

Now, an emerged and embedded identity is not inert, is not a thing but rather an actor. Chapter 3 ends with sketches of how disciplines

---

[3] I can leave to one side issues of physiological and neurological capacities for language. Identity in the guise of human consciousness may be triggered only across the interactions of distinct network settings sustained by such a population.

[4] But not beyond some threshold: the Icelandic sagas developed despite remarkable isolation into an exceptionally powerful skein of stories (Scholes and Kellogg 1966, chap. 2).

switch and hitch and stack with one another. Just as disciplines continue to draw on networks, they also all get drawn into further levels
of social organization, as referred to in chapters 4, 5, and 6. Then chapter 7 examines how actors exactly try to break out of context.

So context transpires on many levels, with many aspects, but there
remains still, also, an overall or global context. Thus, complete specification of context can also require drawing on geography, on biology,
on engineering, and many other specialties, and thereby lies outside
this theory proper. I have offered some pointers throughout. I cite also
guides to ethnography (e.g., Vaughan 2002; Knox, Savage, and Harvey
2006), which is a different take on describing global context.

Context remains crucial, but, I think, is harder to instantiate when
one starts with individualist presuppositions in modeling. I cite the
massive *Foundations* by Coleman (1990). See Emirbayer and Goodwin
(1994) for discussion. But also central is the early paper by Schelling
(1971), "Dynamic Models of Segregation." This is still cited in the
stream of papers that he started using computer simulations to fill out
theory: for example, Edmonds and Hales (2005), Watts (2003).

I draw on such diverse sources for particular modelings that it is
hard to bring to bear the generalized idea of context. I will begin by
supplanting context with boundary, which also satisfies the basic stipulation of applying across both social and cultural aspects.

First comes an abstract appraisal of boundary as construct, then
the applied modelings. After that I turn back to the generalized view
of context.

8.2.1. Boundary as Theory

In natural science theories, boundary has proved to be a crucial and
productive concept.[5] Experimental manipulation there can impose
boundary. That is suggestive, only. To recognize a boundary is not an
innocent activity.

Social phenomena are least predictable and most interesting at
boundaries. The world has long noted these truths, and boundaries are
a basic concept in any folk theory. Charles Tilly (2004) surveys these
mechanisms of social boundary. For a vivid account of the trials and
tribulations of modern organization theory around boundaries, see
Padgett's review essay (1992) on the work of Arthur Stinchcombe.

Boundaries in social action are not given facts but are, instead, subtle
and complex products of action.[6] Boundaries are theories that can

[5] Much of theoretical physics is structured as boundary-value problems (see, for example, Morse and Feshbach 1953).

[6] Only persistent argument from John Padgett brought me to this realization.

cause facts in the practice both of social science and of ordinary life. The business of social organization is ultimately to make boundaries, which native theories attempt to portray.

Boundaries have to be constructed and negotiated and maintained. Boundaries are not a free good, handily available to participant or observer. There are projects of control and disciplines of production that underlie and shape any putative "boundary." One boundary gets recognized from, and as a frequency distribution of, sets of social actions. Another boundary is constructed out of stories to dampen impacts of network.

Social organization is like some impacted, mineralized goo, some amazing swirl of local nuclei and long strands of order among disorder. An economist speaks of firms as "islands of planned co-ordination in the sea of market relations" (Richardson 1972). Social organization is indeed rich in possible boundaries.

Richness in boundaries is a resource for control projects. Ambage, ambiguity and contingency, and their trade-offs, are the calculus of boundaries for analysts. Some agreement on boundaries is the sign for emergence of rhetoric as balancing of diverse control projects. Stories are one form of agreement, communicable speculations by actors about recurrent acts by others. The boundaries of rhetorics are constructs that result from, rather than being causes of, interpenetration between network populations.

Human cultures, each marked by some discourses in story-sets and their values, concentrate on what nuclei of order can be found. Thus, they set a tone of exposition that presupposes more orderliness than is really there. The main business of human discourse is to put an orderly face on the underlying messes.

Human powers of perception are limited, and it is not surprising that some agreed descriptions of boundaries are used for orientation to and within social spaces. What remains to be disentangled is how important are stories and explanations in sharpening some edge of boundary in social action. Stories can be woven together into ideologies that compete with boundaries, as in this account:

> The social transformations which occurred in England during the 16th and 17th centuries culminated in the formation and articulation of abstract ideologies as guides to action, which, when carried out, transformed the world in their image. Common to these ideologies was a sustained attack on particularism, for example, the Puritan emphasis on the "godly community" over ties of kinship and locality, and the common-law emphasis on principled "right" rather than the exercise of particular

"rights." As Weber has made clear, the distinctive feature of the West was the tenacious hold which these universalistic rhetorics held on the pattern and organization of social life. (Bearman 1985)

8.2.2. Brass Tacks

Although actors themselves rely on intuition and context and stereotypes, modeling is an indispensable addition for the observer or analyst. So, whence do the actual specifications and implementations, the brass tacks, come? I will cite many examples of specifying theory by use of an explicit model from boundary. I should say *"attempting* to specify theory," because these modelings are difficult.

The first twenty volumes of *Journal of Mathematical Sociology*, with Pat Doreian as editor, offer a comprehensive guide. More often than not, these papers are using Coleman (1990) for their theoretical framing. This is often made explicit, as for example recently in Miller-Benedict (2006).

It is instructive to begin here with three brief contrasts of alternative approaches to similar phenomena.

Even stripped-down networks are exceedingly complex mechanisms for process, whether of diffusion or manipulation, as we saw, for example, in the early section of chapter 2 on tracing. And modeling depends upon presupposition. The primacy of the network has been challenged by an alternative approach, of considerable age. Instead of the network of pair-ties, turn to how triads of various kinds fit together. This idea was developed by Davis, and then Holland and Leinhardt, as sketched earlier in chapter 2, first for just the multiplex tie. There, with asymmetric ties distinguished, there prove to be thirteen distinct triads. Subsequently, as we saw with the law firm case in chapter 3, this other bottom-up approach was extended to multiple types of tie. It becomes plain that both dyad and triad approaches generate insight on reality. Both can be used to derive network topology from transitivity, asymmetry, and balance theory. Both were part of a Second Wave of math modeling, post-1950s, which also drew on First Wave developments such as balance theory.

How real are the two extremes of liminality and tournament, from the end of chapter 3? In a profound series of analyses of the 1950s, Landau (1950, 1965) proved that the almost universal predominance of perfect linear orders of dominance among flocks in some species of social animals could not be accounted for by any plausible model of impacts from attributes of individuals upon outcomes of particular pair encounters. Landau rigorously proved that some form of heavy dependence upon existing overall social rankings was necessary.

Landau could not establish, just from abstract modeling, the kind of dependence that obtains. But a sociobiologist—that is, a comparative-species sociologist—Ivan Chase (1986), has presented evidence that, for some species, it is a cumulation of perceptions of gaming status. The principal species studied is chickens, who individually are stupid. Ambiguity does not figure, since there is no culture.

Among humans one never finds the near-perfect dominance order that emerges from naive encounters as among chickens. Instead, a tournament may appear, but as a conspiracy, a joint conscious contrivance (Green and Stokey 1983; Rosen 1984). The culture around tournaments is clear-cut, and the form is imposed from the larger setting. The result is that the ostensible basis, the cultural criterion of strength or brains, or what have you, which is used to account for ordering, is completely impossible to validate. Mandated dominance in social relation implies arbitrary placements on a cultural criterion: Landau's work can be reinterpreted to that effect; and Leifer's work, developed in the previous chapter, suggests some sociopsychological mechanisms.

How does it happen that the human species, in our own time and sites, is so enamored of this social form, analogous to a form that is native to a vertebrate species characterized by stupidity? There can be no answer within the ostensible scope of the competing set of individuals. This set may be a squash ladder, but it may equally well be a clutch of otherwise brilliant mathematicians jockeying for pecking order among themselves, possibly reflected in prizes. We must first examine the playing out of gamings for control, via decouplings and embeddings, and specify disciplines and how they may eventuate in hierarchies. Only through several layers of embeddings and story formation might it be possible to predict when and why this stupid form is reproduced and earns establishment.

My 1970 paper "Simon out of Homans by Coleman" argues for a simple stochastic process as an adequate model from James Coleman's (1964) cornucopia of models for deriving from Homans's small group survey (1950) the same empirical generalizations that Simon (1957) hypothesized by solving a model of coupled linear differential equations. This is a math model used to support what is possibly the most venerable analytic device in sociology, the 2x2 table, which certainly is a matter of boundaries. The model derived ultimately from a classic source for the Second Wave of social science modeling, the introduction to stochastic processes by mathematician William Feller (1968); and see Leik and Meeker (1975), Rapoport (1983), and Fararo (1973).

8.2.3. Illustrative Models, by Chapter

An extended survey of explicit examples for modeling of theory would take too much space. I will just cite at least one publication, frequently my own, that carries out more or less complete modeling for a major construct from each of the chapters. Each of these studies can be viewed on-line.

As general background, besides the classic early surveys across classes of models that were cited just before, I point to relatively recent overviews by Edling (1998), by Fararo and Butts (1999), and quite recently by Hedstrom (2005). I have authored a long string of short scans (White 1962, 1963b, 1970b, 1973, 1997, 2000a, 2000b, 2002). I also point out the text from which I first taught math models in social science: Kemeny, Snell, and Thompson (1957), which, like the early surveys, remains a treasure trove of leads.

for **identity**:

Harris (1991) on synonymy
Padgett (1997) and Bonacich (2003) on cellular automata as guide
White (1970e) on masking of identity
Kruglanski and Webster (1996) on switching around cognitive closure

for **networks**:

Moody and White (2003)
White and Johansen (2006)
Watts, Dodds, and Newman (2002)
Add Health (Bearman Moody, and Faris 2002; Bearman, Moody, and Stovel 2004)
Science/industry collaborations (Powell et al. 2005)
Blockmodels (Breiger, Boorman. and Arabie 1975) and Tallberg (2005)

for **disciplines** across dimensions:

Martin (2002) tightness and clarity of group beliefs, entropic models
game theory (Shubik 1984a, b)
timing (Gibson 2005b)
production markets in arts (White 2002, 2006)
queuing as filter (White and Christie 1958)

for **styles**:

turn-taking in committee discourse (Gibson 2005b)
structuring in diffusion (Martin 2002)
combinatorics of stratification (White 1963b)
Simon out of Homans by Coleman (White 1970d)

for **rhetorics** and **organizations**:

Abell (1987) on syntax

Relational equation algebras (Bonacich 1980; Bonacich and McConaghy 1979)

Friedell (1967), and Evans (1975) on semilattices

Ijira and Simon (1977) on size distributions

Padgett (1989, 1997) on plea bargaining, and on hypercycle models of autocatalytic

emergence of organizations as networks of rule sequences

Thompson and Mulac (1991) model of parentheticals

for **institutional systems**:

Boyd (1991)

Gould and Fernandez (1993)

Winship (1978) on time

vacancy chains (White 1970c, e)

for **regimes**:

lattices of political mobilization (Mische and Pattison 2000)

and see Freeman and White (1993)

for **getting action**:

Burt (1992a)

Mische and White (1998)

Eccles and White (1986a, b)

Leifer and White (1986)

Levine (1993)

White (1985)

Now, we can return to considering chapter 7. Firms and industries in the West themselves engage in effective indirect controls over their own careers and careers of other corporate actors and persons. The principle can be extended by analytic continuity to other scopes. Congestion profiles in flow systems, for example, can also be interpreted as supporting a control that is indirect, in fashion analogous to career (Kleinrock 1964; Riordan 1962).

Boundary was introduced as how to frame context in mathematical modeling, and this does work with many of the models, in particular for "Simon out of Homans by Coleman" (White 1970d). But more powerful framing is needed to support all of even only the early models. Boundaries do not seem adequate in the modeling, for example, of values, or of the valuation orderings of disciplines.

8.2.4. The Third Wave in Social Science Modeling

Robert K. Merton convinced us that an important breakthrough in a science would tend to well up independently many times. The great news is that diverse examples of a new vision of modeling are bubbling up in tangible research. The work of Watts and associates, and of Padgett and colleagues, for example, have been cited repeatedly in this manuscript, both as to tangible data and to sophisticated method. Works of Mischel and of Burt that were cited in chapter 4 also fit the bill.

Chapters 5 and 6 have already cited major new developments in network realism, from research groups around Peter Bearman and David Stark—for example, on communities and on shipping networks. I bring in now a parallel comparison between two other studies to hammer home the point that social science grounded in network realism is breaking through to a new phase of power and scope. At the end, I will lead up to the importance for theory of the breakthrough that has emerged.

Chapter 3 featured rich data and analyses by Lazega and collaborators for explaining the council discipline. His work had also invoked network analyses, and I have shown how it fits with style. And now I draw a parallel with a novel set of methods applied by anthropologist Douglas White, with several different collaborators, to very different sets of data.

Begin with an original new conceptualization and measurement of cohesion from embeddedness in a paper by James Moody, also a collaborator with Bearman, who brought the huge Add Health network data under the knife of White's novel algorithms (Moody and White 2003). Those algorithms turn attention away from cliques and blockmodels and the like to focus on overlap. The apparent messiness of multiple, sprawling overlappings is turned into an asset after application of leverage from a deep theorem on connectivity of graphs published in 1927 by Menger.

Moody and White portray cohesion as what I call a style. They are so lucid and provide such complete context that you should consult it in preference to any sketch by me.[7]

One other large data set, on political actions from corporate directors located in an interlock network, from sociologist Mizruchi, was also shown to yield significant predictions using the Moody and White approach. The point is that this approach, powerful and novel, is also en-

---

[7] However, I should note that the account of embeddings of two sorts for production markets, which I will give from my own work in the next section, probably could be sharpened by bringing in this new formulation

tirely independent of the powerful approaches marshaled for the analysis of Lazega's law firm, described in the previous chapter. To me this outcome, reinforced by the many other studies I have cited, is strong support for the reality of and impacts from style as social formation.

Note also that a large range of sizes are included, from the hundred or so in the law firm of Lazega, to thousands in Add Health's high schools and Mizruchi's corporate director network. Indeed, a subsequent (2004) programmatic paper by Douglas White and Moody, joined by sociologists Woody Powell and Jason Owen-Smith, extrapolates the approach to apply to industrial networks of national scope and multiple levels. These papers break important new ground by targeting evolution of what I call a style rather than only testing cross-sectional predictions as to attributes.

Yet even these extrapolations do not get to perhaps the deepest findings. For that, turn to other work of Douglas White, now with a fellow anthropologist, Michael Houseman, centered on kinship systems. Here the obscurity is not from graph theory mathematics, but from the sheer intricacy of kinship description, which is such that few others intrude on anthropologists. The central importance of kinship is that it can also be represented by native theory of some acumen and accuracy, much more clearly and transparently than, say, in the Lazega case. Houseman and White are fully conversant with and active also in nontribal study, such as in their piece following up and improving on the Watts's team study of searchability, not just reachability, in the Small World (White and Houseman 2003).

The climax for me is the recent book by Douglas White and Ulla Johansen (2006). In this remarkable monograph, they call for probing a qualitatively new sort of construct, cohesion. I regard it as a major independent discovery of the gist of what I will argue, in the next section, as the core finding from the present exposition of theory.

8.3. Modeling from Operational Environment

Accounting to context must be a central feature in my theoretical approach. I have discriminated social processes parceled out into six chapters (though without actual derivation) and claim that these distinct sorts can mix and exert joint influence. But this raises a nightmarish specter of theorizing dozens of different joint-nesses. Using boundary as theory was an attempt to sidestep this specter. A generalized construct of context as operational environment, that was introduced in chapter 3, may enable taming of the specter.

But I will show that this generalized context already invokes a paradox. This is parallel to the approach of Niklas Luhmann, laid out most completely in his *Social Systems* (1995). Although Luhmann uses the term *environment*, I stick with *context* for two reasons. First, there are too many extraneous overtones today from *environment*. Second, his usage commits one to general systems theory, and related work such as Spencer--Brown's calculus, both of which pull one away from the main lines of science and modeling. Nonetheless, Luhmann stands out as relevant here for the intensity and consistency of his focus on what I call *context*, and thereby he faces this same specter, now around his functional subsystem distinctions.

My approach to context has to rise above the distinctions among chapters 1–6. So I now emphasize what the chapters have in common. First, each has integral to it the joining of social with cultural, ranging from the *netdom* of chapter 1 through the *realm* of chapter 6. Second, each has to offer accommodation for different levels, where social is integrated with cultural in the discrimination of "levels." But context does evoke paradox. Paradox is unavoidable first because of the endemic switchings, at all scopes, from which meanings derive. And context hovers overall, invoking for any given chapter constructs from other chapters, and thereby often other levels, which is where paradox is especially apparent, around embeddings.

To emphasize that levels are crucial, I have proceeded in two steps. First, in chapter 2, I discussed coupling and decoupling, whose patterns can be intricate but do not seem paradoxical to me. Then I turned in chapter 3 to embedding with decoupling, where paradox appeared. Already providing an example for the subsection that follows on how measures relate with levels in models, I laid out embedding of the production markets in chapters 3 and 5 (and see White 2002). There, I turned from using the generic and thus anodyne term "context," to specifying the multi-level concept of "operational environment."

This chapter will end with sections that cover situations when, counter to my present approach, context is split apart into either cultural or social, rather than joined, as with embeddings. So those sections discuss culture and space as leached versions of context.

8.3.1. Embeddings with Three Dimensions

Context is most helpful analytically when generalized, rather than being specialized according to which of the chapter types are conceived to be adjoined, at what level and in what number. Moreover, switchings are endemic at all levels, and context cannot specify those in any detail. In any case, the analyst wants to use context to succeed in modeling, not to portray context for its own sake. So it makes sense to seek some simplified indexing of context that permits estimation of its impacts on the functioning of a particular social process.

I developed a space for representing possible valuation contexts of a market interface. Detailed results of modeling show for what locations in this index space there is no viable variant of the interface to construct.[8] And yet, indexed contexts across much of the space may sustain two, or even all three, species of discipline. The central region of index space for interfaces turns out to be a "black hole," where it is my conjecture that no variety of any species is viable.

What is not clear and would take extensive development is how to model interaction between disciplines. How can the embedding of identity forms into networks, in parallel and crossing arrangements, be modeled explicitly as population?

Or alternatively, how can one predict and represent the suppression of one alternative discipline by another? A general issue would be how congeries of disciplines are invoked and fit together in larger populations—and what slippage there remains for fresh control. I have discussed this before, as in the chapter 7 section on agenda for agency, and much of the material in chapters 4–6 lays groundwork for such modeling. But there is a need for a more general approach to appraisal.

The market space (White 2002) can be seen as a more abstract sort of social space, which is a by-product of, and enabled by, greater freedom of connection together with less freedom of valuation. Each of the three disciplines discussed in chapter 3 gets its task done only according to embedding—with respect to dependency, to differentiation, and to involution in network population. I now seek to extrapolate that discussion to other formations.

A regime can be seen as embedding constituents, including disciplines, parallel to the way that chapter 3 showed the discipline as embedding its members, and so also for institutions and for styles. As with disciplines, one inquires as to how any particular process formation gets assessed, weighed according to its location in the embedding context. In chapter 3, involution, dependence, and differentiation were defined in abstract and general enough terms to be invoked again here.

---

[8] Others (Bales 1970; Breiger and Ennis 1979) have modeled what is, in my terms, the constitution of interfaces when the complementarity ratio is nil, for example, for free discussion groups. I derived an explicit map of stability for interface discipline, in the ISERP Working Paper 05–01 cited in chapter 3. This map is indexed for moderate complementarity, neither completely involuted nor turned entirely to struggling for attention among cross-stream markets. It arrays contexts according to vulnerability to interventions for control.

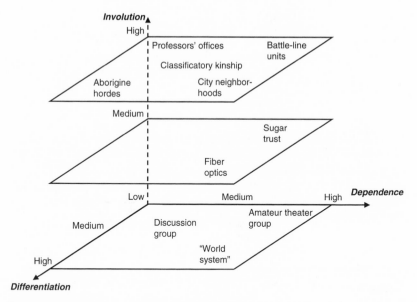

Figure 8.2: The 3-D space for interface discipline

So I use these three dimensions next, defined abstractly as in chapter 3, to index styles, institutional systems, and control regimes.

I go further and argue that there is some parallelism in mechanism between the three disciplines and the three larger forms:

style—interface discipline, involution parameter
institutional system—council discipline, differentiation parameter
control regime—arena discipline, dependency parameter

My speculation is that each of the three process formations is especially focused on, and outcomes shaped especially by, the value of just one parameter ratio. That was already claimed in chapter 3 for disciplines: readers are advised to reread that section (3.2.3 Involution, Differentiation, and Dependency). As there, so also here, there will be secondary variation in outcome according to position of an example on the other two dimensions.

Besides these three abstract parameters that index relative sensitivity, there of course must be a set of tangible scalings, dealing with average size, for modeling a particular case.

The speculation is made tangible in the following three figures, 8.2, 8.3, and 8.4, one for each genre. In the three-dimensional space for that genre, I indicate where various empirical cases might be located. In two of the dimensions, the index calibrates the relative impacts from

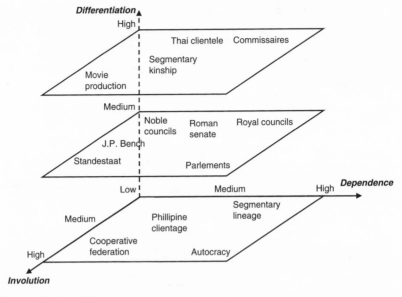

Figure 8.3: The 3-D space for council discipline

prior or upstream as a ratio to impacts from later or downstream. Each index is to be appraised as a ratio of curvatures of valuations. There is also an index for cross-stream. And I make conjectures about the functioning of systems according to values of the ratios. In particular, when the first two ratios are both near unity, there is so little discrimination that only simple forms of social process, such as the catnets of chapter 2, persist.

8.3.2. Spread within and across Cases

All this, of course, oversimplifies how social process formations fit together, which is the nub of context theory. There can be levels building on top of levels, despite confounding by switchings. And a formation from one chapter can embed in one from another.

A production market profile embeds an identity as interface discipline, from chapter 3. But already in chapter 5 it became apparent that such discipline was always sitting among other markets in the institutional system of a production economy. The individual interface discipline itself is embedded into the production economy as a style characterizing that industry. Upstream and downstream of that industry, as well as in the market profile, a characteristic and recognizable sensitivity establishes itself in ripostes characteristic in discourse and ties.

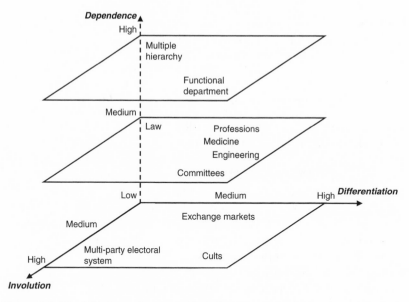

Figure 8.4: The 3-D space for arena discipline

The production economy in turn embeds into the control regime of fiscal economy, which Luhmann identifies as a functional subsystem of society. And any regime is embedding into a context that contains the contrasting realm(s) against which its own valuation is asserted, and so positions on value do result. Yet the environment of the regime goes well beyond specific other regimes, including all sorts of social and technical formations.

8.3.3. Other Measures and Levels for Models

Envelopes were introduced around styles in chapter 4. But envelopes at any scope can also be important indicators for rhetorics, as seen by either participants or observers. This is so even when explicit perception of construction, as in vacancy chains, is not generated or is not possible. Collective protest activities (Tilly 1978) as well as panics (Granovetter and Soong 1983; Milgram 1977) have a phenomenological reality not dependent upon perceptions of cumulation across contingencies.

A stratification system builds around style but out of the same constituent disciplines and ties as an institutional system. Styles can apply even when no rhetorics can be discerned in a stochastic environment. But the usual situation is a stochastic environment that is a context for styles as well as rhetorics, which may or may not themselves be crosscut by positions across roles. Continuing coexistence of network populations in a population envelope depends upon flexibility from their couplings through positions and/or rhetorics.

8.3.4. Control Theory in Engineering Yields Style

Control theory in engineering has a long history, and many independent origins (Bennett 1979 and see the appendix in the 1992 edition). So far it has been referred to social and managerial systems only vaguely and half-heartedly. Although strategic gaming can be present within such systems, too often it is just ignored (for a recent survey, see Shubik 1984a, b). Classical control theory, with emphasis upon mechanical systems and time-path analyses, is particularly associated with the Russian tradition. Control theory with emphasis upon electronic elements and upon frequency-spectrum dissection is associated with the American tradition.

Mundane production control on factory floor is an obvious parallel to and model for triage, which illustrated style in chapter 4, and it leads into the deliberate engineering of control as a process. Governments, like factories, can be surveyed as to whether they are "bang-bang" control systems, or instead more advanced systems. Lurching from crisis to crisis, with engineering controls not cutting in until the window shade has banged against the wall, or the temperature against its floor, is a bang-bang style of control. Washing machines provide another example of this bang-bang style, in which the controls can be preset but are not responsive to the process as it unfolds.

Such classical control systems, even when feedback loops are added, do not seem promising as analogues to guide analyses of social and management phenomena. These phenomena not only are erratic in time but also reflect assessments and efforts made from within the system. After all, control efforts among actors who are always struggling for identities among changing contexts are what generate the space of possibilities.

A basic idea, decoupling, is missing from standard engineering theory of control. It is analogous to discipline as used in chapter 3 because explicitly given goals are assumed. After World War II, more advanced approaches to control theory were introduced, beginning with Wiener (1949). The conceptually important version for social analysis was introduced as "dynamic programming" in this country by Richard Bellman (1957) and in Russia by Pontryagin. A limitation of classical control theory, from the social system perspective, is its focus on an explicit goal, often one to be maximized. Bellman retains this condition but in an attenuated form, where policy supplants goal.

His operationalization of "policy" is a signal contribution. Bellman establishes a new way to operationalize for explicit computation the reality that policy is effective only through particular embeddings in time. He construes a system as a convolution of successive stages, the representation being in a calculus of nested integrations. These yield computations of dependent variables vis-à-vis control goals, which goals themselves are able to shift and be influenced by intervening outcomes. The computations are thus partly decoupled from one another and yet at the same time one embeds the next through setting its boundary conditions. Realistic policy is modeled, as opposed to preset engineering instructions.

In the solution space of classical theory, the curve of constrained optimums, the extremum, is conceived as a locus of points. Bellman's decisive step was to reconceive of the extremal as an envelope of tangents. That is, the optimal approach is decoupled into a sequence of explicitly definable policies, each simplified to be made operational; so the optimal approach is broken down into an evolving profile of choices among a family of possible stances. Analytic machinery is developed, despite the exceptional complexities, to a point permitting generation of at least numerical solutions. More important here, the machinery is sophisticated enough to capture the frequent occurrence of abrupt and discontinuous policy changes (cf. the material on federal budget changes toward the end of this chapter).

Thus, advanced control theory, beginning at least with Richard Bellman, offers insights into how to conceptualize structure and system together. Indeed, it supports the theoretical framing I adopt. Note the parallelism between Bellman's analytic approach and the account of style in chapter 4 in terms of profiles and switches.

A major purpose of advanced control implementations is to decrease the sensitivity of outcomes to the parameters of the structure. Sensitivity is also cut to outside disturbances, which decreases the significance of the distinction between "outside" and "inside."[9] The obverse approach is also used in control applications. One may introduce further structure in order to decrease sensitivity to system discipline. The study by Eccles and Crane (1988) of the rapidly evolving world of investment banking, is vivid on the intertwining of system with structure in attempting to maintain control in a structure bouncing too rapidly for architecture to be of much help.

Against the background of Bellman's innovations, classical control theory itself can also be milked for further insights, and perhaps it can then furnish heuristic guidance in social situations. Bellman's perspec-

---

[9] This conceptualization has become known as a Kalman filter.

tive can be used to enrich the vast range of example solutions from classical engineering applications (Leigh 1987) available for these heuristics. This constitutes enriching a system in order to simplify structure.

8.4. Context Leached into Space

Social space goes beyond the self-consistent field invoked for style in chapter 4. Social space becomes plural, not singular, nor is social space stable. Thus, in social phenomenology, "space" itself is problematic; it is a contingent and changing and egocentric accomplishment. Control projects depend upon intersubjective decouplings and embeddings, among changing spaces, subjective and objective. Participants can each choose differently how to draw bounds to actions, but only within some common rhetorics.

Space, whether social or physical, requires and yields pragmatics of analysis. A leading geographer, Doreen Massey (2005), argues that space matters as the dimension for the social. There are many specifically sociological framings for and contributions about "space," to which I now turn. The Chicago School of urban ecology pioneered the study of social segregation within cities in the 1920s, and of course they drew on Toennies's formulations from the previous century, around "the village."

Watts (1999) pushed the network views reported in chapter 2 much further, with explicit attention to physical space. He elaborated and extended those views to Internet spaces, diffusion, and other topics in a score of papers with many associates, including Peter Dodds, Roby Muhammad, Matt Salganik, and Gueorgi Kossinets, which are available on the Web. A completely different, more traditional, approach is summarized by Gans (2002); in the same issue of *City and Community,* he is challenged from the actor network theory perspective (see chapter 2) by Gieryn, and then stretched in an aesthetic direction by Zukin.

Equally important are new phenomenological explorations of how space feels. The same Sharon Zukin takes us into loft spaces in Manhattan; Diane Vaughan takes us into the crowded, tense eyries of professional air traffic controllers; David Stark and coworkers trace how spaces got reembodied by financial district survivors of 9/11; and Karin Knorr-Cetina with Bruegger (2002) is one of several who explore what space becomes for electronic traders glued to their screens. Wellman (2001; Wellman and Haythornwaite 2002) points out that the whole new world of computer-mediated communication, Internet and so on, has transformed the spatial scope of networking and thus of networks.

8.4.1. Localities

Locality is where social space must somehow be patched together with physical space or geography. Localities are—contrary to common sense--complex and confusing accomplishments of human social structure (cf. Durkheim 1915; Reid 1913; Rose 1960; Zeigler 1974). Social science theory has shied away from locality, except for specialized work by some geographers (Haggett, Cliff, and Frey 1977). To meld social with geographic concepts is very hard, as Koopmans emphasized (1957) within economic theory, and as Alonso demonstrated (1964). In the words of L. J. Sharpe (1979, p 18): "Indications of a spatial variation of power has been treated almost as if all politics could exist on the head of a pin . . . scientific rationalism has a tendency toward uniformity and centralization." Social theorists themselves have noted that the vertical as an earthly dimension is a potent metaphor in social stratification (see, e.g., Schwartz 1981).

In coming to grips with some social actions, a first step is to fix on locales for actors relative to each other within social spaces as well as physical space. Intuition teaches us that physical space provides metaphors for social relations, which then themselves influence perceptions of space. Baxandall earlier (1975) made this vivid through his comparison of Renaissance painting conventions in Italian cities with their emerging commercial routines. He shows how relations shape and are shaped by the newly crisp conventions of placement in art works.

The massive study of the Florentine Renaissance cited in previous chapters expands on this theme:

> The cognitive problem posed by the relational packages of heterogeneous alters and ties is one of establishing comparability (Espeland and Stevens 1998)--how to turn a collection into a portfolio. In accounting, organizing piles of transactions with the same people into current accounts was a crucial step in constructing structured arrays of "customers" and measuring interaction with them in terms of relational credit and profit. In painting, organizing tiles on the floor spatially in simulated three dimensions was a crucial step in clarifying narrative relations among characters on the canvas and also movement between them and the viewer. In patrilineage families, discussing and debating the complicated twists and turns of Roman history was a crucial step in teaching themselves the duties and interaction skills of family members toward each other (Alberti 1971). In each of these Florentine examples, the cognitive function of abstract space was to project heterogeneous social reality onto lower-dimensional arrays of representations that revealed projected lines of movement for oneself. (Padgett and McLean 2006b)

All social action sites in physical space-time. We live among irregular mixings between biophysical space-times and social action. Social action can be modeled as generating its own bubbles of space-time that are somehow adjoined to the biophysical. Such bubbles cannot be personal, one to each individual identity, because they come as networks with populations and nest in levels from disciplines.

It is not easy to tease out what is the more purely social aspect of space-times, wherein to construe action out of control efforts by identities. Every identity is giving some accounting for itself in ties with others, which leads to sets of stories. Different sets may generate and perceive different social spaces, and all depend upon and influence an ecological level, like any other phenomena on earth. Locality as a social construct implies some approximation to a partition of physical space in order to gain self-consistency in the social accounting of localities.

Locality has, over the ages, been the basis of government (Whitney 1970; Massey 2005). Locality seems important in economic realms across diverse periods as well. But the meaning of cities as wholes can be entirely different depending on the kind of localism:

> Basra grew from nothing to more than 200,000 inhabitants in 30 years in the 7th century. The merchant class of the great Islamic cities, of Cairo, Baghdad or Cordoba, was not indigenous as was the upper level of Western cities ... the lack of localism in the Islamic lands deprived the cities of commercial aggressiveness. (Postan and Rich 1987, p. 405)

Blockmodels and localities are two contrasting simplifications of social formations resulting from control struggles. Blockmodels ignore production. Blockmodeling is of formations as seen in purely social space. Sets of ties will be concatenated to suggest meshings with sets of stories. Localities, on the other hand, determine types of networks in terms of productions, weaving together sets of stories for the latter.

Locality is not a separate topic, but an outcome to be predicted and then carried through successive examples. Locality is a dependent variable, one requiring complex articulations within the theory. Localities are intersections between physical space and social networks, which are also embeddings. The main difficulty is modeling the uneasy mix between physical and social spaces required by locality as a construct.

This mix confounds interpretation in two general ways.

First, analogues to physical space confound the proper differentiation of levels within social spaces. Sorting out levels is a difficult puzzle, bound up with stories for disciplines. Only a few classic studies are clear on such levels in interaction with the localities; for example, Sayles and Strauss (1967) on the local trade union.

Localities come into recognition from inducing ritual about physical space in terms of social spaces. This confounds theorists. A recent essay by an urban planner expresses the issues well, using the term *center* for locality:

> Let us define a *generalized center* as a marked place in space or time. . . . Surrounding a center is a structure or pattern that "supports" it and points to it. Centers imply inhomogeneity . . . and in the inhomogeneity there is either fall-off toward the boundary, or the periphery arises from (has its source in) the center . . . centers are often accidents that become facts: chance fluctuations . . . residents claim there is a downtown . . . the historian discovers a primitive act . . . an act of founding . . . a center exists only because it is developed around. . . . Critics need authors and styles to organize the works of art they study . . . one is looking for marked points in space, or in time, or in a collection from which and around which all complexity evolves . . . we can create differentiates of quality, through advertising and art, that make a place locationally justified just because it possesses those created differentiates. (Krieger 1984, pp. 1251–57)

Locality raises difficult subtleties of valuation, as well as of meaning. Locality embeds new levels. Localities build out of story-sets constrained around value.

Localities are constructed out of social networks and physical productions by the suppression of stories about actors. Not all stories correspond to the network etiology of social space. Some stories seem wedded to creating artificial localities—that is, they seem wedded to categorical attributions to sets of actors.[10] Such an account is, however, against the grain of the actual processes. The earliest story-form, the epic, was closer to real network etiology (e.g., Scholes and Kellogg 1966).

That theorists may become confounded by locality appears in the use made of ostensibly obvious geography to solve difficulties with social integration. Nadel (1957) is trenchant in arguing the need to model within theory—in his case, role theory—how the practical person of everyday puts together the disparate social worlds in which s/he has to live. From a philosophical view (cf. Kolb 1986), the only universal claims we can make are local performances, and it is a tempting solipsism to claim these as the interpenetrations of social worlds. Locality, whether in space or time, is used as a folk-surrogate for role integration.

Halevy (1974) gives a classic account of an attempted opposite structuring, of reliance upon local notables to guide and legitimate a whole

---

[10] Much survey research on attitudes presupposes and indeed contributes to such attributions.

system, the nascent Third Republic of France. This was a system in extreme shock, following collapse of the Second Empire in the Franco-Prussian war. Given complete authority, local notables in the aftermath of turbulence were utterly unable to cope. They needed to supply coherent story accounts to a larger population, which is exactly antithetical to their being local notables.

8.4.2. Structuralist versus Atomic

The mixing of geography with social spaces as locality confounds theory in a second general way. This second way is the conundrum of structuralist versus atomic hypotheses, already brought up in the previous chapter. The structuralist conjecture stakes out an extreme position, the antipodes to individualism, namely that all action is shaped mainly by the overall structure.

On the one hand, it is hard to deny that overall context or structure directly constrains and shapes action. This is true even more in social action than in physical systems, since there is a whole additional refraction of totality through perception and its embeddings in rhetorics, and culture, a refraction into multiple spaces. Concrete examples jog this sense:

> Italian history is essentially local history, especially since centralizing forces are conservative and anachronistic (the Holy Roman Empire). . . . Heterogeneity was the essence of the Italian scene; the development of so many centers of contrasting types—trading towns and industrial towns, bankers' towns and agrarian backwaters—cannot be reduced to a single scheme. Each type made some contribution to the complexion of the whole. . . . It is hardly possible to write a local history without at least some working hypothesis as to its relationship with a wider world, so much does the assessment of local manifestations depend on the way in which the general and normal development is envisaged. . . . Those parts of Italy which were effectively linked to the empire of Charlemagne through innumerable local variations follow a single pattern, while those parts which remained outside—the South, the islands and Venice—follow a course which is radically different. . . . By a gradual decline, the German Emperors in Italy passed from being effective though intermittent rulers to become the leaders of a faction until, in the end, they were merely the tools of factions. (Hyde, 1966, pp. 8–9)

On the other hand, it is individual identities that generate the unpredictability at the core of history. And locality is not unrelated to identity: this also was in the Hyde account just quoted, though only implicitly.

The conundrum of structuralist versus atomic hypotheses mixes together boundary with locality issues. This can be shown vividly in a context of religious institution:

> Augustine's theology ... conceives of an (priestly) order almost exclusively with reference to the individual who exercises it. ... Such a view would have been impossible to hold but for the virtual breakdown of the old, jealously corporate notion of the local Church and its local ministry during the two preceding generations. Augustine's theory is in itself a proof that by circa a.d. 400 that idea was extinct as a living force. (Dix 1947, p. 286)

And in a still earlier period:

> Earliest Christianity began as a renewal movement within Judaism brought into being through Jesus ... after ad 70 Pharisaism gained the upper hand in Judaism, and the Christians were excommunicated. ... Wandering charismatics were the decisive spiritual authorities in the local communities, and local communities were the indispensable social and material basis for the wandering charismatics. Both owed their legitimation and existence to their relationship to the transcendental bearer of revelation. It was the homeless wandering charismatics who handed on what was later to take independent form as Christianity ... the local groups of sympathizers remained within the framework of Judaism ... entangled in the old situation. ... Wandering prophets and teachers were still the decisive authorities at the time of the Didache (in the first half of the second century). ... Their superiors were still the "apostles," who were allowed to stay no more than three days in one place. All these wandering charismatics had a higher reputation than local ministers. (Theissen 1982, p. 7)

Localities are spatial analogues to groupings of events in time. Sheer locale in physical space becomes locality only after considerable interpretive work. Anthropological studies have made this clear (e.g., Firth 1957; Fortes 1945; Hart and Pilling 1960; Rose 1960; Spencer and Gillen 1927; Warner 1937).

8.4.3. Events

On a basis of routine, not emergency, accounting conventions are used at higher levels of business and government to generate streams of events that can be used to formulate decouplings of actors in aid of control projects. Events are crafted into localities of explanation. Events are crucial in the realization and elaboration of projects of control, and of the accompanying decouplings and embeddings of production from disciplines. But there is no definite architecture, no overarching system explicitly articulated, in which one can continue to reach through and get action.

Corporate actors shape and are shaped by events. But events themselves may become actors. Eric Foner argues, on a macro scale, the need in us as observers, but implicitly also of the actors in the era of his studies, for a great deal of framing by distinctive events to build social reality, and a social calendar:

> The Civil War had by the end of the 1970's been relegated to the wings . . . [this was] more than a reflection of the overall crisis of academic history in the 1970s. . . . Traditional emphasis on institution and events, politics and ideas was superseded by a host of "social" concerns . . . (new) groups looked to history for a "useable past." . . . As historians intruded into the intimate lives of past generations of Americans, public events and institutions receded into the background. No alternative theory of politics emerged. . . . The Civil War is unintelligible if divided into the various subcategories of contemporary historical inquiry. . . . Problems appeared and disappeared, events simply happened, with no sense of systematic relations or underlying causes. (1980, p. 3)

Translate Foner's eloquent plaint into one for reconstitution of identity, identity construed at a higher level and of greater scope as corporate actor. Confederacy and Union in his account are events as identities of large scope.

As Foner consciously makes clear, historians are social technicians who, ex post, impose a macro story on hunks of social space-in-time which, as seen by a Martian, would be a mere picaresque jumble. Journalists are the analogue in relation to current events, joining historians in discounting ambiguity (Gans 1979; Schudson 1989). Administrators, when general managers, are the line-operation version, with the much more difficult task of suppression **ex ante** (Vancil 1979).[11] And the philosopher Ricoeur argues (1988) that narrative constitutes social time and thus that narrative is the bridge between sidereal and phenomenological time, so one could say that he considers stories as actors in some sense.

8.4.4. Pragmatics of Space-Time

Space operationalizes distance and closeness, which we all find indispensable for orienting ourselves, as well as orienting our analyses. Second, location is the resulting matrix for closeness, and is at the same

---

[11] See the section entitled "General Management" in chapter 7.

time the matrix for dynamics, which embeds time in space for and from a system of actors. Third, space-time can be made to represent and explain context.

Developing a public account for how we view and locate ourselves even in physical space has proved very difficult. In the European histories of engineering and art, satisfactory perspective renderings in plane projections were achieved only a handful of centuries ago. In the modern psychology of perception, Gibson (1950, 1979; and see Restle 1980) and Shepard (1984, 1987, 1989) still are wrestling with these problems.

It should be no surprise that social scientists are as yet groping toward analogous effectiveness in communicable representations of how we see ourselves in, and operate in, social space(s), which in any case cannot be divorced from representations in biophysical space, where production resides. Both modes of network, multiplex and special, do share in a continuing elision of ordinary geographical space. In whatever portrayals finally prove effective for them, social spaces will be multiple in an extreme, with very fragmentary and scrappy topology.

Guidance can be sought (as sketched in chapter 1) in mathematics and also in mathematical formulations of natural science. A science need not construe even physical space either as unique or as a matter of human phenomenology. Hypothetical spaces are vital in natural sciences too, such as a two-dimensional Cartesian space for physical phenomena, in which, for example, wave motion would be impossible (Weyl 1949). And abstract spaces, so-called state spaces, are constructed, to be at hand for particular processes and problems. These state spaces are aids to our perceptions rather than putative arenas of causal contingency.[12] The only state spaces that prove indispensable are those adduced from already successful portrayals of cause.[13] We can learn from principles of perception that spaces are as much the *consequences* as the "real" arenas of causal action.

Boundaries are matters of context, as also are units of measurement. Social organization exhibits historical particularities, but with a continuing tendency toward self-similarity across levels and scope in bio-

---

[12] Some natural scientists also are dismissive of spatial texture; for example, the biologist Gold who has it that (1977, p. 49) "[a] dimension is a label attached to a number that gives the information 'number of what.'"

[13] In the spirit of this dictum are some exploratory efforts in sociology such as those concerning social mobility (e.g., Sorokin 1927; Hauser and Featherman 1977) or social influence (e.g., Levine 1972; Mizruchi and Schwartz 1988). Thermodynamics comes close to being a model for this dictum, with the prior causal discoveries being those by Count Rumford (Brown 1962; Huang 1963; Ziman 1979). Furthest from the causal are "spaces" generated in routine factor analysis, psychometrics, and much econometrics (Leamer 1978).

physical space-time. Only where control efforts jointly yield a discipline are these levels clearly discriminable. However, "level" in this case is well defined only with respect to a given discipline, there being no assured mechanism to separate distinct levels as aggregates. Even the juncture between biophysical and social is somewhat arbitrary. And there is no mechanism for locking social space-times into some unified totality, except vaguely through their ricocheting off biophysical space-time.

Thus arises a chicken-and-egg **conundrum**: disciplines and ties generate social space-times, the shape(s) of which however predetermine(s) what disciplines and ties there can be. This is the principal difficulty of analysis for social structure and process.

There is an auxiliary self-similarity **conundrum**—if approximately separate levels coagulate, will the "laws" be the same at each "level"?[14] The conundrum can be approached analytically: for example, one may conjecture that arenas tend to come in larger contexts where self-similarity obtains, leading to the hieratic style explicated in chapter 7 and self-consistency across levels and time. One can draw parallels to, as well as divergences from, the contexts of natural science, spaces. Attempts to specify self-consistent social space lead to conundrums. These conundrums become paradoxes if not dealt with explicitly.

Let us recapitulate the constituents: any two disciplines may be joined by a tie or ties, so that networks cross between as well as within species, and each discipline has a story-set; and, there are further possible concatenations of embeddings of embeddings among these identity-disciplines, connected by networks of various types of tie. The resulting social space-times are storied and are catenations of incidences, and of embeddings and other operations. The problematics are set by operations unlike those of homogeneous physical space-times.

The whole ensemble must survive being buffeted by chance junctures with work and in play. Sassen (2006, chapter 8) among others argues that the explosive growth in global Internet and other digital communication is leading to new construals of territoriality in terms of mixed spatio-temporal "assemblages." Much the same construals can be discerned even without reference to the Internet (Brenner 2004).

---

[14] For example, in the study of change in investment banking by Eccles and Crane (1988), the shift from sole-bank model for client to competitive multitie model also proved to be associated within each bank with decentralization to network form and thus to "flat" organization. But, by contrast, in Key's (1945) study of Southern politics, the South as a whole region held as a monolith in national politics despite radically different, and differently decentralized, party systems across the constituent states.

8.5. Context Leached into Culture

Some theory has culture standing on its own and yet impacting ongoing processes. I insist that social and cultural are intertwined all the way. This section expands on that insistence rather than critiquing particular freestanding theories of culture. It offers a complement to Swidler (1986) with more abstract and general topics.

Take as the first case, theories themselves, which are also inhabitants of our sociocultural world built from netdoms and identities. Each theory tends to erode others. For example, rational choice theory erodes cultural theorizing from values, but so do less sharp-edged theories. The erosion is assessed by Rieder (1990, p. 204) as follows:

> Recasting moral values and rhetorics in terms of selection dilemmas does not entirely undermine the explanatory status of culture. But notions of repertoire and use, by diminishing culture as a constraint, tend in this direction. To the extent that culture is rendered malleable, its particular manifestation "selected out" by situational contingencies and strategic purpose, it loses its coercive quality. Culture becomes a dependent variable, fickle and lambent, that changes in rhythm with the structural realities that impinge on it and the changing incentives and costs that accompany them.

Much the same erosion might seem to follow from my approach. My point here is that the erosion itself can get enacted only through tangible mobilizations and arguments with no universal meta-theory of what theory survives.

8.5.1. Everyday Roles and Nadel's Paradox

The child will have some role in each of several frames. Take, first, the playground example of chapter 1, where roles could include braggart, bully, docile follower, and the like. Separately, in the home, some menu of roles is available for the child vis-à-vis parents and siblings. Separately again, among gangs, there may be task leader, social leader, follower, and so on (Whyte 1943). These roles sort out in tension from some familiar complementarities into frames. Everyday roles were earlier discussed late in chapter 2.

The point is that there is no phenomenological basis for discriminating roles within some frame until other role frames are activated. One will not be seen as a parent until one is also a workmate or scholar or tribesman; you will not be seen as a playmate until you are also a schoolboy; and so on. This is true even though analysts can infer such roles from structural equivalence patterns on just one network.

One looks for a set of positions within network data as a bridging structure among distinct role frames. The social position of a particular child does not lie in any one such role in a frame of hers, but rather in her being recognized at the same time in a role in other frames. The same position appears as an identity in each of several network populations. Each position can be seen as a bracket specifying which role is selected in each frame and to which blocks in that network population. Such a position may have some tag associated with it, such as, for the child, teacher's pet, butt of ridicule, or big shot.

A particular position thus brings together a set of distinct identities, each possibly supported by a discipline, from distinct network populations. They are brought together into a more-or-less integrated whole. This whole might be equated to the personality or to the scene in everyday usage.

This is my answer to the puzzle posed by the anthropological theorist Nadel (1957). He had provided field reports (1946) well beyond tribal in scope, and he tried to model a whole such social universe in terms of positions across roles in frames. His was a precursor to the Luhmann and Bourdieu visions. He made reference to only a few very general positions; so the question of their being gathered along networks or into disciplines did not arise. The remaining puzzle for him was what sort of diffuse structuring of the larger context might nonetheless be observed and shown to be essential.

The puzzle is only a special case of what DiMaggio has called the Nadel paradox:

> Each relationship contains unique features which render it incomparable to the others. . . . How then can we extract . . . any embracing order while still paying attention to these qualitative characteristics. (DiMaggio 1992, p. 119)

DiMaggio argues, as I do in this book, that one cannot get valid results by pursuing separately just a formalized, abstract reckoning, or on the contrary, by just giving attention to descriptive richness. I think this is an underestimate because there is a third view in terms of situations that must be encompassed. The situational is the central focus for Mische, as I report in chapter 7, and my six chapters are the effort to capture main features of social process, as theory that is robust across the situational. A fourth view, as to flesh-and-blood humans, which I argued against earlier in this chapter, is also in Nadel's thinking, and I will return to that in the next section.

For now, let me return to and expand on the original role puzzle. To elaborate into role frames carries a price, which is the necessity to somehow integrate location in one coherent role frame with locations in other role frames from different network populations, who tell other sets of stories. Positions are to accomplish this. How, Nadel might ask, can an individual make sense out of being, say, father and professor and Yankees fan and taxpayer in different countries? How can one make sense of a context of others, each of whom has quite different combinations of, and different overlaps to, yet others' combinations of roles in frames, from a very large menu of role frames? How is such a common sense to be supported by some context?

Nadel's puzzle, as he expounded with force and lucidity, becomes more severe as identities individually have more options regarding role frames. And individuals do have some options in all save the most involute tribes. Nadel fell back on a generalization of *institution* beyond its standard definition in dictionaries. Nadel distinguished the political realm, economic realm, and so on: these are much like the functional subsystems of Luhmann's analysis.

Nadel then argued that certain generalized resources, such as money and power, were what correlated role frames, joined in a few abstract positions across realms. He failed to produce a plausible system. Each of the present chapters can be seen as one partial solution to Nadel's puzzle. Nadel bypassed the whole idea of some sorts of middle-range orders embracing network populations, as well as the disciplines that can be built from them. Yet it seems clear that no larger ordering that is deterministic in either cultural assertion or social arrangement could sustain and reproduce itself across so many and such large network populations as in the current world. Some sort of stochastic environment must be assumed and requires modeling. Chapter 4 introduced the construct of style as suitable to capturing kinds of contextual orderings in a stochastic environment for networks and disciplines among disparate identities.

It was a mistake for Nadel to take individual persons for granted as universals and just build from them.

Let us turn to another case.

8.5.2. Kinship in a Sinhalese Village

An obscure village in Sri Lanka was a crucial testing field for the overthrow of well-behaved kinship theory bequeathed by his elders that was plotted by Sir Edmund Leach (1961). Leach, despite his brilliance, shown already in the even more famous *Political Systems of Highland Burma* that he researched while a guerilla warrior during World War II, could not overthrow the opposition; he just cast the latest stone in an unending dialogue between behaviorist, statistical theory and overarching systemic value theories. He did not have concepts that were adequate, because the measurement ideas were too crude to suggest or sustain such.

Enter Michael Houseman and Douglas White with "Network Mediation of Exchange Structures" (1998). They did not yet have the power of the later cut-graph theory of embedded cohesion (see chapter 4), but they already mounted innovative dual ways of portraying networks, with ties as nodes and nodes as ties. And the crux is that they had Leach's data of unmatched rigor and coverage and quality—with many dimensions to the networks, notably land ownership and its changes in relation to marriages.

Houseman and White treated gingerly Leach's obsession to wipe out his elders, with numerous admiring references, accompanied by quiet statements about where the evidence really pointed. The general direction of the evidence was toward Bourdieu's habitus, as Brudner and White (1997) had suggested a year earlier in studying similar topics, but for an Austrian village. At that point, Brudner and White had not yet reached the explicit modeling of network cohesion and embeddedness achieved in the next decade (see chapter 4). Bourdieu's habitus can be seen as an intermediate stance between notions of explicit cultural rule systems on the one hand and Leach's rather vague "statistical" structure, which he had as emergent without any explicit brief.

Even without the later technical advances, Houseman and White made a strong case for the emergence of a manifest structure of two sides, often called moieties. The structure is manifest but not enshrined with labels and explicit theory. The point is that this line of work points to erasing false dichotomies with theoretical shoutings back and forth, in favor of explicit portrayal. Then possibilities arise for theorizing what sorts of outcomes should be expected, and how they might change under other circumstances: that is proper theorizing.

What about the Lazega study of a law firm, which we put parallel earlier to Douglas White's work on modeling to context? Probably much the same intermediate position between explicit rule and implicit network emergence will hold. A problem is that the very different technical analytics used by Lazega are not as conducive, it seems to me, to tangible and adjustable network presentation.

8.5.3. Culture as Basis for Social Science

In the snakeskin-shedding view of culture, social formation must at any given time have a carapace, which, however, is outgrown and drops off as a new one comes into place. Antiquarians and aesthetes and dictionary-compilers and university librarians cherish and collect the snakeskins. But surely a culture should be seen as a continuously interacting population of interpretive forms articulated within some social formation.

In Swidler's terms (1986), culture is made up of practices. One can view culture as the interpretive contexts for all social actions so that it can be computed as an envelope from them, as well as shaped by them. Effective practices to that end have evolved that precede, preface, and anticipate social sciences.

Kinship was the first social science. All the paradoxes and difficulties are there, in various peoples' own native constructions (cf. e.g., Spencer and Gillen 1927) of their kinship edifices, constructions in formats that mix observation with analysis and with proclamation. Only a few of these formats have proved able to sustain and reproduce themselves. This first science was lost for a while. Its phenomena are too close and too involving to encourage recognition of abstract similarities in cultural content. Lewis Henry Morgan (re)discovered kinship;[15] it may well be the only preexisting and discoverable social science.

Social scientists may see challenges to their authority from ordinary persons, but only with respect to the phenomenology of everyday life, which most social scientists would concede to them anyway. Yet, even this can confound and obfuscate research. "Networks" are the outstanding example today. Ambitious MBAs, hippies, executives, social workers, journalists—they all agree on the importance of networks. Since sources that diverse all urge the advantages of "networking" as social process, the term must confound many interpretations, and thus it confounds much social science fieldwork attempting to use network terms and concepts.

But, one may object, these laypersons use common sense, so their joint endeavors surely cannot confound codified scientific results regarding more recondite aspects of social organization. Since the laity are no status threat, surely they cannot be besting scientists! However, the "laity" includes the jurists, includes the bankers, includes all sorts of groups and persons preeminent over social scientists within existing social stratification. And sometimes, perhaps, the preeminence exists because their professions' and professional insights are superior, especially for the aspects in which they specialize, whether or not a parallel specialty science, a political science or an economics, is split off.

Whatever the outcome of any such particular argument, the very discussion concedes the basic point, since the discussion is, literally, in lay terms. The language of the present work embeds, and makes as invisible as they are effectual, an enormous array of assumptions about social action. Social science is impregnated with existing culture.

Actual social orders and cultures are much messier and more interesting than are particular rhetorics, or embeddings of rhetorics into

---

[15] Consult Trautmann (1987) for a recent history.

Utopian schematics. But even Utopian schematics do capture aspects of how actors try to perceive their social context, and these schematics do so across a wide range of historical contexts. Berman (1983) has argued an extreme form of this view, in his sweeping canvas of the evolution of legal systems for the whole Western era since the emergence of the papacy. The point is that continual reshaping of meanings to maintain the semblance of coherence in social action requires explicit and reliable interconnections between the framing of sets of stories and the structure of institutions. It is these mappings that make rhetoric possible.

Conscious and proclaimed cultures are sets of rhetorics that encapsulate attempts, often inept, at regularizing social spaces from the perspective of different populations and institutions. Hegemony (Williams 1977; Keohane 1984) reflects the success of a family of such attempts that exhibits some coordination and expertise in an autochthonous theory. The stochastic mode of perception, analysis, and reality is omnipresent just because of the feebleness of culture's hold on the patchy social realities that erect and reerect themselves upon continuing biosocial realities. Hegemony nonetheless testifies to the importance of some order being imposed: the transposable order that is supplied by basis sets of story-lines that can account for whatever happens. Social science theories are recent attempts at hegemony.

The task of social science is to construe boundaries and environments. All analytical sciences work from boundaries: boundary conditions are preeminent. Social analysis is peculiar only in that it must seek out the generation of its own spaces as part of the environment. Since the spaces are plural—and irregular, temporary and ill-connected to boot—the boundaries are difficult to find, subtler than in other sciences, as we saw at this chapter's beginning.

Completion of the task requires systematic measurement and modeling, both of which may be confounded by the existing local insight of elites and professionals. There is a tension between the stories produced and ties counted by a social formation, and the analytic technique believed by the analyst. Padgett and Ansell put the conundrum well when they set out to clarify their general position on the interrelation of social attributes and social networks:

> Obviously (contra some occasionally overstated polemics by social network aficionados), **we do not believe that social attributes are irrelevant:** The particular way in which the Medici recombined social attributes through networks is the heart of the story here. What we object to is the arranging of attributes discretely in groups or spatially as grids. ... Of course actors in the system, as well as researchers, do exactly these cluster-

ing procedures mentally when they analyze their own social structure; this is what "boundedly rational" cognitive classifications are all about. But there is a widely underappreciated gap between these macro cognitive (or "cultural") operations and micro-behavioral "local action," taken by concrete individuals in very particular, heterogeneous and often cross-pressured circumstances. Simplifying social reality into homogeneous subsets "with common interests" rips individuals out of their (often contradictory) multiple network contexts and obscures the very heterogeneity and complexity of which organizations like the Medici party are constructed. (1993, n. 38, p. 1285)

The hardest task will be to unravel the constitutions of the numerous social times that exist. This requires overcoming the lingering astrology in our thinking—the astrology that leads us to merely consult watches, or centuries, to infer social order.[16] Only Marxism among classical strands of theory has a central role for problematics and dynamics of time and thence of development in the large. And only Pareto among classic theorists has a central role for attempts at control that go beyond discipline, go beyond social routine and so turn on timing.

Most early theorists were not able to convert sketches and conjectures on social organization into operational measures and theory. There were heroic attempts, from Marx through Ricardo (consult Morishima 1973) and on through Sorokin (1927), as well as some measures and models still current, mainly of Pareto (1966). Further steps in this direction are timely, steps that presuppose not only these earlier contributions but also the enormously expanded range of measurement, of mathematics, and of analogy from natural sciences, which are available today.[17] It is especially important to operationalize the terms that have been heretofore primitive, mythical, invisible—such as *society* and *person*. Burt, in a work (1992a) quoted in chapter 5, has shown the many payoffs from full operationalization, there in a software package.

This reasoning can, of course, be extrapolated to natural sciences. The living out of some particular field of science is as an invisible college, which is to say as a style. But the specificity of a science is that it aims

---

[16] It is a vain presupposition that the watches on our wrists give us "the" time that orders social life in some self-evident way. There are leads in Abbott (1983, 1984).

[17] Modern analytic and quantitative techniques can be applied both to existing native accountings and to data freshly garnered. These techniques can yield answers to questions and support for conjectures, but explicit formal models will be called for. One can use stochastic processes, for example, to model bruises from ties as triggers of identities. Combinatorial and stochastic analyses can also model the cognitive processes implicated in the generation of stories. Citations to examples of computations have been woven into the text. See Rapoport (1953) for a philosophic overview.

toward and defers to two special rhetorics, called theory and an experimental paradigm that prescribes the relation of the living to the theory. There are levels: these rhetorics for a particular field are held to embed into higher-order versions for more encompassing fields. Realm is embedded into more embracing realm.

I will end with a trenchant summary statement by Sharon Hays:

> I argue that social structure consists of *two* central, interconnected elements: systems of social relations and systems of meaning. Systems of social relations consist of patterns of roles, relationships, and forms of domination according to which one might place any given person at a point on a complex grid that specifies a set of categories running from class, gender, race, education, and religion, all the way to age, sexual preference, and position in the family. Systems of meaning are what is often known as culture, including not only the beliefs and values of social groups, but also their language, forms of knowledge, and common sense, as well as the material products, interactional practices, rituals, and ways of life established by these. While not reducible to systems of social relations, culture matches the other central structure of social life in its power, its patterning, its durability, and its collective and transcendent nature. If one wants to understand the resilient patterns that shape the behavior of any individual or group of individuals, *both* the cultural and the relational milieu must be taken into account. (Hays 1994)

REFERENCES

Abbott, Andrew. 1981. "Status and Status Strain in the Professions." *American Journal of Sociology* 86:819–36.

———. 1983. "Sequences of Social Events: Concepts and Methods for the Analysis of Order in Social Processes." *Historical Methods* 16:129–47.

———. 1984. "Event Sequence and Duration: Colligation and Measurement." *Historical Methods* 17:129–47.

———. 1988. *The System of Professions*. Chicago: University of Chicago Press.

———. 1994. "Review of 'Identity and Control.' " *Social Forces* 72:895–901.

———. 1999. *Department and Discipline: Chicago Sociology at One Hundred*. Chicago: University of Chicago Press.

———. 2001. *Chaos of Disciplines*. Chicago: University of Chicago Press.

Abell, Peter. 1987. *Social Syntax*. Oxford: Clarendon Press.

Agha, Asif. 1993. "Grammatical and Indexical Conventions in Honorific Discourse." *Journal of Linguistic Anthropology* 3:131–63.

Alberti, Leon Battista. 1971. *The Albertis of Florence: Leon Battista Alberti's Della Famiglia*. Lewisburg, PA: Bucknell University Press.

Allison, Graham T. 1971. *Essence of Decision*. Boston: Little, Brown.

Alonso, William. 1964. *Location and Land Use: Toward a General Theory of Land Rent*. Cambridge, MA: Harvard University Press.

Anderson, Perry. 1974. *Lineages of the Absolutist State*. London: New Left Books.

Anheier, Helmut K., Jürgen Gerhards, and Frank P. Romo. 1995. "Forms of Capital and Social Structure in Cultural Fields: Examining Bourdieu's Social Topography." *American Journal of Sociology* 100:859–903.

Antal, F. 1965. *Florentine Painting and Its Social Background: The Bourgeois Republic before Cosimo de Medici's Advent to Power: XIV and Early XV Centuries*. London: Routledge.

Arnoldi, Jakob. 2006. *Frames and Screens: The Reduction of Uncertainty in Electronics Derivatives Trading*. Institut fur Soziologie, Ludwig-Maximilians Universität München.

Arrow, Kenneth J., and Frank H. Hahn. 1971. *General Competitive Analysis*. San Francisco: Holden-Day.

Ashford, Douglas E. 1982. *British Dogmatism and French Pragmatism*. London: G. Allen & Unwin.

Ashley, Richard K. 1980. *The Political Economy of War and Peace*. London: Pinter.

Aspers, Patrik. 2001. *Markets in Fashion: A Phenomenological Approach*. Stockholm: City University Press.

Atiyah, Michael. 1990. *The Geometry and Physics of Knots*. New York: Cambridge University Press.

Aubert, Vilhelm. 1965. *The Hidden Society*. Totowa, NJ: Bedminster Press.

Aubert, Vilhelm, and Harrison C. White. 1959. "Sleep: A Sociological Interpretation." *Acta Sociologica* 4:1–16 and 46–54.

Avrahampour, Yally. 2007. "A Relational and Performative Account of the Adoption of Equity Investment by U.K. Pension Funds." Ph.D. diss., Department of Sociology, Essex University.

Axelrod, Robert M. 1984. *The Evolution of Cooperation*. New York: Basic Books.

Azarian, G. Reza. 2006. *The General Sociology of Harrison White: Chaos and Order in Networks*. New York: Palgrave-Macmillan.

Badian, E. 1958. *Foreign Clientelae, 264–70 b.c.* Oxford: Clarendon Press.

———. 1985. *Publicans and Sinners: Private Enterprise in the Service of the Roman Republic*. Ithaca, NY: Cornell University Press.

Baecker, Dirk. 1997. "Interfaces—A View from Social Systems Theory." Universität Witten/Herdecke.

Bailes, Kendall E. 1978. *Technology and Society under Lenin and Stalin*. Princeton, NJ: Princeton University Press.

Bailey, Norman T. J. 1957. *The Mathematical Theory of Epidemics*. New York: Hafner.

———. 1982. *The Biomathematics of Malaria*. London: Griffin.

Bailey, Robert W. 1984. *The Crisis Regime: The MAC, the EFCB and the Political Impact of the New York City Financial Crisis*. Albany, NY: State University of New York Press.

Bailey, William, and Calvin Morrill. 1989. "The Skinhead Threat: Power, Identity and Social Style." Department of Communication, University of Arizona.

Baker, R. H. 1982. "Clientelism in the Post-revolutionary State: The Soviet Union." In *Private Patronage and Public Power*, edited by Christopher Clapham, pp. 36–52. London: Pinter.

Baker, Wayne. 1984. "The Social Structure of a National Securities Market." *American Journal of Sociology* 89:775–811.

———. 1990. "Market Networks and Corporate Behavior." *American Journal of Sociology* 96:589–625.

Bakhtin, Mikhail. 1968. *Rabelais and his World*. Cambridge, MA: MIT Press.

———. 1981. *The Dialogic Imagination: Four Essays*. Austin: University of Texas Press.

Baldassarri, Delia, and Peter S. Bearman. 2006. "Dynamics of Political Polarization." In *ISERP Working Paper 06–07*: Columbia University. Forthcoming in *American Sociological Review*.

Baldwin, David. 1978. "Power and Social Exchange." *American Political Science Review* 72:1229–42.

Baldwin, Mark P., Peter B. Rhines, Huei-Ping Huang, and Michael E. McIntyre. 2007. "The Jet-Stream Conundrum." *Science* 315:467–68.

Bales, Robert F. 1970. *Personality and Interpersonal Behavior*. New York: Holt-Rinehart-Winston.

Banfield, Edward C., and James Q. Wilson. 1963. *City Politics*. New York: Random House.

Bank, J. 1981. *Verzuiling: A Confessional Road to Secularization, Emancipation and the Decline of Political Catholicism, 1920–1970*. The Hague.

Barkey, Karen. Forthcoming. *Empire of Difference: The Ottomans in Comparative Perspective*. Cambridge: Cambridge University Press.

Barraclough, Geoffrey. 1946. *The Origins of Modern Germany.* Oxford: Blackwell.

Barth, Fredrik. 1965. *Political Leadership among Swat Pathans.* London: Athlone Press.

Battistella, Edwin L. 1996. *The Logic of Markedness.* New York: Oxford University Press.

Baxandall, Michael. 1975. *Painting and Experience in Fifteenth Century Italy.* New York: Oxford University Press.

———. 1980. *The Limewood Sculpture of Renaissance Germany.* New Haven, CT: Yale University Press.

Bearman, Peter S. 1985. "The Eclipse of Localism and the Formation of a National Gentry Elite in England, 1540–1640." Ph.D. diss., Department of Sociology, Harvard University.

———. 1991. "The Social Structure of Suicide." *Sociological Forum* 5:501–24.

———. 1993. *Relations into Rhetorics: Local Elite Social Structure in Norfolk, England 1540–1640.* New Brunswick, NJ: Rutgers University Press.

———. 1997. "Generalized Exchange." *American Journal of Sociology* 102: 1383–415.

———. 2005. *Doormen.* Chicago: University of Chicago Press.

Bearman, Peter S., Robert Faris, and James Moody. 1999. "Blocking the Future: New Solutions for Old Problems in Historical Social Science." *Social Science History* 23:501–35.

Bearman, Peter S., James Moody, and Robert Faris. 2002. "Networks and History." *Complexity* 8:61–71.

Bearman, Peter S., James Moody, and Katherine Stovel. 2004. "Chains of Affection: The Structure of Adolescent Romantic and Sexual Networks." *American Journal of Sociology* 110:44–91.

Becker, Carl L. 1932. *The Heavenly City of the Eighteenth-Century Philosophers.* New Haven, CT: Yale University Press.

Becker, Howard. 1982. *Art Worlds.* Berkeley: University of California Press.

Beik, William. 1985. *Absolutism and Society in Seventeenth-Century France: State Power and Provincial Aristocracy in Languedoc.* New York: Cambridge University Press.

Bellman, Richard. 1957. *Dynamic Programming.* Princeton, NJ: Princeton University Press.

Bendor, Jonathan, and Piotr Swistak. 1991. "The Evolutionary Stability of Cooperation." College Park: University of Maryland Collective Choice Center.

Bennett, S. 1979. *A History of Control Engineering, 1800–1930.* New York: Peter Peregrinus.

Berge, C. 1962. *The Theory of Graphs and Its Applications.* New York: Wiley.

Bergesen, Albert, Roberto M. Fernandez, and Chintamani Sahoo. 1987. "America and the Changing Structure of Hegemonic Production." In *America's Changing Role in the World System,* edited by Terry Boswell and Albert Bergesen. New York: Praeger.

Berkowitz, S.D. 1982. *An Introduction to Structural Analysis: The Network Approach to Social Research.* Toronto: Butterworths.

Berle, Adolf A., and Gardiner C. Means. 1932. *The Modern Corporation and Private Property.* New York: Macmillan.

Berman, Harold J. 1983. *Law and Revolution: The Formation of the Western Legal Tradition*. Cambridge, MA: Harvard University Press.

Bialer, Seweryn. 1987. "Gorbachev's Move." *Foreign Policy* 68:59–87.

Biber, Douglas, and Edward Finegan (Eds.). 1994. *Sociolinguistic Perspectives on Register*. New York: Oxford University Press.

Biddle, Bruce. 1986. "Recent Developments in Role Theory." *Annual Review of Sociology* 12:67–92.

Bilous, Frances R., and Robert M. Krauss. 1989. "Dominance and Accommodation in the Conversational Behaviors of Same-and Mixed-Gender Dyads." Department of Psychology, Columbia University.

Birkhoff, Garrett, and S. MacLane. 1953. *A Survey of Modern Algebra*. New York: Macmillan.

Bjerstedt, Ake. 1956. *Interpretations of Sociometric Choice Status*. Lund: Gleerup.

Blau, Peter M. 1964. *Exchange and Power in Social Life*. New York: Wiley.

Blau, Peter M., and Otis Dudley Duncan. 1967. *The American Occupational Structure*. New York: Wiley.

Bloch, R. Howard. 1977. *Medieval French Literature and Law*. Berkeley: University of California Press.

Boltanski, Luc. 1989. "A New Regime of Justification: The Project-oriented Cité." Department of Sociology, Stockholm University.

Boltanski, Luc, and Eve Chiapello. 2005. *The New Spirit of Capitalism*. New York: Verso.

Boltanski, Luc, and Laurent Thévenot. 1999. "The Sociology of Critical Capacity." *European Journal of Social Theory* 2:359–77.

Bonacich, Phillip. 1980. "The 'Common Structure Semigroup': An Alternative to the Boorman and White 'Joint Reduction.' " *American Journal of Sociology* 81:1384–1446.

———. 2003. "Cellular Automata for the Network Researcher." *Journal of Mathematical Sociology* 27:263–73.

Bonacich, Phillip, and Maureen J. McConaghy. 1979. "The Algebra of Blockmodeling." In *Sociological Methodology 1980*, edited by K. F. Schuessler, pp. 489–532. San Francisco: Jossey-Bass.

Bonilla, Frank. 1970. *The Failure of Elites*. Cambridge, MA: MIT Press.

Boorman, Scott A. 1974. "Island Models for Takeover by a Social Trait Facing a Frequency-Dependent Selection Barrier in a Mendelian Population." *Proceedings of the National Academy of Sciences* 71:2103–7.

———. 1975. "A Combinatorial Optimization Model for Transmission of Job Information through Contact Networks." *Bell Journal of Economics* 6:216–49.

Boorman, Scott A., and Paul R. Levitt. 1980. *The Genetics of Altruism*. New York: Academic Press.

Boorman, Scott A., and Harrison C. White. 1976. "Social Structure from Multiple Networks: Part II, Role Interlock." *American Journal of Sociology* 81: 1384–1446.

Bothner, Matthew S. 2003. "Cooperation and Social Influence: The Diffusion of a Sixth Generation Processor in the Global Computer Industry." *American Journal of Sociology* 108:1175–1210.

Bott, Elizabeth. 1957. *Family and Social Network: Roles, Norms, and External Relationships in Ordinary Urban Families*. London: Tavistock.

Boudon, Raymond. 1993. "Review of 'Identity and Control.' " *Contemporary Sociology* 22:311–14.

Bourdieu, Pierre. 1977. *Outline of a Theory of Practice*. Cambridge: Cambridge University Press.

———. 1980 [1990]. *The Logic of Practice*. Palo Alto: Stanford University Press.

———. 1984. *Distinction: A Social Critique of the Judgement of Taste*. Cambridge, MA: Harvard University Press.

———. 1996a. *The Rules of Art: Genesis and Structure of the Literary Field*. Stanford, CA: Stanford University Press.

———. 1996b. *The State Nobility: Elite Schools in the Field of Power*. Oxford, England: Polity Press.

———. 2000. *Pascalian Meditations*. Palo Alto: Stanford University Press.

Bower, Joseph L. 1986. *Managing the Resource Allocation Process: A Study of Corporate Planning and Investment*. Revised edition. Boston, MA: Harvard Business School Press.

Boyd, John P. 1991. *Social Semigroups: A Unified Theory of Scaling and Blockmodeling as Applied to Social Networks*. Fairfax, VA: George Mason University Press.

Bradach, Jeffery L., and Robert G. Eccles. 1989. "Price, Authority, and Trust: From Ideal Types to Plural Forms." *Annual Review of Sociology* 15:97–118.

Bradfield, Richard M. 1973. *A Natural History of Associations*, Vols. 1 and 2. London: Duckworth.

Brady, Thomas A. 1985. *Turning Swiss: City and Empire, 1450–1550*. Cambridge: Cambridge University Press.

Braudel, Fernand. 1982. *The Wheels of Commerce*. New York: Harper & Row.

Breiger, Ronald L. 1974. "The Duality of Persons and Groups." *Social Forces* 53:181–90.

———. 1990. "Social Control and Social Networks: A Model from Georg Simmel." In *Structures of Power and Constraint: Papers in Honor of Peter M. Blau*, edited by Craig Calhoun, Marshall W. Meyer, and W. Richard Scott. New York: Cambridge University Press.

———. 1991. *Explorations in Structural Analysis*. New York: Garland.

———. 2000. "A Tool Kit for Practice Theory." *Poetics* 27:91–115.

Breiger, Ronald L., Scott A. Boorman, and Phipps Arabie. 1975. "An Algorithm for Clustering Relational Data with Applications to Social Network Analysis and Comparison with Multidimensional Scaling." *Journal of Mathematical Psychology* 12:328–83.

Breiger, Ronald L., and James G. Ennis. 1979. "Personae and Social Roles: The Network Structure of Personality Types in Small Groups." *Social Psychology Quarterly* 42:262–70.

Brenner, Neil. 2004. *New State Spaces: Urban Government and the Rescaling of Statehood*. New York: Oxford University Press.

Bridenbaugh, Carl. 1962. *Mitre and Sceptre: Transatlantic Faiths, Ideas, Personalities, and Politics 1689–1775*. Oxford: Oxford University Press.

Briggs, Charles L., and Richard Baumann. 1992. "Genre, Intertextuality, and Social Power." *Journal of Linguistic Anthropology* 2:131–72.

Brilliant, Elinor. 1990. *The United Way.* New York: Columbia University Press.

Brillouin, Leon. 1962. *Science and Information Theory.* New York: Academic Press.

Brint, Stephen. 1992. "Hidden Meanings: Cultural Content and Context in Harrison White's Structural Sociology." *Sociological Theory* 10:194–208.

Brown, P., and S. C. Levinson. 1987. *Politeness: Some Universals in Language.* New York: Cambridge University Press.

Brown, Roger, and A. Gilman. 1960. "The Pronouns of Power and Solidarity." *In Style in Language,* edited by T. Seboek. Cambridge, MA: MIT Press.

Brown, Sanford C. 1962. *Count Rumford, Physicist Extraordinary.* London: Greenwood Press.

Brownstein, Larry. 1982. *Talcott Parsons' General Action Scheme: An Investigation of Fundamental Principles.* Cambridge: Schenkman.

Brudner, Lilyan A. and Douglas R. White. 1997. "Class, Property and Structural Endogamy: Visualizing Networked Histories" *Theory and Society.* 25: 161–208.

Bryson, Arthur, and Yu-Chi Ho. 1969. *Applied Optimal Control: Optimization, Estimation and Control.* Waltham, MA: Blaisdell.

Brzezinski, Z., and S. P. Huntington. 1964. *Political Power USA/USSR.* New York: Viking Press.

Bueno de Mesquita, Bruce, and David Lalman. 1992. *War and Reason.* New Haven, CT: Yale University Press.

Burns, Tom. 1991. *Erving Goffman.* New York: Routledge.

Burt, Ronald S. 1978a. "Cohesion versus Structural Equivalence as a Basis for Network Subgroups." *Sociological Methods and Research* 7:189–212.

———. 1978b. "Corporate Society: A Time Series Analysis of Network Structure." *Social Science Research* 4:271–328.

———. 1980. "Models of Network Structure." *Annual Review of Sociology* 6:79–141.

———. 1982. *Toward a Structural Theory of Action: Network Models of Social Structure, Perception and Action.* New York: Academic Press.

———. 1983. *Corporate Profits and Cooptation: Networks of Market Constraints and Directorate Ties in the American Economy.* New York: Academic Press.

———. 1987. "Social Contagion and Innovation: Cohesion versus Structural Equivalence." *American Journal of Sociology* 92:1287–1335.

———. 1988. "The Stability of American Markets." *American Journal of Sociology* 93:356–95.

———. 1990. "Kinds of Relations in American Discussion Networks." In *Structures of Power and Constraint: Papers in Honor of Peter M. Blau,* edited by Craig Calhoun, Marshall W. Meyer, and W. Richard Scott, pp. 411–51. New York: Cambridge University Press.

———. 1992a. *Structural Holes: The Social Structure of Competition.* Cambridge, MA: Harvard University Press.

———. 1992b. *Social Contagion.* New York: Columbia University Press.

———. 2000. "The Network Structure of Social Capital." *Research in Organizational Behavior* 22:345–423.

Bynum, Carolyn. 1987. *Holy Feast and Holy Fast: The Religious Significance of Food to Medieval Women*. Berkeley: University of California Press.

Bythell, Duncan. 1978. *The Sweated Trades: Outwork in Nineteenth Century Britain*. London: St. Martin's.

Calabresi, Guido. 1970. *The Costs of Accidents: A Legal and Economic Analysis*. New Haven, CT: Yale University Press.

Calhoun, Craig J. 1980. "Community: Toward a Variable Conceptualization for Comparative Research." *Social History* 5:105–29.

———. 1993. "Review of 'Identity and Control.'" *Contemporary Sociology* 22:314–18.

Calhoun, Craig J., Edward LiPuma, and Moishe Postone. 1993. *Bourdieu: Critical Perspectives*. Chicago: University of Chicago Press.

Calhoun, Craig J., Marshall W. Meyer, and W. Richard Scott (Eds.). 1990. *Structures of Power and Constraint: Papers in Honor of Peter M. Blau*. New York: Cambridge University Press.

Callon, Michel. 1998. *The Laws of the Market*. Oxford: Blackwell.

Cameron, Peter J. 1994. *Combinatorics: Topics, Techniques, Algorithms*. New York: Cambridge University Press.

Campenhausen, Hans von. [1955] 1969. *Ecclesiastical Authority and Spiritual Power in the Church of the First Three Centuries*. Stanford, CA: Stanford University Press.

Cannadine, David, and Simon Price. 1987. *Rituals of Royalty*. Cambridge: Cambridge University Press.

Caporaso, James A. 1989. "The State in a Domestic and International Context." Washington: Department of Political Science, University of Washington.

Carley, Kathleen M. 1986. "Knowledge Acquisition as a Social Phenomenon." *Instructional Science* 14:381–438.

———. 1993. "Coding Choices for Textual Analysis: A Comparison of Content Analysis and Map Analysis." In *Sociological Methodology*, edited by Peter Marsden. Oxford: Blackwell.

Carlton, Dennis W. 1979. "Vertical Integration in Competitive Markets under Uncertainty." *Journal of Industrial Economics* 27:189–209.

Carr, Raymond. 1966. *Spain, 1808–1939*. Oxford: Clarendon Press.

Carter, Anne. 1967. "Changes in the Structure of the American Economy, 1947 to 1958 and 1962." *Review of Economics and Statistics* 49:209–24.

———. 1976. *Structural Change in the American Economy*. Cambridge, MA: Harvard University Press.

Cerulo, Karen A. (Ed.). 2002. *Culture in Mind: Toward a Sociology of Culture and Cognition*. New York: Routledge.

Chafe, Wallace. 1994. *Discourse, Consciousness and Time*. Chicago: University of Chicago Press.

Chamberlin, Edward. [1933] 1962. *The Theory of Monopolistic Competition: A Reorientation of the Theory of Value*. Cambridge, MA: Harvard University Press.

Chandler, Alfred. [1962] 1969. *Strategy and Structure: Chapters in the History of the Industrial Enterprise*. Cambridge, MA: MIT Press.

Chanowitz, Benzion and Ellen J. Langer. 1980. "Knowing More (or Less) Than You Can Show: Understanding Control Through the Mindlessness/Mindfulness Distinction." In *Human Helplessness: Theory and Application*, edited by Martin E. P. Seligman and Judy Garber. New York: Academic Press.

Chase, Ivan. 1991. "Vacancy Chains." *Annual Review of Sociology* 17:133–54.

Chase, Ivan D. 1986. "Explanations of Hierarchy Structure." *Animal Behavior* 34:1265–67.

Chay, John, and Thomas E. Ross (Eds.). 1986. *Buffer States in World Politics*. Boulder CO: Westview.

Chiffoleau, Yuna, Fabrice Dreyfus, Catherine Laporte, and Jean-Marc Touzard. 2003. "La construction des régles and des normes des marchés agricoles de qualité: Une approche interdisciplinaire appliquée aux viticultures du Languidoc et des Bourgogne: Project 2003–2006." INRA-Montpelier et Université de Bourgogne.

Chrimes, S. 1952. *An Introduction to the Administrative History of Medieval England*. Oxford: Blackwell.

Christian, William A. 1981. *Local Religion in 16th Century Spain*. Princeton, NJ: Princeton University Press.

Church, William F. 1976. *Louis XIV in Historical Thought*. New York: Norton.

Cicourel, Aaron V. 1980. "Three Models of Discourse Analysis." *Discourse Processes* 3:101–31.

———. 1987. "Interpenetration of Communicative Contexts: Examples from Medical Encounters." *Social Psychology Quarterly* 50:217–26.

———. 1991."Formal Semantics, Pragmatics, and Situated Meaning." In *Pragmatics at Issue*, vol. 1, edited by J. Vershueren. Amsterdam: John Benjamins.

Clapham, Christopher S. (Ed.) 1982. *Private Patronage and Public Power: Political Clientelism in the Modern State*. London: Frances Pinter.

Cockcroft, Eva, J. Weber, and J. Cockcroft. 1977. *Toward a People's Art*. New York: Dutton.

Cohen, Joel. 1971. *Casual Groups of Monkeys and Men: Stochastic Models of Elemental Social Systems*. Cambridge, MA: Harvard University Press.

Cohen, Michael D., and J. G. March. 1974. *Leadership and Ambiguity: The American College President*. New York: McGraw-Hill.

Coleman, James S. 1957. *Community Conflict*. New York: Free Press–Bureau of Applied Social Research.

———. 1961. *The Adolescent Society*. New York: Free Press.

———. 1964. *An Introduction to Mathematical Sociology*. New York: Free Press.

———. 1973. *The Mathematics of Collective Action*. Chicago: Aldine.

———. 1990. *Foundations of Social Theory*. Cambridge, MA: Harvard University Press.

Coleman, James S., Elihu Katz, and Herbert Menzel. 1966. *Medical Innovation: A Diffusion Study*. Indianapolis: Bobbs-Merrill.

Collins, Randall. 1987. "Interaction Ritual Chains, Power and Property: The Micro-Macro Connection as an Empirically Based Theoretical Problem." In *The Micro-Macro Link*, edited by Jeffrey C. Alexander, Bernhard Giesen, Richard Munch, and Neil J. Smelser. Berkeley: University of California Press.

———. 2002. *Sociology of Philosophies*. Cambridge, MA: Harvard University Press.

Connolly, William E. 1987. *Politics and Ambiguity*. Madison: University of Wisconsin.

Corey, E. Raymond. 1978. *Procurement Management*. Boston: CBI.

Cornell, Stephen. 1988. *The Return of the Native: American Indian Political Resurgence*. New York: Oxford University Press.

Coulborn, Rushton (Ed.). 1956. *Feudalism in History*. Princeton, NJ: Princeton University Press.

Cozzens, Susan E. 1989. *Social Control and Multiple Discovery in Science: The Opiate Receptor Case*. Albany, NY: State University of New York Press.

Crain, Robert L., E. Katz, and D. Rosenthal. 1961. *The Politics of Community Controversy: The Fluoridation Decision*. Indianapolis: Bobbs-Merrill.

———. 1968. *The Politics of School Desegregation: Comparative Case Studies of Community Structure and Policy Making*. Chicago: Aldine.

Crane, Diana. 1972. *Invisible Colleges*. Chicago: University of Chicago Press.

———. 1987. *The Transformation of the Avant-Garde*. Chicago: University of Chicago Press.

Crapo, H. H., and G. C. Rota. 1970. *On the Foundations of Combinatorial Theory: Combinatorial Geometries*. Cambridge, MA: MIT Press.

Crowell, Richard H., and Ralph H. Fox. 1963. *Introduction to Knot Theory*. Boston: Ginn.

Crozier, Michel, and J. C. Thoenig. 1976. "The Regulation of Complex Organized Systems." *Administrative Science Quarterly* 21:547–70.

Cuff, Robert D. 1973. *The War Industries Board*. Baltimore, MD: Johns Hopkins University Press.

Culicover, Peter. 1987. "Situating Linguistics within Cognitive Science." Department of Linguistics, Ohio State University.

Culicover, Peter, and K. Wexler. 1977. "Some Syntactic Implications of a Theory of Language Learnability." In *Formal Syntax*, edited by P. Culicover, T. Wasow, and A. Akmajian. New York: Academic Press.

Culler, Jonathan. 1975. *Structuralist Poetics: Structuralism, Linguistics and the Study of Literature*. Ithaca, NY: Cornell University Press.

Dahl, Robert A., and Charles E. Lindblom. 1953. *Politics, Economics and Welfare*. New York: Harper.

Dalton, Melville. 1959. *Men Who Manage*. New York: John Wiley.

Dauber, Kenneth. 1992. "Object, Genre, and Buddhist Sculpture." *Theory and Society* 21:561–92.

Davies, Bronwyn, and Rom Harré. 1990. "Positioning: The Discursive Production of Selves." *Journal for the Theory of Social Behaviour* 20:43–63.

Davis, G. F., and H. R. Greve. 1997. "Corporate Elite Networks and Governance Changes in the 1980s." *American Journal of Sociology* 103:1–37.

Davis, James A. 1979. "Clustering and Structural Balance in Graphs." *Human Relations* 20:181–87.

De Boer, J., and G. E. Uhlenbeck (Ed.). 1962. *Studies in Statistical Mechanics*. Amsterdam: North-Holland.

De Nooy, Wouter. 2003. "Fields and Networks: Correspondence Analysis and Social Network Analysis in the Framework of Field Theory." *Poetics* 31:305–27.

De Nooy, Wouter. 2006. "Stories, Scripts, Roles and Networks." Rotterdam: Erasmus University.

De Roover, Raymond. 1966. *The Rise and Decline of the Medici Bank: 1397–1494*. New York: Norton.

De Swaan, Abram. 1988. *In Care of the State: Health Care, Education and Welfare in Europe and the USA in the Modern Era*. Oxford: Oxford University Press.

Dejoia, A., and A. Stenton. 1980. *Terms in Systemic Linguistics: A Guide to Halliday*. New York: St. Martin's.

Delaney, John. 1988. "Social Networks and Efficient Resource Allocation: Job Vacancy Allocation through Contacts." In *Social Structures: A Network Approach*, edited by Barry Wellman and S. D. Berkowitz. New York: Cambridge University Press.

Delli Carpini, Michael X. 1994. "Age and History: Generations and Sociopolitical Change." In *Political Learning in Adulthood*, edited by Roberta Sigel. Chicago: University of Chicago Press.

Desan, Philippe, Priscilla Ferguson, and Wendy Griswold. 1989. *Literature and Social Practice*. Chicago: University of Chicago Press.

Deutsch, Karl W. 1953. *Nationalism and Social Communication*. New York: Wiley.

Dibble, Vernon K. 1965. "The Organization of Traditional Authority: English County Government 1558–1640." In *Handbook of Organizations*, edited by James G. March. Chicago: Rand-McNally.

DiMaggio, Paul. 1982. "Cultural Entreprenuership in Nineteenth Century Boston." *Media Culture & Society* 4:33–50; 303–22.

———. 1987. "Classification in Art." *American Sociological Review* 52:440–55.

———. 1992. "Nadel's Paradox Revisited: Relational and Cultural Aspects of Organizational Structure." In *Networks and Organizations*, edited by Robert G. Eccles and N. Nohira. Boston: Harvard Graduate School of Business Administration Press.

———. 2002. "Why Cognitive and Cultural Sociology Needs Cognitive Psychology." In *Culture in Mind: Toward a Sociology of Culture and Cognition*, edited by Karen Cerulo. New York: Routledge.

DiMaggio, Paul, and Walter W. Powell. 1983. "The Iron Cage Revisited: Institutional Isomorphism and Collective Rationality in Organizational Fields." *American Sociological Review* 48:147–60.

Dix, G. 1947. "The Ministry in the Early Church." In *The Apostolic Ministry*, edited by K. E. Kirk. New York: Morehouse-Gorham.

Dixon, R.M.W. 1972. *The Dyirbal Language of North Queensland*. Cambridge Studies in Linguistics. New York: Cambridge University Press.

Dixon, R.M.W., and Barry J. Blake. 1983. *Handbook of Australian Languages*, vol. 3. Amsterdam: Benjamin.

Dodds, P. S., Roby Muhamad, and Duncan J. Watts. 2005. "An Experimental Study of Social Search and the Small World Problem." *Science* 8:827–29.

Donham, Wallace B. 1952. *Administration and Blind Spots*. Boston: Harvard Graduate School of Business Administration.

Doreian, Patrick, and Thomas Fararo. 1998. *The Problem of Solidarity: Theories and Models*. Amsterdam: Gordon and Breach.

Douglas, Mary. 1970. *Natural Symbols: Explorations in Cosmology.* New York: Pantheon Books.

Duby, Georges. 1980. *The Three Orders.* Chicago: University of Chicago Press.

Dumont, Louis. 1986. *A South Indian Subcaste: Social Organization and Religion of the Pramalai Kallar.* Oxford: Oxford University Press.

Duncan, Starkey. 1977. *Face-to-Face Interaction.* Hillsdale, NJ: Erlbaum Associates.

Duranti, Alessandro, and Charles Goodwin (Eds.). 1992. *Rethinking Context.* New York: Cambridge University Press.

Durkheim, Emile. 1915. *The Elementary Forms of the Religious Life.* London: Allen & Unwin.

———. 1947. *The Division of Labor in Society.* Glencoe, IL: Free Press.

———. [1897] 1997. *Suicide.* New York: Free Press.

Eagle, Nathan, Alex Pentland, and David Lazer. 2007. "Inferring Social Network Structure Using Mobile Phone Data." In submission.

Eccles, Robert G. 1981a. "Bureaucratic versus Craft Administration: The Relationship of Market Structure to the Construction Firm." *Administrative Science Quarterly* 26:449–69.

———.1981c. "The Quasifirm in the Construction Industry." *Journal of Economic Behavior and Organization* 2:335–57.

———. 1981d. "The Pursuit of Renascence under the Ambivalence Born of the Confluence of Nascence and Senescence." In *HBS Case Services.* Cambridge, MA: Harvard Business School Press.

———. 1985. *The Transfer Pricing Problem: A Theory for Practice.* Lexington, MA: Lexington Books.

Eccles, Robert G., and Dwight B. Crane. 1988. *Doing Deals: Investment Banks at Work.* Boston: Harvard Business School Press.

Eccles, Robert G., and Harrison C. White. 1986a. "Firm and Market Interfaces of Profit Center Control." In *Approaches to Social Theory,* edited by Siegwart Lindenberg, James S. Coleman, and Stefan Nowak. New York: Russell Sage.

———. 1986b. "Concentration for Control? Political and Business Evidence." *Sociological Forum* 1:131–58.

———. 1988. "Price and Authority in Inter-profit Center Transactions." *American Journal of Sociology, Supplement* 94:S17–S51.

Eckstein, Arthur Myron. 1987. *Senate and General: Individual Decision Making and Roman Foreign Relations, 264–197 b.c.* Berkeley: University of California Press.

Edling, Christopher. 1998. "Essays on Social Dynamics." Department of Sociology, Stockholm University.

Edmonds, Bruce, and David Hale. 2005. "Computer Simulation as Theoretical Experiment." *Journal of Mathematical Sociology* 29:209–32.

Ehrenreich, Barbara and John. 1970. *The American Health Empire.* New York: Vintage Books.

Eisenstadt, Shmuel N. 1956. *From Generation to Generation.* Glencoe, IL: Free Press.

Eisenstadt, Shmuel N., and Rene Lemarchand (Eds.). 1981. *Political Clientelism, Patronage and Development.* Beverly Hills, CA: Sage.

Emerson, Richard. 1962. "Power-Dependence Relations." *American Sociological Review* 27:31–40.

Emirbayer, M., and J. Goodwin. 1994. "Network Analysis, Culture, and the Problem of Agency." *American Journal of Sociology* 99:1411–54.

Emirbayer, Mustafa, and Ann Mische. 1998. "What Is Agency?" *American Journal of Sociology* 103:962–93.

Ennis, Philip. 1992. *The Seventh Stream: A History and Geography of Rock 'n' Roll to 1970.* Middletown, CT: Wesleyan University Press.

Erdos, Paul, and Joel Spencer. 1974. *Probabilistic Methods in Combinatorics.* New York: Academic Press.

Erikson, Emily. 2006. "The English in the East Indies: Economic Integration at the Birth of Capitalism." Ph.D. diss., Department of Sociology, Columbia University.

Erikson, Emily, and Peter S. Bearman. 2006. "Malfeasance and the Foundations for Global Trade: The Structure of English Trade in the East Indies, 1601–1833." *American Journal of Sociology* 111:195–230.

Erikson, Erik H. 1958. *Young Man Luther: A Study in Psychoanalysis and History.* London: Faber and Faber.

Espeland, Wendy N., and Mitchell L. Stevens. 1998. "Commensuration as a Social Process." *Annual Review of Sociology* 24:313–43.

Evans-Pritchard, E. E. 1940. *The Nuer.* Oxford: Clarendon Press.

Evans, Peter. 1975 "Multiple Hierarchies and Organizational Control." *Administrative Science Quarterly* 20:250–59.

———. 1979. *Dependent Development.* Princeton, NJ: Princeton University Press.

———. 1995. *Embedded Autonomy.* Princeton, NJ: Princeton University Press.

Evans, Rowland, and Robert Novak. 1966. *Lyndon B. Johnson: The Exercise of Power—A Political Biography.* New York: New American Library.

Fama, Eugene F., and Michael C. Jensen. 1983. "Separation of Ownership and Control." *Journal of Law and Economics* 26:301–25.

Fararo, Thomas J. 1973. *Mathematical Sociology.* New York: Wiley.

Fararo, Thomas J., and Carter Butts. 1999. "Advances in General Structuralism." *Journal of Mathematical Sociology* 29:1–65.

Faulkner, Robert R. 1971. *Studio Musicians.* Chicago, IL: Aldine.

———. 1983. *Music on Demand: Composers and Careers in the Hollywood Film Industry.* New Brunswick, NJ: Transaction Books.

Favereau, Olivier. 2005. "The Missing Piece in Rational Choice Theory." *Revue francaise de sociologie* 46:103–22.

Feenstra, Robert., and Gary Hamilton. 2006. *Emergent Economies, Divergent Paths: Economic Organization and International Trade in South Korea and Taiwan.* Cambridge: Cambridge University Press.

Feld, Scott. 1981. "The Focused Organization of Social Ties." *American Journal of Sociology* 86:1015–35.

Feller, William. 1968. *An Introduction to Probability Theory and Its Application.* New York: Wiley.

Ferguson, Priscilla P. 2005. "Eating Orders: Markets, Menus, and Meals." *Journal of Modern History* 77:679–700.

Findley, Carter V. 1980. *Bureaucratic Reform in the Ottoman Empire.* Princeton, NJ: Princeton University Press.

Fine, Ben, and Lawrence Harris. 1985. *The Peculiarities of the British Economy.* London: Lawrence & Wishart.

Fine, Gary A. 1979. "Small Groups and Culture Creation: The Idioculture of Little League Baseball Teams." *American Sociological Review* 44:733–45.

Finley, M. I. 1977. *Aspects of Antiquity.* Harmondsworth: Penguin.

Firth, Raymond. 1957. *We, the Tikopia.* London: Allen & Unwin.

Fischer, Claude. 1982. *To Live Among Friends: Personal Networks in Town and City.* Chicago: University of Chicago Press.

Fligstein, Neil. 1985. "The Multidivisional Form." *American Sociological Review* 50:377–91.

———. 1990. *The Transformation of Corporate Control.* Cambridge, MA: Harvard University Press.

———. 2001. *The Architecture of Markets.* Princeton, NJ: Princeton University Press.

Fligstein, Neil, and Jennifer Choo. 2005. "Law and Corporate Governance." *Annual Review of Law and Social Science* 1:64–81.

Fligstein, Neil, and Roberto M. Fernandez. 1988. "Worker Power, Firm Power and the Structure of Labor Markets." *Sociological Quarterly* 29:5–28.

Foner, Eric. 1980. *Politics and Ideology in the Age of the Civil War.* New York: Oxford University Press.

Forgas, Joseph P. (Ed.). 1985. *Language and Social Situations.* New York: Springer.

Forment, Carlos A. 1989a. "Political Practice and the Rise of an Ethnic Enclave." *Theory and Society* 18:47–81.

———. 1989b. "The Emergence of Political Space in Spanish America: 1700–1830." Ph.D. diss., Department of Sociology, Harvard University.

Fortes, Meyer. 1945. *The Dynamics of Clanship among the Tallensi.* London: Oxford University Press.

———. 1949. *The Web of Kinship among the Tallensi.* London: Oxford University Press.

Fortes, Meyer, and E. E. Evans-Pritchard (Eds.). 1949. *African Political Systems.* London: Oxford University Press.

Foster, C. C., A. Rapoport, and C. Orwant. 1963. "A Study of a Large Sociogram." *Behavioral Science* 8:56–66.

Foucault, Michel. 1980. *Power/Knowledge.* New York: Pantheon.

———. 2000. *Power.* New York: New Press.

Freeman, Linton C. 1979. "Centrality in Social Networks." *Social Networks* 1:215–39.

———. 2004. *The Development of Social Network Analysis: A Study in the Sociology of Science.* Vancouver: Empirical Press.

Freeman, Linton C., and Douglas R. White. 1993. "Using Galois Lattices to Represent Network Data." *Sociological Methodology* 23:127–46.

Freeman, Linton C., Douglas R. White, and A. Kimball Romney (Eds.). 1989. *Research Methods in Social Network Analysis.* Fairfax, VA: George Mason University Press.

Freidson, Eliot. 1986. *Professional Powers: A Study of the Institutionalization of Formal Knowledge.* Chicago: University of Chicago Press.

———. 2001. *Professionalism: The Third Logic.* Chicago: University of Chicago Press.

Friedell, Morris. 1967. "Organizations as Semilattices." *American Sociological Review* 32:46–54.

Fuchs, Stephan. 2001a. *Against Essentialism: A Theory of Culture and Society.* Cambridge, MA: Harvard University Press.

———. (Ed.). 2001b. *Networks and Systems.* New York: Rowman & Littlefield.

———. 2001c. "Networks and Systems." In *Talcott Parsons Today: His Theory and Legacy in Contemporary Sociology,* edited by A. J. Trevino. New York: Rowman & Littlefield.

Furnivall, J. S. 1948. *Colonial Policy and Practice: A Comparative Study of Burma and Netherlands India.* London: Cambridge University Press.

Fuss, Melvyn, and Daniel MacFadden (Eds.). 1978. *Production Economics: A Dual Approach to Theory and Applications,* vols. 1 and 2. New York: North-Holland.

Gal, Susan. 1979. *Language Shift: Social Determinants of Linguistic Change in Bilingual Austria.* New York: Academic.

Gans, Herbert. 1962. *The Urban Villagers: Group and Class in the Life of Italian Americans.* New York: Free Press of Glencoe.

———. 1979. *Deciding What's News: A Study of CBS Evening News, NBC Nightly News, Newsweek and Time.* New York: Vintage.

———. 2002. "The Sociology of Space: A Use-Centered View." *City and Community* 1:329–48.

Garfinkel, Harold. 1967. *Studies in Ethnomethodology.* Englewood Cliffs, NJ: Prentice-Hall.

Garnsey, Peter, and R. P. Saller. 1987. *The Roman Empire.* London: Duckworth.

Gennes, Pierre-Gilles de. 1979. *Scaling Concepts in Polymer Physics.* Ithaca, NY: Cornell University Press.

Gergen, Kenneth J. 1985. "The Social Constructionist Movement in Modern Psychology." *American Psychologist* 40:266–99.

Ghurye, Govind S. 1957. *Caste and Race in India.* Bombay: Popular Book Depot.

Gibson, David R. 2003. "Participation Shifts: Order and Differentiation in Group Conversation." *Social Forces* 81:1135–81.

———. 2005a. "Concurrence and Commencement: Network Scheduling and Its Consequences for Diffusion." *Journal of Mathematical Sociology* 29.

———. 2005b. "Opportunistic Interruptions: Interactional Vulnerabilities Deriving from Linearization." *Social Psychology Quarterly* 68:316–37.

———. 2005c. "Taking Turns and Talking Ties: Network Structure and Conversational Sequence." *American Journal of Sociology* 110:1561–97.

Gibson, James J. 1950. "The Perception of Visual Surfaces." *American Journal of Psychology* 100:646–64.

———. 1979. *The Ecological Approach to Visual Perception.* Boston: Houghton Mifflin.

Giddens, Anthony. 1979. *Central Problems in Social Theory.* London: Methuen.

———. 1984. *The Constitution of Society: Outline of the Theory of Structuration.* Cambridge: Polity Press.

Gill, Joseph, S. J. 1959. *The Council of Florence.* Cambridge: Cambridge University Press.

———. 1964. *Personalities of the Council of Florence*. New York: Barnes & Noble.

Girard, Monique, and David Stark. Forthcoming. "Socio-technologies of Assembly: Sense-Making and Demonstration in Rebuilding Lower Manhattan." In *Governance and Information: The Rewiring of Governing and Deliberation in the 21st Century*, edited by David Lazer and Viktor Mayer-Schoenberger. New York: Oxford University Press.

Giuffre, Katherine. 1999. "Sandpiles of Opportunity: Success in the Art World." *Social Forces* 77:815–32.

Givón, Talmy. 1984. *Syntax: A Functional-Typological Introduction*. Philadelphia: Benjamins.

Goffman, Erving. 1955. "On Face Work." *Psychiatry* 18:213–31.

———. 1963. *Behavior in Public Places*. Glencoe, IL: Free Press.

———. 1967. *Interaction Ritual*. New York: Pantheon.

———. 1971. *Relations in Public*. New York: Harper.

———. 1974. *Frame Analysis*. New York: Harper & Row.

Gold, Harvey J. 1977. *Mathematical Modelling of Biological Systems: An Introductory Guidebook*. New York: Wiley.

Gottwald, Norman K. 1979. *The Tribes of Jahweh: A Sociology of the Religion of Liberated Israel, 1250–1050 b.c.e.* Maryknoll, NY: Orbis Books.

Gould, Roger V. 1995. *Insurgent Identities*. Chicago: University of Chicago Press.

———. 2002. "The Origins of Status Hierarchies: A Formal Theory and Empirical Test." *American Journal of Sociology* 107:1143–78.

Gould, Roger V., and Roberto M. Fernandez. 1993. "Structure of Mediation: A Formal Approach to Brokerage in Transaction Networks." In *Sociological Methodology*, edited by Peter Marsden. Oxford: Blackwell.

Grabher, Gernot. 2006. "Trading Routes, Bypasses, and Risky Intersections: Mapping the Travels of 'Networks' between Economic Sociology and Economic Geography." *Progress in Human Geography* 30:163–89.

Grabher, Gernot, and Oliver Ibert. 2006. "Bad Company? The Ambiguity of Personal Knowledge Networks." *Journal of Economic Geography* 6:251–71.

Graham, R. L., M. Grötschel, and L. Lovász. 1995. *Handbook of Combinatorics*, vol. 2. Cambridge, MA: MIT Press.

Granick, David. 1967. *Soviet Metal-fabricating and Economic Development: Practice vs. Policy*. Madison: University of Wisconsin Press.

———. 1972. *Managerial Comparisons of Four Developed Countries*. Cambridge, MA: MIT Press.

———. 1975. *Enterprise Guidance in Eastern Europe: A Comparison of Four Socialist Economies*. Princeton, NJ: Princeton University Press.

Granovetter, Mark. 1973. "The Strength of Weak Ties." *American Journal of Sociology* 78:1360–1380.

———. 1974. *Getting a Job: A Study of Contacts and Careers*. Cambridge, MA: Harvard University Press.

———. 1983. "The Strength of Weak Ties: A Network Theory Revisited." *Sociological Theory* 1:201–33.

———. 1985. "Economic Action and Social Structure: The Problem of Embeddedness." *American Journal of Sociology* 91:481–510.

Granovetter, Mark, and Roland Soong. 1983. "Threshold Models of Diffusion and Collective Behavior." *Journal of Mathematical Sociology* 9:165–79.

Gray, C. G., and K. E. Gubbins. 1984. *Theory of Molecular Fluids*. New York: Oxford University Press.

Greeley, Andrew. 1979. *The Making of the Pope 1978: The Politics of Intrigue in the Vatican*. Kansas City, KS: Andrews & McMeel.

Green, Jerry, and Nancy L. Stokey. 1983. "A Comparison of Tournaments and Contracts." *Journal of Political Economy* 91:349–65.

Greenstein, Fred I. 1982. *The Hidden-Hand Presidency: Eisenhower as Leader*. New York: Basic Books.

Greif, A. 2006. *Institutions and the Path to the Modern Economy: Lessons from Medieval Trade*. Cambridge: Cambridge University Press.

Griffeth, Robert, and Carol Thomas. 1981. *The City-State in Five Cultures*. Santa Barbara: ABC-Clio.

Griswold, Wendy. 1986. *Renaissance Revivals*. Chicago: University of Chicago Press.

Gross, Neal W., S. Mason, and A. W. McEachern. 1958. *Explorations in Role Analysis: Studies of the School Superintendency Role*. New York: Wiley.

Grossetti, Michel. 2005. "Where Do Social Relations Come From? A Study of Personal Networks in the Toulouse Area of France." *Social Networks* 27:289–300.

Grossman, Peter Z. 1987. *American Express*. New York: Crown.

Gruen, Erich S. 1974. *The Last Generation of the Roman Republic*. Berkeley: University of California Press.

Guilarte, Miguel G. 1990. *Semi-periphery in United Nations Parliamentary Process*. New York: Columbia University.

Gulati, Ranjay, and Martin Gargiulo. 1999. "Where Do Interorganizational Networks Come From?" *American Journal of Sociology* 104:1439–93.

Gumperz, John J. 1982. *Discourse Strategies*. Cambridge: Cambridge University Press.

Habermas, Jurgen. 1975. *Legitimation Crisis*. Boston, MA: Beacon.

Hacking, Ian. 1999. *The Social Construction of What?* Cambridge, MA: Harvard University Press.

Hackman, J. Richard.1993. "Teams, Leaders and Organizations: New Directions in Crew-Oriented Flight Traning." In *Cockpit Resource Management*, edited by E. L. Wiener, B. G. Kanki, and R. L. Helmreich. Orlando, FL: Academic Press.

Haggett, Peter, A. D. Cliff, and A. Frey. 1977. *Locational Models*. New York: Wiley.

Haiman, John. 1978. "Conditionals Are Topics." *Language* 54:564–89.

Halas, Elzbieta. 1985. "The Contextual Character of Meaning and the Definition of the Situation." *Studies in Symbolic Interaction* 6:149–65.

Halevy, Daniel. 1974. *The End of the Notables*. Middletown, CT: Wesleyan University Press.

Halliday, M.A.K. 1994. *An Introduction to Functional Grammar*. London: Arnold.

Halliday, M.A.K., and Ruqaiya Hasan. 1976. *Cohesion in English*. London: Longman.

Hamilton, Gary G., and Nicole Biggart, W. 1985. "Why People Obey." *Sociological Perspectives* 28:3–28.

Hamilton, Gary G., William Zeile, and Wan-Jin Kim. 1990. "The Network Structures of East Asian Economies." In *Capitalism in Contrasting Cultures*, edited by S. R. Clegg and S. G. Redding, pp. 105–29. Berlin: de Gruyter.

Hammel, Eugene, and Peter Laslett. 1974. "Comparing Household Structure over Time and between Cultures." *Comparative Studies in Society and History* 16:73–109.

Han, Shin-Kap. 1995. "Mimetic Isomorphism and Its Effect on the Audit Services Market." *Social Forces* 73:637–64.

———. 2000. "Inducing Homogeneity in the Audit Services Market: A Cross-Industry Analysis." *Sociological Forum* 15:511–40.

———. 2003. "Tribal Regimes in Academia: A Comparative Analysis of Market Structure across Disciplines." *Social Networks* 25:251–80.

Han, Shin-Kap, and Ronald L. Breiger. 1999. "Dimensions of Corporate Social Capital: Toward Models and Measures." In *Corporate Social Capital and Liability*, edited by R. Leenders and S. Gabbay, pp. 118–44. Boston: Kluwer.

Hanks, William F. 1990. *Referential Practice: Language and Lived Space among the Maya*. Chicago: University of Chicago Press.

———. 1993. "Metalanguage and Pragmatics of Discourse." In *Reflexive Language: Reported Speech and Metapragmatic*, edited by J. A. Lucy. New York: Cambridge University Press.

Hannan, M. T., and J. H. Freeman. 1989. *Organizational Ecology*. Cambridge, MA: Harvard University Press.

Harary, Frank. 1977. *Graph Theory*. Reading, MA: Addison-Wesley.

Harris, Zellig. 1991. *A Theory of Language and Information*. Oxford: Clarendon Press.

Harrison, Daniel. 2000. "Identity and Control as Critical Theory." Department of Sociology, Florida State University.

Hart, Charles, and Arnold Pilling. 1960. *The Tiwi*. New York: Holt.

Haspelmath, Martin. 1997. *Indefinite Pronouns*. Oxford: Clarendon Press.

Hauser, Robert M., and David L. Featherman. 1977. *The Process of Stratification: Trends and Analyses*. New York: Academic Press.

Hawking, P. R. 1977. *Social Class, the Nominal Group and Verbal Strategies*. London: Routledge.

Hawkins, John A. 1983. *Word Order Universals*. New York: Academic.

Hays, Sharon. 1994. "Structure and Agency and the Sticky Problem of Culture." *Sociological Theory* 11:57–72.

Hechter, Michael. 1987. *Principles of Group Solidarity*. Berkeley: University of California Press.

Heclo, H. Hugh. 1969. "The Councillor's Job." *Public Administration* 47:185–202.

Hedstrom, Peter. 1988. *Structures of Inequality*. Stockholm, Sweden: Almqvist & Wisksell International.

———. 2005. *Dissecting the Social: On the Principles of Analytic Sociology*. Cambridge: Cambridge University Press.

Herredia, Blanca. 1989. "Economic Liberalization and Regime Change: Mexico in Comparative Perspective." Department of Political Science, Columbia University.

Higgins, Michael D. 1982. "The Limits of Clientelism: Towards an Assessment of Irish Politics." In *Private Patronage and Public Power: Political Clientelism in the Modern State*, edited by Christopher Clapham, pp. 114–41. London: Frances Pinter.

Hillmann, Henning. 2004. "Identity from Economic Networks." Ph.D. diss., Department of Sociology, Columbia University.

———. 2006. "Localism and the Limits of Political Brokerage: Evidence from Revolutionary Vermont." Unpublished paper, Stanford University.

Hintze, Otto. 1975. *The Historical Essays of Otto Hinze 1919*. Edited by Felix Gilbert. New York: Oxford University Press.

Hirsch, Paul. 1972. "Processing Fads and Fashions: An Organization Set Analysis of Culture Industry Systems." *American Journal of Sociology* 77:639–59.

Hocart, A. M. 1950. *Caste: A Comparative Study*. London: Methuen.

Hodge, Robert, and Gunther Kress. 1993. *Language as Ideology*. London: Routledge.

Hofstadter, Douglas R. 1979. *Godel, Escher and Bach: An Eternal Golden Braid*. New York: Basic Books.

Hollingshead, S. 1949. *Elmtown's Youth*. New York: Wiley.

Holm, John. 1988. *Pidgins and Creoles*. New York: Cambridge University Press.

Homans, George C. 1950. *The Human Group*. New York: Harcourt, Brace.

Homans, George C., and David Schneider. 1955. *Marriage, Authority and Final Causes: A Study of Unilateral Cross-Cousin Marriage*. Glencoe, IL: Free Press.

Hopper, Paul J. 1995. "The Category 'Event' in Natural Discourse and in Logic." In *Discourse Grammar and Typology*, edited by W. Abraham, T. Givon, and S. A. Thompson, pp. 139–51. Philadelphia: John Benjamin.

Hopper, Paul J., and Elizabeth C. Traugott. 1993. *Grammaticalization*. New York: Cambridge University Press.

Hopwood, Anthony G. 1978. "Towards an Organizational Perspective for the Study of Accounting and Information Systems." *Accounting, Organizations and Society* 3:3–13.

Horwitz, Morton J. 1977. *The Transformation of American Law, 1780–1860*. Cambridge, MA: Harvard University Press.

Houseman, Michael, and Douglas R. White. 1998. "Network Mediation of Exchange Structures: Ambilateral Sidedness and Property Flows in Pul Eliya." In *Kinship, Networks and Exchange*, edited by Thomas Schweizer and Douglas R. White. Cambridge: Cambridge University Press.

Howell, Martha C. 1998. *The Marriage Exchange: Property, Social Place, and Gender in Cities of the Low Countries, 1300–1550*. Chicago: University of Chicago Press.

Howell, Nancy. 1969. *The Search for an Abortionist*. Chicago: University of Chicago Press.

———. 1979. *Demography of the Dobe !Kung*. New York: Academic Press.

―――. 1988. "Understanding Simple Social Structure: Kinship Units and Ties." In *Social Structures: A Network Approach*, edited by Barry Wellman and S. D. Berkowitz, pp. 62–82. Cambridge: Cambridge University Press.

Hsiao, Kung-chuan. 1960. *Rural China: Imperial Control in the Nineteenth Century.* Seattle: University of Washington Press.

Hsu, G., and M. T. Hannan. 2005. "Identities, Genres, and Organizational Forms." *Organization Science* 16:474–90.

Huang, Kerson. 1963. *Statistical Mechanics.* New York: Wiley.

Hull, Isabel 1982. *The Entourage of Kaiser Wilhelm II.* New York: Cambridge University Press.

Hyde, J. K. 1966. *Padua in the Age of Dante.* Manchester, UK: University Press.

―――. 1973. *Society and Politics in Medieval Italy.* London: Macmillan.

Ijira, Yuji, and H. A. Simon. 1977. *Skew Distributions and the Sizes of Business Firms.* Amsterdam: North-Holland.

Ikegami, Eiko. 2000. "A Sociological Theory of Publics: Identity and Culture as Emergent Properties of Networks." *Social Research* 67:989–1029.

―――. 2005. *Bonds of Civility: Aesthetic Networks and the Political Origins of Japanese Culture.* Cambridge: Cambridge University Press.

Inkeles, Alex (Ed.). 1991. *On Measuring Democracy: Its Consequences and Concomitants.* New Brunswick, NJ: Transaction Publishers.

Jacques, E. 1956. *Measurement of Responsibility.* London: Tavistock.

Jakobson, Roman. 1990. *On Language.* Edited by Linda R. Waugh and Monique Monville-Burston. Cambridge, MA: Harvard University Press.

James, John. 1953. "The Distribution of Free-Forming Small Group Size." *American Sociological Review* 18:569–70.

Jasso, Guillermina. 1990. "Methods for the Theoretical and Empirical Analysis of Comparison Processes." In *Sociological Methodology 1990*, edited by Clifford C. Clogg, pp. 369–419. Washington, DC: American Sociological Association.

―――. 1991. "Cloister and Society: Analyzing the Public Benefit of Monastic and Mendicant Institutions." *Journal of Mathematical Sociology* 16:109–36.

Jensen, Eugene C. 1985. "Network Macrostructure Models for the Davis-Leinhardt Set of Empirical Sociomatrices." *Social Networks* 7:203–24.

Jensen, Michael C., and W. H. Meckling. 1976. "Theory of the Firm: Managerial Behavior, Agency Costs and Ownership Structure." *Journal of Financial Economics* 3:305–60.

Johnson, H. T. 1983. "The Search for Gain in Markets and Firms: A Review of the Historical Emergence of Management Accounting Systems." *Accounting, Organizations and Society* 8:139–46.

Johnson, T. J. 1972. *Professions and Power.* London: Macmillan.

Johnson, Walter. 1999. *Soul by Soul: Life Inside the Antebellum Slave Market.* Cambridge, MA: Harvard University Press.

Kahneman, D., P. Slovic, and A. Tversky. 1982. *Judgment under Uncertainty: Heuristics and Biases.* Cambridge: Cambridge University Press.

Kaplan, Robert S. 1982. *Advanced Management Accounting.* Englewood Cliffs, NJ: Prentice-Hall.

Katz, Donald R. 1988. *The Big Store: Inside the Crisis and Revolution at Sears*. New York: Penguin.

Kearns, Doris Helen. 1976. *Lyndon Johnson and the American Dream*. New York: Harper & Row.

Kegan, Robert. 1982. *The Evolving Self*. Cambridge, MA: Harvard University Press.

Keilman, Nico, Anton Kuijsten, and Ad Vossen (Eds.). 1988. *Modelling Household Formation and Dissolution*. Oxford: Clarendon Press.

Kelsall, R. K. 1955. *Higher Civil Servants in Britain*. London: Routledge & Kegan Paul.

Kemeny, John J., Snell, L., and F. L. Thompson. 1957. *Introduction to Finite Mathematics*. Englewood Cliffs, NJ: Prentice-Hall.

Kemp, Jeremy. 1982. "A Tail Wagging the Dog: The Patron-Client Model in Thai Studies." In *Private Patronage and Public Power: Political Clientalism in the Modern State*, edited by Christopher S. Clapham, pp. 142–61. London: Frances Pinter.

Kent, Davis, and D. Shapiro. 1978. "Resources Required in the Construction and Reconstruction of Conversation." *Journal of Personality and Social Psychology* 36:13–22.

Keohane, Robert O. 1984. *After Hegemony*. Princeton, NJ: Princeton University Press.

Key, V. O., Jr. 1945. *Southern Politics in State and Nation*. Knoxville: University of Tennessee Press.

Kim, H., and Peter S. Bearman. 1997. "The Structure and Dynamics of Movement Participation." *American Sociological Review* 62:70–93.

Kitto, H.D.F. 1958. *The Greeks*. Harmondsworth, UK: Penguin.

Kleinfeld, Judith S. 2002. "The Small World Problem." *Society* 39:61–66.

Kleinrock, Leonard. 1964. *Communication Nets: Stochastic Message Flow and Delay*. New York: McGraw-Hill.

Knight, Frank. 1921. *Risk, Uncertainty and Profit*. Cambridge, MA: Houghton Mifflin.

Knorr-Cetina, Karin, and Urs Bruegger. 2002. "Global Microstructures: The Virtual Societies of Financial Markets." *American Journal of Sociology* 107:905–50.

Knox, Hannah, Mike Savage, and Penny Harvey. 2006. "Social Networks and the Study of Relations: Networks as Method, Metaphor and Form." *Economy and Society* 15:113–40.

Kochen, Manfred (Ed.). 1989. *The Small World*. Norwood, NJ: Ablex.

Kohlberg, Lawrence. 1981. *The Philosophy of Moral Development: Moral Stages and the Idea of Justice*. San Francisco: Harper & Row.

Kolb, David. 1986. *The Critique of Pure Modernity: Hegel, Heidegger, and After*. Chicago: University of Chicago Press.

Kontopolous, K. M. 1993. *The Logics of Social Structure*. Cambridge: Cambridge University Press.

Koopmans, Tjalling C. 1957. *Three Essays on the State of Economic Science*. New York: McGraw-Hill.

Kossinets, Gueorgi. 2006. "Effects of Missing Data in Social Networks." *Social Networks* 28:247–68.

Kossinets, Gueorgi, and Duncan J. Watts. 2006. "Empirical Analysis of an Evolving Social Network." *Science* 311:88–90.

Kossman, E. H. 1971. "The Crisis of the Dutch State, 1780–1813." In *Britain and the Netherlands*, edited by J. S. Bromley and E. H. Kossman. The Hague: Martinus Nijhoff.

———. 1978. *The Low Countries*. Oxford: Oxford University Press.

Krackhardt, David. 1987. "Cognitive Social Structures." *Social Networks* 9:1109–39.

Kratchovil, P. 1968. *The Chinese Language Today: Features of an Emerging Standard*. London: Hutchinson.

Krauss, Robert M., and Peter D. Bricker. 1967. "Effects of Transmission Delay and Access Delay on the Efficiency of Verbal Communication." *Journal of the Acoustical Society of America* 41:286–92.

Kreps, David M. 1988. *Notes on the Theory of Choice*. Boulder, CO: Westview.

Kriedte, Peter, Hans Medick, and Jurgen Shlumbohm. 1981. *Industrialization before Industrialization: Rural Industry in the Genesis of Capitalism*. New York: Cambridge University Press.

Krieger, Joel. 1984. *Undermining Capitalism*. Princeton, NJ: Princeton University Press.

Kruglanski, Arie W., and Donna M. Webster. 1996. "Motivated Closing of the Mind: 'Seizing' and 'Freezing.' " *Psychological Review* 103:263–83.

Kuhn, Philip A. 1970. *Rebellion and Its Enemies in Late Imperial China*. Cambridge, MA: Harvard University Press.

Kuhn, Thomas S. 1970. *The Structure of Scientific Revolutions*. Chicago: University of Chicago Press.

Kurosh, A. G. 1965. *Lectures in General Algebra*. Oxford: Pergamon Press.

Labov, William. 1966. *The Social Stratification of English in New York City*. Washington, DC: Center for Applied Linguistics.

Lachmann, Richard. 1985. "Feudal Elite Conflict and the Origins of English Capitalism." *Politics and Society* 14:349–78.

———. 1987. *From Manor to Market*. Madison: University of Wisconsin Press.

———. 2000. *Capitalists in Spite of Themselves: Elite Conflict and Economic Transitions in Early Modern Europe*. New York: Oxford University Press.

Lachmann, Richard, and Stephen Petterson. 1988. "Rationality and Structure in the 'Failed' Capitalism of Renaissance Italy." Department of Sociology, University of Wisconsin—Madison.

Landau, Hyman. 1950–1951. "On Dominance Relations and the Structure of Animal Societies: I. Effect of Inherent Characteristics; II. Some Effects of Possible Social Factors." *Bulletin of Mathematical Biophysics* 13:1–19; 245–61.

———. 1965. "Development of Structure in a Society with Dominance Relation When New Members Are Added Successively." *Bulletin of Mathematical Biophysics* 27:151–60.

Lash, Scott. 2002. *Critique of Information*. London: Sage.

Lasswell, Harold D., and A. Kaplan. 1950. *Power and Society*. New Haven, CT: Yale University Press.

Latour, Bruno. 1999. "On Recalling ANT." In *Actor-Network Theory and After*, edited by J. Law and J. Hassard, pp. 15–25. Oxford: Blackwell.

Laumann, Edward O., and David Knoke. 1987. *The Organizational State: Social Choice in National Policy Domains*. Madison: University of Wisconsin Press.

Laumann, Edward O., and Franz V. Pappi. 1976. *Networks of Collective Action: A Perspective on Community Influence Systems*. New York: Academic.

Lazega, Emmanuel. 2001. *The Collegial Phenomenon: The Social Mechanisms of Co-operation among Peers in a Corporate Law Partnership*. Oxford: Oxford University Press.

Lazega, Emmanuel, and Olivier Favereau (Eds.). 2002. *Conventions and Structures*. London: Elgar.

Lazega, Emmanuel, and David Krackhardt. 2000. "Spreading and Sifting Costs of Lateral Control in a Law Partnership: A Structural Analysis at the Individual Level." *Quantity and Quality* 34:153–75.

Lazega, Emmanuel, and Philippa Pattison. 1999. "Multiplexity, Generalized Exchange and Cooperation in Organizations: A Case Study." *Social Networks* 21:67–90.

Lazerson, Mark. 1995. "A New Phoenix? Modern Putting-Out in the Modena Knitwear Industry." *Administrative Science Quarterly* 40:34–59.

Leach, Edmund R. 1954. *The Political Systems of Highland Burma*. Boston: Beacon.

———. 1961. *Pul Eliya, a Village in Ceylon: A Study of Land Tenure and Kinship*. Cambridge: Cambridge University Press.

Leamer, Edward. 1978. *Specification Searches: Ad Hoc Inference with Non-experimental Data*. New York: Wiley.

Leavitt, Harold J., and Thomas L. Whisler. 1958. "Management in the 1980s." *Harvard Business Review* 36: 41–8.

Lee, Richard B. 1979. *The !Kung San*. Cambridge: Cambridge University Press.

Lehmbruch, G., and P. C. Schmitter (Eds.). 1982. *Patterns of Corporatist Policy-Making*. Beverly Hills: Sage.

Leifer, Eric M. 1983. "Hierarchies of Ends: Uncertain Preferences in Strategic Decision Making." Ph.D. diss., Department of Sociology, Harvard University.

———. 1985. "Markets as Mechanisms: Using a Role Structure." *Social Forces* 64:442–72.

———. 1990. "Enacting Networks: The Feasibility of Fairness." *Social Networks* 12:1–25.

———. 1991a. *Robust Action*. New York: Garland.

———. 1991b. "Organizing for Involvement: The Evolution of League Sports in America." Department of Sociology, Columbia University.

———. 1998. *Making the Majors: The Transformation of Team Sports in America*. Cambridge, MA: Harvard University Press.

Leifer, Eric M., and Harrison C. White. 1986. "Wheeling and Annealing: Federal and Multidivisional Control." In *The Social Fabric: Issues and Dimensions*, edited by James F. Short. Beverly Hills: Sage.

———. 1988. "A Structural Approach to Markets." In *Intercorporate Relations: The Structural Analysis of Business*, edited by Mark Mizruchi and Michael Schwartz. New York: Cambridge University Press.

Leigh, J. R. 1987. *Applied Control Theory.* London: Peter Peregrinus.

Leik, R. K., and B. F. Meeker. 1975. *Mathematical Sociology.* Englewood Cliffs, NJ: Prentice-Hall.

Lenin, V. I. [1902] 1966. "What Is to Be Done?" In *Essential Works of Lenin,* edited by H. M. Christman. New York: Bantam.

——. 1976. "The Development of Capitalism in Russia." In *Collected Works.* Moscow: Progress Publishers.

Leontief, Wassily W. 1966. *Input-Output Economics.* New York: Oxford University Press.

Lepenies, Wolf. 1988. *Between Literature and Science: The Rise of Sociology.* New York: Cambridge University Press.

Lévi-Strauss, Claude. 1969. *The Elementary Structures of Kinship.* Boston: Beacon.

Levine, Joel H. 1972. "The Sphere of Influence." *American Sociological Review* 37:14–27.

——. 1990. *World Atlas of Director Interlocks.* Hanover, NH: Worldnet.

——. 1993. *Exceptions Are the Rule.* Boulder, CO: Westview.

Levins, Richard. 1966. "The Strategy of Model Building in Population Biology." *American Scientist* 54:421–31.

Levinson, Stephen C. 1983. *Pragmatics.* New York: Cambridge University Press.

Levy, Hermann. 1944. *Retail Trade Associations.* New York: Oxford University Press.

Levy, Marion J. 1948. "A Note on Pareto's Logical-Non-logical Categories." *American Sociological Review* 13:756–57.

Lewontin, Richard C. 1974. *The Genetic Basis of Evolutionary Change.* New York: Columbia University Press.

Libecap, Gary. 1978. "Economic Variables and the Development of the Law: The Case of Western Mineral Rights." *Journal of Economic History* 38:338–62.

Lieberson, Stanley. 2000. *A Matter of Taste: How Names, Fashion and Culture Change.* New Haven, CT: Yale University Press.

Lijphart, Arend. 1968. *The Politics of Accommodation.* Berkeley: University of California Press.

Lindenberg, Siegwart. 1989a. "Choice and Culture: The Behavioral Basis of Cultural Impact on Transactions." In *Social Structure and Culture,* edited by Hans Haferkamp, pp. 175–200. Berlin: DeGruyter.

——. 1989b. "Social Production Functions, Deficits, and Social Revolutions." *Rationality and Society* 1:51–77.

Link, Bruce G., and Jo C. Phelan. 2001. "Conceptualizing Stigma." *Annual Review of Sociology* 27:363–85.

Lipset, S. M., and Rokkan, S. 1967. *Party Systems and Voter Alignments: Cross-National Perspectives.* New York: Free Press.

Livingston, Eric. 1986. *Ethnomethodological Foundations of Mathematics.* London: Routledge & Kegan Paul.

Livingston, James. 1994. *Pragmatism and the Political Economy of Cultural Revolution 1850–1940.* Chapel Hill: University of North Carolina Press.

Llewellyn, Karl N. [1933] 1989. *The Case Law System in America.* Chicago: University of Chicago Press.

Lodge, R. Anthony. 1993. *French: From Dialect to Standard*. London: Routledge.

Luckham, Robin. 1971. *The Nigerian Military: A Sociological Analysis of Authority and Revolt, 1960–1967*. Cambridge: Cambridge University Press.

Lucy, John A. (Ed.). 1993. *Reflexive Language: Reported Speech and Metapragmatics*. New York: Cambridge University Press.

Luhmann, Niklas. 1989. *Ecological Communication*. Cambridge: Polity/Blackwell.

———. 1995. *Social Systems*. Palo Alto: Stanford University Press.

———. 2004. *Law as a Social System*. Oxford: Oxford University Press.

Lynes, Russell. 1954. *The Tastemakers*. New York: Greenwood.

Ma, Shang-keng. 1973. "Introduction to the Renormalization Group." *Review of Modern Physics* 45:589–613.

Macmahon, A. W., John D. Millett, and Gladys Ogden. 1941. *The Administration of Federal Work Relief*. New York: Social Science Research Council.

Macneil, Ian R. 1978. "Contracts: Adjustment of Long-Term Economic Relations under Classical, Neo-classical and Relational Contract Law." *Northwestern Law Review* 72:854–906.

———. 1986. "Exchange Revisited: Individual Utility and Social Solidarity." *Ethics* 96:567–93.

MacPherson, C. P. 1962. *The Political Theory of Possessive Individualism*. Oxford: Oxford University Press.

Maine, Henry Sumner. 1861. *Ancient Law*. London: J. Murray.

Maines, David R. 1993. "Narrative's Moment and Sociology's Phenomena: Toward a Narrative Sociology." *Sociological Quarterly* 34:17–38.

Major, J. Russell. 1960. *Representative Institutions in Renaissance France: 1421–1559*. Madison: University of Wisconsin Press.

Mannheim, Karl. [1929] 1936. *Ideology and Utopia: An Introduction to the Sociology of Knowledge*. London: Routledge.

Mansfield, Edwin. 1968. *The Economics of Technical Change*. New York: Norton.

———. 1975. *Microeconomics: Theory and Applications*. New York: Norton.

March, James G., and Johan P. Olsen. 1976. *Ambiguity and Choice in Organizations*. Bergen: Universitetsforlaget.

———. 1989. *The Organizational Basis of Politics*. New York: Free Press—MacMillan.

March, James G., and Herbert A. Simon. 1958. *Organizations*. New York: Wiley.

Marriott, McKim. 1968. "Caste Ranking and Food Transactions: A Matrix Analysis." In *Structure and Change in Indian Society*, edited by Milton Singer and Bernard S. Cohn. Chicago: Aldine.

Marshall, Alfred. 1891. *Principles of Economics*. London: Macmillan.

Martin, John L. 2002. "Some Algebraic Structures for Diffusion in Social Networks." *Journal of Mathematical Sociology* 26:123–46.

———. 2003. "What Is Field Theory?" *American Journal of Sociology* 109:1–49.

Martines, Lauro. 1968. *Lawyers and Statecraft in Renaissance Florence*. Princeton, NJ: Princeton University Press.

Massey, Doreen B. 2005. *For Space*. London: Sage.

Mayer, Adrian C. 1960. *Caste and Kinship in Central India*. Berkeley: University of California Press.

McAdam, Douglas. 1988. *Freedom Summer*. New York: Oxford University Press.

McAdam, Douglas, and R. Paulsen. 1993. "Specifying the Relationship between Social Ties and Activism." *American Journal of Sociology* 99:640–67.

McPherson, M., L. Smith-Lovin, and J. M. Cook. 2001. "Birds of a Feather: Homophily in Social Networks." *Annual Review of Sociology* 101:415–44.

McPherson, Miller, and James Ranger-Moore. 1991. "Evolution on a Dancing Landscape: Organizations and Networks in Dynamic Blau Space." *Social Forces* 70:19–42.

Merton, Robert K. 1968. *Social Theory and Social Structure*. New York: Free Press.

———. 1985. *On the Shoulders of Giants: A Shandean Postscript*. New York: Harcourt Brace Jovanovich.

Meyer, Marshall. 1993. "Order from Disorder? Review of 'Identity and Control.'" *Contemporary Sociology* 22:309–11.

Milgram, Stanley. 1967. "The Small World Problem." *Psychology Today* 2:60–67.

———. 1975. *Obedience to Authority: An Experimental View*. New York: Harper & Row.

———. 1977. *The Individual in a Social World*. Reading, MA: Addison-Wesley.

Miller-Benedict, V. 2006. "How Do Non-linear Relations of Social Macro-Variables Arise from Aggregation of Individual Reason?" *Journal of Mathematical Sociology* 30:137–58.

Milroy, Lesley. 1980. *Language and Social Networks*. Oxford: Blackwell.

Mintz, Beth, and Michael Schwartz. 1985. *The Power Structure of American Business*. Chicago: University of Chicago Press.

Mische, Ann. 2007. *Partisan Publics: Contention and Mediation across Brazilian Youth Activist Networks*. Princeton, NJ: Princeton University Press.

Mische, Ann, and Philippa Pattison. 2000. "Composing a Civic Arena: Publics, Projects, and Social Settings." *Poetics* 27:163–94.

Mische, Ann, and Harrison C. White. 1998. "Between Conversation and Situation: Public Switching Dynamics across Network Domains." *Social Research* 65: 295–324.

Mischel, Walter. 1968. *Introduction to Personality: A New Look*. New York: Holt, Rinehart & Winston.

———. 1990. "Personality Dispositions Revisited and Revised: A View after Three Decades." In *Handbook of Personality Theory and Research*, edited by L. Pervin. New York: Guilford.

Mizruchi, Mark S. 1991. "Urgency, Motivation, and Group Performance: The Effects of Prior Success on Current Success among Professional Basketball Teams." *Social Psychological Quarterly* 54:181–89.

Mizruchi, Mark S., and Michael Schwartz. 1988. *Intercorporate Relations: The Structural Analysis of Business*. New York: Cambridge University Press.

Mohr, John, and Vincent Duqenne. 1997. "The Duality of Culture and Practice: Poverty Relief in New York City, 1888–1917." *Theory and Society* 26:305–51.

Moody, James, and Douglas R. White. 2003. "Social Cohesion and Embeddedness: A Hierarchical Conception of Social Groups." *American Sociological Review* 68:1–25.

Moon, J. W. 1968. *Topics in Tournaments*. New York: Holt, Rinehart & Winston.

Moore, Basil J. 1988. *Horizontalists and Verticalists: The Macroeconomics of Credit Money.* Cambridge: Cambridge University Press.

Moore, Mignon. 2006. "Lipstick or Timberlands? Meanings of Gender Presentation in Black, Lesbian-Headed Households." *SIGNS: Journal of Women in Culture and Society* 32:113–39.

Moote, A. Lloyd. 1971. *The Revolt of the Judges: The Parlement of Paris and the Fronde, 1643–1652.* Princeton, NJ: Princeton University Press.

Morgan, Lewis Henry. 1877. *Ancient Society.* Gloucester, MA: Smith.

Morishima, Michio. 1973. *Marx's Economics.* New York: Cambridge University Press.

Morrill, Calvin. 1995. *The Executive Way: Conflict Management in Organizations.* Chicago: University of Chicago Press.

Morris, Martina. 1993. "Epidemiology and Social Networks: Modeling Structured Diffusion." *Sociological Methods and Research* 22:99–126.

Morse, Philip M., and Herman Feshbach. 1953. *Handbook of Theoretical Physics,* parts 1 and 2. New York: McGraw-Hill.

Mousnier, Roland. 1971. *La Venalite des Offices Henri IV et Louis XIII.* Paris: Press Universitaires de France.

———. 1984. *Institutions of France under the Absolute Monarchy 1578–1789.* Chicago: University of Chicago Press.

Muetzel, Sophie. 2002. "Constructing Berlin: Capital City Journalism." Ph.D. diss., Department of Sociology, Columbia University.

Muth, John F. 1959. "Rational Expectations and the Theory of Price Movements." In *Research Memorandum,* Office of Naval Research and Graduate School of Industrial Administration, Carnegie Institute of Technology.

Myrdal, Gunnar. 1954. *The Political Element in the Development of Economic Theory.* Cambridge, MA: Harvard University Press.

Nadel, S. F. 1946. *A Black Byzantium.* Oxford: Oxford University Press.

———. 1957. *The Theory of Social Structure.* London: Cohen & West.

Najemy, John M. 1982. *Corporations and Consensus in Florentine Electoral Politics, 1280–1420.* Chapel Hill: University of North Carolina Press.

Nakano, Tsutomu, and Douglas R. White. May 2006. "Power-Law and 'Elite-Club' in a Complex Supplier-Buyer Network: Flexible Specialization or Dual Economy?" Working Papers Series, Center on Organizational Innovation, Columbia University. Available on-line at http://www.doi.columbia.edu/pdf/nakano_white_de.pdf.

Namier, Lewis. 1961. *The Structure of Politics at the Accession of George III.* London: Macmillan.

Napier, Augustus, and C. A. Whitaker. 1978. *The Family Crucible.* New York: Harper & Row.

Needham, Rodney. 1962. *Structure and Sentiment.* Chicago: University of Chicago Press.

Nelson, Elizabeth White. 2004. *Market Sentiments: Middle-Class Market Culture in 19th-Century America.* Washington, DC: Smithsonian Books.

Neumann, John von, and Oskar Morgenstern. 1944. *The Theory of Games and Economic Behavior.* Princeton, NJ: Princeton University Press.

Newcomb, Theodore M. 1961. *The Acquaintance Process.* New York: Holt, Rinehart & Winston.

Newell, Allan, and Herbert A. Simon. 1972. *Human Problem Solving.* Englewood Cliffs, NJ: Prentice-Hall.

Newman, John Henry. 1876. *The Arians of the Fourth Century.* London: Pickering.

Newman, Peter. 1965. *The Theory of Exchange.* Englewood Cliffs, NJ: Prentice-Hall.

Niebuhr, Reinhold. 1959. *The Structure of Nations and Empires.* New York: Scribner.

Nissen, Hans J. 1988. *The Early History of the Ancient Near East: 9000–2000 b.c.* Chicago: University of Chicago Press.

Nohria, N., and R. G. Eccles (Eds.). 1992. *Networks and Organizations: Structure, Form, and Action.* Boston: Harvard Business School Press.

Nolan, Patrick. 1983. "Status in World System." *American Journal of Sociology* 89:410–19.

Oberman, Heiko. 1981. *Masters of the Reformation.* New York: Cambridge University Press.

Ochs, Elinor, and Carolyn Taylor. 1992. "Family Narrative as Political Activity." *Discourse and Society* 3:301–4.

Opie, Peter, and Iona Opie. 1969. *Children's Games in Street and Playground: Chasing, Catching, Seeking, Hunting, Racing, Duelling, Exerting, Daring, Guessing, Acting, Pretending.* Oxford: Clarendon Press.

Ore, Oystein. 1965. *Theory of Graphs.* Providence, RI: American Mathematical Association.

Padgett, John F. 1980a. "Bounded Rationality in Budgetary Research." *American Political Science Review* 74:354–72.

———. 1980b. "Managing Garbage Can Hierarchies." *Administrative Science Quarterly* 14:583–604.

———. 1981. "Hierarchy and Ecological Control in Federal Budgetary Decision-Making." *American Journal of Sociology* 87:75–129.

———. 1990a. "Plea Bargaining and Prohibition in the Federal Courts: 1908–1934." *Law and Society Review* 24:413–50.

———. 1990b. "Mobility as Control: Congressmen through Committees." In *Social Mobility and Social Structure,* edited by Ronald L. Breiger. New York: Cambridge University Press.

———. 1992. "Review Essay: The Alchemist of Contingency Theory." *American Journal of Sociology* 97:1462–70.

———. 1997. "The Emergence of Simple Ecologies of Skill: A Hypercycle Approach to Economic Organization." In *The Economy as an Evolving Complex System II,* edited by Brian Arthur, Steven Durlauf, and David Lane. Reading, MA: Addison-Wesley/Santa Fe Institute.

———. 2001. "Organizational Genesis, Identity, and Control: The Transformation of Banking in Renaissance Florence." In *Markets and Networks,* edited by Alessandra Cassella and James Rauch. New York: Russell Sage.

Padgett, John F., and Christopher Ansell. 1993. "Robust Action and the Rise of the Medici, 1400–1434." *American Journal of Sociology* 98:1259–1319.

Padgett, John F., and Paul D. McLean. 2006. "Organizational Invention and Elite Transformation: The Birth of Partnership Systems in Renaissance Florence." *American Journal of Sociology* 111:1463–1568.

Palmer, Donald. 1984. "Broken Ties: Interlocking Directorates and Intercorporate Coordination." *Administrative Science Quarterly* 28:40–55.

Pareto, Vilfredo. 1935. *The Mind and Society.* New York: Harcourt, Brace.

———. 1966. *Sociological Writings.* New York: Praeger.

Parry, John H. 1971. *Trade and Dominion: The European Overseas Empires in the Eighteenth Century.* New York: Praeger.

Parry, Jonathan P. 1979. *Caste and Kinship in Kangra.* London: Routledge and Kegan Paul.

Parsons, Talcott. 1937. *The Structure of Social Action.* New York: McGraw-Hill.

Parsons, Talcott, Robert F. Bales, and Edward A. Shils. 1953. *Working Papers in the Theory of Action.* Glencoe, IL: Free Press.

Parsons, Talcott, and Edward A. Shils (Eds.). 1951. *Toward a General Theory of Action.* New York: Harper & Row.

Partee, Barbara H. 1996. "Allegation and Local Accommodation." In *Discourse and Meaning: Papers in Honor of Eva Hajicova,* edited by Barbara H. Partee and Petr Sgall, p. 65. Amsterdam: Benjamins.

Patterson, Nerys T. 1981. "Material and Symbolic Exchange in Early Irish Clientship." In *Proceedings of the Harvard Celtic Colloquium,* edited by James E. Doan and C. G. Buttimer, pp. 53–61. Cambridge, MA: Harvard University Press.

Patterson, Orlando. 1982. *Slavery and Social Death: A Comparative Analysis.* Cambridge, MA: Harvard University Press.

Pattison, Philippa. 1993. *Algebraic Models for Social Networks.* Cambridge: Cambridge University Press.

Pattison, Philippa E., and Ronald L. Breiger. 2002. "Lattices and Dimensional Representations." *Social Networks* 24:423–44.

Payne, P. L. 1974. *British Entrepreneurship in the 19th Century.* London: Macmillan.

Perinbanayagam, R. S. 1991. *Discursive Acts.* New York: de Gruyter.

Perry, Martin K. 1989. "Vertical Integration: Determinants and Effects." *Handbook of Industrial Organization* 1:183–255.

Peterson, Richard A. (Ed.). 1976. *The Production of Culture.* Beverly Hills, CA: Sage.

Pettigrew, Andrew. 1985. *The Awakening Giant: Continuity and Change in Imperial Chemical Industries.* Oxford: Basil Blackwell.

Phelan, J. C., B. G. Link, A. Diez-Roux, I. Kawachi, and B. Levin. 2004. "'Fundamental Causes' of Social Inequality in Mortality: A Test of the Theory." *Journal of Health and Social Behavior* 45:265–85.

Piore, Michael, and Charles Sabel. 1984. *The Second Industrial Divide: Possibilities for Prosperity.* New York: Basic Books.

Pizzorno, Alessandro. 1991. "On the Individualistic Theory of Social Order." In *Social Theory for a Changing Society,* edited by Pierre Bourdieu and James Coleman, pp. 209–31. Boulder, CO: Westview.

Plumb, J. H. 1967. *The Growth of Political Stability in England, 1675–1725*. London: Penguin.

Pocock, J. A. 1975. *The Machiavellian Moment*. Princeton, NJ: Princeton University Press.

Podolny, Joel M. 2001. "Networks as the Pipes and Prisms of the Market." *American Journal of Sociology* 107:33–60.

———. 2005. *Status Signal: A Sociological Study of Market Competition*. Princeton, NJ: Princeton University Press.

Poggi, Gianfranco. 1978. *The Development of the Modern State*. Stanford, CA: Stanford University Press.

———. 1983. "Clientelism." *Political Studies* 31:662–68.

Polanyi, Karl, Conrad M. Arensberg, and Harry W. Pearson. 1957. *Trade and Market in the Early Empires*. Glencoe, IL: Free Press.

Polanyi, Michael. 1958. *Personal Knowledge*. Chicago: University of Chicago.

Polletta, Francesca. 1998. "'It Was Like a Fever': Narrative and Identity in Social Protest." *Social Problems* 45:137–59.

———. 2005. "How Participatory Democracy Became White and Other Stories of Organizational Choice." *Mobilization* 9:271–88.

Pool, Ithiel de Sola, and Manfred Kochen. 1978. "Contacts and Influence." *Social Networks* 1:1–51.

Pooler, Victor H. 1964. *The Purchasing Man and His Job*. New York: American Management Association.

Porter, Michael E. 1976. *Interbrand Choice, Strategy and Bilateral Market Power*. Cambridge, MA: Harvard University Press.

Postan, M., and E. Rich (Eds.). 1987. *The Cambridge Economic History of Europe*. Vol. 2, *Trade and Industry in the Middle Ages*. New York: Cambridge University Press.

Powell, Walter W. 1985. *Getting into Print: The Decision-Making Process in Scholarly Publishing*. Chicago: University of Chicago Press.

———. 1987. "Hybrid Organizational Arrangements: New Forms or Transitional Development?" *California Management Review* 30:67–87.

Powell, Walter W., Douglas R. White, Kenneth W. Kogut, and Jason Owen-Smith. 2005. "Network Dynamics and Field Evolution: The Growth of Interorganizational Collaboration in the Life Sciences." *American Journal of Sociology* 110:1132–1205.

Prince, Harold. 1974. *Contradictions*. New York: Dodd Mead.

Prins, A.H.J. 1953. *East African Age-Class Systems*. Groningen: Wolters.

Project Solarium. 1988. "The Challenge of Leadership in Foreign Affairs." New York: School of International Affairs, Columbia University.

Radford, Andrew. 1990. *Syntactic Theory and the Acquisition of English Syntax: The Nature of Early Child Grammars of English*. Oxford: Blackwell.

Radner, Roy. 1975a. "A Behavioral Model of Cost Reduction." *Bell Journal of Economics* 6:196–215.

———. 1975b. "Satisficing." *Journal of Mathematical Economics* 2:254–62.

Ragin, Charles, and Howard Becker (Eds.). 1992. *The Logic of Social Inquiry: What Is a Case?* New York: Cambridge University Press.

Rapoport, Anatol. 1953. "Spread of Information through a Population with Socio-structural Bias. II. Various Models with Partial Transitivity." *Journal Bulletin of Mathematical Biology* 15.

———. 1983. *Mathematical Models in the Social and Behavioral Sciences*. New York: Wiley.

Rawls, Anne W. 1989. "Language, Self and Social Order: A Reformulation of Goffman and Sachs." *Human Studies* 12:147–72.

Reader, W. J. 1975. *Imperial Chemical Industries: A History.* Oxford: Oxford University Press.

Reid, James S. 1913. *The Municipalities of the Roman Empire*. Cambridge: Cambridge University Press.

Reme, Petronille. 2005. "Harrison C. White: Une theorie generale des marches." Ph.D. diss. Paris: Panthéon Sorbonne.

Restle, Frank. 1980. "The Seer of Ithaca." *Contemporary Psychology* 291–93.

Richardson, G. B. 1972. "The Organization of Industry." *Economic Journal* 82:883–96.

Ricoeur, Paul. 1988. *Time and Narrative*, vol. 3. Chicago: University of Chicago Press.

Rieder, Jonathan. 1990. "Rhetoric of Reason, Rhetoric of Passion." *Rationality and Society* 2:190–213.

Riggs, Fred. 1964. *Administration in Developing Countries: The Theory of Prismatic Society.* New York: Houghton Mifflin.

———. 1966. *Thailand*. Honolulu: East-West Center.

Riker, William H. 1982. "Implications from the Disequilibrium of Majority Rule for the Study of Institutions." In *Political Equilibrium*, edited by Peter Ordeshook and Kenneth Shepsle. Boston: Kluwer-Nijhoff.

Riordan, J. 1962. *Stochastic Service Systems*. New York: Wiley.

Romo, Frank, and Helmut K. Anheier. 1991. "The Omega Phenomenon: A Study of Social Choice." Working paper. New York: Russell Sage Foundation.

Romo, Frank P., and Michael Schwartz. 1995. "The Structural Embeddedness of Business Decisions: The Migration of Manufacturing Plants in New York State, 1960 to 1985." *American Sociological Review* 60:874–907.

Rose, Frederick G. G. 1960. *Classification of Kin, Age Structure, and Marriage amongst the Groote Eylandt Aborigines*. Berlin: Akademie-Verlag.

Rosen, Sherwin. 1984. "The Distribution of Prizes in a Match-Play Tournament with Single Eliminations." In *Discussion Paper Series*. Chicago: National Opinion Research Center.

Rosenberg, Hans. 1958. *Bureaucracy, Aristocracy and Autocracy: The Prussian Experience 1660–1815*. Cambridge, MA: Harvard University Press.

Roseveare, Henry. 1973. *The Treasury: 1660–1870*. New York: Barnes & Noble.

Rowen, Herbert H. 1978. *John de Witt, Grand Pensionary of Holland, 1625–1672*. Princeton, NJ: Princeton University Press.

———. 1988. *The Princes of Orange: The Stadtholders in the Dutch Republic*. New York: Cambridge University Press.

Ryder, Norman B. 1965. "The Cohort as a Concept in the Study of Social Change." *American Sociological Review* 30:843–61.

Salganik, Matthew J., Peter S. Dodds, and Duncan J. Watts. 2006. "Experimental Study of Inequality and Unpredictability in an Artificial Cultural Market." *Science* 311:854–56.

Salter, Malcolm S., and W. A. Weinhold. 1979. *Diversification through Acquisition.* New York: Macmillan.

Salzinger, Leslie. 2004. "Revealing the Unmarked: Finding Masculinity in a Global Factory." *Ethnography* 5:5–28.

Samuelson, Paul. 1947. *Foundations of Economic Analysis.* Cambridge, MA: Harvard University Press.

Sarfatti-Larson, Magali. 1977. *The Rise of Professionalism.* Berkeley: University of California Press.

Sassen, Saskia. 2006. *Territory, Authority, Rights: From Medieval to Global Assemblages.* Princeton, NJ: Princeton University Press.

Sattinger, Michael. 1980. *Capital and the Distribution of Labor Earnings.* New York: North-Holland.

Savage, Michael, Katherine Stovel, and Peter Bearman. 2001. "Class Formation and Localism in an Emerging Bureaucracy: British Bank Workers, 1880–1960." *International Journal of Urban and Regional Research* 25:284–306.

Sawyer, Keith. 1992. "The Pragmatics of Play: Interactional Strategies during Children's Pretend Play." *Pragmatics* 3:259–82.

Sayles, Leonard. 1979. *Leadership: What Effective Managers Really Do . . . and How They Do It.* New York: McGraw-Hill.

Sayles, Leonard R., and George Strauss. 1967. *The Local Union,* rev. ed. New York: Harcourt, Brace & World.

Scarf, H. 1967. "On the Approximation of Fixed Points of a Continuous Mapping." *SIAM Journal on Applied Mathematics* 15:1328–43.

———. 1973. *The Computation of Economic Equilibria.* New Haven, CT: Yale University Press.

Schachter, Stanley, Frances Rauscher, Nicholas Cristenfeld, and K. Tyson Crone. 1994. "The Vocabularies of Academia." *Psychological Science* 5:37–41.

Schama, Simon. 1987. *The Embarrassment of Riches: An Interpretation of Dutch Culture in the Golden Age.* New York: Knopf.

Schelling, Thomas C. 1960. *The Strategy of Conflict.* Cambridge, MA: Harvard University Press.

———. 1971. "Dynamic Models of Segregation." *Journal of Mathematical Sociology* 1:143–86.

———. 1978. *Micromotives and Macrobehavior.* New York: Norton.

Scheppele, Kim L. 1988. *Legal Secrets: Equality and Efficiency in the Common Law.* Chicago: University of Chicago Press.

Schiffrin, Deborah. 1987. *Discourse Markers.* New York: Cambridge University Press.

Schmitter, Philippe C. 1975. "Liberation by Golpe: Retrospective Thoughts on the Demise of Authoritarian Rule in Portugal." *Armed Forces and Society* 2:5–33.

Schneider, David M. 1968. *Kinship and Social Organization.* New York: Humanities Press.

Scholes, Robert, and R. Kellogg. 1966. *The Nature of Narrative*. New York: Oxford University Press.

Schudson, Michael. 1989. "How Culture Works: Perspectives from Media Studies on the Efficacy of Symbols." *Theory and Society* 18:153–80.

Schurmann, F. 1968. *Ideology and Organization in Communist China*. Berkeley: University of California Press.

Schwartz, Barry. 1981. *Vertical Classification: A Study in Structuralism and the Sociology of Knowledge*. Chicago: University of Chicago Press.

Schwartz, Michael. 1966. "Introduction to Social Relations: Notes on Social Organization." Department of Social Relations, Harvard University.

———. 1976. *Radical Protest and Social Structure*. New York: Academic Press.

Schwartzman, Kathleen C. 1989. *The Social Origins of Democratic Collapse: The First Portuguese Republic in the World Economy*. Lawrence: University of Kansas Press.

Searle, Eleanor. 1988. *Predatory Kinship and the Creation of Norman Power*. Berkeley: University of California Press.

Segal, Alan F. 1986. *Rebecca's Children: Judaism and Christianity in the Roman World*. Cambridge, MA: Harvard University Press.

Seligman, Martin E. P., and Judy Garber (Eds.). 1980. *Human Helplessness: Theory and Application*. New York: Academic Press.

Selznick, Philip. 1952. *The Organizational Weapon: A Study of Bolshevik Strategy and Tactics*. New York: McGraw-Hill.

———. 1955. *The TVA and the Grass Roots: A Study in the Sociology of Formal Organization*. Berkeley: University of California Press.

Sengers, Jan V., and Anneke L. Sengers. 1968. "The Critical Region." *Chemical and Engineering News* 46:104–18.

Senturk, Recep. 2006. *Narrative Social Structure: Anatomy of the Hadith Transmission Network, 610–1505*. Stanford, CA: Stanford University Press.

Sewell, William H., Jr. 1994. *A Rhetoric of Bourgeois Revolution*. Durham, NC: Duke University Press.

Shanon, Benny. 1990. "What Is Context?" *Journal for the Theory of Social Behavior* 20:159–66.

Shapiro, Martin. 1980. "Appeal." *Law and Society Review* 14:629–61.

Sharpe, L. J. 1979. *Decentralization Trends in Western Democracies*. Beverly Hills, CA: Sage.

Shepard, R. W. 1953. *Cost and Production Function*. Princeton, NJ: Princeton University Press.

Shepard, Roger N. 1984. "Ecological Constraints on Internal Representation: Resonant Kinematics of Perceiving, Imagining, Thinking and Dreaming." *Psychological Review* 91:417–47.

———. 1987. "Evolution of a Mesh between Principles of the Mind and Regularities of the World." In *The Latest and the Best: Essays on Evolution and Optimality*, edited by J. Dupre. Cambridge, MA: MIT Press.

———. 1989. "Internal Representation of Universal Regularities: A Challenge for Connectionism." In *Neural Connections, Mental Computations*, edited by L. Nadel, L. A. Cooper, Peter Culicover, and R. M. Harnish. Cambridge, MA: MIT Press.

Shotter, John. 1993. *Cultural Politics of Everyday Life: Social Constructionism, Rhetoric and Knowledge of the Third Kind.* Buckingham, UK: Open University Press.

Shubik, Martin. 1984a. *Game Theory in the Social Sciences: Concepts and Solutions.* Cambridge, MA: MIT Press.

———. 1984b. *A Game Theoretical Approach to Political Economy.* Cambridge, MA: MIT Press.

Shuman, Amy. 1986. *Storytelling Rights: The Uses of Oral and Written Texts by Urban Adolescents.* New York: Cambridge University Press.

Silver, Allan. 1989. "Friendship and Trust as Moral Ideals: An Historical Approach." *European Journal of Sociology* 30:274–97.

———. 1990. "Friendship in Commercial Society: Eighteenth-Century Social Theory and Modern Society." *American Journal of Sociology* 91:1474–1504.

Silverstein, Michael. 1998. "The Improvisational Performance of Culture in Realtime Discursive Practice." In *Creativity in Perfomance*, edited by R. Keith Sawyer. Greenwich, CT: Ablex.

Simirenko, Alex. 1982. *The Professionalization of Soviet Society.* New Brunswick, NJ: Transaction Books.

Simmel, Georg. 1955. *Conflict and the Web of Group-Affiliations.* New York: Free Press.

Simon, Herbert A. 1945. *Administrative Behavior.* New York: Macmillan.

———. 1957. *Models of Man.* New York: Wiley.

Simon, Herbert A., D. Smithburg, and V. Thompson. 1950. *Public Administration.* New York: Knopf.

Skinner, G. William. 1965. "Marketing and Social Structure in Rural China." *Journal of Asian Studies* 24:3–43, 195–228, 363–99.

Skocpol, Theda. 1992. *Protecting Soldiers and Mothers: The Political Origins of Social Policy in the United States.* Cambridge, MA: Harvard University Press.

Skvoretz, John V., and R. H. Conviser. 1971. "Interests and Alliances." *Man* 9:53–67.

Skvoretz, John V., and Thomas J. Fararo. 1980. "Languages and Grammars of Action and Interaction: A Contribution to the Formal Theory of Action." *Behavioral Science* 25:9–22.

Skvoretz, John V., Thomas J. Fararo, and Nick Axten. 1980. "Role-Programme Models and the Analysis of Institutional Structure." *Sociology* 14:49–67.

Sloan, Alfred P. 1963. *My Years with General Motors.* New York: Doubleday.

Smith, Charles W. 1989. *Auctions: The Social Construction of Value.* New York: Free Press.

Smith, J. Maynard. 1985. *Evolution and the Theory of Games.* New York: Cambridge University Press.

Smith, Michael G. 1975. *Corporations and Society.* Chicago: Aldine.

Smith, Tammy. 2006. "Narrative Networks and the Dynamics of Ethnic Conflict and Conciliation." Department of Sociology, Columbia University.

Sorokin, Pitirim A. 1927. *Social and Cultural Mobility.* New York: Harper Bros.

———. 1937–1941. *Social and Cultural Dynamics.* New York: American Books.

Spencer, Baldwin, and Francis James Gillen. 1927. *The Arunta: A Study of a Stone Age People.* London: Macmillan.

Spilerman, Seymour. 1977. "Careers, Labor Market Structure and Socioeconomic Achievement." *American Journal of Sociology* 83:551–93.

Star, Susan Leigh. 1989. *Regions of the Mind: Brain Research and the Quest for Scientific Certainty.* Stanford, CA: Stanford University Press.

Stark, David. 2001. "Ambigous Assets for Uncertain Environments: Heterarchy in Postsocialist Firms." In *The Twenty-First-Century Firm: Changing Economic Organization in International Perspective,* edited by Paul DiMaggio. Princeton, NJ: Princeton University Press.

———. 2006. "For a Sociology of Worth." Published in Italian as "Appello per una Sociologia della Grandezza." *Sociologia del Lavoro* 104:200–223.

Stark, David, and László Bruszt. 1998. *Postsocialist Pathways: Transforming Politics and Property in East Central Europe.* New York: Cambridge University Press.

Stark, David, and Balazs Vedres. 2006. "Social Times of Network Spaces: Network Sequences and Foreign Investment in Hungary." *American Journal of Sociology* 111:1368–1411.

Stark, Rodney, and W. S. Bainbridge. 1979. "Networks of Faith." *American Journal of Sociology* 85:1376–95.

Stedry, A. C. 1960. *Budget Control and Cost Behavior.* Englewood Cliffs, NJ: Prentice-Hall.

Steenstrup, Carl. 1987. "The Legal System of Japan." In *Law and the State in Traditional East Asia,* edited by Brian McKnight. Honolulu: University of Hawaii Press.

Stenton, Frank. 1965. *The First Century of English Feudalism.* Oxford: Oxford University Press.

Stephan, Frederick. 1958. "Two Queues under Preemptive Priority with Poisson Arrival and Service Rates." *Operations Research* 6:399–418.

Stevenson, G. H. 1939. *Roman Provincial Administration.* Oxford: Blackwell.

Stewman, Shelby. 1976. "Markov Models of Occupational Mobility: Theoretical Development and Empirical Support; Part I, Careers." *Journal of Mathematical Sociology* 4:201–45.

———. 1988. "Organizational Demography." *Annual Review of Sociology* 14:173–202.

Stewman, Shelby, and S. L. Konda. 1983. "Careers and Organizational Labor Markets: Demographic Models of Organizational Behavior." *American Journal of Sociology* 88:637–85.

Stinchcombe, Arthur. 1993. "Review of 'Identity and Control.' " *European Sociological Review* 9:333–36.

Stone, Lawrence. 1965. *The Crisis of the Aristocracy, 1558–1641.* Oxford: Oxford University Press.

———. 1972. *The Causes of the English Revolution, 1529–1642.* London: Routledge.

Stouffer, Samuel A., Arthur A. Lumsdaine, Marion Harper Lumsdaine Jr., Robin M. Williams, M. Brewster Smith, Irving L. Janis, Shirley A. Star, and Leonard S. Cottrell Jr. 1949. *The American Soldier.* Princeton, NJ: Princeton University Press.

Strang, David, and Nancy B. Tuma. 1993. "Spatial and Temporal Heterogeneity in Diffusion." *American Journal of Sociology* 99:614–40.

Strathern, Andrew. 1971. *The Rope of Moka*. Cambridge: Cambridge University Press.

Street, David, R. Vinter, and C. Perrow. 1966. *Organizations for Treatment*. New York: Free Press.

Stuart, Toby. 1998. "Network Positions and Propensity to Collaborate." *Administrative Science Quarterly* 43:668–98.

Suleiman, Eza N. 1987. *The Notaries and the State*. Princeton, NJ: Princeton University Press.

Suolahti, Jaakko. 1955. *The Junior Officers of the Roman Army*. Helsinki: Finnish Academy of Sciences.

Svalastoga, Kaare. 1959. *Prestige, Class, and Mobility*. Copenhagen: Gyldendal.

Swales, J. M. 1990. *Genre Analysis: English in Academic and Research Settings*. New York: Cambridge University Press.

Swanson, Guy E. 1988. *Ego Defenses and the Legitimation of Behavior*. New York: Cambridge University Press.

Swart, Koenraad W. 1949. *Sale of Offices in the 17th Century*. The Hague: Nijhoff.

Swidler, Ann. 1986. "Culture in Action: Symbols and Strategies." *American Sociological Review* 51:273–86.

Syme, Ronald. 1968. *The Roman Revolution*. Oxford: Oxford University Press.

Tallberg, Christian. 2005. "A Bayesian Approach to Modeling Stochastic Block-structures with Covariates." *Journal of Mathematical Sociology* 29:1–23.

Tarrow, Sidney. 1977. *Between Center and Periphery: Grassroots Politicians in Italy and France*. New Haven, CT: Yale University Press.

Taylor, Lily Ross. 1949. *Party Politics in the Age of Caesar*. Berkeley: University of California Press.

Tellenbach, Gerd. 1966. *Church, State and Christian Society at the Time of the Investiture Contest*. Oxford: Blackwell.

Theissen, Gerd. 1982. *The Social Setting of Pauline Christianity*. Philadelphia: Fortress Press.

Thompson, Bard (Ed.). 1961. *Liturgies of the Western Church*. Cleveland, OH: World.

Thompson, Sandra A., and Anthony Mulac. 1991. "A Quantitative Perspective on the Grammaticalization of Epistemic Parentheticals in English." In *Approaches to Grammaticalization*, edited by Elizabeth C. Traugott and B. Heine. Amsterdam: Benjamin.

Thrupp, Sylvia L. 1948. *The Merchant Class of Medieval London, 1300–1500*. Ann Arbor: University of Michigan Press.

Tillich, Paul. 1963. *Systematic Theology*, vol. 3. Chicago: University of Chicago Press.

Tilly, Charles. 1975. "Reflections on the History of European State-Making." In *The Formation of National States in Western Europe*, pp. 3–83. Princeton, NJ: Princeton University Press.

———. 1978. *From Mobilization to Revolution*. Reading, MA: Addison-Wesley.

———. 1990. *Coercion, Capital and European States, a.d. 990–1990*. Cambridge, MA: Blackwell.

Tilly, Charles. 1996. *Citizenship, Identity and Social History.* New York: Cambridge University Press.

———. 2002. *Stories, Identities, and Political Change.* London: Rowman & Littlefield.

———. 2004. "Social Boundary Mechanisms." *Philosophy of the Social Sciences* 34.

———. 2006. *Why?* Princeton, NJ: Princeton University Press.

Traugott, Elizabeth C. (Ed.) 1986. *On Conditionals.* New York: Cambridge University Press.

Trautmann, Thomas R. 1987. *Lewis Henry Morgan and the Invention of Kinship.* Berkeley: University of California Press.

Tuck, R. H. 1965. *An Essay on the Economic Theory of Rank.* Oxford: Blackwell.

Tukey, John. 1977. *Exploratory Data Analysis.* Reading, MA: Addison-Wesley.

Turner, Victor. 1969. *The Ritual Process.* Chicago: Aldine.

———. 1974. *Dramas, Fields and Metaphors.* Ithaca, NY: Cornell University Press.

Udy, Stanley. 1959. *Organization of Work.* New Haven, CT: Human Relations Area Files.

———. 1970. *Work in Traditional and Modern Society.* Englewood Cliffs, NJ: Prentice-Hall.

———. 1990. "Structural Inconsistency and Management Strategy in Organizations." In *Structures of Power and Constraint: Papers in Honor of Peter M. Blau,* edited by Craig Calhoun, Marshall W. Meyer, and W. Richard Scott. Cambridge: Cambridge University Press.

Urban, Greg. 1993. *A Discourse-Centered Approach to Culture: Native South American Myths and Rituals.* Austin: University of Texas Press.

Urban, Michael E. 1987. "Centralization and Elite Circulation in a Soviet Republic." *British Journal of Political Science* 19:1–23.

Urton, Gary, and Carry J. Brezine. 2005. "Khipu Accounting in Ancient Peru." *Science* 309:1065–67.

Uzzi, Brian. 1996. "The Sources and Consequences of Embeddedness for the Economic Performance of Organizations: The Network Effect." *American Sociological Review* 61:674–98.

Van Doosselaere, Quentin. 2004. "A State Formation Dynamic in Feudal England: Public Finance Numerical Procedures." Department of Sociology, Columbia University.

———. 2006. "From Feudal to Modern: Social Dynamics and Commercial Agreements in Medieval Genoa." Department of Sociology, Columbia University.

Van Schendelen, M.P.C.M., and R. J. Jackson (Eds.). 1987. *The Politicisation of Business in Western Europe.* London: Croom-Helm.

Van Vleck, J. H. 1932. *The Theory of Electric and Magnetic Susceptibilities.* New York: Oxford University Press.

Vancil, Richard F. 1979. *Decentralization: Managerial Ambiguity by Design.* Homewood, IL: Dow Jones-Irwin.

———. 1984. "How CEOs Use Top Management Committees." *Harvard Business Review* 62: 65–73.

Vaughan, Diane. 2002. "Signals and Interpretive Work: The Role of Culture in a Theory of Practical Action." In *Culture in Mind: Toward a Sociology of Culture and Cognition*, edited by Karen Cerulo. New York: Routledge.

———. 2006. "The Social Shaping of Commission Reports." *Sociological Forum* 21:291–306.

Velthuis, Olaf. 2006. *Talking Prices*. Princeton, NJ: Princeton University Press.

Venkatesh, Sudhir A. 2000. *American Project: The Rise and Fall of a Modern Ghetto*. Cambridge, MA: Harvard University Press.

———. 2007. *The Other Economy*. Chicago: University of Chicago Press.

Viala, Alain. 1988. "Prismatic Effects." *Critical Inquiry* 14:563–73.

Vichniac, Judith E. 1985. "Union Organization in the French and British Iron and Steel Industries in the Late Nineteenth Century." In *Political Power and Social Theory*, edited by M. Zeitlin. Greenwich, CT: JAI Press.

von Gierke, Otto. 1950. *Natural Law and the Theory of Society, 1500–1800*. Cambridge: Cambridge University Press.

Wachter, Matthias. 2001. "Rational Action and Social Networks in Ecological Economics." Working paper, Swiss Federal Institute of Technology.

Walder, Andrew G. 2006. "Ambiguity and Choice in Political Movements: The Origins of Beijing Red Guard Factionalism." *American Journal of Sociology* 112:710–50.

Waley, Daniel. 1969. *The Italian City Republics*. New York: McGraw-Hill.

Walker, Gordon. 1985. "Network Position and Cognition in a Computer Software Firm." *Administrative Science Quarterly* 30:103–30.

Waller, Willard. 1932. *The Sociology of Teaching*. New York: Wiley.

Wallerstein, I. 1974. *The Modern World-System*, vol. 1. New York: Academic Press.

———. 1980. *The Modern World-System*, vol. 2. New York: Academic Press.

Warner, W. Lloyd. 1937. *A Black Civilization*. New York: Harper.

Warriner, Charles K. 1981. "Levels in the Study of Social Structure." In *Continuities in Structural Inquiry*, edited by Peter Blau and Robert K. Merton. London: Sage.

Wasserman, Stanley, and Katherine Faust. 1994. *Social Network Analysis: Methods and Applications*. Cambridge: Cambridge University Press.

Watkins, Susan C. 1990. "From Local to National Community: The Transformation of Demographic Regimes in Western Europe, 1870–1960." *Population and Development Review* 16:241–72.

Watt, Ian. 1957. *The Rise of the Novel*. Berkeley: University of California.

Watts, Duncan J. 1999. *Small Worlds: The Dynamics of Networks between Order and Randomness*. Princeton, NJ: Princeton University Press.

———. 2003. *Six Degrees: The Science of a Connected Age*. New York: Norton.

———. 2004. "Networks and Collective Behavior: A Research Program." Columbia University, Department of Sociology.

Watts, Duncan J., Peter S. Dodds, and M.E.J. Newman. 2002. "Identity and Search in Social Networks." *Science* 296:1302–5.

Weber, Max. 1978. *Economy and Society*. Berkeley: University of California Press.

Weick, Karl E. 1968. "The Panglossian World of Self-Justification." In *Theories of Cognitive Consistency*, edited by R. Abelson, E. Aronson, W. McGuire, T. Newcomb, M. J. Rosenberg, and P. Tannenbaum, pp. 706–15. Chicago: Rand-McNally.

———. 1976. "Educational Organizations as Loosely Coupled Systems." *Administrative Science Quarterly* 21:1–19.

Wellman, Barry. 1981. "The Community Question." *American Journal of Sociology* 84:1201–31.

———. 2001. "The Rise of Networked Individualism." In *Community Informatics*, edited by Leigh Keeble and Brian Loader, pp. 17–42. London: Routledge.

Wellman, Barry, and S. D. Berkowitz (Eds.). 1988. *Social Structures: A Network Approach*. Cambridge: Cambridge University Press.

Wellman, Barry, Peter J. Carrington, and Alan Hall. 1988. "Networks as Personal Communities." In *Social Structures: A Network Approach*, edited by Barry Wellman and S. D. Berkowitz, pp. 130–84. New York: Cambridge University Press.

Wellman, Barry, and Caroline Haythornwaite (Eds.). 2002. *The Internet in Everyday Life*. Oxford: Blackwell.

Weyl, Hermann. 1949a. *Philosophy of Mathematics and Natural Science*. Princeton, NJ: Princeton University Press.

———. 1949b. "Shock Waves in Arbitrary Fluids." *Communications on Pure and Applied Mathematics* 2:102–22.

White, Douglas R., and Michael Houseman. 2003. "The Navigability of Strong Ties: Small Worlds, Tie Strength, and Network Topology." *Complexity* 8:72–81.

White, Douglas R., and Ulla C. Johansen. 2006. *Network Analysis and Ethnographic Problems: Process Models of a Turkish Nomad Clan*. Oxford: Lexington Books.

White, Douglas R., Jason Owen-Smith, James Moody, and Walter W. Powell. 2004. "Networks, Fields and Organizations: Micro-Dynamics, Scale and Cohesive Embeddings." *Computational and Mathematical Organization Theory* 10:95–117.

White, Douglas R., and Karl Reitz. 1983. "Graph and Semigroup Homomorphisms on Networks and Relations." *Social Networks* 5:193–234.

White, Harrison C. 1962. "Chance Models of Systems of Casual Groups." *Sociometry* 25:153–72.

———. 1963a. *An Anatomy of Kinship*. Englewood Cliffs, NJ: Prentice-Hall.

———. 1963b. "Cause and Effect in Social Mobility Tables: Combinatorial Models." *Behavioral Science*:14–27.

———. 1964. "The Cumulation of Roles into Homogeneous Structures." In *New Perspectives in Organization Research*, edited by William W. Cooper, Harold J. Leavitt, and M. W. Shelly II. New York: Wiley.

———. 1970a. "Search Parameters for the Small World Problem." *Social Forces* 49:259–64.

———. 1970b. *Chains of Opportunity: System Models of Mobility in Organizations*. Cambridge, MA: Harvard University Press.

————. 1970c. "Matching, Vacancies and Mobility." *Journal of Political Economy* 78:97–105.

————. 1970d. "Simon out of Homans by Coleman." *American Journal of Sociology* 76:307–24.

————. 1970e. "Stayers and Movers." *American Journal of Sociology* 76:307–24.

————. 1973. "Everyday Life in Stochastic Networks." *Sociological Inquiry* 43:43–49.

————. 1981a. "Where Do Markets Come From?" *American Journal of Sociology* 87:517–47.

————. 1981b. "Production Markets as Induced Role Structures." In *Sociological Methodology 1981*, edited by Samuel Leinhardt, pp. 1–57. San Francisco: Jossey-Bass.

————. 1982. "Review Essay: Fair Science?" *American Journal of Sociology* 87:951–56.

————. 1985. "Agency as Control." In *Principals and Agents: The Structure of Business*, edited by John Pratt and Richard Zeckhauser. Boston: Harvard Graduate School of Business Administration Press.

————. 1991. "Values Come in Styles, Which Mate to Change." In *Toward a Scientific Analysis of Values*, edited by Michael Hechter and Lynn Nadel. Stanford, CA: Stanford University Press.

————. 1993. *Careers and Creativity: Social Forces in the Arts*. Boulder, CO: Westview.

————. 1995. "Social Networks Can Resolve Actor Paradoxes in Economics and in Psychology." *Journal of Institutional and Theoretical Economics* 151:58–74.

————. 1997. "Can Mathematics Be Social? Flexible Representations for Interaction Process and Its Socio-Cultural Constructions." *Sociological Forum* 12:53–71.

————. 2000a. "Modeling and Discourse around Markets." *Poetics* 27:117–33.

————. 2000b. "Parameterize." *Sociological Theory* 10:504–9.

————. 2002. *Markets from Networks: Socioeconomic Models of Production*. Princeton, NJ: Princeton University Press.

————. 2006. "Probings of Market Process." Working paper, University of California–Irvine.

White, Harrison C., Scott A. Boorman, and Ronald L. Breiger. 1976. "Social Structure from Multiple Networks. I. Blockmodels of Roles and Positions." *American Journal of Sociology* 81:730–80.

White, Harrison C., and Lee S. Christie. 1958. "Queuing with Preemptive Priorities or with Breakdown." *Operations Research* 6:79–95.

White, Harrison C., and Emily Erickson. 2005. "Taboo." In *Oxford Encyclopedia of Economic History*.

White, Harrison C., and Frédéric Godart. 2007. "Märkte als soziale Formationen." In *Märkte als soziale Strukturen*, edited by Jens Beckert, Rainer Diaz-Bone, and Heiner Ganßmann. Frankfurt: Campus.

White, Harrison C., Frédéric Godart, and Victor Corona. 2007. "Mobilizing Identities: Uncertainty and Control in Strategy." *Theory, Culture & Society*.

White, Harrison C., Forthcoming. "Produire en contexte d'incertitude. La construction des identités et des liens sociaux dans les marchés." *Sciences de la Société*.

White, Harrison C. and John W. Mohr. Forthcoming. "How to Model an Institution." *Theory and Society*.

White, Harrison C., and Cynthia A. White. 1993. *Canvases and Careers: Institutional Change in the French Painting World*. New York: Wiley.

White, Hayden. 1980. "The Value of Narrativity in the Representation of Reality." *Critical Inquiry* 7:5–27.

Whitford, Joshua. 2002. "Pragmatism and the Untenable Dualism of Means and Ends: Why Rational Choice Theory Does Not Deserve Paradigmatic Privilege." *Theory and Society* 31:325–63.

———. 2005. *The New Old Economy: Networks, Institutions, and the Organizational Transformation of American Manufacturing*. Oxford: Oxford University Press.

Whitford, Joshua, Solon Simmons, and Susan Helper. 2006. "Contested Collaboration: Toward a Behavioral Theory of the Network Firm." Working paper, MIT Institute for Work and Employment.

Whitney, Joseph R. R. 1970. "China: Area, Administration and Nation Building." In *Research Papers*. Department of Geography, University of Chicago.

Whyte, William F. 1943. *Street Corner Society*. Chicago: University of Chicago Press.

Wiener, Norbert. 1949. *Time Series*. Cambridge, MA: MIT Press.

Wildavsky, Aaron. 1975. *Budgeting: A Comparative Theory of the Budgetary Processes*. Boston: Little, Brown.

Williams, George H. 1981. *The Mind of John Paul II*. New York: Seabury Press.

Williams, Raymond. 1977. *Marxism and Literature*. New York: Oxford University Press.

Williamson, Oliver E. 1970. *Corporate Control and Business Behavior*. Englewood Cliffs, NJ: Prentice-Hall.

———. 1975. *Markets and Hierarchies: Analysis and Antitrust Implications*. New York: Free Press.

Willis, G. G. 1950. *Saint Augustine and the Donatist Controversy*. London: SPCK.

Willis, Paul. 1977. *Learning to Labour*. London: Gower.

Wilson, Kenneth G. 1979. "Problems in Physics with Many Scales of Length." *Scientific American* 241:140–57.

Wilson, E. O. 1970. *Insect Societies*. Cambridge, MA: Harvard University Press.

———. 1979. *Sociobiology: The New Synthesis*. Cambridge, MA: Harvard University Press.

Wilson, John. 1989. *The Boundaries of Conversation*. London: Pergamon.

Windeler, Arnold, and Jorg Sydow. 2001. "Project Networks and Changing Industry Practices—Collaborative Content Production in the German Television Industry." *Organization Studies* 22:1035–60.

Windmuller, John. 1969. *Labor Relations in the Netherlands*. Ithaca, NY: Cornell University Press.

Winship, Christopher. 1978. "The Allocation of Time among Individuals." In *Sociological Methodology*, edited by K. Schuessler. San Francisco: Jossey-Bass.

Winship, Christopher, and Michael Mandel. 1984. "Roles and Positions: A Critique and Extension of the Blockmodeling Approach." *Sociological Methodology* 14:314–44.

Wittgenstein, Ludwig. 1965. *The Blue and Brown Books*. New York: Harper & Row.

Wolfe, Alvin W. 2006. "Review of 'Network Analysis and Ethnographic Problems.' " *International Journal of Middle East Studies* 38:603–5.

Wolfe, Thomas. 1980. *The Right Stuff*. New York: Bantam.

Wolin, Sheldon S. 1987. "Democracy and the Welfare State: The Political and Theoretical Connections between Staatsrason and Wohlfahrts-staatsrason." *Political Theory* 15:467–500.

Wrapp, H. Edward. 1983. In *Strategic Management*, edited by R. G. Hamermesh. New York: Wiley.

Wynne-Edwards, V. C. 1985. *Evolution through Group Selection*. Oxford: Blackwell.

Yoshino, M. Y. 1968. *Japan's Managerial System*. Cambridge, MA: MIT Press.

Yoshino, M. Y., and Thomas Lifson. 1988. *The Invisible Link: Japan's Sogo Shosha in the Organization of Tradition*. Cambridge, MA: MIT Press.

Zadeh, Lotfi, K. Fu, K. Taneka, and M. Shimura (Eds.). 1975. *Fuzzy Sets and their Applications to Cognitive and Decision Processes*. New York: Academic Press.

Zajac, Edward E. 1985. "Perceived Economic Justice: The Example of Public Utility Regulation." In *Cost Allocation: Methods, Principles, Applications*, edited by H. Peyton Young. New York: Elsevier.

Ziegler, Rolf. 1974. *Anwendung mathematischer Verfahren zur Analyse sozialer Ungleichheit und sozialer Mobilität*. Kiel, Germany: Christian Albrecht Universität.

Ziman, John M. 1979. *Models of Disorder: The Theoretical Physics of Homogeneously Disordered Systems*. Cambridge: Cambridge University Press.

Zipf, George K. 1949. *Human Behavior and the Principle of Least Effort: An Introduction to Human Ecology*. Cambridge: Addison-Wesley.

Zuckerman, Ezra W., Tai-Young Kim, Kalinda Ukanwa, and James von Rittmann. 2003. "Robust Identities or Nonentities? Typecasting in the Feature-Film Labor Market." *American Journal of Sociology* 108:1018–74.

INDEX

Abbott, Andrew, xvii, 257
Abell, Peter, 233
ability as random process, 37
academic disciplines, 265
accidents, 9, 13; as population boundaries, 149; as source of identities, 9
accountings, 36, 176, 185, 187, 287, 336,
343; tie distinction, 36
acquaintance dance, 96; as arena discipline, 96; as realm, 95
acquaintances, scope of, 22
actions, local, 287
actors: action generates, 154; identities of,
24; personal, 141, 186, 188, 291
Add Health Survey, 56, 351–52
administrators maintaining coherence, 314
agency, 293; calculus of, 296; for control,
292; by delegation, 293
agendas, 294–95
ambage, 57–58, 72, 214–15, 229, 271; high,
181; intimacy as lowered, 151; low, 315
ambiguity, 57–58, 214–15, 229; in councils,
93; cultural, 57; high, 315; low, 181
American academic science, 268–70
annealing, 325–26; popular rebellion
as, 325
Antal, Fredrick, 48
anthropology, xviii
anti-careers, 194
anticategorical imperative, 48
arena disciplines: acquaintance dance as
example of, 96; caste system as, 101;
committees as, 102–3; control regimes,
355; defined, 64–65; exchange markets
as, 99; flows in, 64–65; 3D space for,
357; valuations, 98
arenas. *See* arena disciplines
attention, selective, 217
attitudes, 50–51, 144, 229; person as, 51
attributes, catnets from similarity of, 53
authority, 82, 84, 162, 294
autocracies, 166

averages, dispersions as opposed to, 337
Avrahampour, Yally, xvi, 327, 329
Axelrod, Robert M., 230

Bailey, Robert, 317
Baldassarri, Delia, 21
Baldassarri and Bearman model of partisan polarization, 21–22
bar, similarity of attributes in, 53
Bearman, Peter, xv, 21, 35, 124, 351
Bellman, Richard, 358
"big men" in New Guinea, 152
blocking action, 198, 220, 253, 279,
310, 312
blockmodeling analysis, 266
blockmodels, 69; use of term, 55
Bob Dylan values example, 234
Boltanski and Thévenot disputes and net-
works, 182, 225–27
Boorman, Scott A., xv, 55
Bott, Elizabeth, 47–49
boundaries, 61, 141, 345–46; arena disci-
plines and, 64
Bourdieu, Pierre, xvi, 96, 114, 222, 241–42
Bower, Joseph, 281
Boyd, John, 192
bracketing, disallowing of , 12
Breiger, Ron, 52, 55
budget, construction of, 191
budgets, 218; federal, 216
Burma, 169, 324; direct rule, 324
Burt, Ronald, 60, 131–33

calculus, use of term, 72
capitalism, 244, 275–76; emergence of, 242
careers, 171, 185–86, 190–95, 307–8, 350;
as patterns of switchings, 3
Carley, Kathleen, 338
caste, 262–68
catnets, 53; definition of, 52
causes, variabilities as, 154
CEO, 102; as arena discipline, 102
Chafe, Wallace, 335